INSIDE
RELIGIOUS
PUBLISHING

INSIDE RELIGIOUS PUBLISHING

A LOOK BEHIND THE SCENES

Leonard George Goss & Don M. Aycock
EDITORS

ZondervanPublishingHouse
Academic and Professional Books
Grand Rapids, Michigan

A Division of HarperCollinsPublishers

Inside Religious Publishing
Copyright © 1991 by Leonard George Goss and Don M. Aycock

Requests for information should be addressed to:
Zondervan Publishing House
Academic and Professional Books
1415 Lake Drive S.E.
Grand Rapids, Michigan 49506

Library of Congress Cataloging-in-Publication Data

Inside religious publishing : a look behind the scenes / [edited by] Leonard George Goss and Don M.
Aycock.

    p.   cm.
   Includes bibliographical references.
   ISBN 0-310-35861-2
   1. Christian literature — Publication and distribution. 2. Christian literature — Authorship.
I. Goss, Leonard George. II. Aycock, Don M.
BR44 .I57   1991   91-24875
070.5 — dc20   CIP

All Scripture quotations, unless otherwise noted, are taken from THE HOLY BIBLE: NEW
INTERNATIONAL VERSION (North American Edition), copyright © 1973, 1978, 1984 by the
International Bible Society. Used by permission of Zondervan Bible Publishers.

Edited by L. G. Goss and Gerard Terpstra
Interior designed by L. G. Goss
Cover designed by Gary Gnidovic

Printed in the United States of America

91 92 93 94 95 96 / AM / 10 9 8 7 6 5 4 3 2 1

For Carolyn,
With love and gratitude and admiration.
Thanks for your support, your faith, and your encouragement.
L.G.G.

To Carla, who greets each new publication of my words with almost as much joy as I do.

To my boys, Chris and Ryan, who are beginning to discover the Word on their own.

To the memory of George Buttrick, who knew more about words and the Word than anyone else I have ever known.

To the saints of First Baptist Church of Gillis, Lake Charles, Louisiana, who are fellow servants of the Word.

To all the writers of the Word who will be helped by this book.
D.M.A.

Contents

Introduction

Charlie Shedd tells the story of a mighty dragon that lived in a cave on the side of a mountain high above a peace-loving village. Every day — sometimes all day — the mighty dragon would stand outside the cave and roar, with a roaring that could be heard far and wide. Looking up, the fearful people of the village saw the dragon brooding, glowering, and threatening, and they wrung their hands and were sad that they had to live in the shadow of this fearsome monster. It is no wonder that even the bravest people in the village were afraid.

Then one day, a certain small boy announced that he would go to fight the dragon. With great maturity, he said, "I will not live where fires cannot be lighted; where children do not go outside to play; and where men stay away from the fields because they live in fear."

"I will go and face the dragon," the boy proclaimed. And though the elders of the village and all his fellow villagers tried to dissuade him, he went. As the boy made his way up the mountain, he discovered a strange thing. The closer he came to the dragon's cave, the smaller the dragon seemed to be. At last when the boy arrived at the cave opening, the mighty dragon had become a creature so small that the boy could hold him in the palm of his hand. Whereupon our boy hero took the tiny monster and carried it back to the village.[1]

Thus the mighty dragon turned out to be less fearsome than once imagined. The tale of the dragon is a parable of publishing, and it reveals what will happen when you become acquainted with the mysterious industry. For both the reader looking in from the outside and the person inside who wants a larger view, publishing may look like an awful dragon. You may think of publishers and those who work for them as monsters in the entrance to a cave. The contributors to this book want to assure you that people who work at writing and publishing are very much like people in any other creative endeavor. Some are tall; some are short. Some are thin; some are fat. Some are friendly; *most* are friendly. What moral or lesson can be drawn from the tale of the mighty dragon? It is that those who work in this field are exactly like all other mortals both inside and outside the industry, neither better nor worse. Well, not much worse.

This collection of essays is meant to open up religious publishing to you, the reader — to let you know that this is a burgeoning field, one in search of and in great need of talented new people. Many of you want to know more about the publishing enterprise in the hopes of becoming a part of it. This book will tell you what you need to know.

It is true that no area of publishing is easy to enter anymore, but like all the others, it can be cracked. *Inside Religious Publishing: A Look Behind the Scenes* will reveal what the practice of religious publishing is all about, offering the "big picture" of what is going on in there. Some chapters discuss the diversity among religious publishing houses and their personnel. Others cover the job opportunities available in this branch of publishing. And some suggest what skills or attributes are needed to get into the field. Many of the chapters emphasize the publishing of religious books, but other chapters deal with magazines, newsletters, curriculum, and script-writing.

This book puts to work good writers, publishers, editors, and agents to describe the overall scope of religious publishing and takes readers step by step into the important enterprise of writing, editing, advertising, and selling religious books and other materials. Each provocative chapter is written by a leader in the field.

Religious publishing is built on a very long and deep and wide platform, from inspirational and devotional books and novels that have an underlying religious theme, to theological and biblical scholarship for students and professors and, at a deeper intellectual level, for thought leaders in religion and philosophy. Religious magazines are also widely varied. They are published for every conceivable audience and deal with virtually every imaginable subject area, including social and political problems. My own house, Zondervan, is an example. We publish books under many imprints, from romance fiction to devotions, from self-help books to Bible study resources for laypeople, from youth and children's books to general nonfiction that challenges, informs, and inspires. We publish titles for preachers and pastors and missionaries as well as for counselors, church planters, and Bible teachers. There are reference works like dictionaries, encyclopedias, and commentaries. We also publish textbooks, thought-provoking studies, and monographs in the theological disciplines such as theology, biblical studies, church history, apologetics, ethics, and integrative studies in the humanities and social sciences. From Zondervan alone one can see the wide sweep of the enterprise that is religious publishing.

That is something about *what* we publish. The question of *why* we publish is a little more difficult to answer. Why do people want to go into religious publishing? What reasons can there be beyond the economic or pragmatic one of having a job? We are, after all, in the "book business" or the "magazine business." People in religious publishing, like others in publishing generally, love books and magazines and love to read. Yes, we know that the things we produce are commodities, products with covers, pages with ink on them, and bindings. But we know that they are much more than this, that beyond this, publishing is about promoting ideas that can spread as intensely as wildfire and even change the lives of readers.

The real business of religious publishing is not only selling what it is that we produce, important as that is. Our real business is promoting *ideas*. God has given us the gift of words. We publish them for people who, like us, love and want the value of books and periodicals in order to develop their own thoughts, to participate in dialogue with others, to leave something for another generation, and to build a deep foundation of faith. It is no exaggeration to say that we hold in our hands the power to mold minds, and we work in this field with a deep sense of responsibility. We try to offer answers to readers through writing and publishing in the same way the Gospels tell us Jesus offered answers to his hearers on the vital religious, political, and social issues of his day — by mooring them in stories of personal accountability. Through stories the entire Bible conveys the good news that God has entered into the story of his creation. Our challenge in religious publishing is to communicate that marvelous good news. No idea is more worth promoting.

— Leonard George Goss

NOTES

1. Charlie W. Shedd's version of the dragon story is in *If I Can Write, You Can Write* (Cincinnati: Writer's Digest Books, 1984), 49.

Acknowledgments

Grateful acknowledgment is made for permission to reprint the following articles:

"The Pursuit of Excellence" by Sherwood Eliot Wirt, from *The Making of a Writer* (Minneapolis: Augsburg Publishing House), copyright © 1987. Reprinted by permission.

"Art and Propaganda" and "The Pitfalls of Christian Writing" by Philip Yancey, from *Open Windows* (Nashville: Thomas Nelson Publishers), copyright © 1985. Reprinted by permission.

"Marks of a Creative Editor" by Judith E. Markham, copyright © 1990 by *Interlit* of the David C. Cook Foundation, Elgin, Illinois. Reprinted by permission.

"Searching for the Great Commission" by John P. Ferré and "Moving the World with Magazines" by Stephen Board, from *American Evangelicals and the Mass Media*, ed. Quentin J. Schultze (Grand Rapids: Zondervan Publishing House), copyright © 1990. Reprinted by permission.

Part 1
The Art and Ethics
of Religious Publishing
and Writing

Chapter 1

The Pursuit
of Excellence

Sherwood Eliot Wirt

In Christian literature we have the greatest subject in all history, the man from Nazareth. We have the greatest source of truth, the Bible; the greatest message of hope, eternal life; the greatest benefit to offer, salvation from sin; the greatest motivator to the good life, the gospel. More than that, Christianity has provided the world with its most thrilling music, has inspired the finest in architecture and art, and has stirred the sublimest passions and the noblest sacrifices in individuals.

Now in the late twentieth century, when all this has been made available to us through the miracle of mass communication, I ask you, why shouldn't it evoke great writing from among us? What's holding us back from literary excellence?

I believe that God, who fashioned the galaxies with his supernatural sense of timing, has used that same sidereal timing to cause you to read this page and to put this question to you. He is driving his scribes out of the temple, telling us we've been cogitating in there long enough. He wants us out in the middle of things like Amos and Jeremiah, discovering

Sherwood Eliot Wirt is the former editor of *Decision* magazine and the founder of the Decision School of Christian Writing. He is the author of numerous books, including *Spiritual Awakening*, *Topical Encyclopedia of Living Quotations*, and *The Making of a Writer*. He is active as a teacher at writings schools and conferences all over the country.

what's going on and writing about it. He wants us to take the lid off the Christian message. He wants us to write the love language of the 1980s and 1990s. He is showing us all the outlets — print, film, television, radio, cassettes, videocassettes, pulpit — ready to go to work for him. He wants us to use the media to make things happen.

"Proclaim this message. . . . Stand at the gate of the LORD's house and there proclaim. . . . Write in a book all the words I have spoken to you" (Jer. 3:12; 7:2; 30:2). Over and over the sacred Scriptures tell us to forget about ourselves and to start talking up God, to concentrate on objective truth. All the reasonings of men can lead us only to Hiroshima and Beirut, but in Christ lies the promise of peace.

We all know these things, or should; but as writers we are asking further, how do we communicate truth to our generation? What does it take, as we approach the year 2000, to achieve literary excellence or even come near it? *Genius?* Forget it. That quality was left out of our makeup. *Zeal?* Well, we have a little. *Vocabulary?* We're still having trouble with words like "egregious," "arcane," and "desideratum." *Fasting?* Let's see, when is coffee break? *Imagination? Brain Power?* We pass.

Let's admit that we don't have it, and start from there. Let's say frankly that for us to compose a decent sentence takes blood, toil, tears, and sweat, and turning out a really sparkling page of copy means an enormous amount of rewriting.

Now at least we're on bedrock. Like the Pilgrim in the Slough of Despond, we have touched the bottom and found it to be sound.[1] The apostle Paul wrote some words to the Corinthians (1 Cor. 1:26–29) that we might adapt to our situation: "You see your calling, brothers and sisters, that not many talented are among us, not many gifted; not many giants or best-sellers; but God has chosen the hacks of the world to show up the literary elite, that *The New York Times* reviewers might not glory in his presence." But the apostle added that he was struggling together with us toward the mark of excellence (Phil. 3:14).

But when we speak of the pursuit of excellence, of going for the gold medal, we need to distinguish between great literature as the world acknowledges it and great Christian literature. In many respects the standards are the same, but there is one important difference. It is not the use of religious phrases of religious themes. The difference lies between merely descriptive writing and writing that motivates. Thomas de Quincey once named three categories: the literature of *irrelevance*, the literature of *knowledge*, and the literature of *power*. We all know about the literature of *irrelevance;* there is far too much of it in our Christian bookstores. There is also the literature of *knowledge*, whose function is to teach. It is basically cognitive, and appeals to the mind. But the literature of *power* is not just cognitive, it is causal; its function is to move. Thus we might call the horoscope column in the daily newspaper the literature of irrelevance; the discourses of Epictetus the literature of knowledge; but the *Communist Manifesto* and the epistle to the Galatians would be the literature of power.

It is not enough for the copy we turn out to wear a cross on its escutcheon, not enough that we maintain our orthodoxy and express ourselves clearly and earnestly. What we write has to do things to people, to motivate them. It has to be causal if it is to be great: "Put on the full armor of God. . . . Stand firm and do not let yourselves be burdened again by a yoke of slavery. . . . Go into all the world and preach the good news" (Eph. 6:11; Gal. 5:1; Mark 16:15). Martin Luther once wrote, "Oh, it is a living, creative, active, mighty thing, this faith."[2] That is the way to think of great Christian writing. It is more than beauty, more than entertainment, more than richness of style, even though it may contain all three. It is the literature of power.

So when we speak of the pursuit of excellence, we are not thinking of cleverness, brilliance, elegance, facility of expression, or even clarity of thought. Hemingway, Maugham, Mailer, and Pynchon wrote from motives different from ours. But having said that, we cannot ignore the rules of good writing or those who have mastered them. A true professional learns both from his peers and his competitors. Paul learned from Menander; Augustine learned from Virgil.

One can also learn from a good editor. Let me share with you a portion of a letter written to me by an editor after I had submitted a nonfiction book manuscript. These are the editor's words:

> There is one problem with your manuscript that overarches all others: the story is emotionally flat. There is no drama, no pathos, where there should be. I am not drawn along by the story at all, not caught up in the drama of this man's life. You have succeeded in talking to all the necessary people and getting the facts of the story straight, but you have not added to the factual account those storytelling elements that provide life and color, that reach the reader's emotions as well as his intellect. The result is that as I read the manuscript, I feel very much as though I am having a story told to me, as opposed to feeling I am reading a marvelous story. There is only the narrator telling rather than showing what was going on. The story is always at arm's length; I never feel as though I am there. In short, I think you need to go through another draft of the manuscript. I realize I am asking a great deal of you, but I believe it is in the best interests of the book.

And there followed some technical suggestions.

As the words sank into my consciousness, and my skin began to crawl, I began to see myself as one of the great mediocre writers of the world. But I had recently read Tom Wolfe's book, *The Right Stuff*, and on an impulse I reread the description of John Glenn's feelings as he was coming into the atmosphere after his pioneer voyage in outer space. Many things might be said about Wolfe's writing, but he is not mediocre. He puts you in that capsule, and you watch the broken pieces of the heatshield come flying past your window, and you realize that you are about to be burned to a crisp. You are lost, lost in space, and a stranger to the earth.

Well, after that little ride, I went back to my Memorywriter with a vengeance. The biggest hurdle was my own laziness. Once over that, I had a clear vision of what needed to be done, and proceeded to do it. The book was published and has gone into a third printing.

In the writing of twenty books I have been taught many things about this fascinating field of writing: how to do it and how not to do it; how to tell a marketable idea from a poor one; how to make friends with editors and how to keep that friendship; how to strive for a style that pleases the reader; and most important, how the Holy Spirit can use literature to bring glory to God.

In working with different writers' groups I have learned what leads to professional competence and success, and what holds writers back. Many factors are involved in the making of a writer; some are spiritual, some physical, some psychological. In this book we shall limit ourselves to the craft itself, and the craftsman as such. We shall concentrate on the pursuit and achievement of excellence. To do that, we shall wade into the stream of history and swim alongside some of the writing men and women who have interpreted truth down through the ages and have passed the word to us. We shall become aware of the joy, the color, the music, the elixir, the mystique that goes with writing. We shall not talk about our lack of preparation, the mistakes we made in our studies, the books we haven't read. Forget all that. We're starting with now.

NOTES

1. John Bunyan, *Pilgrim's Progress.*
2. Luther's Preface to the Epistle to the Romans.

Chapter 2

Words and the Word
Theological Musings on Christian Writing

Don M. Aycock

In the Beginning . . .

A story is told of a meeting between a theologian and an astronomer. The astronomer said to the theologian, "I don't understand why you theologians fuss so much about things like predestination and supralapsarianism, about the communicable and the incommunicable attributes of God, of imputed or infused grace, and the like. To me Christianity is very simple — it's the Golden Rule: 'Do unto others as you would have others do unto you.'"

The theologian thought about that for a moment and then replied, "I think I see what you mean. I get lost in all your talk about exploding novas, the expanding universe, theories of entropy, black holes, and the like. To me astronomy is very simple — it's 'Twinkle, twinkle, little star. . . .'"

The urge to reduce every discipline to its simplest terms is understandable but sometimes laughable. Astronomy has its worldview, its technical language, and its methods of accomplishing its work. So does

Don M. Aycock is a pastor and the prolific author of more than ten books and dozens of articles. He is co-author, with Leonard George Goss, of *Writing Religiously: A Guide to Writing Nonfiction Religious Books* and is co-editor of *Inside Religious Publishing: A Look Behind the Scenes.*

theology. Theological methodology is a branch of systematic theology that seeks to understand how theology does its work. Fortunately, this chapter is not on theological method. I mention it because we Christian writers need to be aware that theology is not our enemy.

Theology troubles us though. We might be tempted to think of it as a needless encumbrance to our work, the same way high school kids think math is the most useless subject ever invented. Most people do not like to do reflective work that dissects and analyzes a subject. Someone once said, "I hate botany, but I love flowers." We could read that as, "I hate theology, but I love God."

Botany and theology are not the same, of course. Botany is characterized by its subject — flora. But theology is characterized by its object — God. The word *theology* is literally *Theos logos*, thinking about God. Theology is not just the narrow contemplation of God and "religious" concepts. Medieval theologians supposedly debated about how many angels could dance on the head of a pin. Who cares!? Theology is an awareness of otherness that provides the perspective from which Christians think and write.

One contemporary theologian has written that theology is "involved in the practical task of acquiring an understanding of life and world."[1] This same theologian says, "Theology is not or ought not to be a haven for all inarticulate sputterings about human life or Christian faith nor the sort of lunatic asylum where everyone does his or her own thing without facing the responsibility of giving an account for such speaking, writing, or gesticulating which is, or purports to be, of theological significance."[2] The Christian writer will give such an account. Did not Jesus say, "But I tell you that men will have to give account on the day of judgment for every careless word they have spoken [or written?]" (Matt. 12:36)?

I am not attempting in this chapter to offer a full-scale theology for writers. I simply want to pique your curiosity about some elements of writing that go beyond form and style. To do this I will tell you some stories about writing and open some windows to let in some fresh air and light. And to change the metaphor, we will gather nectar from many flowers to make our pound of honey. At the end of the chapter you will not have a systematic theology of Christian writing. What I hope you will have is a renewed sense of appreciation for your calling as a writer (and I do think it is a calling) and a new perspective from which to work.

We all have a theology whether we are aware of it or not. The writer who is a Christian is influenced by his or her concept of God, relationship to Christ, involvement or lack of it in a church, and so on. The question is not, "Do I have a theology?" but rather, "Is my theology a good one or a defective one?" Billy Graham, C. S. Lewis, Frank Peretti, Beverly

LaHaye, and Kenneth Hagin all have a theology. You do, too, even if you are someone who says you hate theology.

My fundamental conviction in this chapter is that Christian writers need a sound, biblical understanding of human life and of God's will. That is theology. You need not have a Ph.D. in systematic theology, but you do need to possess a well-rounded basis from which to write. Please understand that I am *not* pleading for writers to sound "orthodox" by peppering their manuscripts with religious-sounding words. There is probably too much of that already. What I am after is to get us writers to be thoughtful with the words we do use. Words are words. There are no "Christian words" but only words that can be used to convey Christian meaning. The late H. Grady Davis once said, "A Christian may use language for a Christian purpose, but, as there is no such thing as 'Christian' wood or stone or metal, so there can be no such thing as 'Christian' or 'sacred' or 'holy' language. Even in the Bible, especially in the Bible, language is human, true to the reality of human life." Yes, I am aware of the holy usages of language in the Bible, but it is mostly everyday language that is filled with new meaning and infused with grace.

One obvious reason for this need for writers to have a sound theology is that there is so much ignorance about the basics of our faith. A Church of England publication listed the following children's answers to church-school questions:

- Noah's wife was called Joan of Ark.

- The fifth commandment is: Humor thy father and thy mother.

- Lot's wife was a pillar of salt by day, but a ball of fire by night.

- When Mary heard she was to be the mother of Jesus, she went off and sang the Magna Carta.

- Salome was a woman who danced naked in front of Harrods.

- Holy acrimony is another name for marriage.

- Christians can have only one wife. This is called monotony.

- The Pope lives in a vacuum.

- Today wild beasts are confined to Theological Gardens.

- Iran is the Bible of the Moslems.

- A republican is a sinner mentioned in the Bible.

- Abraham begat Isaac and Isaac begat Jacob and Jacob begat twelve partridges.

- The natives of Macedonia did not believe, so St. Paul got stoned.

- The first commandment was when Eve told Adam to eat the apple.[3]

Pure nonsense? Give a biblical/theological test to nearly anyone you know and you will likely get similar results. Christian writers cannot afford the luxury of ignorance but often we are ignorant anyway. We are like Columbus in search of the new world. He did not know where he was going when he left Spain, did not know where he was when he arrived at the new world, and did not know where he had been after he returned home.

Carl F. H. Henry, founding editor of *Christianity Today*, once said that theology is important because "an empty head committed to Christ will sooner or later be vulnerable to other commitments. Unless one can give a reason for the hope he has, he soon will be whiplashed by illusionary hopes."[4]

Could this lack of a theological foundation account for some of the items in contemporary Christian bookstores? Another theologian has written, "Evangelicals are generally afraid to compete in the marketplace of ideas with the modern secularist. They would rather separate themselves from the 'world' to avoid the embarrassment of intellectual defeat. They still prefer their devotional, self-help publications to decisive refutations of the naked illogic of unbelief." This writer continues, "Instead of the great classics in defense of the faith . . . what are the stores selling? Little Prudy Dottie Dimple's joybells quiet-time books, how-to-be-blessed-out-of-your-socks manuals, and ball-point pens with suitable Bible verses inscribed thereon."[5]

I am not suggesting that writers need to become professional theologians. My point is that our message of the gospel is too important to leave it to "I'll just let the Spirit move me" whims. Someone has observed that too many people who have said, "I have half a mind to write a book," do so!

. . . Was the Word . . .

Words are tools that can move the world and shape consciences for Christ. Words are cheap little gimmicks that can be spun in any way to produce the maximum effect desired by the writer. Which of these two statements is true? Both are true. Words can be used to influence wills and shape consciences toward Christ; they can also be used to manipulate people for a writer's selfish purpose. Christian writers — I hope — aim for the former and not the latter.

Have you noticed the devaluation of words lately? I often have the sense that there is a terrible inflation in the economy of language and that words are worth much less now than before. The National Council of Teachers of English speaks of "verbal pollution." This is doublespeak —

the attempt to convey a simple idea by using high-sounding words. The NCTE offers the following examples: In some regions a gas bill is now called an "energy document." The stock market crash of October 1987 was merely a "fourth-quarter equity retreat." Chrysler laid off 5,000 workers but called the move a "career alternative enhancement program." Did you know that jumping off a building could lead to "sudden deceleration trauma" upon landing?

Even everyday objects and actions are not immune to this double-speak. Zippers are "interlocking slide fasteners," toothbrushes are "home plaque removal instruments," and a spanking is an "intensive adverse intervention." Janitors are now "entropy control engineers." The military is into this mess, too: war is now "lethal intervention," an event that could lead to "excess mortality."[6]

The federal government is probably more guilty of verbal inflation than anyone else. A tongue-in-cheek example is from a government lawyer who took the line from the Lord's Prayer that reads, "Give us this day our daily bread" and phrased it in "governmentese": "We respectfully petition, request, and entreat that due and adequate provision be made, this day and the date hereinafter subscribed, for the satisfying of these petitioners' nutritional requirements and for the organizing of such methods of allocation and distribution as may be deemed necessary and proper to assure the reception by and for said petitioners of such quantities of baked cereal products as shall, in the judgment of the aforesaid petitioners, constitute a sufficient supply thereof."

Biblical language knows no such devaluation. What is striking about the language of the Bible is its sparseness and its frugality. Words are the servants of the Word. The prophet Jeremiah knew this fact. He once complained that God had tricked and deceived him. But after the complaint Jeremiah said, "But if I say, 'I will not mention him or speak any more in his name,' his word is in my heart like a fire, a fire shut up in my bones. I am weary of holding it in; indeed, I cannot" (Jer. 20:9).

The word is God's creative act. In Genesis God spoke, and creation came into being. In the prophets the word defies every effort to silence it, whether by the godly prophets, such as Jeremiah or Jonah, or by false prophets. "'Is not my word like fire,' declares the LORD, 'and like a hammer that breaks a rock in pieces?'" (Jer. 23:29). In Isaiah the word is said to be like rain that falls to earth to nourish the seeds in the soil. The Lord says of his word, "So is my word that goes out from my mouth: It will not return to me empty, but will accomplish what I desire and achieve the purpose for which I sent it" (Isa. 55:11).

Finally, the Word of God became flesh in Jesus of Nazareth. As John's gospel puts it, "In the beginning was the Word, and the Word was

with God, and the Word was God. He was with God in the beginning"
(1:1–2). Death and the grave could not silence him. This Word is the
supreme power at work in the world, a power to which all knees will
ultimately bend (Phil. 2:10–11). Christian writers are servants of the
Word with their words.

When all is said and done, our message is something given to us. We
do not invent it. Although we have great latitude to be creative in finding
ways to communicate the Gospel, the central message is still something
given to us. As King David once prayed, "Everything comes from you,
and we have given you only what comes from your hand" (1 Chron.
29:14). While the core message is given to us, the means of communicating it is not. When I was in seminary, I was a professor's assistant in
homiletics class. My job was to grade student sermons. Several students
became very upset with me because I gave them less than an A on their
sermon outlines. They would say, "God gave me this sermon! How can
you give me a C?" I sometimes wanted to say, "I think God can spell
better than this." I understood what they meant. They felt a sense of
inspiration in formulating the idea of the sermon. What they did not
realize is that although the central idea may have been inspirational, the
communicating of that idea required hard work. I admit that I was long in
learning this lesson myself. I am still learning it. Writing — whether of
sermons, articles, or books — is difficult work. The old adage is still true:
writing is 10 percent inspiration and 90 percent perspiration.

We owe a debt to our readers to convey this message in clear,
compelling language. The problem with much popular Christian writing
is banality. The problem with much scholarly Christian writing is
obscurity. Why cannot there be both clarity and art? I think there can be
if Christian writers are willing to work on both the message and the form
of communicating it.

Clarity is essential. John Wesley, a cofounder of the Methodist
denomination, published a book of sermons in 1746. He wrote in his
introduction:

> I design plain truth for plain people; therefore, of set purpose, I
> abstain from all nice and philosophical speculations; from all
> perplexed and intricate reasonings; and, as far as possible, from even
> the show of learning. I labor to avoid all words which are not easy to
> be understood, all which are not used in common life; and, in
> particular, those kinds of technical terms that so frequently occur in
> Bodies of Divinity; those modes of speaking which men of reading are
> intimately acquainted with, but which to common people are an
> unknown tongue.[7]

As Paul put it, "In church I would rather speak five intelligible words to instruct others than ten thousand words in a tongue. Brothers, stop thinking like children. In regard to evil be infants, but in your thinking be adults" (1 Cor. 14:19–20).

Being "adult" in our thinking does not mean being obscure, pseudointellectual, or showy in our use of language. Some theological literature is like a black hole. It is so dense that no light can escape from it. Why not instead write in a jack-in-the-box style that promises a surprise and a delight? One reason why C. S. Lewis is so popular is that he paid the price of thinking deeply but clothing his thought in bright garments. Everyone is more attracted to a party costume than a funeral shroud.

Allow me to give a personal example of what I mean by this. I earned the Doctor of Theology degree in systematic theology in 1986. At the time I was pursuing my degree and writing my dissertation I was also the pastor of a church. I could sit in my seminars at seminary and discuss great books and write scholarly papers all I wanted. But when I went back home to my parish the people did not want or need purely academic theology. They had no interest in my reciting great recipes. They just wanted to know if there was anything to eat.

During the time I was writing my dissertation, I felt a strong internal need to write something of a completely different nature. I was captivated by Galatians 5:22 — "The fruit of the Spirit is love, joy, peace," and so on. I preached sermons on the fruit of the Spirit and also wrote a book about it entitled *Walking Straight in a Crooked World.*[8] There is a lot of me in that book. I remember that the book seemed to tumble out of me, and writing it was a joy.

Shortly after that book was published, I was invited to speak at a writers conference in Tacoma, Washington. The invitation came partly because of another book I had written — *Writing Religiously.*[9] The conference was a general one, and I was one of two people representing religious writing. I led a workshop and also shared in a panel discussion. On that panel were editors from several large publishing houses, and five agents from New York. When the discussion turned to religious writing, the editors and agents seemed to snort in contempt. They said they thought religious writing was junk, and none of them would touch it. One agent in particular seemed to be proud of her refusal to consider anything so far beneath her as inspirational writing. I felt a bit bruised by that experience, but I knew they were partially right.

That evening the conference officials invited me to take a dinner cruise on Puget Sound. One woman, who was my host at the conference, came up to me and said, "I just read your book, *Walking Straight in a*

Crooked World. I thought you said you wrote religious stuff." I stared at her for a moment and said, "I do. That book is a religious book." She said, "No it's not! I wouldn't be caught dead reading a religious book, but I read yours and loved it. I read it all the way through. I like your style. But it's not a religious book." We talked about it more, and I realized she had a prejudice against anything labeled "religious." She thought everything in that area was designed to force particular opinions down unwilling throats. For her and the agents and editors on the panel discussion, religious literature was propaganda that is merely an ugly stepchild of legitimate publishing.

I do not mention this experience to tout my book. It is not great, but it is folksy and, I hope, warm and alive. What I learned from that experience is the perspective many people have on Christian writing. They think of it as boring, shallow tripe with no real connection to contemporary life. Christian writers may be like the gnat in a story Aesop told. A gnat landed on the horn of a bull and then apologized. The bull said, "It doesn't matter. Actually, I didn't even know you were there." Are we Christian writers just gnats swarming around the horns of "real" publishers? I think not! But we do have a reputation of being uninformed, unintelligible, and uninteresting. Those three sins are unforgivable to secular publishers. They are finally becoming unforgivable to religious publishers, too.

... *And the Word Was with God* ...

How do we Christian writers move beyond drivel and trivia to works of significance? In a word, the answer lies in passion. To have passion is to be committed to our work the way a lover is committed to his beloved. This precludes writing that is as cold as an iceberg or as speculative as the stock market. Great writers are passionate people. The passionate writer gives himself or herself to the work at hand. The writing comes from the inside as something deeply felt and believed. When it emerges on the page, it is alive and moves. Such writing is sometimes a guard dog that snaps at our heels while we run away. At other times it is a lap dog that snuggles next to us and warms us with its breath. Passionate writing, though, is never a stuffed puppy to be tossed around at will.

Sherwood Anderson has said that a real writer is a lover. Consider his counsel.

> The disease we all have and that we have to fight against all our lives is, of course, the disease of self. I am pretty sure that writing may be a way of life in itself. It can be that, because it continually forces us

away from self toward others. Let any man, or woman, look too much upon his own life, and everything becomes a mess. I think the whole glory of writing lies in the fact that it forces us out of ourselves and into the lives of others. In the end the real writer becomes a lover.[10]

Writing *does* something. It changes the writer and also the reader. The story — whatever you are writing about — is both a personal offering and a sacred act. The late Jewish writer Martin Buber used to tell a story about a rabbi whose grandfather had been a pupil of the founder of Hasidism, the Baal Shem Tov. This rabbi was once asked to tell a story. He said, "A story ought to be told so that it is itself a help." Then he told this story: "My grandfather was paralyzed. Once he was asked to tell a story about his teacher and he told how the holy Baal Shem Tov used to jump and dance when he was praying. My grandfather stood up while he was telling the story and the story carried him away so much that he had to jump and dance to show how the master had done. From that moment, he was healed. That is how stories ought to be told."[11]

The passionate storyteller jumps and dances while telling a tale of jumping and dancing. The passionate writer puts herself into her work and emerges as a different person. J. B. Priestly referred to this as being "engrossed by an art." He compared himself with other earlier writers and concluded,

> The difference between us was not ability, but in the fact that while at heart they did not really much care about authorship, but merely toyed with the fascinating idea of it, I cared like blazes. And I suspect that in any form of art, it is this caring like blazes, while you are still young, that counts. Because you care and the dream never fades, other things, looking like those gifts of the gods, are added unto you. The very passion of the heart draws power. In some mysterious fashion, I suspect, you orientate your being so that such gifts as observation, invention, and imagination are pulled your way. . . .
>
> A mere desire for the rewards, no matter how constant and burning that desire may be, will not do the trick. You have to be fascinated from the first by the art itself, engrossed and spellbound, and not simply dazzled by the deceptively superior life of its successful practitioners. In this matter you have, in short, to be pure in heart before you can be blessed.[12]

He "cared like blazes." That is passion — in the quality that Christian writers need. It is internal heat that strikes sparks and warms the words in service of the Word.

Where does the source of our writing originate? Is it simply that we do market research and find something that will sell? Market research is critical, but that does not produce writing that is both timely and timeless. The poet Robert Frost was often asked about the sources of his poems. He answered his questioners this way:

> A poem is never a put-up job, so to speak. It begins as a lump in the throat, a sense of wrong, a homesickness, a love sickness. It is never a thought to begin with. It is at its best when it is a tantalizing vagueness. It finds its thought and succeeds or doesn't find it and comes to nothing. I suppose it finds it lying around with others not so much to its purpose in a more or less full mind.[13]

That lump in the throat or sense of wrong is like Jeremiah's fire in his bones and like Paul's "woe to me if I do not preach the gospel." Christian writing will improve when our works are less commissioned by the marketplace and more compelled by the living God.

Passion — another name for love — gives writers not only a voice but also eyes and ears. Conventional wisdom says that love helps us overlook the faults in others. That is only half true. Love helps us genuinely see and hear other people. A very wise seminary professor wrote a book about preaching and said that preachers, like writers, must learn to see and hear. Pay attention to his council and substitute "writer" in place of "pastor," and "writes" instead of "preaches."

> When a pastor preaches, he doesn't sell patent medicine; he writes prescriptions. Others may hurl epithets at the "wealthy" but the pastor knows a lonely and guilt-ridden man confused by the Bible's debate with itself over prosperity: Is prosperity a sign of God's favor or disfavor? Others may display knowledge of "poverty programs" but the pastor knows what a bitter thing it is to be somebody's Christmas project. He sees a boy resisting his mother's insistence that he wear the nice sweater that came in the charity basket. He can see the boy wear it until out of Mother's sight, but not at school out of fear that he may meet the original owner on the playground. There are conditions worse than being cold. Others may discuss "the problem of geriatrics" but the pastor has just come from the local rest home and he still sees worn checkerboards, faded bouquets, large print King James Bibles, stainless steel trays, and dim eyes staring at an empty parking lot reserved for visitors. Others may analyze "the trouble with the youth today" but the pastor sees a fuzzy-lipped boy, awkward, noisy, wishing he were absent, not a man, not a child, preoccupied with ideas that contradict his fourteen years' severe judgment against the girls.[14]

Are you awake and seeing? There is little room for theological Rip Van Winkles.

... And the Word Was God ...

Writers are lovers, and lovers are seers. That is what made Jesus, the Word, so effective with words. He was passionate about what he said, not that he shouted all the time but rather that he was totally present in his encounters with people. Think about his life as portrayed in the gospels. Jesus was observant of everyday life. He communicated with wit and humor, giving us pictures of religious leaders who strained out gnats and swallowed a camel, and blind people leading blind people. He turned potentially embarrassing situations into object lessons through his repartee: a coin with Caesar's image enabled him to teach the disciples to give to Caesar the things that are Caesar's and to God the things that are God's.

Jesus spun homey images: a woman looking for a lost coin, a father waiting for a lost son. He collected pictures from nature: the lilies of the field and the birds of the air taken care of by God. He invested himself in the lives of individuals: Zacchaeus the tax collector and Mary of Magdalene. He borrowed from traditional wisdom and renewed its meaning: "You have heard it said . . . but I say to you." He felt deeply about life: he wept at the death of Lazarus and was angry with moneychangers in the temple.

When Jesus spoke, people listened. Mark 1:22 says, "The people were amazed at his teaching, because he taught them as one who had authority, not as the teachers of the law." The word *authority* here is from the Greek *exousia*. *Ex* means "out of" and *ousia* means "essence" or "inner reality." Jesus spoke out of his inner reality.[15] His message was self-validating and authentic. Jesus never wrote anything that exists today, but his spoken words collected in the New Testament indicate a man who was alive at the center. He had imagination, wit, strong emotions, tender love, powerful language abilities, and an inviting personality. He is the model for Christians in general and for Christian writers in particular.

When all is said and done, what is Christian writing? Like all other writing, it strives for excellence. Christian writing communicates its vital message with metaphors. Its words are bouillon cubes that melt in the mind of the reader to provide concentrated nourishing sustenance. Its sentences are springs, coiled, compressed, and ready to spring loose in the reader's mind to produce surprise and effect. Its paragraphs are lozenges to dissolve slowly on the mental tongue to soothe and heal. Its pages are Jalapeño peppers that look harmless enough, but after one bite the reader will know he has chomped down on something significant.

Like all writing, Christian writing strives to spin its tales to keep the reader's attention. We are like Scheherazade who told stories to a caliph who married many brides successively and had them beheaded the next day. Scheherazade told him such an enthralling and suspensefull story that the sultan stayed the execution a day so he could hear the end of the story. That went on night after night. Sheer interest in the story kept the girl alive. Today readers can execute a writer with a yawn.

Christian writing aims to produce a Rice Krispies effect. We want our message to go "snap, crackle, pop" in the minds of readers. A writer succeeds when a reader says, "Hmm, I've never thought of it that way before," or, "I didn't know that," or even, "I don't agree with this at all!" To jump start the reader's brain is a worthy goal. Empty words will not do that. As Ecclesiastes 6:11 says, "The more the words, the less the meaning, and how does that profit anyone?"

Christian writing uses similes to hang pictures on the gallery of the mind. A Christian writer is like a midwife struggling to assist in the birth of a new manner of conveying the Word. Or he is like a circus clown who brings joy and laughter and humanity to a theater of absolute skills and death-defying stunts. Or again, he is like the sculptor Michelangelo who could look at a block of marble and see an angel. The writer can look at a blank page and see a story wanting to take shape and life.

The Christian writer is like a carpenter who crafts his structure piece by piece. His care and commitment to excellence are evident in the finished product. The Christian writer is like a star thrower. Anthropologist Loren Eisley was once walking along a beach where he saw people gathering shells. One man was collecting starfish that had washed up on the beach that night. Whenever he found one still alive, the man would throw it back into the water. Eisley began to throw the starfish back, too. He said that was like sowing, the sowing of life. That is the Christian writer. She is an enabler of life rather than a cataloger of death. She offers hope, truth, and life rather than tragedy and destruction.

Christian writing is oxymoronic. An oxymoron is a figure of speech in which an effect is created by a paradoxical coupling of terms. The word literally means "sharp fool." Christian writing is a romantic disenchantment. The imagined romantic life of a writer jetting off to exotic locations, working in a lavish office with the latest equipment, and living off fat royalty checks is tempered with the disenchantment of the reality. We who are writers would live far below the poverty line if we depended on royalties alone. We might take the bus across town if we can find the right change. Our office might be a corner of the pantry equipped with an ironing board, a #2 pencil, and a Big Chief school tablet.

Christian writing is a boring challenge. We crank an 8½-by-11-inch battle zone into the IBM Selectric or boot up Microsoft Word on the

Macintosh or scratch a Bic pen on loose-leaf paper. Any of those actions creates anxiety and excitement. The writer knows that communicating by this medium can be challenging and boring at the same time. Writing is work, and work can be drudgery. It can also be exhilarating as we discover things about ourselves and our world we never before imagined.

Christian writing is a contemporary anachronism. It seems out of date and out of sequence in time. Who talks of God anymore? Yet the question of God is never far from most people, even the outwardly nonreligious. The Christian writer poses the God question in many different ways, sometimes obliquely, sometimes overtly. It may be done as Charles Stanley does it or as Walker Percy did it. But whatever the approach, the question of ultimate reality forms and informs our work.

Christian writing is a joyful tyranny. To be a writer is to be possessed by some inner need to write. This need can be tyrannical. Do "normal" people spend a fortune on writing equipment and resources? Do "normal" people stay up at all hours of the night punching the keyboard in the slight hope that someone may actually read their work? To be a writer can be a terrible joy. It holds terrors with one arm and lilting joy with the other. We writers are hugged with both arms at the same time. No wonder we can be a bit eccentric!

... In Him Was Life, and That Life Was the Light of Men ...

I said at the beginning of this chapter that my purpose was not to construct a systematic theology of Christian writing. Instead, what I wanted to do was to take this diamond and turn it a bit to allow different facets of light to emerge. The basic conviction of Christianity is that Jesus is the light of the world. As light, he forces out darkness and keeps the terrors of the night at bay. We who write are mere candles to this sun. But light is light, whether much or little.

To make our light shine, we must overcome several attitudes and situations that strangle our writing. One attitude is a false stress on humility. I am thinking here about an attitude among some Christians that goes something like this: "Jesus said we must deny ourselves. But if I seek publication in my writing, then I am promoting myself and thereby sinning." My answer to that? Hogwash! Any writer who thinks like this has some inner fantasy about becoming famous and then losing zeal for Christ. You can forget it. You will not become famous as a Christian writer, so you can escape from this false humility. A writer is a servant of the Word with words. But a servant is still a servant, and there is no room for "stars" or "celebrities" among us. The recent televangelist scandal taught us this fact.

Another situation that hurts our writing is the nonconnectional nature of our lives. Christian writers are not like Nashville songwriters. We do not gather in taverns to guzzle beer, swap stories, argue, posture, and write songs. I am not suggesting that we do so. We have churches and maybe even writers' clubs, but most writers work in isolation. Proverbs 27:17 says, "As iron sharpens iron, so one man sharpens another." I often wish for closer contact with others who share my interest in writing. My editor friends are greatly valued, but I see them irregularly. A good writers' conference is useful in breaking the sense of isolation and sharpening us.

Some writers are simply lazy. They will not hustle, sweat, study, write, and re-write; in short, they will not pay the price of being a writer. Writing is not a dainty pastime. It is real work with real demands and rewards. I have friends who tell me they envy me my work. I try to point out that they can write also if they are willing to pay the price in time and energy. They want to have written and enjoy the finished product. They do not want to write and put up with the anxiety and sweat involved in the process.

One attitude that affects some Christian writers is presumption. This is seen in the person who says, "God will give me the message and write it for me." That is pure presumption. God gave us minds with which to think and hands with which to write. God inspires and energizes us through his Spirit, but the work is left up to us. The late Red Smith once said, "Sure, writing is easy. All you have to do is sit down and open a vein."

A narrow understanding of holiness holds back some Christian writers. James 1:27 tells us to keep ourselves from "being polluted by the world." We want to heed that warning, but what does it mean? Some Christians seem to think that they can avoid worldly pollution by simply being ignorant of life around them. If that is the case, what do they have to offer people? The trick is to be in the world but not of the world, to be aware of life and issues but not to be dragged down by attitudes and actions apart from God.

Playing loose with facts is another attitude that hurts Christian writers. One editor speaks of some Christians who speak and write "evangelastically."[16] Truth is not elastic and will not stretch. I am not referring here simply to making mistakes. Everyone does that. My point is that some writers feel free to disregard facts or to spin them in their favor. Others will not bother to check the accuracy of so-called facts before acting on them. One case in point is the supposed petition from

Madelyn Murray O'Hair to have religious broadcasting banned. Over a decade and a half the Federal Communication Commission has received millions of letters protesting this atheistic intrusion. The only problem is that there is no such thing as the O'Hair petition. It never existed. It got started as a rumor and took on a life of its own. The Christian writer, of all people, must be accurate with facts and check things out. We can be creative and imaginative in our writing but we cannot invent truth or dream up facts.

Fear of failure holds back some Christian writers. They do not like rejection. If they never send out manuscripts, they will never be rejected. But to fail to try is a worse failure than trying and being turned down. Besides, we are in good company if our manuscripts seem like boomerangs that keep coming back. Successful people in all walks of life face rejection. Actor Dustin Hoffman was rejected four times from the Actors Studio before he finally made it through. Sidney Poitier was once thrown out of a theater group for black actors. Watercolorist Dong Kingman did not make it at the Oakland School of Painting, yet at a recent auction one of his watercolors received a higher bid than a Picasso. I can speak to this matter from personal experience. I once had a book manuscript turned down by 87 publishers. The 88th published it, and it became a main coselection by the Religious Book Club. Accept rejection as a temporary setback but never quit.

So go ahead. Write. Seek publication. Be salt and light in this dark and decaying world. You will not get rich and famous (but if you do, remember me in your will). Give to others what Christ has given to you. The blessing is in the doing. Write. Right now.

NOTES

1. Theodore W. Jennings, Jr., *Introduction To Theology* (Philadelphia: Fortress, 1976), 6.

2. Ibid., 7.

3. This humorous list was published in *Parables* (May 1990), 3.

4. Carl F. H. Henry, quoted in a special mini-report, "Trends in the Church," from "National and International Religion Report," no date given.

5. John Warwick Montgomery, "The Emperor's Clothes," in *Moody Monthly* (April 1987), 10.

6. "Doublespeak Tries to Sneak By," a Scripps Howard News Service story in *The Commercial Appeal* (Memphis, 4 July 1988), A2.

7. John Wesley, quoted in W. E. Sangster, *Power in Preaching* (London: Epworth, 1958), 68.

8. *Walking Straight in a Crooked World* (Nashville: Broadman, 1986).

9. Co-authored with Leonard Goss (Grand Rapids: Baker, 1984).

10. Sherwood Anderson, quoted by Charles L. Wallis, ed., *Speakers' Illustrations for Special Days* (New York: Abingdon, 1956), 55. The original source is Howard Mumford Jones, ed., *Letters of Sherwood Anderson* (Boston: Little, Brown, n.d.).

11. This tale of the Baal Shem Tov is told many places. This one came from Martin E. Marty, *By Way of Response* (Nashville: Abingdon, 1981).

12. J. B. Priestley, quoted by Halford E. Luccock, *In The Minister's Workshop* (Nashville: Abingdon, 1944), 34. The original source is *Rain upon Godshill* (New York: Harper & Bros., 1939), 164.

13. Robert Frost, in a letter to Louis Untermeyer, 1 January 1916, quoted in Stanley Burnshaw, *Robert Frost Himself* (New York: George Braziller, 1986), 282.

14. Fred Craddock, *As One Without Authority*, rev. ed. (Enid, Okla.: Phillips University Press, 1974), 82.

15. If you are interested in reading more about this, consult chapter 3 of my book *Eight Days That Changed the World* (Nashville: Broadman, 1990).

16. Chip Bailey, "Editor's Notebook," *Remnant Christian Magazine* (September 1990), 19.

SUGGESTED READING

Bausch, William J. *Storytelling: Imagination and Faith*. Mystic, Conn.: Twenty-Third Publications, 1984.

A theology of storytelling developed in the telling of stories. Characteristics of stories, parables, and paradoxes. A book to inform the abilities and affect the will.

Brueggeman, Walter. *The Prophetic Imagination*. Philadelphia: Fortress, 1978.

The unique ways in which the Old Testament prophets and Jesus learned to see differently from their countrymen; instructive for helping writers to "see" differently.

Carpenter, Humphrey. *The Inklings: C. S. Lewis, J. R. R. Tolkien, Charles Williams, and Their Friends*. New York: Ballantine, 1981.

The literary origins and effects of the works of this circle of writers. A fine study of how writers can learn from one another and spur each other on to better things.

Fischer, Kathleen R. *The Inner Rainbow: The Imagination in Christian Life*. Ramsey, N.J.: Paulist, 1983.

How imagination is linked to everything from spirituality to the arts to morality to ministry.

Forbes, Cheryl. *Imagination: Embracing a Theology of Wonder*. Portland, Oreg.: Multnomah Press, 1986.

Imagination as a gift of God that is not to be mistreated or ignored.

Lockerbie, D. Bruce. *The Liberating Word: Art and the Mystery of the Gospel*. Grand Rapids: Eerdmans, 1974.

An insightful look at creativity and the creative process.

Luccock, Halford E. *In the Minister's Workshop*. Nashville: Abingdon, 1944.

A book on preaching, but, more than that, about communication.

Young, Robert D. *Religious Imagination: God's Gift to Prophets and Preachers*. Philadelphia: Westminster, 1979.

A look at God's activity and creativity and how that affects Christians who seek to communicate God's message.

Chapter 3

Art and Propaganda

Philip E. Yancey

If someone were to tell me that it lay in my power to write a novel explaining every social question from a particular viewpoint that I believed to be the correct one, I still wouldn't spend two hours on it. But if I were told that what I am writing will be read in twenty years' time by the children of today, and that those children will laugh, weep, and learn to love life as they read, why then I would devote the whole of my life and energy to it.

The man who wrote those words, Leo Tolstoy, vacillated continually between art and propaganda. Twenty years, even seventy years, after his death people are still laughing, weeping, and learning to love life as they read his books, but others are also reflecting on, arguing with, and reacting to his particular viewpoint on social, moral and religious questions. Although in this quote Tolstoy claims to come down firmly on the side of art, veins of "propaganda" run throughout his novels, inspiring some readers and infuriating others. In nonfiction works like *What is Art?*

Philip Yancey is a free-lance writer and editor-at-large for Christianity Today, Inc. He served as general editor of *The Student Bible* (NIV) and is the author or co-author of numerous books, including four that have received the ECPA Gold Medallion Award: *Disappointment with God, Fearfully and Wonderfully Made, In His Image,* and *Where Is God When It Hurts.*

the great novelist leans toward propaganda, even, as some conclude, at the expense of true art.

Like a bipolar magnet, the Christian author today feels the pull of both forces: a fervent desire to communicate what gives life meaning counteracted by an artistic inclination toward self-expression, form, and structure that any "message" might interrupt. The result: a constant, dichotomous pull toward both propaganda and art. Propaganda is a word currently out of favor, connoting unfair manipulation or distortion of means to an end. I use it in a more acceptable sense, the original sense of the word as coined Pope Urban VIII. He formed the College of Propaganda in the seventeenth century in order to disseminate the Christian faith. As a Christian writer, I must readily admit that I do strive for propaganda in this sense. Much of what I write is designed to convert or to cause others to consider a viewpoint I hold to be true.

Counterbalancing the literary tug away from propaganda, many evangelicals exert an insidious tug away from art. They would react to Tolstoy's statement with disbelief — to choose a novel that entertains and fosters a love for life over a treatise that solves every social (or, better, religious) question of mankind! How can a person "waste" time with mere aesthetics — soothing music, pleasing art, entertaining literature — when injustice rules the nations and the decadent world marches ineluctably to destruction? Is this not fiddling while Rome burns? Currently novels written by evangelicals tend toward the propagandistic (even to the extent of fictionalizing Bible stories and foretelling the Second Coming) and away from the artful.

Somewhere in this magnetic field between art and propaganda the Christian author (or painter or musician) works. One force tempts us to lower artistic standards and preach an unadorned message; another tempts us to submerge or even alter the message for the sake of artistic sensibilities. Having lived in the midst of this tension for over a decade, I have come to recognize it as a healthy synthetical tension that should be affirmed. Success often lies with the extremes: an author may succeed in the evangelical world by erring on the side of propaganda. But ever so slowly, the fissure between the Christian and secular worlds will yawn wider. If we continue tilting toward propaganda, we will soon find ourselves writing and selling books to ourselves alone. On the other hand, the Christian author cannot simply absorb the literary standards of the larger world. Our ultimate goal cannot be a self-expression, but rather a God-expression.

C. S. Lewis explored the polarity in the address "Learning in Wartime," delivered to Oxford students who were trying to concentrate on academics while their friends fought in the trenches of Europe and staved off the German aerial assault on London. How, asked Lewis, can creatures who are advancing every moment either to heaven or hell spend any fraction of time on such comparative trivialities as literature, art, math, or biology (let alone Lewis' field of medieval literature)? With great perception, Lewis noted that the condition of wartime did not change the underlying question, but merely accelerated the timing by making it more likely that any one person would advance *soon* to heaven or hell.

The most obvious answer to the dilemma is that God himself invested great energy in the natural world. In the Old Testament he created a distinct culture and experimented with a variety of literary forms which endure as masterpieces. As for biology and physics, everything we know about them derives from painstakingly tracing his creative activity. For a Christian, the natural world provides a medium to express and even discover the image of God. Nevertheless, while Lewis affirms the need for good art and good science, he readily admits that Christianity knocks culture off its pedestal. The salvation of a single soul, he says, is worth more than all the poetry, drama, and tragedy ever written. (A committed Christian must acknowledge that intrinsic worth, and yet how many of us react with dismay when reading of such terrible tragedies as the burning of the library in Alexandria, the destruction of the Parthenon during the Crusades, and the bombing of cathedrals in World War II while scarcely giving a thought to the thousands of nameless civilians buried in the rubble of those edifices?)

The dilemma of art and propaganda is essentially a tremor of the seismic human dilemma of living in a divinely created but fallen world. Beauty abounds, and we are right to seek it and to seek to reproduce it. And yet tragedy and despair and meaninglessness also abound, and we must not neglect addressing ourselves to the human condition. That is why I affirm both art and propaganda. As an author, I experiment with different forms and I hope to express my propaganda (if the word offends you, read "message") as artfully as possible and to imbue my art with a worthwhile message. I embrace both art and propaganda, rejecting the pressures to conform to one or the other.

In dealing with the tensions of art and propaganda over the years, I have learned a few guidelines that allow for a more natural wedding of the two. Whenever I have broken one of these guidelines, I have usually awakened to the abrupt and painful realization that I have tilted too far toward either art or propaganda. In either case my message gets lost, whether through pedantic communication or through a muddle of empty verbiage. Because Christian writers are mainly erring on the side of propaganda, not art, my guidelines speak primarily to that error.

1. An artful propagandist takes into account the ability of the audience to perceive.

For the Christian writer (or speaker) who wants to communicate to a secular audience, this caution cannot be emphasized too strongly. In effect, you must consider two different sets of vocabulary. Words which have a certain meaning to you as a Christian may have an entirely different, sometimes even antithetical, meaning to your secular listener. Consider a few examples of fine words which have had their meanings spoiled over time. Pity once derived from piety: a person dispensed pity in a godlike, compassionate sense. By responding to the poor and the needy, one was mimicking God, and therefore pietous, or full of pity. Similarly, as any reader of the King James Version knows, charity was an example of God's grace, a synonym for love (as in the famous 1 Corinthians 13 passage). Over the centuries, both those words lost their meaning until they ultimately became negatively charged. "I don't want pity!" or "Don't give me charity!" a needy person protests today. The theological significance has been sucked away.

Similarly, many words we now use to express personal faith may miscommunicate rather than communicate. The word *God* may summon up all sorts of inappropriate images, unless the Christian goes on to explain what he or she means by God. Love, a vital theological word, has lost its meaning — for popular conceptions of it, merely flip a radio dial and listen to popular music stations. The word redemption most often relates to trading stamps, and few cultural analogies can adequately express that concept. Blood is as easily associated with death as with life.

As words change in meaning, Christian communicators must adapt accordingly, selecting words and metaphors which precisely fit the culture. Concepts, too, depend on the audience's ability to absorb them, and often we must adapt downwards to a more basic level. If I see a three-year-old girl endangering herself, I must warn her in terms she can understand. For example, what if the child decides to stick her finger first into her mouth and then into an electrical outlet. I would not respond by searching out my *Reader's Digest Home Handyman Encyclopedia* and launching into an elaborate monologue on amps, volts, and electrical resistance. Rather, I will more likely slap her hand and say something like "There's fire in there! You'll be burned!" Although, strictly speaking, the outlet box contains no literal fire, I will choose concepts that communicate to the comprehension level of a three-year-old.

Andrew Young reports that he learned an essential principle of survival during the civil rights struggle. "Don't judge the adversary by how you think," he says. "Learn to think like the adversary." He voiced that principle in the days of the Iran hostage crisis when news accounts were using such adjectives as "insane, crazed, demonic" to describe Iranian leaders. Those labels, said Young, do nothing to facilitate communication. To understand Iran, we must first consider their viewpoint. To the militants, the Shah was as brutal and vicious as Adolf Hitler; therefore they were reacting to the U.S. as we would respond to a country that deliberately sheltered a mass murderer like Hitler.

In a parallel way, when Christians attempt to communicate to non-Christians, we must first think through their assumptions and imagine how they will likely receive the message we are conveying. That process will affect the words we choose, the form and, most importantly, the content we can get across. If we err on the side of too much content, as Christians often do, the net effect is the same as if we had included no content.

Alexander Solzhenitsyn, who has walked a tightrope between art and propaganda all his life, learned this principle after being released from the concentration camps when his writing finally began to find acceptance in Soviet literary journals. In *The Oak and the Calf* he recalls, "Later, when I popped up from the underground and began lightening my works for the outside world, lightening them of all that my fellow countrymen could hardly be expected to accept at once, I discovered to my surprise that a piece only gained, that its effect was heightened, as the harsher tones were softened."

(We must use caution here, as Solzhenitsyn learned. A new danger may seep in: the subtle tendency to lighten too much and thus change the message. *Just drop this one offensive word*, the Soviet censors coaxed Solzhenitsyn. *There's really no need to capitalize God—that's archaic. If you want us to publish* One Day in the Life of Ivan Denisovich, *merely cross out this one problematic line.* Solzhenitsyn resisted those last two requests; he capitalized God and left the controversial sentence, "I crossed myself, and said to God: 'Thou art there in heaven after all, O creator. Thy patience is long, but thy blows are heavy.'" Acceding to such pressure would efface his whole message, he decided.)

Whenever a Christian addresses a secular audience, he or she must maintain a balance between leaving the message intact and adapting it to that audience. We who are Christians stumble across God everywhere. We ascribe daily events to his activity. We see his hand in nature and the Bible. He seems fully evident to us. But to the secular mind, the question is how is it even possible to find God in the maze of cults, religions, and television mountebanks, all clamoring for attention against the background of a starving, war-torn planet. Unless we truly understand that viewpoint, and speak in terms the secular mind can understand, our words will have the quaint and useless ring of a foreign language.

2. Artful propaganda works like a deduction rather than a rationalization.

Recently, psychologists have begun to define an instinctual process of rationalization in the human mind, sometimes labeled the theory of cognitive dissonance. Basically, it means that the human mind, intolerant of a state of tension and disharmony, works to patch up inconsistencies with a self-affirming process of rationalization.

I am late to a luncheon with a publisher. Obviously, according to this theory, it cannot be my fault — I start with that assumption. It must be the traffic. Or my wife. Or the others at the meeting, who showed up on time.

My article is rejected. Instantly I start consoling myself with the knowledge that hundreds of manuscripts were rejected that day. The editor could have had a bad breakfast. Perhaps no one even read my manuscript. Any number of factors arise to explain my rejection. My mind tries to quiet the jarring cacophony caused by this bit of news.

I define the process of rationalization very simply: it occurs when a person knows the end result first, and reasons backwards. The conclusion is a given; I merely need to find a way to support that conclusion. I ran headlong into an example of the process of rationalization while researching an article about Wycliffe Bible Translators. Since rumors of Wycliffe's CIA involvement proliferate, I felt it essential to try and track them down. I telephoned outspoken critics of Wycliffe all over the country. One, a professor in a New York university, insisted that Wycliffe was definitely subsidized by the CIA. I asked for proof. "It's quite obvious," he replied. "They claim to raise their $30 million annual budget from fundamentalist churches. You and I both know there's not $30 million available from that source. Obviously, they're getting it from somewhere else." Had that professor done a little research, he would have discovered that each of the five top television evangelists pulls in over $50 million annually from religious sympathizers. Certainly the pool of resources in the United States is large enough to account for Wycliffe's contributions. But he started from a foregone conclusion and reasoned backward.

Solzhenitsyn encountered a startling case of rationalization when the Soviet editor Lebedev said to him, "If Tolstoy were alive now and wrote as he did then (meaning against the government) he wouldn't be Tolstoy." Lebedev's opinion about his government was so firmly set that he could not allow a plausible threat to it and so he rationalized that Tolstoy would be a different man under a new regime.

Sadly, much of what I read in Christian literature has an echo of rationalization. I get the sense that the author starts with an unshakable conclusion and merely sets out to discover whatever logical course could support that conclusion. Much of what I read on depression, on suicide, on homosexuality, seems written by people who begin with a Christian conclusion, and who have never been through the anguished steps that are the familiar path to a person struggling with depression, suicide, or homosexuality. No wonder the "how-to" articles and books do not ring true. No conclusions could be so flip and matter-of-fact to a person who has actually endured such a journey.

A conclusion has impact only if the reader has been primed for it by moving along the steps that lead to it before being confronted with the conclusion. The conclusion must be the logical outgrowth, the consummation of what went before, not the starting place.

C. S. Lewis, Charles Williams, and J. R. R. Tolkien struggled with these issues intensely as they worked on fiction that reveals an underlying layer of Christianity. Lewis and Tolkien particularly reacted with fire against well-meaning Christians who would slavishly point to all the symbolism in their books, such as labeling the characters of Aslan and Gandalf as Christ-figures. Even though the parallels were obvious, both authors vigorously resisted admitting that had been their intent. Those characters may indeed point to Christ, but by shadowing forth a deeper, underlying cosmic truth. One cannot argue backwards and describe the characters as mere symbolic representations — that would shatter their individuality and literary impact. (I often wonder if Lewis erred on the side of propaganda with Aslan and thus limited his non-Christian audience, whereas Tolkien's greater subtlety may last for centuries.)

In one article I alluded to several novels by Tolstoy and Dostoyevsky which begin with poignant quotations from Scripture. Their authors selected those verses because they summarize a central message. Yet are the novels (*Anna Karenina, Resurrection, The Idiot,* and *The Brothers Karamazov*) propaganda? Only a hardened cynic would say so. The novels, rather, incarnate the concept behind the Bible references so compellingly and convincingly that the reader must acknowledge the truth of what he or she reads. To be effective, a Christian communicator must make the point inside the reader before the reader consciously acknowledges it.

3. Artful propaganda must be "sincere."

I put the word sincere in quotes because I refer to its original meaning only. Like so many words, sincere has been preempted by modern advertising and twisted so badly that it ends up meaning its opposite.

Consider, for example, a shy, timid salesman, who doesn't mix well at parties and cannot be assertive on sales calls. He is sent by his manager to a Dale Carnegie course to improve his self-confidence. "You must be *sincere* to be a successful salesman," he is told, and he practices various techniques for sincerity. *Start with the handshake—it must be firm, confident, steady. Here, try it a few times. Now that you have that down, let's work on eye contact. See, when you shake my hand, you should be staring me right in the eye. Don't look away or even waver. Stare straight into me—that's a mark of sincerity. Your customer must feel you really care about him.*

For a fee of several hundred dollars, our insecure salesman learns techniques of sincerity. His next customers are impressed by his conscientiousness, his confidence in his product, and his concern for them, all because he has learned a body language. Actually, an acquired technique to communicate something not already present is the opposite of the true meaning of sincere. The word, a sculptor's term, derives from two Latin words, *sine cera*, "without wax." Even the best of sculptors makes an occasional slip of the chisel, causing an unsightly gouge. Sculptors who work with marble know that wax mixed to the proper color can fill in that gouge so perfectly that few observers could ever spot the flaw. A truly perfect piece, however, one that needs no artificial touch-up, is *sincere*, without wax. What you see is what you get — there are no embellishments or cover-ups.

Propaganda becomes bad propaganda because of the touch-up wax authors apply to their work. If we can truly write in a sincere way, reflecting reality, then our work will reflect truth and reinforce our central message. If not, readers will spot the flaws and judge our work accordingly.

When I read *The Oak and the Calf*, I laughed aloud as I read the Soviet censors' advice to Solzhenitsyn, because their script could have been written by an evangelical magazine editor. Three things must not appear in Russian literature, they solemnly warned Solzhenitsyn: (1) Pessimism, (2) Denigration, and (3) Surreptitious sniping. Cover up your tendencies to realism with a layer that might soften the overall effect, they seemed to be saying.

Biography and fiction written by evangelicals too often show wax badly gaumed over obvious flaws. We leave out details of struggle and realism that do not fit neatly into our propaganda. Or, we include scenes that have no realism just to reinforce our point. Even the untrained observer can spot the flaws, and slight bulges here and there can ruin a work of art.

All three of these temptations to propagandize in the bad sense increase with a captive, supportive audience. When we no longer have to win people over to our point of view, for example, realism can become an impediment. The Christian public will applaud books in which every prayer is answered and every disease is healed, but to the degree those books do not reflect reality, they will become meaningless to a skeptical audience. Too often our evangelical literature appears to the larger world as strange and unconvincing as a Moonie tract or *Daily Worker* magazine.

For models of these three guidelines of artful communication, we can look to the Creator himself. He took into account the audience's ability to perceive in the ultimate sense — by flinging aside his deity and becoming the Word, one of us, living in our cramped planet and within the limitations of a human body. In his communication through creation, his Son, and the Bible, he gave only enough evidence for those with faith to follow the deductions to truth about him, but yet without defying human freedom. And as for being sincere, has a more earthy, realistic book ever been written than the Bible?

A friend of mind, a hand surgeon, was awakened from a thick sleep by a 3 A.M. telephone call and summoned to an emergency surgery. He specializes in microsurgery, reconnecting nerves and blood vessels finer than human hairs, performing meticulous twelve-hour procedures with no breaks. As he tried to overcome his grogginess, he realized he needed a little extra motivation to endure this one marathon surgery. On impulse he called a close friend, also awakening him. "I have a very arduous surgery ahead of me, and I need something extra to concentrate on this time," he said. "I'd like to dedicate this surgery to you. If I think about you while I'm performing it, that will help me get through."

Should not that be the Christian author's response to God — an offering of our work in dedication to him? If so, how dare we possibly produce propaganda without art, or art without meaning?

To those few who succeed and become models of artistic excellence, the Christian message takes on a new glow. Looking back on T. S. Eliot's life, Russell Kirk said, "He made the poet's voice heard again, and thereby triumphed; knowing the community of souls, he freed others from captivity to time and the lonely ego; in the teeth of winds of doctrine, he attested the permanent things. And his communication is tongued with fire beyond the language of the living."

Chapter 4

Pitfalls of Christian Writing

Philip E. Yancey

T hou hast conquered, O pale Galilean, and the world has grown gray with Thy breath." Thus concluded the poet Charles Swinburne about the wearisome effect of Christianity on culture at large.

I can speak comfortably only about the field of writing, and that indeed has grown gray in recent years. Walk into any Christian bookstore and thumb your way through the orderly, monochrome rows of self-help books, lifeless theological works, and personal testimonies. Very few seem interesting or appealing enough to attract readers from the general populace. Those who browse in the religious stores, surveys show, represent a scant ten percent even of the forty million born-again Christians who supposedly live tucked away in the corners of America.

Fortunately for Christian publishing, that ten percent is large enough to support a passel of evangelical publishers and a burgeoning industry of six thousand Christian bookstores. The sales figures are indisputable: three evangelical books placed on the top-twenty-of-the-decade list and several million-copy sellers appear annually. And yet, is

Philip Yancey is a free-lance writer and editor-at-large for Christianity Today, Inc. He served as general editor of *The Student Bible* (NIV) and is the author or co-author of numerous books, including four that have received the ECPA Gold Medallion Award: *Disappointment with God, Fearfully and Wonderfully Made, In His Image,* and *Where Is God When It Hurts.*

Christian literature penetrating culture, or is the fissure separating Christian readers from the broader public yawning ever wider?

I will leave the consumer buying habits for marketers to worry over, but an underlying question haunts me as a Christian author: why should anyone read anything religious? Hundreds of Christian books have crossed my desk in the last decade and, I must admit, after a time they do seem to look and sound alike. I have watched literary sparks flare up in the Jewish and Catholic subcultures, but why have evangelicals produced such mediocrity?

Sales may well continue to double every five years, but I care more about the quality of Christian writing. I have tried to analyze trends in the books I have seen in order to erect "Caution!" signs around the pitfalls of Christian writing. Below, I outline four criticisms of Christian writing, criticisms that I accept for myself, as a Christian author. I do not intend to point to specific negative examples and therefore must paint "Christian writing" with a very broad brush. Will high standards of quality improve sales? Who knows? I am convinced, however, that we Christian authors must strive for higher literary standards for our work to be taken seriously in the world at large. A captive audience will read indiscriminately; a skeptical or even hostile audience must be lured.

Thought Without Art

Too often Christian writing performs a kind of literary decapitation: we render the head without the body, the thought without the art. We allow someone to speak to us with his or her brain only, while keeping concealed the background and context which produced those thoughts. For example, we will record Christian leaders' thoughts about lifestyles without delving into how they spend their own money and free time. In our profiles of Christian leaders, we give little regard to the stages of development and processes that contributed to form their opinions.

Numerous examples in the secular world should teach us how a person's head can be artfully connected to his body, and John McPhee is one of the best practitioners. McPhee resists the moniker of nonfiction, and why indeed should a category of writing be labeled by what is not? Preferring "the literature of fact," he has led the way in showing how fact can be written as good literature.

I think especially of McPhee's book, *Encounters With the Archdruid*, in which he sets conservationist David Brower against the forces that would destroy his beloved nature. Of the scores of articles and books I have read analyzing the clash between industrial growth and natural resource

48

conservation, none comes close to McPhee's artful presentation. He sets the stage by describing the adversaries.

Brower hardly resembles the stereotyped Forest Ranger or mountain hiker: he is balding and, except for a pot-belly, seems frail, with pale legs like toothpicks protruding from his shorts. But he has led the fight for conservation, first with the Sierra Club and then with the John Muir Institute. (And, incidentally, he has climbed nearly every mountain in America over 14,000 feet.)

Floyd Dominy is Brower's exact opposite: a tall, good-looking cowboy who wears a ten-gallon hat, smokes a fat cigar, and spins one yarn after another. Starting back in Dust Bowl days, Dominy devoted his life to building dams and eventually rose to the position of head of the Bureau of Land Management. He and Brower constantly lock horns, especially in courtrooms, as Brower seeks injunctions to halt Dominy's latest dam project. Everything you would want to know about the complex growth/no growth decisions confronting civilization is contained in McPhee's book, but embodied in an absorbing style. Entertaining personalities come to stand as archetypes for the philosophies they represent.

In one sequence, McPhee takes a rafting trip down the Colorado River with Brower and Dominy. There, in the surging rapids of the Colorado, between the gorges of the Grand Canyon, around a fire on the great river's banks, we get to know the two men and observe the collision of two powerful movements in Western civilization. Perhaps McPhee does not include as many histrionic facts about the clash as other reporters and journalists might have done, but no one I have read captures the conflict more graphically. McPhee gives us the ideas behind each movement in an unforgettable narrative form.

George Plimpton accomplished the same result in a different arena with an article in *Harper's*. He wished to feature Marianne Moore, a demure Catholic poet. But who today reads articles on poets, even if this poet is one of the greatest? In a stroke of great ingenuity, Plimpton succeeded by linking her with one of the worst poets, but most colorful characters, of our time. He set up a luncheon between Moore and Muhammad Ali, and simply recorded what happened.

What happened was that Muhammad Ali decided to honor Marianne Moore by letting her participate with him on a joint effort. His topic: a fight with Ernie Terrell. Plimpton describes the hilarious interaction of Ali and the utterly intimidated Moore. The two finally do produce a "poem." Writes Plimpton, "While we waited, he told me that he was going to get the poem out over the Associated Press wire that afternoon. Mrs. Moore's eyes widened. The irony of all those years struggling with *Broom* and all the other literary magazines, and now to be with a fighter who promised instant publication over a ticker. It did not help the flow of inspiration. She was doubtless intimidated by Ali's presence, especially at his obvious concern that she, a distinguished poet, was having such a hard time holding up her side. In his mind speed of delivery was very much a qualification of a professional poet."

In his indirect way, Plimpton exposes American culture and its values and the role of art and entertainment in that culture. He achieves that in a holistic and incarnational manner. His treatment is memorable, but not shrill; in fact, he never draws the moral for his readers. The article itself is the message — the implication of that bizarre lunch being the only way to gain national exposure for Marianne Moore.

In contrast to McPhee and Plimpton, Christian authors tend to give *only* the ideas and thoughts, without tracing the personalities involved and the context of how those thoughts developed. Too often religious books are organized and written like sermons, with an outlined structure superimposed on the content.

Many successful evangelical authors are not authors at all; they are speakers who make their living by speaking at churches and conferences. One can hardly blame them for organizing their written material in the same way as their spoken material, and often it sells well. But speakers who write books in the same style defy the basic rules of communication. Writers cannot merely list facts and hope to penetrate readers' brains. They must take readers on an emotional journey to hold their attention. People do not read the same way they listen, and a book-speech is effective only among an audience previously committed to agree with the material. It cannot reach out to a noncaptive audience such as a world skeptical of Christian ideas. That requires books created according to the rules of written communication.

An author cannot captivate an audience with his or her own personal magnetism as a speaker can. Authors must use such techniques as a gripping narrative style, well-placed anecdotes, suspense, and a structure that compels a reader to follow the train of thought. To a diverse audience, ideas come across best when they are embodied and live within a visual, imaginable context.

Of contemporary Christian writers working in the field of "nonfiction," I know of no one who finds more consistent artistic success than Frederick Buechner. He tackles formidable tasks in his choice of material: retold Bible stories (*Peculiar Treasures*); jazzed up theology (*Wishful Thinking*); sermons (*Magnificent Defeat, The Hungering Dark*); and even a fictionalized biography of a saint (*Godric*). In each of these genres

Buechner applies his sharply honed novelist's skills, and one cannot fault the books for didacticism or boredom.

In *Telling The Truth*, Buechner constructed a book around one thematic sentence: "The gospel is, in some ways, like a tragedy, a comedy and a fairy tale." It covers old ground but, through wise use of images and allusions to literary sources as disparate as *King Lear* and *The Wizard of Oz*, Buechner makes the basic facts of the gospel glow as though he has just discovered the truth in a pottery jar in the Middle East.

Is it merely incidental that some of the most effective Christian apologists in this century — C. S. Lewis, Dorothy Sayers, George MacDonald, G. K. Chesterton — drank deeply at the well of fiction? There, they learned the need to construct even their more theological works with the flair of a novelist.

Supernature Without Nature

G. K. Chesterton proposed a theory to explain the Dark Ages, that wasteland of painting, music, writing, and the other arts. Could they, he asked, be a necessary interlude after the Roman and Greek defilement and before the discovery of the true Romance? Nature had, in fact, been spoiled. "It was no good telling such people to have a natural religion full of stars and flowers. There was not even a flower or a star that had not been stained. They had to go into the desert, the monasteries, where they could find no flowers or even into the cavern where they could see no stars. . . . Pan was nothing but panic. Venus was nothing but venereal vice."

Gradually against this gray background beauty began to appear, something fresh and delicate. In St. Francis of Assisi, the flowers and stars recovered their first innocence, fire and water were deemed worthy to be the brother and sister of a saint. The purge of paganism was complete at last, and Christians began to rediscover nature with a rush. The greatest blossoming of art in all of history, the Renaissance, immediately followed.

Several centuries later, however, the scientific revolution sent new shock waves through the church, from which we have not yet recovered. Nature and supernature split apart. The church abandoned nature to the physicists and geologists and biologists, retreating to the more limited purlieu of theological speculation. The scientists, in turn, abandoned the supernatural to the church and the paranormalists.

Too often today Christian writers tiptoe around God's creation; it is simply "matter," unworthy of the attention granted supernatural issues. (Similarly, says Jacques Ellul, science avoids questions of supernature to such an extent that it puts on blinders and severely restricts intellectual thought.) It is time for Christian writers to rediscover our natural environment and the characteristics of true humanity. By avoiding nature we divorce ourselves from the greatest images and carriers of supernature, and our writing loses its chief advantage, the ability to mimic creation. When Tolstoy describes spring, the wonder of tiny flowers poking up through the thawing tundra, he invests in it the same exuberance and significance that he gives to a description of Christian conversion. It too is an expression of God's world. As a result, both passages stir up the feeling of longing in a sensitive reader. People live in the world of nature; we must first affirm that and plumb its meaning before leading them on to supernature.

Recently some fine authors have led the way in attempting to reveal nature as a carrier for supernature. Annie Dillard's *Pilgrim at Tinker Creek* was a landmark in that genre. Lewis Thomas applies the same approach but from a less explicitly religious viewpoint. Response to these two authors demonstrates the hunger in readers for a more holistic approach to the world. Nature and supernature are not two separate worlds; they are different expressions of the same reality, and effective writing must deal with both.

In a brief passage, Pablo Neruda shows what can be done with the subject of writing itself, the choice of words as carriers of expression:

> You can say anything you want, yes sir, but it is the words that sing; they soar and descend. I bow to them, I love them, I cling to them, I run them down, I bite into them, I melt them down. I love words so much: the unexpected ones; the ones I wait for greedily are stalked until, suddenly, they drop. Vowels I love: they glitter like colored stones, they leap like silver fish. They are foam, thread, metal, dew. I run after certain words. They are so beautiful I want to fit them all into my poem. I catch them in mid-flight as they buzz past. I trap them, clean them, peel them. I set myself in front of a dish: they have a crystalline texture to me: vibrant, ivory, vegetable, oily, like fruit, like algae, like agate, like olive. And then I stir them, I shake them, I drink them, I gulp them down, I garnish them, I let them go. I leave them in my poem like stalactites, like slivers of polished wood, like coal, pickings from a ship wreck, gifts from the waves. Everything exists in the word.

Such enthusiasm for words should spill over into the whole process of presenting both the natural and supernatural. The concept of creation is, at heart, a Christian concept. That thought did not exist among the Greeks, who instead used the word *techna*, from which we derive our word "technological." The great Greek poets and playwrights thought in terms of arranging or manufacturing their works; they had no model of divine *creatio ex nihilo* to mimic. It staggers me that we Christians so blithely forfeit our opportunity to explore that magnificently created world. We fly instead to a supernatural world so far elevated from our fringe readers that they cannot possibly make the leap.

Conversely, when we discuss the realm of the supernatural, we must do so with unflinching realism. An article I read recently described a solemn vigil in which the author, standing before the Washington monument, listened reverentially as someone read aloud the names of thousands of those killed by the Hiroshima bomb. He was participating in some anniversary sponsored by an antiwar group. He described a terrible dilemma: while doing his very best to concentrate on the horrible immolation of Hiroshima's victims, his mind ineluctably dragged him back to the more immediate pain of his aching feet. His weak arches could not bear this vigil. Similarly, why cannot we be honest about such spiritual acts as praying and truly portray the dilemma of unholy people performing holy acts while contemplating fallen aches, twitching eyelids, and wobbly knees?

In short, we need a more supernatural awareness of the natural world and a deeper natural sensitivity to the supernatural world. In our art the two must come together, and fuse.

Action Without Tension

Sometimes when I read Christian books, especially in the fields of fiction and biography, I have a suspicion that characters have been strangely lobotomized. It's as if an invasion of body snatchers has sucked out the humanity I know and replaced it with a sterilized imitation. Just as a lobotomy flattens out emotional peaks and valleys, Christian writers can tend to safely reduce life's tensions and strains to a more acceptable level.

A biblical book such as *Jeremiah* or *Hosea* spends a full chapter describing, in graphic terms, Israel's resemblance to a harlot who goes a-whoring, sleeping with every nation that comes down the street. We tend to take those same thoughts and express them as "God is mad at us," or "God is disappointed in Israel." Tragically, we also miss the emotional force of forgiveness that follows such gross adultery. We lobotomize the relationship between God and ourselves, and ourselves and other people.

We express theological concepts without the emotion, the drama, or the tension. Old Testament Jews understood the full impact of words like atonement and forgiveness: they watched as the priest slid a knife across the spurting artery of a fear-stiffened lamb.

A perverse fear of overstatement keeps us confined to that flatland realm of "safe" emotions and tensions — a fear that seems incredible in light of the biblical model. Why is it that three-hundred-page novelizations of biblical characters somehow seem more stereotyped than the five-page description in the original source? As a beginning, we must turn to the masters of good writing and learn how tension and emotion can be expressed in print. Of modern authors, few excel James Dickey, John Updike, and William Faulkner in ability to take the most ordinary event, say, a dinner conversation, and render it in a captivating manner. As for drama, Dickey can sustain a climb up a one-hundred-foot cliff for fifty pages, keeping the reader's heart pounding violently all the way. These skills can be acquired, but *only* through intense study and effort.

Far more difficult is the task of weaving morality into the fabric of the narrative. We Christian writers lapse into thinking of the world in terms of good or evil instead of the inseparable mixture of good *and* evil present in every person and nearly every action. Earlier times yearned for caricatured saints; they ascribed miracles when there were none. Our time scoffs at miracles and debunks saints. In order to communicate to a skeptical audience, Christian writers must temper their portrayal of good with a strong emphasis on realism.

Again, successful models abound. Consider Dostoyevsky, perhaps the greatest "interior" novelist, who displayed such profound insight into the human psyche. His Christ figure, the protagonist of *The Idiot*, appears as a strange, unpredictable epileptic prince. His goodness, though, is unquestioned, and *The Idiot's* final scene presents perhaps the most moving depiction of grace in all of literature: the "idiot" prince compassionately embracing the man who has just killed his lover. In *Crime and Punishment*, Dostoyevsky presents the darkest side of human nature, but even there the deranged murderer softens in the glow of Sonya's love. Somehow Dostoyevsky accomplishes both justice and forgiveness. In *The Brothers Karamazov* Dostoyevsky presents a truly good man, but counterbalances that character with two brothers. How is it that, a hundred years after Dostoyevsky, Christian literature has, by and large, fallen back into a heroes-and-villians mentality?

A few novelists manage a believable blending of good and evil. Interestingly, these all present a badly flawed protagonist, seemingly a *sine qua non* of modern literature. Consider the whiskey priest in Graham Greene's *The Power and the Glory*, Mauriac's irascible curmudgeon in *Viper's Triangle*, Bernanos' frail saint in *Diary of a Country Priest* and Buechner's tragicomic evangelist in the Leo Bebb series.

Light Without Darkness

Reading religious books sometimes reminds me of traveling through a mile-long mountain tunnel. Inside the tunnel, headlights provide the crucial illumination; without them I would drift dangerously toward the tunnel walls. But as I near the tunnel exit, a bright spot of light appears that soon engulfs my headlights and makes them useless. When I emerge from the tunnel, a "check headlights" sign reminds me that I still have them on. In comparison to the light of day they are so faint that I have lost awareness of them.

Christian books are normally written from a perspective outside the tunnel. The author's viewpoint is already so flooded with light that the author forgets the blank darkness inside the tunnel here many of his or her readers are journeying. We forget that, to someone in the middle of the mile-long tunnel, descriptions of blinding light can easily seem unreal.

When I pick up many Christian books, I get the same sensation as when I read the last page of a novel first. I know where it's going before I start. We desperately need authors with the skill to portray evolving viewpoints and marks of progression along the spiritual journey as accurately and sensitively as they show the light outside the tunnel.

I think of William Faulkner's *Sound and the Fury* or Ken Kesey's *One Flew Over the Cuckoo's Nest* as examples of shifting points of view. Kesey tells his tale through the viewpoint of a mute Indian who, at the beginning, is thoroughly insane. As McMurphy weaves his liberating spell on twelve fellow inmates, however, the qualities of courage, hope, and self-confidence suddenly seep into that human prison. You can watch the Indian edge toward sanity as the book progresses; his own narrative begins to make more sense. Near the end of the book Kesey slips in an unexpected hint that perhaps there is only one truly insane person in the entire asylum — McMurphy, the one who seemed defiantly sane. At last McMurphy is lobotomized and brought back to the ward strapped to a frame in a symbolic cruciform posture, and the captives (twelve) finally rebel. The movie version, of course, did not capture that subtlety; the medium cannot sustain it.

Kesey's book succeeds because he writes as compellingly from the insane person's point of view as from the sane person's, just as Dostoyevsky in *Karamazov* argued the agnostic's views as strenuously as the believer's. Christian books should allow the reader to understand lack of faith as well as faith; if not, they will be read only by those predisposed to belief. The insanity must sound like insanity, not just glimmers of insanity as recalled by the sane. Doubt must sound like true doubt. In the middle of the tunnel, where one can barely fathom a headlight, pure daylight may blind.

These four criticisms of religious writing I accept for myself. Other Christian authors share my perceptions and are working hard to raise the standards of religious publishing.

Dorothy L. Sayers dedicated one of her books "In the name of One who assuredly never bored one in the thirty-three years He passed through the world like a flame." But we Christian authors must confess to having bored plenty of people. So far the evangelical reading public has been tolerant, buying millions of books of uneven quality each year. But a saturation point is inevitable. If Christian writing is not only to maintain interest in the forgiving Christian audience, but also to arouse interest in the skeptical world beyond the Christian subculture, it must grow up.

If we need models of how to do it well, we need only look as far as the Bible. Only ten percent of the Bible's material, the epistles, is presented in a thought-organized format. The rest contains rollicking love stories, drama, history, poetry, and parables. There, humanity is presented as realistically as in any literature.

Why else do the paired books of Samuel, Kings, and Chronicles exist, if not to give a detailed context to the environment in which angry prophets were to deliver their messages? Can we imagine a more skillful weaving of nature and supernature than the great nature psalms, the theological high drama of Job and the homespun parables of Jesus? What literary characters demonstrate a more subtle mixture of good and evil than David, or Jeremiah, or Jacob? And, from the despair of Ecclesiastes to the conversion narratives of Acts, is any wavelength on the spectrum of faith and doubt left unexpressed on the Bible's pages?

C. S. Lewis once likened his role as a Christian writer to an adjective humbly striving to point others to the Noun of truth. For people to believe that Noun, we Christian writers must improve our adjectives.

Chapter 5

A Code of Ethics for Christian Writers

Harold Ivan Smith

If there is a word that has captured the interest of the American public recently, it is the word *ethics*.

This chapter deals with the ethics of Christian writing. The *how* and the *why* of writing is as important as what one writes.

Ethics is relevant to Christian writers because we publish in a culture that prefers to think of rights rather than obligations or responsibilities — a culture that demands immediate rather than delayed gratification. We work with some colleagues who would rather get ahead than make ethical choices.

The issue of ethics is clouded by personal definitions. Webster defines ethics as "the principles of conduct governing an individual or a group" or "the discipline dealing with what is good and bad and with moral duty and obligation." Unfortunately, ethics is easier to define or debate than to implement.

Increasingly, governmental bureaucrats have come under scrutiny for violating government ethics codes and for conflict of interest. Key

Harold Ivan Smith is president of Harold Ivan Smith and Associates, a consulting firm that focuses on the role of single adults in the workplace. He holds graduate degrees from Scarritt Graduate School, Vanderbilt University, and Rice Seminary. He is the author of more than twenty books, including *Once in a Lifetime: Reflections on the Death of a Father, A Singular Devotion,* and *Fortysomething and Single.*

leaders in Congress have been forced to resign their offices or redesign their aspirations because of ethics violations; others are currently under investigation.

Business schools have begun to require courses in ethics and offer refresher courses for the business community.

Physicians have been faced with questions of patients' rights and disclosure of HIV-positive blood status.

No profession is immune from the ethics crisis.

The Ethics Issue in Christian Writing

The issue of ethics may be more pronounced among Christian writers in the days to come. The scandals of televangelism have had consequences on the print media as well. All the enterprises of the church have felt the fallout.

In a sense, Christian writing may be particularly vulnerable to ethical confusion. While Ephesians mentions evangelists, teachers, exhorters, preachers, and "those who do good works," the distinctive ministry of Christian writing has only recently been recognized.

The first Christian writers, generally clergy, simply extrapolated ethical principles from the ministry and adapted them. Publishers made ethical policies that became more complicated as the publishers grew in size. Today the issue is front and center in the world of Christian literature. More writers, editors, and publishers are asking, "What *should* I do?"

Clearly, the reputation of Christian writing suffered when a well-known writer was publicly charged with plagiarizing. The allegation became more newsworthy when the individual charged was a pastor who had publicly excised the sins of colleagues. If the issue had remained within the writing world, it might have been resolved quietly; however, the accuser went to the newspapers and wire services with his allegations. The issue is complicated because the accuser is also a Christian author, though not the author of the work plagiarized.

Before that flap died down, another pastor — author of eighteen Christian books — was charged with plagiarism and responded that he did not know it was "necessary" to footnote material from another author.

What impact do such front-page allegations have on the religious community and on a growing community of religious writers who want their work to be taken seriously? Does an "I didn't mean to . . . " excuse such behavior? Does it cast a lingering shadow over the integrity of all religious writers?

Consider the 1988 presidential campaign of Senator Joseph Biden of Delaware. During a campaign stop in the primary in Iowa, Biden used material from a speech by British Labour Party leader Neil Kinnock without crediting Kinnock.

Within a few weeks, Biden withdrew from the presidential race, his reputation tarnished and his judgment questioned, particularly by political operatives working for other candidates. Would Biden have been forced to drop out if he had been running for county judge?

In 1988 one of the nation's leading psychiatrists was forced to resign his tenured professorship at Harvard·Medical School after a graduate student uncovered his plagiarism while surveying twenty-year-old medical journals. Would he have been forced to resign at a less prestigious institution?

Is there a higher standard for the world of government and medicine? Aren't religious leaders supposed to be authorities on ethical issues?

A Biblical Standard

Scripture does not pinpointedly address ethics for Christian writers. It does offer guidance that bears considering, such as, "Do your best to present yourself to God as one approved, a workman who does not need to be ashamed and who correctly handles the word of truth" (2 Tim. 2:15).

Recall our discussion of the pastors: both writers made choices (if not to plagiarize then to be careless in methodology) that led to their being "ashamed." Neither of them properly "handled the word of truth."

Let us consider another case in point. Much of William Barclay's commentary was not copyrighted. Across the years, ministers and writers have freely quoted and paraphrased Barclay. When sermons are converted into manuscripts, errors in footnoting can be made: credit for a quote can be left out or quotation marks can be overlooked by a typist.

Let's say a pastor is asked to write for a Sunday school quarterly. Say he pulls out one of these old sermons and say several passages slip through without being cited as Barclay's. One Sunday morning in Sunday school, a college student points out that the material in the quarterly has been "plagiarized" from Barclay. An embarrassed Sunday school teacher writes a denominational editor asking, "How could this happen?" The credibility of the writer and publisher come into question. Paul's words to young Timothy seem appropriate: "Watch your life *and* doctrine closely" (1 Tim. 4:16). The accuracy of our doctrine can be impugned by the sloppiness of our writing methodology.

Moreover, Paul said, "Set an example for the believers in speech, in life, in love, in faith and in purity" (1 Tim. 4:12). Should Paul have added *"in writing"*?

Christian writers must "give the enemy no opportunity for slander" (1 Tim. 5:14). A working understanding of ethics is a major step toward fulfilling that injunction.

We cannot — despite the contemporary cultural milieu — lightly dismiss our active involvement in the "community" of Christian writers. Peter wrote, "Each one of us [not most of us] should use whatever gift he has received to serve others . . . " (1 Peter 4:10). Peter went on to say, "If anyone speaks, he should do it as one speaking the very words of God" (4:11). Dare we substitute the words *writes* and *writing* in that passage?

The Christian writer cannot ignore the implications of Paul's words to the church at Ephesus, "It was he who gave some to be apostles, some to be prophets, some to be evangelists, and some to be pastors and teachers, to prepare God's people for works of service, *so that* the body of Christ may be built up *until we all* reach unity in the faith and in the knowledge of the Son of God and become mature, attaining to the whole measure of the fullness of Christ" (Eph. 4:11–13, italics mine).

So much of Christian writing is taught through an informal apprenticeship or through an increasing number of Christian writer's conferences. The next generation of Christians who write must be trained to practice high standards of ethics as well as grammatical accuracy. Otherwise, we end up with a contemporary adaptation of Judges 21:25: "In those days Israel had no king; everyone did as he saw fit." Without ethics, literary anarchy prevails. Paul's phrase "until we all" reminds us of our community ties, which are not easily ignored.

What does it mean to be a professional? F. E. Bullett defined profession as "a field of human endeavor with a well-defined body of knowledge, containing basic principles common to all practitioners skilled and experienced in applying these techniques, dedicated to the public interest."[1]

A code of ethics is essential for a profession to develop, let alone flourish. Moreover, a profession must expect compliance with the good practices of the profession.

As we have seen, the price of a single failure can have implications for more than the writer, indeed, for the entire body of believers. In response to one such incident, one major Christian publisher now requires that all quotes be footnoted and that xeroxed copies of the original page(s) be submitted with the manuscript.

Consider the impact of James' words, particularly in substituting "writer" for "teacher": "Not many of you should presume to be [writers], my brothers, because you know that we who [write] will be judged more strictly" (James 3:1).

Let's examine some basic ethical principles for Christian writers.

Principle One: Faith

Christian writers are committed to sharing the Gospel effectively. Christian writers believe in the dignity and worth of the individual. They realize the failure of man through any other means than Jesus to be restored to wholeness and relationship with God. Therefore, Christian writers are careful to avoid slurs, petty wordisms, accusations, broadsides, or stereotypes that would further alienate the reader. Christian writers are cautious not to "bear false witness," especially through sweeping generalizations and stereotypes.

Christian writers are deliberate in the use of Scripture, recognizing that "all Scripture is God-breathed and is useful for teaching, rebuking, correcting and training in righteousness, so that the man of God may be thoroughly equipped for every good work" (2 Tim. 3:16). For us, "throughly equipped" implies being thoroughly prepared to write, as well.

Christian writers, in preparing materials based on scriptural exposition, use commentaries and other resources only for enrichment, corroboration, and contradiction. Commentaries should never be a crutch to prop up the writing. Nor should Scripture be used to shore up weak logic.

Some editors have noticed a tendency by some authors to rely too heavily on particular commentaries and, in some cases, to deliberately use outdated commentaries. Sometimes this happens because of time pressures. Authors, too busy "in ministry" to "dig" in the Word, reach for the old tried-and-true answers. Ethical writers establish time priorities to include adequate research and thinking *before* writing.

Additionally, after consulting one or two commentaries, one should avoid writing statements like "commentators agree or suggest. . . ." The qualifier *some* would be essential to an accurate use.

Christian writers use Scripture as a scalpel, never as a club. A Christian writer is prepared to admit that other writers may interpret the passages differently — without questioning their credibility or spirituality.

I have long been interested in the prophet Jonah in the Old Testament. I grew up thinking the book of Jonah had a great deal to do with whales. Imagine my surprise at age thirty-five when I learned that the whale is only a sideroad, not the main thoroughfare [the whale disappears after Jonah 2]. The issue in the book of Jonah is Jonah's prejudice against the residents of Nineveh. He wants the Lord to annihilate them.

One popular children's book about Jonah for ages ten to twelve made no mention of Jonah 4. In reading the book, one would assume that the Scripture ends with 3:10 and the storybook line "they all lived happily ever after." Admittedly, chapter 4 might be inappropriate for a young child's level of theological comprehension. Unfortunately, however, if we skip that chapter in family devotions, our children grow up to be adults who missed the lesson of an angry, sulking prophet.

Ethically Christian authors must be hesitant and careful in prooftexting. Scripture texts are not to be misued in the way jig-saw puzzle pieces may sometimes be misused — forced into place. For example, in writing on the issue of homosexuality, Romans 1:27 is used repeatedly as the ultimate prooftext (sometimes with a "Boy, this will nail them!" mentality). The cautious writer must also consider the implications in the context of the verse, specifically what follows in chapter 2: "You, therefore, have no excuse, you who pass judgment on someone else . . . " (v. 1). Christian writers must take "the *whole* counsel of God" rather than convenient proof-texts.

Christian authors are deliberate in their use of Scripture.

Principle Two: Competence

Christian writers are committed to maintaining high standards of competence and recognizing their own limits of competence. We should not attempt to write on subjects outside the recognized boundaries of our expertise.

I am not a theologian or a biblical scholar. I am a lecturer and writer. Certainly there are areas of theology in which I have hunches and thoughts, but I must be careful to label them as such. Even the apostle Paul qualified his statements on virgins by saying, "I have no command from the Lord, but I give a judgment as one who by the Lord's mercy is trustworthy" (1 Cor. 7:25).

For Christian writers today, it is tempting to begin believing the publicist's media kits. We must realize our levels of competence and stay within them. That may mean saying no to a publisher.

For example, what about authors who write on psychological "hot" topics without solid academic and theological training?

Sometimes these books develop because a topic that is "hot" becomes a new market for a proven writer on a related topic. Sometimes a publisher cannot or will not say no to an author. The book sells, not because of good content, but because of the name on the cover. Such books may be quite damaging — although not by intent — to readers struggling with these psychological issues. Moreover, inferior books on a topic steal the limelight that should go to a competent author.

Christian writers recognize that maintaining high standards of professional competence is a responsibility shared by all Christian writers.

Principle Three: Integrity

Christian writers must be honest in dealing with publishers, colleagues, and others in the Christian community, seeking to eliminate deceit.

One area of growing ethical concerns is the hot potato of endorsements. Authors seem always on the lookout for a famous colleague who will claim, "This is *the* book of the year!" or "*must* reading by every Christian." In the Christian community, these endorsements are often looked on as favors or IOUs. On some occasions, a publicist and/or author may prepare the endorsement and read it over the phone to the endorser for approval. And some authors will endorse books as a marketing tool for their own career because it keeps their name before the public.

Potential readers assume that an endorser has read the book. That may not be so. In one instance, I was asked to read a manuscript on single adults, my field of competence. After careful review (as a professional courtesy without compensation) I was concerned with twenty-six statements in the manuscript. I called the editor and cited the errors. I also inquired about the author's limited personal experience in light of sweeping generalizations linked to all single adults. I said I would give an endorsement only if there was some adjustment of the troublesome passages.

Imagine my surprise at seeing the book in a bookstore and discovering that none of my suggestions had been used. I read the back jacket and was stunned when I saw the names of those who had given endorsements. A particular passage that had concerned me was one in which the author insisted that single adults, when tempted to masturbate, should begin speaking in tongues until the temptation passed. Several of the endorsers — friends of mine — are not charismatic and would reject such counsel. However, their endorsements were glowing: "Must reading by every single adult." Had they read the entire manuscript? If so, how had they overlooked the passage on masturbation? Would not readers assume the endorsement to be a full endorsement of the contents?

Later a magazine editor asked me to review the same book. I was obviously biased by my experience with the manuscript and by the fact that I had a book on the same topic forthcoming. My integrity demanded that I not review the book.

Principle Four: Research Responsibilities

Statistics can be used as drunks use lightposts: for illumination to find one's way home or for holding up oneself. So it is with research. You can use stats to prove almost anything.

Since I regularly write on the issue of divorce, I was incredulous when I noted that one prominent author had written in a new book that the divorce rate had dropped and that the decline was a result of the election of a particular candidate for president (who ironically happened to be the first divorced occupant of the White House). I checked the cited source of the information. The last paragraph of this particular Bureau of the Census Report noted that these were *preliminary* statistics and that there was no expectation that the divorce rate had declined.

Immediately other authors borrowed author no. 1's interpretation and cited him rather than the census report. Suddenly, everyone was thanking the Lord that the divorce rate had declined.

Author no. 1 had not read the report in its entirety. The same census document noted that the number of live-ins had increased 300 percent. Many couples who would have been prime candidates for a divorce had elected not to marry but to live together. So, even if one interpreted the slight drop in the divorce rate as a moral victory, I saw it as a hollow one.

Christian writers use research that has been carefully selected to meet three criteria: the data must be *accurate, current* and *appropriate*. In the book on single adults, the major piece of "research" to back up the author's statement that "even secular sociologists agree" was a quotation from a 1958 sociological journal. The information was dated.

In another sexually related counseling book, published by a house known for its academic orientation, I was dismayed by the number of citations from *People* magazine and the absence of quotations from scholarly journals.

Christian writers are aware that a statement or a quotation may mislead or deceive because it makes only a partial disclosure of relevant facts.

Christian writers do not borrow research from another writer without giving credit, particularly by using that author's footnotes as one's own rather than the more precise: *"as quoted in . . . ."*

Christian authors are careful to quote accurately and in light of the context. Even an elipsis mark can change the original writer's meaning. Several Christian authors have had their reputations tarnished by a writer's "lifting" an offensive quote — alleged to make the author sound "new age" — out of a text that modifies its meaning.

In one example, a writer used dated books by several prominent authors. He did not, however, contact any of them to ask, "Do you *still* believe what you wrote in . . . ?" Or "Would you still state this as strongly . . . ?" Integrity demands that an author contact a colleague before possibly misrepresenting him or her.

Chuck Colson may have instituted a whole new standard of excellence in his books *Loving God* and *Kingdoms in Conflict*. He includes a section entitled, "With Gratitude," in each book. In that section in *Loving God* Colson wrote:

> The point is made in the section on the church that the Christian life cannot be lived alone. To follow Christ is to become part of a new community. The same may be said about writing a book on the Christian life. It can never be written in a vacuum; the author is inevitably influenced by the lives and writing of others.

This section is not in footnotes. Deliberately, Colson gives credit for ideas. Colson reveals those religious authors he has read. He goes a step further and discloses that Ellen Santilli, a writer on the staff of Prison Fellowship, "did much of the research" for the book. Colson is generous: "Ellen's assistance was invaluable both in drafting some material herself and editing much of mine."

Colson also revealed that two writers — Harold Fickett and Tim Stafford — were directly involved in the writing process.[2]

In *Kingdoms in Conflict*, Chuck Colson listed those who had helped "write" the book. Again, he mentioned Ellen Santilli — "this time my colleague in the fullest sense" — and included her name on the title page. Colson also disclosed that background material for some of the chapters was done by Tim Stafford and by a research assistant, Michael Gerson, who provided what Colson calls "provocative" research.[3]

This is a radical but welcome innovation in the field of Christian writing. Colson was under no legal obligation or precedent to give this credit; however, ethically he believed he was.

Ethical Christian authors give credit to those who have contributed to the publication in proportion to their contributions.

This leads to a major issue that is almost a scandal in the Christian community: the use of ghostwriters. In 1982 *Christianity Today* approached the issue in a provocative article entitled, "Ghostwriting: A Borderline Deceit?"

Consider Dr. Jones, a busy pastor with a growing beyond-the-parish speaking ministry. Obviously, he is marketable, so an acquisitions editor approaches him and suggests that he consider writing a book.

"I'm not a writer," he says, or, "I'm too busy," before initially dismissing the suggestion.

The editor offers the services of a ghostwriter to take Dr. Jones' sermon tapes, and "create" a manuscript. Six months later, Dr. Jones has signed on the dotted line, and the manuscript is in process. Meanwhile, a publicist is hard at work "creating" the author side of Dr. Jones.

Indeed, once the book is published, Dr. Jones receives more invitations to speak. However, he has a problem: How is he to respond to the reader who says, "Dr. Jones, I just loved your book. Especially page twenty. That helped me so much." If the book was ghost-written what should he say?

Has pastor-author Jones stolen the credit that partially belongs to a nameless ghostwriter?

Legally, Dr. Jones has stolen nothing. Besides, he could argue, the ghostwriter was well paid and understood the arrangement.

Ethically the conflict is more difficult to resolve. Some key words could be helpful:

And denotes a collaborator's contribution to the book — e.g., *The Church* by Dr. Jones and David Redding.

With is another common option. *The Church* by Dr. Jones with David Redding. This accurately acknowledges David Redding's involvement but suggests that Dr. Jones was the creative genius behind the book.

One other alternative is *"as told to."* This suggests that the collaborator was a stenographer who merely took Dr. Jones' thoughts, cleaned up his grammar, and made the manuscript shine.[4]

However, some may insist that the collaborator's name be in smaller type or on the title page rather than on the cover. Most readers may never know of David Redding's contribution to the book.

The issue is complicated when publishers have policies that override an author's desire to recognize a collaborator. Some publishers attempt to dissuade the author from recognizing the ghostwriter.

Simply, Christian authors give credit where credit is due.

Principle Five: Writer-Editor Relationship

Christian writers inform their prospective publisher of developments in their personal life that might alter or terminate an existing or potential relationship.

In light of recent events, some publishers have reexamined their contracts. One standard clause reads, "If, by reason of willful acts of the Author, the public reputation of the Author shall have been so degraded as to render the Publisher's continued identification with the author materially damaging to the Publisher's public reputation, the Publisher may terminate this agreement by giving written notice of its election to do so."

Another publisher has an ad hoc understanding: talk to us early so that we can assess the damage.

Christian writers never suppress disconfirming data. They acquaint the publisher with the existence of alternative hypotheses and explanations of their findings. At times, because of the expertise of the author on the particular subject and an editor's level of understanding, a painstaking explanation may be in order. Simply, it cannot be taken for granted that the editor understands all the implications of a particular statement.

One publisher thought a "dream" author team had been formed for a major book on a hot social topic. However, the second author could not — with his academic training — agree to the interpretation of the data by the first author. Ethically, he felt obligated to disclose to the publisher how the data could be understood in a different manner. The publisher chose to side with the first author, and the writing team was dissolved.

This particular author also turned down opportunities to review the book because of his involvement. He considered his responsibility completed when he disclosed his objections to the editor.

Christian writers also have responsibility to see that a publisher does not overstate an endorsement. On a certain book jacket I found a favorable endorsement by a colleague. I was surprised because under his name was the name of a professional organization, on whose board I serve. That particular organization has a written policy against endorsing books of individuals who are not members of the organization. In this case, the publisher had "assumed" the organization's de facto endorsement but promised, after consultation, to remove it from the book jacket.

Christian writers respect the rights and good names of professional colleagues. In a competitive world, like Christian publishing, it can be a temptation to promote oneself by putting down colleagues (particularly when the colleague has published a book that competes with yours).

Increasingly, in the days of a litigious society, Christian authors must be cautious in sharing information about a colleague's personal life. What if an author becomes aware of a moral failure in another author's life? Is he or she responsible for disclosing that to an editor who is about to extend a contract to that author? Is there an obligation based on loyalty to a publishing house to disclose data on moral failure by a fellow author?

Increasingly this is a place for caution.

Principle Six: Personal Responsibility

Christian writers are aware of cultural myths, biases, and prejudices common among the Christian community, just as they are aware of tired clichés and evangelical jargon and stereotypes: "All evangelicals believe ...." Writers should avoid using such in their work.

Christian writers are aware that simplistic answers or solutions won't resolve complex issues.

Christian writers are careful not to appeal to a reader's fear or anxiety.

Christian writers seek to avoid misrepresentation through sensationalism, exaggeration, or superficiality. They are guided by a primary obligation to aid their readers in developing informed judgments, opinions, and choices.

Christian writers are aware that their personal values may affect the selection and presentation of materials. When dealing with topics that may give offense, they recognize and respect the diverse attitudes that readers may have toward the issue.

Christian writers know that they bear a heavy social responsibility because their recommendations and professional actions influence and may alter the lives of readers. Thus these writers are alert to personal, social, organizational, financial, or political situations and pressures that might lead to misuse of the writer's influence.

Christian writers do not claim, either directly or by implication, professional qualifications exceeding those actually attained.

Christian writers monitor closely the adjectives used by publishers: "The nation's leading expert on ...," or "*the* authority on ...." Such statements, although flattering, contribute to the "celebrity" status among Christian writers that is not conducive to one's servanthood as a writer or to a sense of collegiality among other writers.

Summary

To understand the issue of ethics, one has only to listen to the "folklore" exchanged at Christian writer's conferences. Doom, woe, and laments as in "somebody done me wrong" are sometimes offered as fact, particularly by inexperienced authors.

The Hebrews were warned not to be "talebearers" among the people. That is sound advice for authors, too.

Many editors have been hurt by talebearing by inexperienced authors. Moreover, in the minds of many novices, a foe-adversary relationship exists between editors and authors. My experience has been the opposite. However, harmonious relationships do rely on recognition of boundaries and dismantling the subtle temptation to be a "prima donna."

The world of ethics and Christian writing appears to many to be a confusing, frustrating, even menacing world. However, the time to be a professional is from the beginning. Ethics should not suddenly become an issue after we have established our careers.

In the rush to get into print, some people take shortcuts that come back to haunt them. One colleague has resisted having certain of his earlier works brought back into print. They are, he argues, best left alone in deep graves.

One young author I know is habitually embarrassed by the creative "borrowing" (those he copied called it plagiarizing) in his first books. Today, his reputation is still somewhat suspect, because Christian writers and editors have long memories.

Many Christian authors think there is the world of Christian writing and also the world of secular publishing. I think many "real world" readers are interested in what Christians have to say. However, they may have legitimate questions about the ethics *lite* approach of many Christian writers.

As the profession matures, so will our code of ethics. Christian writers are not called to be "cops" policing the ethics of other writers. But we do have a responsibility to protect the profession.

Christian writers are deeply committed to the conviction that we are a community, a body. We are only as strong a profession as our weakest members.

These days call for excellence.

NOTES

1. F. E. Bullett, "Why Certification?" *Certification Registration Information 1981.* Research Report (Washington, D.C.: American Production and Inventory Control Society, 1981), 5.
2. Charles Colson, *Loving God* (Grand Rapids: Zondervan, 1983), 245–48.
3. Charles Colson, *Kingdoms in Conflict* (Grand Rapids: Zondervan, 1987), 373–75.
4. Paul Fromer, "Ghostwriting: A Borderline Deceit?" *Christianity Today* (17 September 1982), 12–14.

SUGGESTED READING

Bell, A. Donald, and John C. Merrill. *Dimensions of Christian Writing*. Grand Rapids: Zondervan, 1970.

Help in examining the Christian writer's values and exploring the delicate issue of balance, as offered by two professors of journalism at the University of Missouri.

Barzun, Jacques, and Henry F. Graff. *The Modern Researcher*. 4th ed. San Diego: Harcourt, Brace, and Jovanovich, 1985. Chapter 3, "The Searcher's Mind and Virtues," 43–59.

A strong call for "accuracy" and honesty in doing research, particularly at the hypothesis stage.

Colson, Charles W. *Kingdoms in Conflict*. Grand Rapids: Zondervan, 1987, 373–78.

In Colson's acknowledgments, "In Gratitude," an excellent model for disclosing the role of others in writing a book and also his recognition of those who assisted in the research.

Evans, Glen, ed. *Complete Guide to Writing Non-Fiction*. San Francisco: Harper & Row, 1988, 847–50.

Notably "The Code of Ethics and Fair Practices" as developed over several years by the American Society of Journalists and Authors, a professional group that maintains a Committee on Editor-Writer Relations.

Fromer, Paul. "Ghostwriting: A Borderline Deceit?" *Christianity Today* (17 September 1982), 12–14.

A provocative and disturbing article, particularly as it applies to the commandment "You shall not bear false witness."

Chapter 6

Publishing Philosophies

Leslie H. Stobbe

For today's writer, one of life's great mysteries is the publishing philosophy of Christian book publishers. These special nuances of the executive team are not emblazoned on buildings, inscribed on letterheads, enunciated by editors at writers' conferences, or included in handouts for first-time book authors. They are, it sometimes seems, designed to be more of a fence than a filter.

What, then, is a publishing philosophy? It may be defined as the particular point of view regarding new-product acquisition held by publishing-house executives controlling the acquisition process.

The Entrepreneurial Perspective

In the case of the publishing house owned by an entrepreneur, the publishing philosophy may reflect the guiding vision that led the owner to found the publishing house and according to which he selects the book

Leslie H. Stobbe has been a bookseller, writer, editor, and publisher since he entered journalism more than thirty-five years ago. He is the author or co-author of twelve books and has participated in editing and marketing for six curriculum and book publishers. Currently he is president of Here's Life Publishers and is active in the Evangelical Christian Publishers Association. His most recent book, co-authored with Jim Talley, is *Life After Divorce*.

manuscripts for publication. For example, Bob Hawkins, Sr., founder and owner of Harvest House Publishers, says, "Our philosophy is to publish books to help the hurts of people." Thus a look through the catalog of Harvest House will disclose many books for those who hurt. But that is not all one sees. There is also a liberal sprinkling of books on other kinds of subjects, often by nationally known authors. In actual fact, the entrepreneur's publishing philosophy may at times become very pragmatic, dictated more by the condition of the cash flow and an opportunity to publish books that are certain to be well received in the marketplace.

A classic example for Harvest House was the book on the Song of Solomon by David Hocking entitled *Romantic Lovers*. Another was the full-color tour de force by Hal Lindsey, *A Prophetical Walk Through the Holy Land*.

Entrepreneurial publishing entails a risk that it will not generate a strong backlist. It is common to publish a relatively high number of books in an effort to see which kinds will stick and become durable titles. It is true in secular as well as religious publishing that the sheer number of books provides the research and development that produces enough winners to keep the publishing house growing. For many years this was true of Baker Book House, Zondervan, and Word, each established by an entrepreneur. These publishers also dominated the bookstore shelves by sheer force of numbers.

A prolific output by publishers might appear to be a real boon to authors, since more of their books get published. Yet when the royalty checks are tallied, few B- and C-level authors at such houses ever earn enough to cover the investment of their time and effort. The A-level authors, the "glamour people" of the book industry, obviously get the promotional effort — just as the Heisman Trophy candidates in college football get the hype — and rack up the sales.

At times entrepreneurs may not bother with literary niceties such as editorial fine-tuning. As one entrepreneur said recently, "I've never seen a well-edited book sell more than a poorly edited book, so why waste money on editing?" You have to wonder if that is the reason many of his books appear to have only a two-year lifespan.

The Entrepreneurial Niche Publisher

Some entrepreneurs develop a niche market and stick with it, and this in time can make them successful. Robert Kregel, for example, decided old was better than new, so he selected the best of the books he considered classics and began publishing reprints. The older the better seems to be his publishing philosophy, though he is highly selective in what he publishes. Every once in a while he wanders from that beaten path and publishes new originals, but these are usually in the category of a personal mission.

Another example of an entrepreneurial niche publisher is Accent Books, an outgrowth of Baptist Publishing House, founded to serve fundamental, independent Baptist churches. There was no question about the publishing philosophy of Robert Mosier, for he stood squarely on the agreed-upon "fundamentals" of separatistic Baptists. A change in ownership could result in some erosion of those values.

Denominational houses, by contrast, often seem to take exactly the opposite route to the freewheeling entrepreneur with his focus on publishing to suit popular trends and subjects. Their publishing philosophy becomes "If it's good for the denomination, it's good for us." The depth of the market represented by a publishing house like Broadman Press, owned by the Southern Baptist Convention, means that books by pastors who have become visible through convention activity will usually sell well enough to warrant their publication. Those written because of some curriculum need have an automatic sale large enough for the publishing house to recoup its investment. More than one Southern Baptist preacher has used this initial launch from Broadman as a springboard to a publishing house with a broader interest base.

A writer seeking exposure may well find that his denominational house represents a fine opportunity to get started. Many are still publishing a small list, so each author gets more attention. That would seem to be the case at Herald Press, a division of Mennonite Publishing House, which restricts its list to books "consistent with Scripture interpreted in the Anabaptist Mennonite tradition that are conducive to spiritual growth among readers." Such a narrow publishing philosophy does not produce many best-sellers, though Herald Press did publish a best-selling cookbook, *More with Less*.

The scene changes dramatically when we consider Augsburg Publishing House or Concordia Publishing House, since both not only draw from a large constituency, but also have had winning series that achieved sales well beyond their denominations. These houses have a strong market-driven philosophy beyond the denominational basics.

A happy mating of avant-garde art and text made the children's book series, the Arch Books, almost synonymous with Concordia for many years. Yet this publishing house of the Lutheran Church — Missouri Synod publishes much more than best-selling children's books that revealed crossover potential. Concordia has also focused heavily on curriculum and curriculum-related products.

Ministry-Related Publishing

For a ministry-related or ministry-owned publishing house the philosophy may be a straightforward extension of the mission philosophy of the parent. Here's Life Publishers, for example, describes its mission as "moving Christians toward ministry, and then resourcing these ministering Christians with the tools for evangelism, discipleship and leadership." This filter is indeed rather narrow, but the publishing philosophy at Here's Life Publishers is to interpret that mission in a broadening sense as the book list grows.

For years InterVarsity Press had lists that catered mainly to the university student or the well-educated layperson. Its publishing philosophy, well-honed and rather fully developed under the stable editorial leadership provided by James Sire, enabled it to publish somewhat provocative books that were evocative of the freer thinking found on university campuses. Yet even there, change came, and suddenly a more market-driven publishing philosophy became visible in the new books.

What may effect changes in a publishing house's philosophy of publishing?

Changing Philosophies for Changing Times

Publishing philosophies may shift rather quickly to a primarily more pragmatic "But will it sell?" attitude if either the publishing house falls on hard times or the financial support of the parent is significantly reduced or withdrawn.

In the case of InterVarsity Press, the parent's impatience with the financial performance of its subsidiary, coupled with personnel changes, resulted in a much more market-driven staff and publishing philosophy.

This stronger orientation to the marketplace may also happen at subsidiaries of ministries when the parent will not provide the capital necessary to expand beyond what can be generated from operational income. This may occur because the parent considers other opportunities and activities more central to its mission, as would appear to have been the case in recent years at NavPress and at Here's Life Publishers. Or it may result from shrinking income at the parent, as happened at Moody Press as the seventies became the eighties, with many long-term books dropped to keep cash available for Bible publishing.

For authors these shifts can be traumatic. At one such publishing house a number of manuscripts already under contract were either returned or placed with other publishers. At another house eight authors in one season were informed that their books would not be released in a second printing because of cash constraints. Since these shifts often occur without significant warning, authors may find themselves caught in the middle, both financially and in terms of the ministry objectives they envisioned for their books. They may also discover either depleted editorial staffs or struggling new editors unable to serve the writers as quickly as before.

Publicly Owned Publishers and the Bottom Line

Shareholder-owned publishing house must of necessity provide a more significant return to the investors than ministry-owned publishing houses. Higher profit levels become mandatory as a result. Not long after ABC acquired Word Books, for example, closer attention to the bottom line resulted in large inventory sell-offs at bargain prices to free up cash.

These moves affected authors seeking publication at Word rather quickly, since the availability of cash made a more aggressive acquisitions policy possible. Then the already successful author could become the primary target of the Word Books editorial team, leaving the new-book author or second-level author fighting for a "place in the sun" against what some have dubbed the "big five" — Graham, Dobson, Schuller, Landorf, and Swindoll. Even more disheartening, the size of the list was cut because of the sales volume generated by these major authors (an opposite strategy to the aforementioned approach of accumulating sales through proliferation of titles). In addition, the theological base was broadened, in effect reducing the opportunities of evangelical writers.

At one stage at Zondervan Publishing House the necessity to maintain healthy asset-to-liability ratios resulted in an inflated inventory of largely unsalable books. When the company discovered this, it was forced to sell off large inventories of such books at significant losses and to heavily curtail new-book acquisition.

The new publishing philosophy was to reduce the number of new titles and focus on winners. Authors with manuscripts in house at the time found themselves in a quandary, since it was either wait their turn — and that could take two years — or see if another publisher could be found who would provide a faster turnaround. In addition, the focus on sure-fire titles slowed down new-book acquisition significantly, reducing the number of slots available for new books.

Hardly had this crisis passed, as well as the impact of the huge advance on royalty given John DeLorean for his personal story, when Zondervan experienced a major change in editorial leadership and acquisition editors. When that happens — as it did at Thomas Nelson, Fleming H. Revell, and NavPress several years later — the writer is again hard put to determine what the publishing philosophies of the new teams will be.

How are these publishing philosophies expressed?

Determining Publishing Philosophies

Since there is no public body holding publishing houses accountable, and since only publicly held publishers release annual reports, publishing philosophies are usually more implicit than explicit. Thus a would-be author will have to study a publisher's list, query editors when they appear at writers' conferences, and talk to veteran booksellers who are usually astute observers of the product mix released by a publishing house. Even after all that, an author may miss the real essence of the decision-making philosophy in situations where the person holding the balance of power is never seen or heard in public and may act rather capriciously at times.

Slogans may seem to provide some guidance, yet they may actually have little relationship to the publishing philosophy of the house. Marketing slogans are designed to win over booksellers and attract customers, and that's really all the freight they carry. For example, the slogan "The Name You Can Trust," which was the flag Moody Press waved for many years, did not explain that the publisher had a strong evangelistic, missionary, and Christian-education component.

Changes at the top can confuse authors for quite some time if they do not stay in touch with personnel changes. Prior to 1978, for example, executives at Moody Press considered their publishing effort an extension of the emphases taught in the classroom. Textbooks reflected a diversity of scholarship, with writers selected on the basis of their potential contribution to a specific topic, not their personal theological stance. Evangelistic tools and missionary books were designed to promote the fulfillment of the Great Commission, and the specific theological stance of the writer was important only as it related specifically to content. Each fiction book, whether for children or adults, had to contain evangelistic content, but the writer did not have to hold personally to the dispensational theology taught in the classrooms of the Moody Bible Institute.

The departure of the veteran executive team at Moody Press over a two-year period from 1978 to 1980 brought younger, less experienced persons into leadership positions. Concern grew about the attitudes of Moody Bible Institute donors toward books by Moody Press. Less flexible positions were taken, and a rather rigid adherence to the total theological stance of Moody Bible Institute was required of authors as mandated by the Institute's board. Books by authors not willing to agree to this theological position were quietly removed from the list. Gordon MacDonald's *Ordering Your Private World*, for example, was dropped because of the author's position on women in ministry and was subsequently published elsewhere. A more cautious publishing philosophy emerged.

The inauguration of a new president and the appointment of new upper management may again give Moody Press greater flexibility, as evidenced in the release of *Agony of Deceit* (edited by Michael Horton and released in 1990), which contained several chapters by writers whose theology does not match Moody's.

Finding Publishing Philosophy Stability

Where may one find publishing philosophy stability?

The publishing houses with the most stable long-term publishing philosophies are undoubtedly the denominational houses serving major denominations. These tend to be controlled by veteran boards that quickly deal with an innovator trying to move the publishing house onto a different track.

With a history tracing back to 1842, Augsburg Publishing House has carried the standard of the American Lutheran Church. With the merger of several Lutheran denominations in 1988, Augsburg was combined with Fortress Press, which had been the publishing arm of the Lutheran Church in America. In the merged publishing house the chief executive officer is also the executive secretary of the Board of Publication. The new corporation has as its mission "to bring the Gospel to as many people as possible through the ministry of the printed word and other media."

Yet despite this obvious Lutheran orientation, Augsburg has long been more eclectic in its book-publishing philosophy. Authors from a variety of denominational backgrounds have found a home on the list of Augsburg. Exemplifying this pragmatic approach is best-selling counselor-author Alan Loy McGinnis, with more than a million copies of *The Friendship Factor* sold and more than two hundred thousand of *Bringing Out the Best in People* sold.

Broadman Press of the Baptist Sunday School Board of the Southern Baptist Convention is a younger house, but its constituency is larger. Pastors of large churches in the denomination are expected to stick with this publishing house even though it has never truly marketed its books aggressively beyond its natural market. The flip side is that though some book projects may not provide a full payback, they may still be published because "we feel we must do them." Rarely will a non-

Baptist author make it onto the Broadman list, because its publishing philosophy focuses its efforts on Southern Baptist writers.

Publishing Philosophy Accountability

Two houses that have shown consistency in publishing philosophy are Bethany House Publishers and Multnomah Press. Both grew out of a Bible-institute environment, and both have retained their founding leaders for many years. This has produced a publishing environment that combines the theological and philosophical accountability as an outreach of a school having a strong missions emphasis with the entrepreneurial vitality of young people possessing a clear publishing focus.

Early on, Bethany's emphasis reflected its charismatic renewal roots, with a steady diet of books on revival and missions. Larry Christensen's book on raising children (*The Christian Family*, 1970) sold so well that it put the new publisher on the map. With a publishing philosophy of releasing books that would encourage Christian growth, Gary Johnson and his wife, Carol, expanded the line. They struck gold with the prairie romances of Janette Oke, and the success of these books has enabled them to be more experimental while retaining their core emphasis.

At about the same time (about 1970) a little booklet written by a faculty member at Multnomah School of the Bible, Pamela Reeves, and assembled by her students caught the fancy of bookstore customers. *Faith Is* became so popular it encouraged many imitators, but more importantly its success established the publishing arm of Multnomah School of the Bible as an exciting opportunity.

Through the years Multnomah Press became known successively for its full-color inspirational books, then its Critical Concern series, but most of all for its books by Charles Swindoll. The enormous success of this author's books gave the publisher the clout to recruit other nationally known authors, who have enhanced the image of Multnomah Press as an exciting publisher.

Currently Multnomah's stated publishing philosophy is to provide a balanced perspective on key issues of the Christian life and to encourage Christians to evangelize non-Christians.

A Publishing Philosophy Honed in England

A newer face on the American scene is Lion Publishing, although its philosophy of publishing has been honed through years of publishing books for the crossover market in Great Britain. From the beginning, the publisher's goal was to bring Christian books into the secular marketplace, so they were designed to be more attractive graphically than the usual British Christian book. The publisher resorted to full-color illustrations throughout its books; as a result these books found favor not only in the British marketplace, but also on the Continent, where Lion books were published in several European and Scandinavian languages.

How Important Is Publishing Philosophy?

Is knowing the publishing philosophies of the various publishing houses really that important? Don't their books all go into basically the same bookstores, where shelf space for face-out display may be far more important than a clear publishing philosophy? Yes, but booksellers do get to know what kinds of books a given publisher releases, and they expect books from that publisher to reflect a certain kind of slant. Changing that too quickly confuses the bookseller, though rarely the end user. Authors also need to feel comfortable with the "feel" of a book list. "Birds of a feather flock together" definitely applies to authors as well.

Writers overeager to be published pay little attention to the publishing philosophy of the house offering a contract, an attitude that may find them on a list with books written by authors with perspectives and doctrinal beliefs quite different from their own. Being mismatched with a publisher may also shorten the shelf-life of their books, reduce their income from the book, and leave them disillusioned about the publishing environment.

Wise homebuyers check out the house they are thinking of buying, coming back two or three times to determine if they really like it as much as it seemed at first impulse. They may bring out a contractor-friend to examine the structural integrity of the house, the quality of the roof covering, and the amount of insulation used. In many communities they will call for an inspection by a termite-exterminating firm. Yet that same buyer will place his or her manuscript with the first publisher offering a contract, without checking with experts on the publisher's record of performance. Certainly some of the questions that need to be asked are, "What is the publishing philosophy of your house? What examples best reveal your publishing philosophy? How stable is your editorial team?" If you are willing to share your royalty, these questions can be answered by that new phenomenon in the Christian world, a literary agent.

SUGGESTED READING

Dessauer, John P., ed. *Christian Book Publishing and Distribution in the United States and Canada.* Tempe, Ariz.: Joint Research Project of the Christian

Booksellers Association, the Evangelical Christian Publishers Association, and the Protestant Church-Owned Publishing Association, 1987.

A landmark study of the historical context, present profile, consumer markets, and key trends into the twenty-first century.

Herr, Ethel. "Evaluating a Book Idea." In *An Introduction to Christian Writing*. Wheaton, Ill.: Tyndale House, 1983.

Guidance for writers to evaluate not only a book idea, but also potential publishers.

Stuart, Sally E. *Inspirational Writers' Market Guides*. San Juan Capistrano, Calif.: Joy Publishing, 1989.

The most up-to-date guide to religious markets, with extensive information on publishers.

Part 2
Particular Issues
of Religious Publishing
and Writing

Chapter 7

Writing for Publication

Wayne E. Oates

People who are considering writing for publication for the first time may overlook two important axioms. The first is that authors address their message to other people. Many prospective writers may view a book or article as a soliloquy. Not so! It is a dialogue. An author writes to a specific audience. In this respect, writing for publication has much in common with writing a letter to someone. The readers are specific individuals and groups. A corollary to this axiom is that the audience is specific and not comprising the whole world.

The second neglected axiom is that this audience is composed of enough people willing and able to *buy* the article or the book. Publication is done by publishers who have to make sure that the book will sell enough copies to justify its publication. Here the sales and marketing divisions of a publishing house have as much to say about the feasibility of publishing as does the editor. Your book or mine may be of the best value imaginable, but if the publisher does not believe it will *sell*, it will not be published.

Wayne E. Oates is professor of psychiatry emeritus, School of Medicine, University of Louisville, and senior professor of psychology of religion at the Southern Baptist Theological Seminary. He is the author of forty-eight books, the most recent of which are *The Presence of God in Pastoral Counseling, Behind the Maskes: Personality Disorders in Religious Behavior*, and *Temptation: A Biblical and Psychological Approach*.

The latter axiom must be modified somewhat. The book that will not sell for one publisher may very well sell for another. Publishing houses themselves have different audiences, especially in the realm of religious publication. For example, Doubleday has a distinct Catholic audience for its religious book section. Westminster and John Knox have a Presbyterian audience. One publisher may appeal to a more conservative audience, and another publisher aim its books at a more liberal audience. Still another publisher may maintain access to both conservatives and moderates. But all of them, regardless of their audience, have one thing in common: they will not publish a book if they do not have confidence it will sell.

However, if one has a very technical manuscript of unique scholarly value that will appeal to a very small scholarly audience, a university press may well be interested in it. It can do so because the publication is subsidized in one way or another. Then, too, many publishers depend on the massive sales of one book to underwrite another book of limited audience. For example, Abingdon has covered the sales of many smaller works with its smashing success with *The Interpreter's Bible*. Mix all I have said here with a generous portion of chance and providence, and your book may get published. The important thing is not to despair when one publisher turns your manuscript down. *The main admonition is: Be clear as to who your audience is and see to it that the publisher whose acceptance you are seeking also addresses that audience.*

Writers' Hindering Fantasies

Several fantasies in the writer's mind, quite often conscious but inarticulate, hinder him or her from getting started on a manuscript and staying with it until it is finished. Let me suggest a few:

1. Authors float in the fantasy that they can get the whole world's attention and that their book will be a best-seller. Therefore, they write with this in mind, but what they are actually doing is writing a soliloquy, with themselves as an audience. A strong dose of reality is an antidote. It takes this form: wise authors choose a specific audience. If the book is to be a text book, they choose the students of a specific discipline as their audience. If it is a handbook for pastors, then pastors are the faces their mind's eye visualizes as they write. If the audience is a lay churchpersons' audience, then the author takes into consideration age differences and chooses to be all-inclusive or age-group specific. Choose your audience and form a mental covenant with them that you are not going to leave or forsake them. You are faithful to your audience. Such fidelity will innoculate you against any undue anxiety as to what any other audience

of people might say. You may get a review later by someone who complains because you did not address his or her needs. I shrug reviews like this off. You can do so, too.

2. Another fantasy that besets us as authors is that we are going to say the final word on our subject. I suppose there is an inherent perversity in all of us that makes us want to have the last word on any subject. But this is a source of much noise in our heart as we struggle to say that *perfect* word. The reality antidote for this fantasy is as follows: Have the courage of imperfection and invite your readers to think *with* you as you and they develop *hypotheses* on your subject and test them out together. Fellow authors will delight in collaborating with you and giving you ideas you had not thought of. Furthermore, remember the wisdom and humility of the apostle John. He said that his book was only a beginning and the world could not contain what could be written on his subject (John 21:24–25). Choose a topic that has a minimal number of other books on it, consult these other books closely, and move your discussion beyond theirs, all the while giving them credit for your indebtedness to them.

3. A third fantasy plagues us. We fantasize that we have unlimited time and an unlimited number of pages available. Somewhere in my college years, I was told that Immanuel Kant said that the human mind functions in the categories of time and space. This applies crucially to the task of writing for publication. Avoidance of the discipline of time and page limitations leaves you floating in the filmy substance of this fantasy. The antidote for this is to use self-imposed deadlines by which you will have a certain chapter or a given number of pages written. Push other duties down the list of your priorities and place this set of decisions high on your use of time. A fine excuse for people who impose on your time is simply to say no and explain that you are pushed by a writing deadline to which you *must* give top priority.

If you have a publisher's contract for a certain date of completion, then set *your* deadlines well within theirs and get your manuscript to them ahead of their deadline. Publishers have heard long stories from authors about the circumstances of broken deadlines. They tend to rely heavily on people who actually beat their deadlines. If you cannot become disciplined to meet time and space restrictions, I would suggest that you choose some other use of your time that is in line with what you really want to do with your life. Otherwise, you will write like a slave scourged and sent to the dungeon each night when you realize you have procrastinated one more day! Then, again, if procrastination is a way of life for you, as it is indeed for many people, you may not even think about having once more put your writing off until some time in the indefinite future. If this is the case, be sure not to tell your friends that you are "writing a book." They will soon begin not taking you seriously on other issues either. At any rate, it is a fine discipline not to tell your friends and co-workers that you are writing a book. Wait until you have finished it and then tell them. Dr. Gaines Dobbins, when asked if he liked to write, said, "Let us say that *I like to have written!*" Dr. Dobbins was my mentor in writing for publication. He taught me to write some copy every day. For example, if you write two pages a day, within a month you will have written 60 pages. Within three months you will have written 180 pages. If circumstances prevent you from writing two pages one day, then write four pages the next day.

A fourth fantasy that hinders some writers from completing a manuscript is the fond thought that they are going to have one whole day in which to do nothing but write. Or they may assume that they are going to have whole weeks or months to retreat to a mountain or seashore cabin to do nothing but write. If this latter dream should come true, they will realize that the library, their most valuable asset, is not there! The antidote to this fantasy is to learn to use what I call *the ungleaned corners of our time.* You spend much time waiting for people. While you are doing this, you can write a few lines or a page if you carry a writing pad with you. I have written on the backs of envelopes, the backs of restaurant place mats, and anything else that was handy. You may have an appointment with someone and that person fails to show up. You then have a whole hour in which to write. Or you can "twist the clock" by arising an hour or two earlier than other people do and use that time to write. Or, if you are a P.M. and not an A.M. personality, you can use the late hours of the evening. Some people seem to get a fresh burst of energy around 9:30 P.M. You may be one of them.

A fifth fantasy that hinders us from putting down our thoughts on paper is that we should read everything that has ever been written on our subject before we start writing. Thus we simply keep reading. I like the method of Paul Tillich, who was a prolific writer. He would write down *de novo* what he himself thought about his subject before he read thoughts of others. Then he would go afield in his own library and in the university library for the thoughts of other people on his subject. Then on a second draft he would rewrite the changes that the thoughts of others had provoked in him.

A good procedure for you and me is first to write down on three or four pages our title and several possible chapter headings with lots of space between. Include as many random thoughts as you wish to use. This is the writer's equivalent of brain-storming. Then find three or four *primary* sources on your subject and read them. By primary sources I mean the works of people who did the original work on the subject. For example, if you are dealing with the subject of the freedom we have in Christ, of course Paul's letter to the Galatians would be a primary source. Another primary source would be Martin Luther's *Treatise on Christian Liberty*. Secondary sources would be commentaries on Galatians and books about Martin Luther. Keep this process going and reshape your outline on the basis of your reading.

A sixth fantasy inheres in all of us. We would like to think that the first draft of what we have to say is some sort of living flesh that cannot be cut, added to, or modified. It is *our* baby! We are reluctant even to trim the fingernails and toenails! This fantasy is akin to the one that makes us feel we must say the final word. An antidote to this fantasy is to listen closely to our editors. They are our teachers as to how to revise our manuscript. There is an adage that says, "Anybody can write, but it takes a writer to rewrite!" Do not think of your first draft as sacrosanct; think of it only as a good draft that can be made better by revision.

Pretesting the Content of a Book in the Making

Your subject and the work you have done on it at this point in its development is still thoroughly subjective to you. You need to get some objective idea as to whether the subject will "fly" or remain at the end of the runway, earthbound. Several ways to test it before you write the entire book are as follows.

1. If you are a teacher or professor in a school, present your ideas in their outline form to a class of students. Get their reactions. Assign research tasks to them on varied aspects of the subject and suddenly a community of learning comes into being. Some years ago I published a text book entitled *The Psychology of Religion* with Word Books. I gave a lecture on all the chapters of the book on one day of classes. The next day two students presented *other* material and their own ideas on the subject. The third day I engaged the class in dialogue about the subject, making careful written note of comments and questions they presented. Throughout the revised text appear such statements as "A student asks: . . . ," "A student comments: . . ." Then I dedicated the book to all of them and expressed appreciation in the acknowledgments.

If you are a Sunday school teacher or an adult discussion leader, you can "run your material by" your students and get their reactions. I wrote a small book, *Confessions of a Workaholic*, published by World Books some years before they went out of business. Before I published it, I pretested the material with an adult discussion group in my church. Then I wrote a brief journal article for *Pastoral Psychology*. I received excellent feedback including many fresh ideas I had not thought of. One of the responses was from one of the editors of World Books. He offered me a contract to make the article into a book with more intensive attention to each of the topics in the article.

You can readily see that this pretesting of material greatly enriches your writing and creates a community of concerned people who contribute much needed criticism and commentary. This calls for fortitude on your part so that you will not become defensive but will keep your mind open and teachable by the reader or listener. If someone has the grace to listen to my untested materials, I ought to have the grace to take his or her feedback with gratitude.

2. By this time you are ready to get the feedback of a publisher. It is very important that you have someone whom both you and the publisher know read your material and make suggestions. Have an understanding with such a reviewer that if he thinks it is worth publication he will recommend you and your manuscript to the publisher. How can you go about doing this?

The best way to do this is to prepare a prospectus of your book. By all means do *not* prepare a whole, completed manuscript. Prepare a prospectus that gives clear ideas as to what your book will be about. The following outline is as good as any in preparing a prospectus.

a. Give a clear, concise subject title to your book that will let a prospective reader know what the book is all about.

b. Describe plainly what your *purpose* in writing the book is.

c. Describe in detail the audience to whom you are addressing the book. Include a list of schools, churches, agencies, groups, and individuals who will be likely to use the book.

d. Write a first chapter that will give a sample of your writing style. Write in inclusive language that is not pitched toward either gender in your audience. One of the best ways of doing this I have found is to write in the second personal singular or plural. For example, "You as a reader have a right to know my basic purpose in writing this book." If this pattern is followed throughout, you will use specific gender references when you are speaking definitely about a particular man or woman. Furthermore, this second person writing is an I-thou meeting between you and your reader. It is personal and not abstract. Write this chapter not only as a sample of your writing style but also as a means of letting the editor(s) know the direction, depth, and intention of the prospective manuscript.

e. Provide the editor with a list of the rest of the chapters of the book. This gives him or her a good idea of where you plan to take the book.

f. Provide the editor with a description of your sources of materials. Are you going to use a questionnaire, a controlled interview, a survey or overview of the existing literature on the subject, or a series of consultations of a selected group of people? By all means provide a bibliography of the primary sources and the secondary sources that you plan to use.

With a prospectus like this, the editor can enter with you into the process of producing the manuscript. This saves you a lot of wear and tear in revisions and gives you access to the wisdom and experience of the editor. Your editor can call your attention to other books by other publishers as well as those of his or her own publishing house. In this way you will know what your competition is. Further, this will enable you to refine your subject and approach so that they will stand out as unique.

Look on your editors as your "coaches" in this game of publishing. Ordinarily they will not tamper with what you want to say but will make suggestions as to how to say it better. Publishing a book is far more of a continuing education than anything else I know. Listen closely to what the editors have to say. My editors have always strengthened my manuscript with their suggestions. Even if they decide they cannot publish your manuscript, you would do well to request their editorial advice on how to improve it.

Why Editors Reject Manuscripts

Let me tell you some of the most common reasons why an editor rejects a manuscript. Knowing these reasons ahead of time may save much self-recrimination and *feelings* of rejection. Note the following possibilities of rejection — not of you, remember, but of your manuscript.

1. Each publishing house holds staff conferences in which they will decide on the kinds of books they are planning to produce over a particular time span. If, for example, they are going to take on a major project of publishing a set of commentaries on the books of the Bible, this crowds out some other kinds of books. Therefore, when you submit a book that does not suit their "publishing policy," they will tell you that your manuscript does not fit their plans for publishing at that time.

2. In addition, some publishers may have a set policy not to publish graduate theses, poetry, novels, etc. If your manuscript is your graduate thesis, go back to the drawing boards and prepare a prospectus such as indicated previously and do not propose it as a graduate thesis for publication.

3. The publisher may be publishing a book on your topic and for that reason cannot take on another that would be in competition with it.

4. Your audience may not be their audience. If so, their editors and sales people will veto your book. For example, you may have a book on faith healing. A publisher for a Christian Science audience or a Pentecostal audience would be more likely to publish your book than a publisher who represents a tradition that is not particularly dedicated to faith healing. On the other hand, they might be greatly interested in a book on religion and medicine.

5. Your audience may be restricted to one denomination, and if your manuscript is not written from an ecumenical point of view, you should approach your denominational press. Broadman publishes Southern Baptist books, Augsburg publishes Lutheran books, Abingdon publishes Methodist books, Westminster and John Knox publish Presbyterian books, etc. In the religious publishing business, parochialism is very evident. Be tuned to these nuances as you write. If your denomination is your audience, then forget about ecumenism unless you want to make a case for ecumenism to your denomination. If you aim at a larger audience than your denomination, then delete most references to your own denomination.

Do not take a rejection of your prospectus as a rejection of you personally and respond with anger and defiance. Channel your energies into finding another publisher, rewriting your manuscript, or making plans for a new one. Keep trying.

Once Your Manuscript Is Accepted

Publishing a book is a small business venture between you and your publisher epitomized in a very specific legal document, a contract. Read it carefully before you sign it. You will ordinarily get 10 percent royalty on the retail price of the book that a publisher accepts. For the book that sells unusually well, your contract most often has a slightly higher royalty percentage for copies sold above a certain number.

Now that your book has been accepted on the basis of the prospectus, your next task is to write the rest of the chapters and put the manuscript into letter-perfect form for the publisher. They may send you their style guide; if they do not, you should ask for it. They may have their own idiosyncratic expectations. In this day of personal computers, they may ask for a floppy computer disk with your manuscript on it, preferably one that is compatible with their computers. Caution: Always keep a copy of your manuscript in a safe place. Terror strikes you when a manuscript of which you do not have a copy is lost!

Once you have sent your manuscript or disk to the publisher, you wait a good while as their content and copy editors go through your manuscript with microscopic attention. After a while they may send you a copy of your edited manuscript, asking a variety of "author queries" of you. Give these your immediate attention and get the copy back to them within the week you get it. They are in full swing in the publishing process and do not want you to sit on a queried copy.

The next time you see your work it will be in page-proof form. The first proofs are sent to you for your own microscopic copy editing. You should not change long blocks of material unless it is to correct an important factual error. However, you may make a reasonable number of word changes that you feel are important. Return the proofs by the publisher's deadline. If you and the editors have agreed on having an index to the book, you will be sent a set of second proofs after a few weeks. You can already have prepared a list of subjects for the index from the manuscript. Now all you have to do is insert the page numbers from the page proofs. This is one of the more tedious aspects of preparing a book for publication.

Promoting Your Book

Now you may think that your work is done! Not so! Now you will receive from your publisher a standard promotional guide-list. They will want you to give them the names, addresses, and — if possible — the telephone numbers of persons who would write good reviews of your book. In addition, they will ask for names of agencies and institutions who would be expected to use your book. In short, they want all the information you can give them to help them introduce you and your book to the possible reading audience you have chosen. They especially will want the names of persons to whom they can send a copy of the manuscript for writing an endorsement to be used on the jacket of the book. Or, they may well have chosen people whom they know and will ask them to write endorsements.

Even after the book is published, your publisher will more than likely ask you for a list of your public appearances for lectures, sermons, workshops, conventions, etc. They will ask for a "contact person" at each place so that they may make arrangements for your book to be on display at a book exhibit. This is very important because many books will be sold when the author is there in person and particularly if the book includes the material you are presenting. You will be asked to autograph copies of your book.

The Publication Date

Publishers will ordinarily give you a publication date. Thus you can plan your teaching, lecturing, workshops, etc., around that date. A few days or weeks before the publication date you will be sent an advance copy of your book. You will see it in its final published form.

One Thing More

In your contract, you may find an "option" clause. This is an agreement on your part with the publisher that you will give them first option on the publication of any future book you publish. They invested a considerable amount of time, money, and energy in *introducing* you to a reading public. They want to capitalize on that investment. Some publishers do not include this option, but if they do, it is very important that you know what you are signing. This is a legal contract, but the more important aspect of it is your faithfulness to your agreement and your relationship to the editorial staff.

May you find new friends and enlarge your world through this arduous adventure of having a book published! And may your book be beloved by your readers!

SUGGESTED READING

Crews, Frederick. *The Random House Handbook*. 5th ed. New York: Random House, 1987.

Feeters, Peggy. *How to Get Started Writing*. Cincinnati: Writers' Digest Books, 1985.

The Letters of Thomas Wolfe. Edited by Elizabeth Newell. New York: Charles Scribner's Sons, 1956.

The New York Times Manual of Style and Usage. New York: Random House, Times Books, 1976.

Strunk, William, Jr., and E. B. White. *Elements of Style*. 3d ed. New York: Macmillan, 1979.

Chapter 8

Communicating the Presence of God Through Writing

Wayne E. Oates

T he writers of the Old and New Testaments certainly communicate the presence of God to you and me as we read what they wrote. However, I doubt that they set about doing just that when they wrote. They were caught up in their own awareness of God, and we experience the presence of God as we empathize with them in their experience. That is what this chapter is all about: Christian authors' being in communion with God as they write, with the hope and prayer that their readers' empathy is attuned with them so that readers experience for themselves the living presence of God. Communication of the presence of God is the spontaneous result of the authors' seeking the knowledge of God in the face of Jesus Christ as they write.

Therefore, for you as an author, this kind of writing is a form of prayer. You faithfully seek communion with God yourself. Essentially, this kind of writing is the secondary result of your cultivating an awareness of the presence of God. This commitment in writing is important and significant because so much religious writing is *about* God,

Wayne E. Oates is professor of psychiatry emeritus, School of Medicine, University of Louisville, and senior professor of psychology of religion at the Southern Baptist Theological Seminary. He is the author of forty-eight books, the most recent of which are *The Presence of God in Pastoral Counseling, Behind the Masks: Personality Disorders in Religious Behavior,* and *Temptation: A Biblical and Psychological Approach.*

not an encounter with God on the part of the writer. This is not to say that therefore religious writing *about* God is inferior to communicating the presence of God through writing. It is to say that the two kinds of writing are *different;* neither is superior or inferior to the other. For example, John Baillie wrote an extremely valuable book entitled *The Knowledge of God*, which is an exceptionally helpful book to guide our thinking *about* God. He wrote another book, *A Diary of Private Prayer*, which conveys directly a personal conversation with God. Both books are equally valuable, and each book is in its own right an exceptionally meaningful book. For the writer of religious reading matter, then, there is a time to write about God and there is a time to share and communicate the presence of God.

My own experience with these two kinds of writing has helped me to formulate my position that the communication of the presence of God is a uniquely different kind of writing. Also, my reading the Old and New Testaments enables me to distinguish the book of Job, for example, as a serious dialogue devoted primarily to discussions about God. It seeks to justify the ways of people with the ways of God in the divine-human encounter. On the other hand, the book of Psalms is a book that communicates the presence of God. The writers are pouring out their feelings and thoughts in a direct conversation with God. They are communicating his very presence.

This leads us to an overview of the substance of this chapter. The first section deals with the preparation of the author himself or herself for writing that communicates the presence of God. The second section describes different literary forms that such writing can take; in other words, it discusses which literary vehicles carry this message best. The third section deals with hazards to avoid in this kind of writing. The fourth section considers the hopes of an author as he or she writes in such a way as to communicate the presence of God.

The Writer's Preparation

What are some specific steps to take in preparation for writing to communicate the presence of God? Let me suggest a few.

First, review again the books that have conveyed to you a profound awareness of God's presence. Your list will be very different from mine, but both yours and mine will be illustrative of the kinds of books that create this God consciousness. One of the earliest such books in my pilgrimage was a book by Harold Tribble entitled *What Baptists Believe*. One of the things he said was that Baptists and indeed, Christians of all faiths believe that God is Spirit and not human with all of the limitations of humanity. This is an obvious fact to any one brought up from babyhood in the church. I had not been so reared. I was a nineteen-year-old person seeking after the knowledge of God. That God was Spirit and nearer to me than hands and feet and closer to me than breathing came alive to me in a profound way.

A second such book was one by George Buttrick — *Jesus Came Preaching*. It spoke to me at the time that I was contemplating entering the ministry. Buttrick made it clear that Jesus as a preacher was Emmanuel, God with us. The direct revelation of God in Jesus Christ as a preacher filled me with awe, wonder, and mystery when I realized the guiding pesence of the Risen Lord with me as I fumbled and sputtered in my first efforts at preaching.

More recently, *Markings* by Dag Hammarskjöld brought the presence of God vividly alive to me as I followed the inner thoughts of this very public man — a man who had a very private walk with God. He wrote those thoughts with no intent to publish them. They were published posthumously. In fact, many of your own writings that convey the reality of God may have been written with no plan to publish them at all.

Of course, the disciplined reading of the Scriptures is important for such writing. And you can find no better models for conveying the presence of God to the reader than the writers of Scripture themselves. For example, the apostle Paul in Philippians 1:3–11 writes in this way by engaging his readers in a prayer that he prays for them. Another example is the high priestly prayer of Jesus recorded in the seventeenth chapter of the Gospel of John. Also, Jude 24 creates that same sense of the presence of God.

Second, examine closely the events around you that provoke an awareness of God's presence in you. Make careful notes of these events. They become the "stuff" of your writing that conveys this awareness of God. These observations of your own encounters with the presence of God are authentically yours. When you tell the story of having had this experience, its very authentic quality is free of the reader's asking if it ever really happened at all or if it is just a story to help you make a point of some kind or other.

Third, write an autobiographical account that points away from you to the experiences that are "common to all of us." This has a way of creating a communion between you and your reader that often becomes an Emmaus Road experience of the Risen Lord walking with you. I had such a thing happen to me in writing my autobiography. I wrote the first draft as a straightforward telling of my own story. I was dissatisfied with the manuscript. I had worked with my editor on other books for thirty years. He knew me very well. I sent the manuscript to him and asked for his response. He suggested that I rewrite the last chapter and that at the end of each chapter I invite my readers into the dialogue by telling *their* life stories. We titled my book *The Struggle to Be Free: My Story and Your Story.* The involvement of my reader in dialogue resulted in my receiving well over two hundred letters in which the writers of the letters told me their stories. In this way a sense of the providence of God and the presence of God in our lives became very vivid.

Fourth, develop the discipline of writing your prayers. Make them as honest and forthright as you can. These prayers can at times be interspersed in your manuscripts or can be made into a book of prayers. They need not be ethereal prayers that you write in a vacuum. They can be prayers written as you are doing the day's work. A friend of mine who is a banker wrote a book of prayers entitled, *From Nine to Five: Prayers in the Day's Work.* I teach a course on pastoral care in human crises. For each day of the course I wrote a prayer for the class to concentrate our attention, memory, and ministry on the needs of persons in that particular crisis. Another friend of mine who has the care of AIDS patients is writing a book of prayers that include prayers of the AIDS patient, his or her family members, doctors, nurses, and ministers. I have read part of his manuscript and an awesome sense of the Holy comes through to me from the written page. Published examples of this kind of writing are Walter Rauschenbusch's *Prayers of the Social Awakening*, Carmen Bernos De Gatztold's *Prayers from the Ark*, and John Baillie's *A Diary of Private Prayer*, to name a few.

Literary Forms for Communicating the Presence of God

It may well be said that any particular literary form can communicate the presence of God. The Bible consists of documents written in many different forms: historical books, such as 1 and 2 Samuel; poems, such as the Psalms; short stories, such as the books of Esther and Ruth; and drama, such as the book of Job. However, some literary forms are more easily used than others. Let me suggest the following literary forms.

1. The biographical account of an event, a series of events, or a chronic stress of life calling for daily renewal of your awareness of the presence of God can be an effective literary form. For example, I have just listened to a minister friend whose wife is diabetic, has had to have one of her legs removed, and is on kidney dialysis. He and she are very close to each other and he is very caring of her. Both of them become exhausted and need to interrupt the stress they are bearing. He speaks of

the daily providence of God in giving them strength for each new day and their gratitude for another day to be together. Theirs is a story of God's presence of which Frederick Buechner speaks in his book *The Hungering Dark* (New York: Seabury, 1968). I actually struggle with them as we pray. If I should have their permission to tell their story, the presence of God would become very real to you in reading it. This is not a story I made up nor is it one I got from a book of illustrations.

When you recount events in the life story of people, events you have directly seen and heard, you become an "eyewitness." In your writing, the things you have seen and heard and handled become lively conveyors of the pesence of God.

2. A well-kept diary told in earthy, realistic words that record the break-through of the presence of God in the muck and mire of the day's work is another literary form you can use. A good example of this is George Bernanos's *Diary of a Country Priest*. He says, for instance,

> My parish! The words cannot be spoken without a soaring kind of love. . . . But as yet the idea behind them is so confused. I know that my parish is a reality, that we belong to each other for all eternity; it is not an administrative fiction, but a living cell of the everlasting Church. But if only the good God would open my eyes and unseal my ears so that I might behold the face of my parish and hear its voice![1]

Another such diary is Denise and Timothy George's book *Dear Unborn Child*. It is composed of meditations about the child while it was yet in the mother's womb. They reveal their own yearnings, hopes, and anticipations before its birth. Their life of prayer and feeling of the presence of God spontaneously generates some of those same feelings in their readers.

3. If you are a poet, an effective way of communicating the presence of God in your writing is to intersperse some of your poetry in the manuscript of your prose writing. Sometimes prose becomes too restrictive for your feelings of either ecstasy or desolation as you write. To break out of that bondage and put your thoughts and feelings into poetry produces this same response in your reader . However, do not plan to publish a whole book of poetry unless you already have a contract from a publisher to put your poems into print. I have heard a litany of rejections of books of poetry by publishers. I personally am not a poet and have never tried to publish poetry, but I have sought to help several authors get their books of poems published — without success. Nevertheless, you can intersperse your poetry in a prose manuscript without worrying about this bit of publishing doom and gloom.

4. A book of prayers is one of the most effective ways of communicating the presence of God. You will notice this as you read books of children's prayers overheard by an adult who is a parent, a Sunday school teacher, etc. I have always wished for a book of prayers written by a student pastor — his or her own prayers expressing the person's real feelings from day to day when the congregation is not listening! Or, I would like to have a book of prayers of a pastor for a group of new Christians as they go through the first year of their Christian life, after their confirmation or their adult baptism as the case may be. It would be an excellent guide for new Christians. I have already seen a book of prayers for newlyweds during the first fifteen days of their marriage written by Leland Foster Wood many years ago and now out of print. This needs to be done again for this generation.

5. The letter is an illustrious form for conveying the awareness of the presence of God. You can take the apostle Paul as a role model in using this method of communicating the presence of God. The letters that Dietrich Bonhoeffer wrote while in prison vibrate with an awareness of the presence of God. C. S. Lewis' *Screwtape Letters* combines humor with revelatory insight to create a sense of God's presence in an ambiguous and clearly evil world. A book of letters written to a wide variety of Christians in different stations of life would be an extension of pastoral prayers. For instance, write a letter to the mother and father of a newborn baby, to a person whose aging parent has just been placed in a nursing home, to a father who has to travel a great deal to make a living, and to a church board member who has led the church along with you through a severe crisis.

When you show empathy to such persons in the church in this way, perhaps all of your parishioners will eventually receive a letter from you. Your affirmation of them comes as a gift from God. And God's presence is made real to them in that moment. Should your letters some day be published, they may strike a responsive chord in the hearts of many readers.

Hazards of Communicating the Presence of God in Writing

The responsibility of communicating the presence of God is a heavy one and carries with it several specific hazards. I am sure that you would not deliberately cause a reader distress, but inadvertently you might do so. I have done so. Because some of the persons wrote me about their misunderstanding, I was able to make amends in one way or other. I wonder about those who did not take the time to write. A few of the hazards I can envision are as follows.

1. Misrepresenting God as a magician. In our eagerness to reinforce positively people's hopes that God will do just what they want, we can easily portray God as a magician. This is one of the hazards of much literature of the positive-thinking variety. The response of Shadrach, Meshach, and Abednego to Nebuchadnezzar is worth pondering: "If it be so, our God whom we serve is able to deliver us from the burning fiery furnace; and he will deliver us out of your hand, O king. But if not, be it known to you, O king, that we will not serve your gods or worship the golden image which you have set up" (Dan. 3:17–18 RSV). These men were not asking for any magic.

2. Misrepresenting God as ruthless fate who wills every bad thing that happens. Rabbi Kushner brought great relief to many people in their feeling that bad things that happened to them were the result of punishment from a vengeful God.

3. Mistaking our own spirit for the Spirit of God. Writing is a therapeutic experience for us when we are under severe personal duress. My great anxiety is that I may project my own concerns on a cosmic scheme as I write and cause my reader to assume that these are the intentions of God. If any one of us stands at this point, we need to take heed lest we fall. It is a slippery slope!

4. Falling into a mood of exhortation, spouting shoulds and oughts that merely frustrate the reader. The frustration lies in the generality of exhortations that are so nonspecific as to leave the reader with nothing but a vague and undefinable sense of guilt. There is a very solid place in literature for godly admonition and exhortation, as in the book of Proverbs. Nevertheless, this kind of writing should be done with care and should be balanced by words of assurance from God and words of praise for God, as in the book of Psalms.

The Hopes of Communicating the Presence of God

We cannot end this discussion with the pitfalls of communicating the presence of God. The main focus is the humble hopes of the author as a communicator of this awesome presence.

The primary hope that spurs you on as an author in the communication of the presence of God is that to do so is to fulfill the purpose for which you have been created by God. That chief purpose is to glorify God and to enjoy him forever. We never more fully realize our purpose in living than when we are pointing away from our own wisdom and calling our reader's attention to the glory of God. We are at the peak of enjoyment in writing when we are enjoying the presence of God as we do so.

Another conviction that we authors have in communicating the presence of God is that we know in part and prophesy in part. In a sense, we never *completely* communicate this ineffable reality. We always do so in part. This is not a false humility, but a real one. To realize the full weight of this tempers and modifies all that we write about anything. I have felt this keenly as I have written this chapter. What I have written here is not a full flaming truth but sparks from my anvil that shed a little light. As Alfred, Lord Tennyson says:

> We have but faith: we cannot know,
> For knowledge is of things we see;
> And we trust it comes from thee,
> A beam in darkness, let it grow.
> *In Memoriam*, lines 21–24

Beams in darkness though our words communicating the presence of God are, nevertheless that God is the God of the darkness and the light. For darkness and light are the same to the God of Abraham, Isaac, Jacob, Jesus, and Paul. That God provides our daily bread and our daily wisdom.

NOTES

1. London: Fontana, 1937, 28.

SUGGESTED READING

Marty, Martin E. *A Cry of Absence: Reflections for the Winter of the Heart*. San Francisco: Harper & Row, 1983.
May, Gerald. *Addiction and Grace*. New York: Harper & Row, 1988.
Oates, Wayne E. *The Presence of God in Pastoral Counseling*. Waco: Word, 1986.
Steere, Douglas. *Together in Solitude*. New York: Crossroad, 1982.
Terrien, Samuel. *The Elusive Presence: The Heart of Biblical Theology*. New York: Harper & Row, 1979.

Chapter 9

To Attend or Not to Attend a Christian Writers' Conference

David R. Collins

They come in all shapes and sizes — the retired schoolteacher from Boise, the accountant from Topeka, the housewife from Atlanta — each carrying his or her own experiences and aptitudes. Some are beginning writers, sensitive and vulnerable to criticism, novices in the competitive world of publication. Others wear a tougher shell, having endured the pain and disappointment of rejection, yet buoyed also by actual publication credits. All are conferees at a writers' conference, drawn by the hope that they may gather skills and pointers on the road to publication.

Secular writing conferences are usually designed with the general writer in mind and offer a wide range of writing workshops and activities to meet the needs and wishes of any and all writers. Such conferences usually feature a smorgasbord of offerings, including lectures, seminars, and workshops on fiction, nonfiction, poetry, juvenile writing, etc.

The nonsecular, or Christian, writing conference has a slightly different focus and awareness. Not only is it designed to meet the needs

David R. Collins has been a full-time English instructor in Moline, Illinois, since 1962. He is the author of fifty-four children's books published since 1970, including six biographies in the popular Media Mott Sowers Series. He has been awarded a Junior Literary Guild and Cornelia Meigs Prize.

of just any writer seeking to better his own writer's voice; it is also charted with the assumption that the conferee is also seeking to carry the message of God's love. Generally there is a feeling that the Christian writer has not only chosen to write for publication but has also been "called" into a special service by a power beyond himself or herself. The Christian writers' conference is likely to feature special vespers or spiritually uplifting events in hopes of providing motivating help to the core workshops. But, more important, the workshops themselves, when taught by quality leaders, provide more than a knowledge of the essentials of good writing; they provide the writer with a sense of calling.

Is a Christian writers' conference for you? It's a question you should ponder with care. Such a conference requires an investment of both time and money. Some attend such conclaves regularly, receiving much personal help and inspiration. Others attend and, when they leave, feel short-changed and disappointed. Perhaps you should consider your need for the stimulation that a writers' conference can give you. After all, isn't writing a lonely business?

That's a question I hear often. Actually I have never found writing to be "lonely." The activity demands solitude, a quiet collection of one's thoughts, but as I create characters, human and animal (I specialize in juvenile writing), loneliness is no part of my world. My writing room gets crowded with characters talking and milling about, I have all I can do to keep some semblance of order. No, I do not find writing lonely. As with everything else I do, I pray for God's constant presence. I know He is there. I know I am never alone.

However, I do enjoy bursting from my web of solitude occasionally and casting myself into the midst of kindred spirits — the kind of atmosphere provided by a writers' conference. I share my experiences and listen to others share theirs; I'm always looking for craft tips and shortcuts. New markets spring up all the time, and old ones die; talking with editors and with other writers is exciting — as well as useful to my writing career. And I often find, particularly at a Christian writers' conference, some individual who has been especially gifted with expression by God. It helps to get me back in focus when I stray (and I do stray) from the true mission of my writing.

Whether or not you should attend a Christian writers' conference is ultimately your decision, of course. But in making that decision, you might consider a few additional points:

1. Are you ready for a Christian writers' conference? Do you lack inspiration and direction in your writing? Have you gleaned everything possible from reading about writing? Have you "picked the brains" of

your local writing group? (The latter can be invaluable as a source of writing help.)

2. Have you studied the Christian writers' conferences available to you? An annual listing of these is provided in *Writer's Digest* and *The Writer*. Smaller writers' magazines also offer lists. All you have to do is write to the conference directors or registrars. Request a brochure. Notice what lectures and seminars are being offered. Do you need help in any of those areas? Are the instructors writers who are actively publishing? Is the conference feasible — financially and geographically — for you?

3. How many conferees usually attend the conference you have in mind? Are you comfortable in a group of that size?

4. Is there opportunity for personal meetings with workshop leaders and/or staff? Can you submit a manuscript or manuscripts for critiquing or discussion? Often a one-to-one conversation can provide specific assistance that a lecture presentation cannot.

Should you decide you're ripe for the writers' conference, plan to get the most out of the experience. Be ready to ask questions of your instructors, the conference staff, and other conferees. By all means, take a few manuscripts, but don't go thrusting them into everyone's face. Have them ready to share if an appropriate forum presents itself and if other conferees want to exchange.

Carry an ample amount of writing materials such as pens, paper, etc. Some may be supplied, but don't count on it. Be prepared to take quick notes. If you plan to tape any sessions, ask for permission to do so, as a professional courtesy. Depending on your schedule, you may or may not want to take a portable typewriter or computer.

If you are staying at a conference site overnight, you will want to include an alarm clock. Often conferences are held at colleges and universities, where overnight accommodations may be spartan; therefore you may need your own pillow, hangers, blanket, and personal toiletries. Find out in advance.

But it is not the tangible items that will afford the greatest potential rewards available from a writers' conference. Such items will only maximize physical comfort. It is what you carry within you that is most important. You must be ready and willing to critically analyze your strengths and weaknesses, to consult with anyone who might help you, and to be willing to share your own ideas and experiences — both in and out of the classroom, with both instructors and colleagues. Be especially on the alert for editors, publishers, or agents. They are looking for good writers.

Finally, don't overlook the opportunity to reach out for God's help.

After all, it was the Lord's words and actions as he went about "his Father's business" that gave direction, meaning, and purpose to our lives. If our words are to have any value at all, they must reflect his example. We must make of ourselves the best writers we can be. Attending a Christian writers' conference may help us do exactly that!

ANNUAL WRITING CONFERENCES

Arizona Christian Writers Conference

> Contact: Reg Forder, P.O. Box 5168, Phoenix, AZ 85010

Blue Ridge Christian Writers' Conference

> Contact: Yvonne Lehman, P.O. Box 188, Black Mountain, NC 28711

Christian Writers Conference

> Contact: CWC, The Community of Living Water, P.O. Box 443, Cornville, AZ 86235

Christian Writers Institute/Conference

> Contact: June Eaton, CWI, 388 E. Gunderson Drive, Wheaton, IL 60188

Green Lake Christian Writers Conference

> Contact: Green Lake Conference Center/ABA, Green Lake, WI 54941

Guideposts Writers Workshop

> Contact: Guideposts Writers Workshop, 747 Third Avenue, New York, NY 10017

IRWA Writing Workshop

> Contact: Marvin Ceynar, 300 Cherry Hill Road, N.W., Cedar Rapids, IA 52405

Lamplighters Inspirational Writers Conference

> Contact: Sharon Stanhope, Box 415, Benton, KS 67017

Maranatha's Christian Writers Seminar

> Contact: Leona Hertel, Maranatha Bible and Missionary Office, 4759 Lake Harbor Road, Muskegon, MI 49441

Mid-America Christian Writers Conference

Contact: Elaine Wright Colvin, P.O. Box 11337, Bainbridge Island, WA 98110

Moody Write-to-Publish Conference

Contact: Leslie Keylock, 820 N. LaSalle Drive, Chicago, IL 60610

Mount Herman Christian Writers Conference

Contact: David Talbott, Mount Herman Association, P.O. Box 413, Mount Herman, CA 95041

Oregon Association of Christian Writers Seminar

Contact: Stanley Baldwin, 17901 S. Canter Lane, Oregon City, OR 97045

Pikes Peak Christian Writers Seminar

Contact: Madalene Harris, P.O. Box 8118, Colorado Springs, CO 80933

Review and Herald Publishing Association Conference

Contact: Review and Herald Association, 55 West Oak Ridge Drive, Hagerstown, MD 21740

St. Davids Christian Writers Conference

Contact: Shirley Eaby, SDCWC, 1775 Eden Road, Lancaster, PA 17601

Seattle Pacific University Christian Writers Conference

Contact: Linda Wagner, Humanities Dept., Seattle Pacific University, Seattle, WA 98119

Southern Baptist Writers Workshop

Contact: Bob Dean, 127 Ninth Avenue N., Nashville, TN 37234

Spokane Christian Writers Conference

Contact: Elaine Wright Colvin, SCWC, P.O. Box 11337, Bainbridge Island, WA 98110

Warm Beach Christian Writers Conference

Contact: Jane Fries, Warm Beach Camp and Conference Center, 20800 Marine Drive, Stanwood, WA 98292

SUGGESTED READING

Periodicals offering conference listings:

The Christian Communicator
Joy Publishing
P.O. Box 827
San Juan Capistrano, CA 92675

The Writer
120 Boylston Street
Boston, MA 02116

Writer's Digest
1507 Dana Avenue
Cincinnati, OH 45207

Books offering conference listings:

Christian Writers' Market Guide
Sally E. Stuart, Editor
Joy Publishing
P.O. Box 827
San Juan Capistrano, CA 92675

Religious Writer's Marketplace
William H. Gentz, Editor
Running Press
125 South 22nd Street
Philadelphia, PA 19103

Chapter 10

Selling Your Book

Sally E. Stuart

Y ou have an idea that would make a great book! You've been working the idea over for a long time, but you're not ready to write it yet. You need to think about it some more, do a little research. Maybe no one would be interested in it anyway. Besides, you've never written a book. You don't even know if you can write a book — you have always been a lot better with devotionals. What if you get a contract and then can't write another word?

That's a familiar scenario, but one that can have a happy ending — even for you. Looking at a finished book and trying to visualize that you were the one who created every word can be overwhelming even for a veteran writer. But writing a book and getting it published is accomplished in the same way as you eat an elephant — one bite at a time. The only secret is in figuring out how to carve it up. This chapter will define each bite and tell you how to cut and chew it before moving on to the next one. The result will be a simple, step-by-step process that will produce a publishable manuscript you can sell.

Sally E. Stuart has been a full-time free-lancer for the last eight years and a writer for twenty-four. She is the author of seventeen books, including the 1991–92 edition of *Christian Writers' Market Guide* and more than 800 published articles. A resident of Aloha, Oregon, she is a nationally recognized marketing expert and is a contributing editor to *The Christian Communicator* and *Living Streams*.

Contrary to what many writers may think, a book is not sold to a publisher after it's written. Today, most books are sold on the basis of a book proposal, rather than from a completed manuscript. First-time authors will usually have to finish writing a manuscript before they will get a contract, but the idea is to find a publisher who is at least interested in your idea before you put the time and effort into writing a whole book. That is the purpose of a proposal — to establish interest.

Also, by presenting your idea in proposal form, it gives the publisher the opportunity to have input into the project before it is completely written. That can save the author a great deal of unnecessary rewriting. Sometimes a publisher will ask the author to reorganize the material, leave out or add a section, strengthen one area and play down another, or do whatever is necessary to give the book the appropriate slant or emphasis for that particular publisher. For that reason it is to the author's advantage to wait to write the book until he finds an interested publisher who can give that kind of real direction to the project.

In addition to the reasons given above for selling a book from a proposal, there are other reasons why the selling of a book should not happen after it is written. A book must be written to sell. That's more than a matter of semantics — it's called marketing. Unfortunately, many writers see marketing as a secondary part of writing, which is why many do not sell. Unless marketing becomes the focus of all you do in the process of putting a book together, chances are that book won't sell. Not because the subject is wrong or the writing is bad, but because it's off target.

Because marketing is not a step that comes at the end of the writing process, we cannot wait until then to do our homework and still expect to sell our book. The steps we will be dealing with will start with your initial idea and take us, step-by-step, to the editor's desk. Not just any editor's desk, but the one where your idea will most likely find a warm and open reception. That will mean doing your homework and not simply groping blindly in the book section of the market guide.

What you learn about marketing this book will serve as a master plan for every book you might write in the future. It will also serve as a plumbline to help you determine which of the many ideas you may come up with are actually publishable in book form. Too many writers treat writing like a game of Russian roulette, in hopes that if they come up with enough ideas, one of them might click with some publisher. Most aspiring writers would have much greater success if they would play darts instead — each idea sharply honed and carefully aimed at the appropriate target.

If you are going to sell your book, or find an interested publisher based on a proposal, you need to know exactly what to offer, and to whom. That's not as hard as it may seem. Again, it's simply being able to identify a course of action and take the appropriate steps. Those steps can become second nature to you as you become intimately familiar with them and then practice putting them to work. And to work we must go.

Your Book Idea

All books must start originally with an idea. It may be a general topic or theme. It may be an intriguing title. It may be the burning desire to share an idea, concept, lifestyle, or pathway to spiritual growth or enrichment. It may be a story — true or fictional — that cries out to be told. Once you can define that idea and put it into words, you have made the first step toward writing a book.

However, you must be very clear about what that idea is. It is not enough to say, "I will write a book on marriage." Marriage may be your general topic or theme, but it is not a full-blown book idea. Until you reach the point where you can describe your book idea succinctly in one or two statements, you are not ready to begin. For example, your book on marriage may be described like this: "This is a book about some specific activities married couples can participate in to enrich their marriages. It will provide the diagnostic tools to identify areas of conflict and then give them valuable exercises to overcome problems in those areas." Whatever the topic of your book, you must be able to complete the sentence, "This is a book about. . . ."

That is not as easy as it sounds. Some writers may spend weeks writing and rewriting that statement until they can put their idea into a nutshell. Don't rush this step. The refining of idea and focus are well worth the investment of time. One of the reasons many writers fail when they try to write a book is that they don't clearly see the bull's-eye for their dart.

An Idea Folder

Once your idea starts to take shape, even if you are still refining your focus, write a working title (or simply the subject) on the tab of a file folder. If you have arrived at your descriptive statement — or thesis statement — write it on the outside of the folder as a constant reminder of where you are going.

Begin to fill that folder with everything you have accumulated or that you find on your topic: newspaper and magazine articles or clippings; random thoughts that come to you; names, addresses, and phone numbers of resource people or authorities; titles of reference books or books on the same topic; potential quotes and their source; snatches of dialogue or description; ideas for the title or chapter titles; and anything else that might be valuable in the writing of your book. Put this folder near your work area and continue to fill it with anything that will expand your idea and contribute to your planned theme.

Chapter Divisions

When your folder begins to bulge, it will be time to expand this single file. Sit down on the floor or at a large table and empty the contents of the folder. Go through each item and begin to divide the items into related categories. As you do this, these natural divisions will likely suggest chapter topics. Some of these may still be blurred, but do your best to sort everything into an appropriate pile. Make a new file folder for each of these piles, giving them an identifying title, or a chapter title if one comes to mind. Each of these folders will now represent a potential chapter in your book. If an order for the chapters is not readily apparent, simply arrange them alphabetically so you can quickly find the folder you want.

Again, put these folders near your desk and continue to add pertinent data, this time putting each item into what seems to be the appropriate chapter folder. All this can and will be sorted more definitively later, so don't worry too much about determining which folder is appropriate at this point. These new divisions will soon become very familiar to you and will help you become more aware of what you should be looking for in your reading, research, or contacts.

Discovering a Book Structure

Eventually your chapter folders will fill up, and you will be ready for your next step. Take some time to go through each folder and become familiar with its contents. During this process, you will discover that some folders cover much too broad a range, while others are pretty thin. The too-big areas may have to be broken down into two or even three chapters, while the thin ones may be dropped or integrated into one of the other chapters. As you work through your material chapter by chapter and begin to see the overall direction your research is taking, you may detect one or more potential themes for your book. Because that theme may be different from the one you originally envisioned, you may need to rewrite your thesis statement to refine or even refocus it. This is only the beginning of the "wet putty" stage, so you can still work and rework your material until it begins to take a shape you feel most comfortable with.

After reviewing the contents of the folders, you will become aware of areas that need to be researched further. At this point you will want to do enough research to round out your material and reveal any aspects of your topic you have overlooked. You will not want to do extensive research until you know there is an interest in your book idea, but you do want to be sure the information you need will be available. Add folders for any new chapter divisions you discover in your research.

After you get the chapter folders readjusted, adding some and deleting some, it will be time to arrange them in order and make up a tentative table of contents. Determine the most logical order for the chapters. When you find what seems to be the best order for now, number the chapter folders accordingly and return them to your work area.

Studying the Market

Having come this far, most writers will be tempted to sit down and start writing. Don't. This is where the preliminary work of marketing must begin. Marketing at this stage is a many-faceted process, so we will examine one facet at a time.

If you haven't already been doing so, start looking for and reading every other book you can find on the same topic (both Christian and secular, if available). Making trips to your local Christian bookstores, church libraries, or Christian university libraries is a good beginning. Check the shelves in the appropriate section for similar books, or use the card catalog. Describe your book to the clerk or librarian and ask what they have available like it. If you can, buy or check out any books that seem to be in competition with your book idea, and read them. If you can't take them with you, at least write down the titles, authors, and publishers of all the books you discover as well as where you found them.

While you are out doing your research, talk to the clerk or librarian about how timely they feel your topic is, and how often they are asked for that type of book. Also find out which of the books available on the topic is currently the most popular. (Be sure you read that one, even if you can't read them all.)

After you read these books, it will be time for some serious soul-searching before you go any further. Very honestly answer these questions: Is my book really different from those already on the market? In what ways does it differ? Does it say anything new? Does it say it better?

The cold, hard truth is that unless you have something new to say, or can say it a whole lot better than others have said it, there's no place for your book in the marketplace. With all the books on the market today, there simply isn't room for the rehashing of old ideas. It is much better to realize that fact before you begin to write than to put months of work into a book that will never sell and should never have been written.

If, in your research, you find few or no books on your topic, it is not necessarily cause for joy. It could mean one of several things. It could mean that you have a truly unique idea whose time is ready, or an idea whose time is not ready, or an idea that is so obscure as to never be ready. It will be your job to determine which. A good way to do that is to talk with book clerks or librarians, Sunday school classes or church groups, your pastor, and even your friends and acquaintances (not your mother; she'd like anything you suggested). Try to determine if anyone else would be interested in what you have to say. Be objective. You don't have the time or emotional energy to put into a book that has no chance of selling.

What About an Agent?

At this point, you may be wondering if you should be looking for an agent. If you are a first-time author, with no books to your credit, then you would be wasting your time even considering an agent. Most agents are not interested in representing anyone who doesn't have a successful track record. Even if you have sold previous books, you don't need an agent in the Christian market, nor are there many available. Only prolific authors who don't want to spend valuable writing time selling their own manuscripts should even consider finding an agent. Another chapter in this book will give you more detailed information on the subject of agents.

Discovering Potential Markets

If the above research reveals that you have a potentially good idea and you are comfortable about moving ahead, you can go to the next step in the marketing research. It's time to find out which book publishers are potential markets.

Check the list of books and publishers you made during the last step. If you found that these books have a different slant from your own, start making a list of the publishers who published them. They may be interested in more books on the subject with a fresh, new slant. Realize, however, that a publisher will not normally accept a new book that would be in direct competition with one they already have on the market.

You may wish to make another trip to the bookstore to do additional research. The bookstore is an excellent place to find potential markets, especially if you are doing something out of the ordinary, such as writing on a specialized topic that wouldn't be mentioned in a market guide. You will want to check several things while you're at the bookstore: (1) Look at books published by any publishers you are considering. Are the covers attractive and enticing to potential buyers? Do the illustrations, type size, quality of the paper, and the like appeal to you? Eliminate any publishers from your list whose books don't come up to the standard you would want for your book. (2) Ask to talk with the book buyer (you may have to make an appointment ahead of time in the larger stores). Describe the book you wish to write and ask the buyer which publisher, or publishers, he would go to first if he wanted to order such a book. Most writers don't realize that a book buyer is one of their most knowledgeable resources when it comes to selecting an appropriate publisher. Even though there are dozens of Christian book publishers, most of those publishers have specialty areas in which they do the bulk of their publishing, or their most recognized publishing. For example, even though they do books in a number of areas, one will specialize in Christian education materials, one in children's books, one in teen fiction, one in adult novels, one in Bible studies, one in gift books, and so on. Your job, and one the book buyer can help you with, is discovering which publisher or publishers are strongest in the category your book would fall into. The publisher your book buyer associates with that particular topic is the one you will want to publish your book.

You may be delighted that XYZ Publisher has agreed to publish your adult novel, especially since it's the first one they've ever accepted. It may be flattering to think yours was the best one they ever found, but the truth is that your book will suffer as a result. If the book buyers don't know that publisher has published a novel — and especially if they know the publisher doesn't have a line of adult novels — they will probably never know that your book exists, or at least not bother to order it.

So in this step of the marketing process, your job is to try to discover which publisher is associated with and sells the most books in the area you are interested in writing about. Chances are that would include more than one potential publisher, especially if you are dealing with a rather broad, general-interest topic. In more specialized areas, the choice of publishers will be much more limited.

Checking the Market Guide

Now go to the library and in the current issue of the *Christian Writers' Market Guide* look up the publishers you are interested in pursuing. The

Guide will provide the latest and most complete information on those publishers. Read the listing on each of your selected publishers in the alphabetical listing of book publishers. That listing will give you their general terms of publication — whether they pay an advance or pay on a royalty basis and the usual percentage; the number of books they publish per year; and whether they want to see a query letter, a proposal, or a complete manuscript. The *Guide* will also indicate the availability of writers' guidelines and book catalogs. Send for both from any publishers you are interested in.

In the *Market Guide* also check the topical listing for the topic you plan to write about and find which publishers say they are interested in that topic. Read the primary listings and send for guidelines and catalogs for any that look as if they might also be potential markets.

Studying Guidelines and Book Catalogs

As the guidelines and catalogs arrive, spend some time reading and studying them. The guidelines will give you specific instructions as to submission requirements and the particular slant a given publisher wants. Read through the guidelines for general information and then set them aside for more careful study later if you decide to submit your work to that particular publisher.

Study each catalog closely to determine whether your book might fit in that publisher's line. First, review the catalog as a whole: What types of books are most prevalent? Is their approach to important topics consistent with your personal beliefs? Would you be proud to have your book in this catalog?

Next, find the section of the catalog where your book would be listed — e.g., marriage/family, children's, youth, Bible studies, or whatever. Is there a substantial section? Do you see a book that appears to be in competition with yours? Would your book complement the section? Are the books written by a wide variety of authors? Are they all written by celebrities? Pastors? Men? Doctors? Women? College professors? Theologians? Are they individual volumes or part of a series (such as Bible studies, children's books, and youth books)? Are they closed series (all written by the same author) or open and ongoing (all different authors)? Would your book fit in one of the existing series? Could you expand your idea into a series of its own?

Continue studying the catalog and asking yourself appropriate questions until you feel certain your book would fit in the catalog and in exactly what form. Repeat this procedure with each catalog you receive. As you do this, begin to rate the potential publishers. By the time you finish evaluating all the catalogs, you should be able to make a list of potential publishers in the order of greatest interest (your interest in them and their interest in your topic) or probability of interest.

Approaching a Publisher

Again review each publisher on your list, carefully reread their guidelines, and determine what you need to do to approach each of them with your idea. Mark one of the following options next to each publisher.

1. If the publisher asks for a *query only* initially: Send only a business letter describing your idea. Your letter should include a brief description of your book idea, including that thesis statement you have been working on. (If you can't describe your book idea clearly and succinctly in a paragraph or two, you are not ready to write your book or approach a publisher.) Tell how your book fits into the market, how it differs from what is already out there, why you are the one to write it, and why you feel they are the right publisher to publish it. (Show that you've done your homework.) Keep your letter to a page or two in length, if possible. You may include a separate sheet of your writing credits or educational credits, if applicable.

Keep in mind that your query is a sales letter and you need to do your best to convince the editor that this is a book they can't afford to pass up.

2. If the publisher wants a *query letter and a book proposal* initially: Send the query letter described above, along with a chapter-by-chapter synopsis (a one-paragraph description of the specific content of each chapter) and 1 to 3 sample chapters. (The *Market Guide* will tell you how many chapters they prefer.) Most publishers prefer to see the first chapter and the most "risky" chapter if there is one. (A risky chapter is one that might be controversial socially or theologically.) You will want to send the one you feel contains your best material or arguments. Some publishers want you to send everything you have written so far.

3. If the publisher wants a *complete manuscript:* Go ahead and write the whole book, following their guidelines and writing it to fit their particular needs as closely as you can.

Query Only

If more than one publisher wants to see only a query letter initially, you can send those queries simultaneously to all of them. Just be sure to mention in your query letter that you are making simultaneous queries.

If you should get more than one positive response to your query letter, you will then have to decide which publisher you want to give first chance to review your manuscript or proposal (depending on what the publishers request). You should not send your material simultaneously at this point. After you have selected the publisher to send it to first, send notes to any others who asked to see it and tell them it is being considered by another publisher but that if it should be returned, you will give them an opportunity to review it at a later date. You don't ever want to close the door on a potential publisher.

If you get the go-ahead from a publisher to complete a manuscript (when no contract is offered), you will be completing the book on speculation. This means the publisher has no obligation to purchase it and will do so only if the completed manuscript meets their expectations. Pay careful attention to any feedback you may get from a publisher at this point as to making any changes or adding new content. That kind of input will make your job easier and increase your chances of selling that publisher the finished manuscript.

You must realize, however, that the publisher may decide against offering you a contract when you have submitted the final manuscript. If that happens, carefully evaluate any comments the editor has made as to why your manuscript was rejected (some will give you no reasons at all) and learn what you can from this experience, but then determine that you will send your work out again as soon as possible. Since you now have a complete manuscript, you can send the whole thing to any publishers who consider complete manuscripts, if you want. However, since most still prefer a proposal, you will also have to go back to sending a proposal only. Now it will be easy to prepare the chapter-by-chapter synopsis based on what you have written, rather than on what you thought you might write.

In your cover letter, you may want to mention that the manuscript is completed and that you can send it immediately on request; but also make it clear that even though it is finished, you will be willing to rewrite it as necessary to fit their particular needs. Publishers are looking for writers who are flexible and open to making any changes or revisions that might be called for.

Selling a book manuscript takes an unusual amount of determination and belief in your work. I know writers who sent out a manuscript or proposal two or three or even up to six times and then gave up because they lost faith in their work. Unless you have a book idea you believe in completely, based on the market study you did as described in this chapter, you have no business taking it into the marketplace. And once you have taken it to market, you have no business withdrawing it until it has sold or you have exhausted every possible market lead. The only exception is if you find in the marketing process that your approach is wrong, the writing is not polished enough to compete, or the topic is no longer valid. You can usually pick up those problems from reading the evaluations of publishers who have read it. Don't take one editor's word for it, but if you get similar comments from all of them, subject your manuscript to an objective appraisal or find a published writer or writing teacher to give you his or her opinion. Don't ask your spouse, your mother, or a close friend. You need a professional opinion.

If you determine that your book is not marketable in its current form, you will have several options: polish the writing, sharpen the focus, find a new focus or slant, do a complete rewrite, or abandon your work entirely. This is never an easy decision, no matter which option you choose. Start by completely rereading your manuscript now that you have enough distance from the writing process to give it a more objective evaluation. Many first manuscripts should never be sold; they are simply a part of the learning process. If you decide to leave this manuscript behind, move forward, encouraged by the knowledge that you did your homework and are capable of doing what so many others only dream about. You not only know the steps that need to be taken — you have walked in them — and you will again.

If the Publisher Offers a Contract

At any point in this process, you could get a phone call or letter advising you that the publisher wants your manuscript and a contract will be forthcoming. After you pick yourself up off the floor or after normal breathing resumes, you will have some important decisions to make. We can't go into all the ramifications of a book contract here (it is covered extensively in another chapter), but I do want to make one caution.

Be reminded that you are now a professional and need to view this contract and your negotiations with the publisher as a professional. I have seen too many Christian writers who looked at a book contract as a gift from God that should not be questioned or tampered with. Although I believe in God's gifts, I have never believed that a book contract was one of them. He may have gifted me with writing talent, but a book contract is something that came because I did my homework and wrote a professional manuscript that was worthy of a publisher's notice. Whether your book was written for money or ministry, you do every other writer a disservice by accepting a contract without question.

I do not know of a major Christian publisher that would try to cheat an author, but it simply makes good business sense to realize that a book contract is written originally for the greatest benefit of the publisher. Any author who accepts the original contract without question makes it harder for writers who, like me, must support themselves with what they make from their writing and simply can't afford to accept a lower royalty or no advance. Writers have a responsibility to evaluate a publishing contract as closely as they would a contract for a new home. When every Christian writer starts to ask for better terms, not only will the writers benefit, but the quality of Christian writing will also improve.

In Closing

Writing a book can be one of the most time- and energy-consuming jobs you may ever tackle — and one of the most satisfying and fulfilling. They tell us there is at least one book inside every person. That may be true, but I know from experience that most people will never write it.

Writing a book takes more discipline than almost anything else you will attempt in your lifetime. Selling it will take even more determination. If you never try, or if you give up too soon, the message you care about may never reach the world.

SUGGESTED READING

Gentz, William H., ed. *Religious Writer's Marketplace*. Philadelphia: Running Press, 1989.

Stuart, Sally E. *Christian Writers' Market Guide*. San Juan Capistrano, Calif.: Joy Publishing. Published annually.

Chapter 11

De-Mystifying the Agent's Role

Lois L. Curley

A writer in Florida sent me a letter introducing herself and enclosing a chapter-by-chapter précis of her first novel. Her captivating style and the general direction of the work intrigued me. Her writing had texture and depth. On the basis of what I saw, I was interested in reading the complete manuscript, which the writer said was in draft form.

Yes, some further development of the characters and some polishing was needed; a few unresolved issues were yet to be thought through; some portions needed to be cut where they slowed the action, etc. But as I read, the feeling grew within me that this work had the ingredients of a great story.

The names of several editors who would be interested in reviewing this work came to mind. I told the writer I'd be happy to talk about representing her for placement of the manuscript in the religious book market. We agreed to team up. I expressed my thinking about this initial manuscript seeming to be only the beginning of what the writer had in

Lois Curley, who has been in religious publishing for more than twenty-five years, is an independent agent in San Diego, focusing on nonfiction properties for the religious and general markets. From a background of teaching English, she entered publishing as a writer, then became an editor in a religious publishing house. She became an agent at the urging of two authors whose book manuscripts she had originally acquired and edited for publication.

mind. My suggestion that she summarize what she would envision for a second and a third book in a trilogy received her ready response.

When I received her proposed overview for books two and three, I called four editors and described the project. Each was interested in reviewing our proposal for a trilogy. Within weeks the author and I had selected the contract we preferred for the three books. It came from a publisher whose advance royalty was not the largest, but one whose quality of books and recognized success in marketing inspirational fiction was proven. To us, this was more important in the long run than a larger up-front payment from a publisher whose marketing track record for fiction was less impressive.

Soon after that I negotiated an audio contract scheduled for production when all three books are published. An option for a video adaptation is in hand, and multiple European language rights for the trilogy are currently being pursued.

With no intention of putting the writer's possible efforts in poor light, I cite this case for two reasons: first, to report how one religious book project was developed and placed for publication by an agent. Also, to indicate some of the ways an agent was able to market the project, probably more quickly and profitably than the author would have accomplished for herself. If the writer had spent her time, money, and creative energy contacting editors one by one — none of whom she knew by name — with the one-book manuscript she originally envisioned, I wonder if she would have developed these several facets of the market. Perhaps; although she says, "No way!" (I need to point out here that the sudsidiary potential in this project are not necessarily inherent within all book projects.)

The phone rings and I hear something like this — again: "My name's Jim Jenkins. You're an agent? The kind that helps writers get their book manuscripts published? Maybe I need that kind of help. How do you go about it? What do I have to do?"

Interest seems to be increasing in what an agent familiar with the religious publishing field can do to maximize one's publication potential. But the persistent, questioning voices of published and unpublished writers alike asking similar questions lead me to believe there's something of a mystery about the agent's role.

Perhaps I can de-mystify the agent's role by focusing on what the agent does to benefit the author and publisher in religious book publishing. I will assume that you are reading this chapter from the viewpoint of one writing for publication. You may have published works to your credit, or you may be anticipating this accomplishment. In the process of our discussion, I hope you will discover how the agent's part can complement both the writer's and the publisher's roles. With this information I believe you can understand how working with an agent could enhance the creative writing gifts God entrusts to some of his children.

Why Be an Agent? or, How to Fall into Agenting

Let me assure you that there are many avenues into agenting. Most of them seem to have come from some area in the publishing industry. Mine is one of those journeys that is fairly typical. And this is the way it looks from my view eleven years later:

In my many years on the editor's side of the desk in religious book publishing, I had but one agent call me. But the one who did and the others I talked shop with did not seem to be informed about or sensitive to the viewpoints and concerns of many who write for religious markets. This scarcity of knowledgeable agents working within the distinctives and diversity of the religious book world was a strong influence in nudging me to become an agent specializing in religious books. Cheering me on in my decision were three authors whose books I had participated in publishing earlier. They became my first clients and today continue also as good friends.

The network of people I had met during my years in publishing within the American Booksellers and the Christian Booksellers associations became valued resources in my new career. With publishing experience and these networking possibilities, I launched the agency. To my surprise, I found myself almost immediately facing a segment of the religious book industry who had deep and subtle misgivings about the agenting role.

Agents — A Tradition to Some, a Threat to Others

General trade book publishers have traditionally preferred to work with agents in the acquisitioning and contracting stages of a project. They recognize that the agent screens out numerous works that might otherwise end up on their manuscript piles; also, that she serves as a scout to make them aware of writers and desirable book projects. Because it's her business to know the kinds of material editors in the various houses are looking for, she can be counted on to bring to an editor's attention those writers and works that fit these interests.

Religious book publishers, however, have been slower to recognize the benefits of working with agents in a similar manner. Perhaps there are some valid reasons for the mistrust and misunderstandings some of these publishers have expressed: that agents seem ignorant of and insensitive to the varying distinctives within religious audiences; that agents are hard-nosed and adversarial; that they make unreasonable demands; that they push for a more favorable contract for their clients than religious book publishers are accustomed to giving; that agents corrupt innocent authors with illusions of unrealistic expectations; that agents think they're protecting the author from the publisher and thereby hinder the process. . . . One editor told me on the side that he thinks agents "know too much" and just complicate negotiations by their requests for contract adjustments.

Such feelings may or may not have some basis of truth. And those that a few editors have expressed cannot be ignored, though I believe most are without factual foundation. I am pleased that these perceptions and understandings are changing, and some of my most highly regarded friends and acquaintances are contacts in the religious book publishing arena. However, the potential benefits of author-agent-publisher relationships are beginning to be recognized among religious publishers, and savvy agents are becoming warmly accepted by the new generation of leaders in religious book publishing.

A Look at Agenting Developments in Religious Book Publishing

First, some background. There was a time earlier in the century when a skillful writer of pertinent religious works could without difficulty find in one of the few exclusively religious book houses a publisher (often the owner) who would agree to publish his book. Perhaps in consultation with an editor, or perhaps without this benefit, the publisher would make that publishing decision because, in his opinion, the work was a worthy one and said something that needed saying — a sufficient reason, indeed, to justify its publication. Whether the potential number of readers was large, small, or even nonexistent was not of great concern.

Customarily then, after publication of his book, the author submitted his works thereafter to that publishing house and began a long and possibly rewarding relationship. It was not uncommon for the agreement to publish be made with a handshake, followed sometime before publication of the book with a contract the author often would sign without discussion or even a reading of the terms.

Some vestiges of long-observed patterns may yet be evident, for publishing traditions and tales persist. It seems there's an aura about writing and publishing that allows aspiring authors to assume even today that there is an eager publisher around every corner awaiting the manuscripts generated by their state-of-the-art word processors. This is a lovely dream.

Now for some present-day realities. General and religious publishers alike give priority consideration to books for which their marketing teams can identify a significantly large and defined audience of potential book buyers. An editor's enthusiastic recommendation of a work is not usually in itself sufficient to justify the financial risk of its publication.

Translated, this means that in the current religious book market, what editorial persons, regardless of rank, may believe are good and valid reasons for publishing a manuscript may not be the weightiest part of the decision-making equation. What those responsible for the company's marketing functions see as the sales potential of a fairly well-defined book-buying audience that they may be able to target successfully is the factor that more often than not weights the decision to publish, or not to publish.

A note here to writers who may be offended by this pressure to sell as crass, unspiritual, below the role of an author: Remember that the marketing side of publishing is the key to distribution of what you write. You may feel that I am exaggerating the intensity, sophistication, and focus of the publishers' marketing role in the religious book industry, especially as compared to the attention that should be given to the creative functions. I fully intend to keep my observations realistic and honest so that you, the author, can grasp the mandate to be visible in every way that is possible for you. How to make yourself and your book(s) known in effective ways is a matter of importance for discussion with your agent and your publishers.

Another fact of publishing today is that personnel changes are to be expected. There's no guarantee that the editor who arranges your contract will be on hand to parent your book through the hoops of editing, production, and promotion on its way to publication and distribution — all vital stages in the birth of a book.

The number of new religious book publishers being launched each year is surprising. The list of new titles from new and established companies is overwhelming. Few new works bring significantly fresh perspectives or communicate with distinction. Market competition is at the same time fierce and stimulating. The race for editors' attention and publishers' promotional dollars has markedly increased the pitch and the pace in this dynamic publishing arena.

Clearly, the preceding brief rehearsal of publishing indicators does not give you the complete picture. But my obvious intent for mentioning even these few is to point out why, in my opinion, more and more religious book writers are depending on their agents to interpret the prevailing winds and maneuver them through the storm and tides of the shifting scene.

There are published and unpublished writers who continue to go the rounds of publishing houses, trying to get an editor's attention. If successful, they warily work through negotiations of a publishing contract, never quite sure that what they have achieved is all they could have hoped for, as compared to what they believe they deserve. . . . ("Muddling through, without knowing all your options," is how one writer expressed it.)

In some cases I have seen writers who are usually quite in control of their responses take on the role of an adversary when faced with negotiating a contract. Was it their uncertainties about the ways of publishing that put them on the defensive? Was it their inexperience and resulting fear in working with editors and publishers that made them consciously or otherwise express their apprehension? Could it have been a suspicion that anyone issuing a contract is out to get them? Whatever the reason, an attitude barrier raised consciously or otherwise can result in a strained writer-editor relationship right from the start. Unfortunately, that is seldom improved through the publication and marketing processes.

Early in my agenting career I learned that money — advances and royalty — holds the potential for becoming another major point of contention between authors and editors who together negotiate a publishing contract. Recently a call came from a widely published author who was experiencing some contract-related tension with his editor and was looking for help to sort out the tangled threads. I agreed to represent him for future books. But it was not appropriate that I become involved at this point in the problem. And what followed in the development of his book made it evident that the editor and the marketing team were less than wholehearted in following the manuscript through the steps toward publication in the manner it deserved. Both the author and the publisher were the losers.

Other instances reported by unhappy authors have further strengthened my belief that an agent's competent handling of contractual business matters can usually foresee and forestall communication and money problems — the most common sources of potential irritation. In the event something unforeseen does arise to threaten the smooth inter-workings of author and editor, the agent in representing the author, with the good of the editor also in mind, serves as a mediating influence in clearing the way to publication.

The import of a mutually respectful and enabling author-editor-publisher partnership cannot be overemphasized. And the agent's role in preparing the way for this kind of a relationship to develop can be invaluable. To represent both the author and the work to appropriate publishers with the goal of maximizing the publication process and the marketing potential is an agent's primary responsibility.

Some religious book writers know what it is to be sought out by acquisition editors who recognize the status and marketing value of that author's name and titles in their list. Yet, from time to time I hear from thus blessed authors who want to be relieved of what one has termed "the tedious parts" of making publisher contacts and negotiating contracts. Another author, weary of "generally selling myself," as she expressed it, asked for representation so she could "be sure that all this will be taken care of properly so [I] can get on with [my] writing." For such a person the author-agent partnership offers a particularly happy solution.

A View of the Agent-Person

'Midst the impermanence and competitiveness of today's publishing scene the author-agent relationship can offer a welcome measure of stability. I think of an agent as a service-oriented, independent business person. Whether or not he is a part of an agency staff, he develops an interdependent relationship with each author he represents. Each of his client's successes are his successes. To serve his constituency, he maintains a current network of publishing contacts and builds good working relationships with each. To serve well a "stable" (the industry's term) of productive religious book authors is for him a deeply satisfying process. He is committed to be there for his authors and to represent them with energy and integrity.

Diane Cleaver explains it this way: The agent "serves as your link to the publishing industry. In fact, as publishing has changed — bigger companies, increased competition for books, higher costs everywhere — it has evolved that the agent is often the *only* permanent force in an author's career."[1]

An agent serves his client best as a knowledgeable business partner and by encouraging and screening her creative efforts. By freeing the writer to focus on her task, he does a service to the publishing world as well as to the author. There are a number of ways an agent can achieve that goal.

His contribution to his client's career is not easily measured. These immeasurables often include guidance in alerting clients to issues and concerns that point to trends of thought and areas of interest the writer is equipped to consider for a future book project. Usually this guidance includes suggestions for organizing and focusing ideas in ways that communicate to a specific and viable market of book buyers. The agent's responsibility here also includes steering a client away from less market-worthy topics he may have chosen, or a subject area he may not be skilled to handle.

Much of an agent's value to her clients is in who and what she knows: the kinds of books editors are buying; their personal subject interests and editorial strengths; the kinds of books their houses market effectively, the kinds of marketing they do, and how well they actually sell books; the makeup and extent of a publisher's list of current titles, as well as its backlist (long and steady sellers); the publishers who value their authors, and how they show it; the ranges of royalty advances the various religious book publishers are paying; those who promptly pay and accurately report taxable earnings to authors and to the IRS; which companies have a history of financial stability — or of losing ground; publishers who run a tight ship, and those whose business operations and administrative practices are somewhat casual, or less than tidy; et cetera. Few authors seem aware that these factors are vital in the process of contacting publishers and identifying those who are among the best positioned to market the kind of project the author proposes. Without good insider information, "Just any publisher, Lord!" becomes the prayer of many a writer.

Preparation and presentation of his clients' book proposals so that they capture editors' interests and sell manuscripts is at the heart of every successful author-agent partnership. Alert agents include in their manu-script proposals any angles that could enhance promotion and sales of the work. This kind of information is usually ammunition that the editor appreciates and needs to help him sell the project to both his editorial and marketing decision-makers.

The manuscript consideration process is often a long one at best. To speed the proposal and manuscript presentation process, agents discuss proposals with several editors at a time. In the religious book field editors are beginning to accept this procedure long accepted in general publishing. Realizing that others are simultaneously reviewing the same proposal, editors who see good possibilities in it for their list, usually respond with more than customary promptness to express their interest to the contacting agent.

Before ushering a simultaneous submission through even the initial editorial consideration process, savvy editors will call the agent to discuss the work and get additional information on the author's project(s) and to talk about the author's rationale, focus, schedule of manuscript comple-tion, and other pertinent items. Also important for an editor to know — prior to moving a manuscript through his company's editorial and marketing review processes — is what interest has been expressed by other publishers in this project. (The agent is careful not to give one publisher unfair advantage over another when there is obvious interest from several publishers in a project.) If there is a high level of interest from other publishers, an editor's timing for approval of this project is motivated and may be planned accordingly.

Simultaneous submissions — which an agent must be up front about with editors to whom he submits proposals — are not usually regarded with favor in religious book publishing when they come from writers. Fair or not, most houses expect authors to contact editors and send out proposals one at a time and then to wait perhaps many weeks for an answer before possibly going through the process again — and again. This procedure could require a matter of years before an author would be able to get proposals to all possible publishers. The delays and hurdles in this route has done as much as anything to interest writers in seeking the aid of an agent.

On the business side of the partnership, the agent's sale of each manuscript for publication should be emotionally as well as financially beneficial to the client, to the publisher, and to the agent. And on the nitty-gritty side of operations, the agent serves as trustee recipient of the author's earnings from royalties, reviews publishers' sales reports and royalty earnings in light of the contract terms, makes prompt disbursement of net earnings to the author, accurately accounts for receipts, and files the appropriate tax reporting forms on client earnings.

Lest you think agents do about everything but write (and they do that, too, in some zanier instances) let me correct any such impression. An agent does not teach you how to write a salable manuscript, prepare the basic rationale and overview of your work for an editor's consideration, or guarantee that a publisher will publish it. But you should realistically be able to count on your agent's genuine interest in your work and in seeing your book(s) succeed.

What Does the Author-Agent Relationship Look Like?

I discovered early in my agenting experiences that as an agent I was more than an initial contact and spokesperson for my clients. I became an editorial consultant, a reviewer of manuscripts, a recommender of ways to fix what was fixable, a bouncer of ideas for new projects, an encourager of writing capabilities. I became a business partner representing each author's interests in ways that promote the successful publishing and marketing of works to bookbuyers of religious/inspirational books. I became a confidant, a therapeutic ear when creative energies falter and deadlines become oppressive. My "antennae" became alert to anything that might hinder smooth working relationships between author and editor.

Agent Diane Cleaver describes the writer-agent relationship as "intimate and tenuous."[2] Although some authors and agents may never become close friends, or even meet face to face, yet theirs is an intimate relationship because they are each in their respective roles handling a book, which is far more than just a product to be marketed. It's a deeply personal thing, involving both author's and agent's egos in their mutual agreement on the manuscript's worthiness for publication and involving their mutual commitment to see it published. Their relationship must, therefore, hold degrees of intimacy and interdependence that require mutual respect and admiration on both sides.

This relationship includes some tenuous implications, too, because mutual trust is its foundation: To communicate skillfully by writing a quality work, this the agent trusts the writer to accomplish. To encourage the writer in expressing his ideas, to appropriately showcase the work to its best advantage before potential publishers, and to make every effort to sell those ideas reflected in his book, this the author trusts the agent to do. Trust and support on both sides is vital to keeping faith and interest in the project alive over the months that may be required to find a publisher.

Tenuous feelings may surface if an author thinks that his agent may not fully understand what the project is basically saying; that the agent is primarily interested in the big books, the big-name authors, and potentially big-money projects; that the agent has too many other clients to care about him; that his book is not his agent's priority; that the agent isn't trying hard enough to find a publisher; et cetera. Looking honestly at these concerns, an author will realize, of course, that he and his work cannot always be his agent's primary interest, for his is one among many projects the agent is monitoring and caring for concurrently. (This issue is usually clarified in the standard working agreement that agents and clients use as their basis for understanding.) But rather than allow those tenuous feelings to grow without due cause, the writer needs to remember he has a direct line to his agent. It is her responsibility to keep it open and to make herself available to discuss the client's concerns and forthrightly answer his queries.

How Do Authors Find the Right Agent for Their Needs?

Your first step is to decide you want to investigate the pros and cons of working with an agent representing you and selling your book projects to the religious publishing trade. When you are serious about that decision, you are ready to begin your search.

The agent I believe you are looking for as your partner is service minded: she has a mind and heart to serve as a business partner and editorial consultant. She is someone able to maximize your creative energies and find the editorial and marketing group that is able to publish, sell, and distribute your work. With these characteristics in mind, here are some ways for expediting your search:

You can find agents who specialize in the religious book market listed in references at your public library. Look for sources such as *Religious Writer's Marketplace*,[3] a periodically updated guide to Christian and Jewish religious markets. Also, you will find names and locations of agents, with religious books as a speciality, in standard references such as *Literary Agents in North America* (LANA) and *Literary Marketplace* (LMP). If you know authors and publishing personnel who are working happily with agents in the religious book market, checking with these sources first may expedite your search.

The next step is to make contact with agents on your list. Start by crafting (and I do mean *crafting*) a thoughtful query letter to briefly introduce yourself. Don't be bashful! Do be succinct! Your publishing résumé is the place to describe your current book project(s) and also your published articles and books by title, publisher, and date (if you have such). Indicate that you are investigating possibilities for working with an agent to place your book projects for publication.

Enclose an overview or chapter-by-chapter précis of your best manuscript. Be sure to include a self-addressed and stamped envelope if you expect a reply — hopefully, with a request to see some or all of the manuscript. Some agents charge a review fee, so ask what the agency's fee schedule is.

When you receive an agent's positive response to your query, promptly send the material she has requested by registered mail or other reliable carrier. Include a self-addressed mailing envelope/package and correct return charges in the event the agent, after reviewing your material, may not be open to representing you or if you decide as a result of your interaction that she is not the person to represent you.

Call and talk informally with the agent if you receive no response within two weeks after the agency's receipt of your materials. If she responds with genuine interest in your manuscript, be prepared with a list of items to discuss and notate for later reference as a basis for making your eventual selection of the one to represent you. Meeting face to face for this discussion may be helpful, but not necessary or perhaps not even possible. (At least half of our clients are located in places on the globe that make it improbable we will ever meet. We've found that it is possible to work quite satisfactorily together by mail, phone, and FAX.

You can be confident that an agent who is honestly enthusiastic about the publishing potential of your work will respond (in a phone conversation that you initiate at a time convenient for him) to your sincere interest in

1. Reasons and events that led to his being an agent.
2. Some authors and titles of books he has sold during the year, and the publishers involved.
3. Terms of his working agreements, particularly as related to commissions and any other charges involved in services rendered. (Some agents provide a schedule of guidelines that give information about how they work with clients.)
4. Some characteristics or insights related to his religious pilgrimage.

You may think of other items for your agent-information file, but the responses you receive in these four subject areas above should help you gather data, form opinions, and get a feel for personality characteristics and interaction styles that would be evident in a working relationship. To some writers their comfort level in talking and working with their agent is the determining selection factor. Others give top priority to an agent's marketing record. The rating scale you devise will, of course, reflect what is important to you and the religious sensitivities that influence your life and writings.

Author-Agent Working Agreements

When you and an agent decide to team up, I think it's wise to make a mutually beneficial working agreement a matter of record. Understanding at the start what expectations each of you has for this important relationship can go a long way to keeping communications and results based on the realities stated in the agreement.

Not all agents use a written form of agreement, but those who do so use documents that are basically similar in their intent. Be thorough in your review of any agreement your agent uses to indicate the guidelines of your work relationship. You should not be pressured into signing it. When you have reviewed all of the items it includes and discussed any of the terms you do not fully understand with the agent and anyone else with whom you may choose to consult, only then are you and the agent you select ready to indicate your full agreement by signing the terms of your partnership.

Know the time period for which you are committing yourself to this agent's representation. Two to three years is common. Be aware that some agreements have self-renewing terms of one or two years. If you do not want this or some other feature included, talk about your reasons and request the removal of such stipulations.

Also, consider carefully the terms for ending this agreement in the event either you or the agent need to terminate the relationship prior to the agreed period.

Some agents use agreements only on a book-by-book basis. These do protect the author's and the agent's interests but do not include the expectation that the agent will handle the author's other works, unless specifically agreed to.

Except for a possible fee for reviewing manuscripts, there's no money to be made by the agent until she sells manuscripts, and she can work a long time before that happens. When a book manuscript is sold, the "agent's clause" is incorporated into the publisher's contract, stating that all monies earned by the author on sales of that book are paid to the agent for her disbursement of the net receipts (the earnings less agent's commission, as stated in the author-agent agreement) to the author.

When you are reviewing and considering an agreement, check the wording to be sure you are not expected to pay a commission on all your creative works. For instance, if an agent is handling placement of your book manuscripts, and you are selling on assignment or as a free-lance writer to periodicals, you may not want to pay an agent's commission on those earnings. While not all agents expect to handle both book and periodical manuscripts for authors, you will be wise to inquire concerning this matter.

Rates of agents' commissions continue to be adjusted by the realities of the economy. For many years 10 percent was the standard commission. Now agents are charging 15 percent, though I know some who charge 20 percent. In the religious book publishing arena, where royalties are historically far below those paid by the general trade, agents cannot serve their authors well and survive on less than 15 percent in this market. There is an unfortunately low rate of survival for those who have tried.

Working with Your Agent

Now, with all this information and counsel, we can assume that you and the agent you have selected to represent you agree that your common objective is to see your work published. A few more suggestions here can help you work profitably by allowing your agent to be the agent and you to be the author:

1. Provide quality manuscripts your agent believes are readily

salable and prepare proposal data the agent can use in her promotion of you and your writings to editors. (Your agent will provide guidance in preparing the type of proposal she needs from you.)

2. Follow your agent's instructions promptly.

3. Be patient while your agent is contacting and interacting with editors to place your book with a publisher appropriate for your work — a process that can take months, many of 'em.

4. Give your agent any information that might provide a marketing angle for your book — such as your speaking and platform schedule to indicate the kinds of appearances with which the sale of books could be coordinated by the publisher and all contacts you may have with radio, TV, bookstores, organizations, institutions, etc., that could serve as a base for making your book known.

In the Final Analysis . . .

Whether you are a career author or someone who writes a single or occasional work, you can undoubtedly understand the rationale we have suggested for working with an agent in negotiating the hills, turns, and twists of the manuscript promoting and selling routes of religious book publishing. We have considered many facets of the agent's role in his goal of encouraging, enabling, and enriching the author whose works involve him in religious book publishing.

If you know writers whose eagerness to obtain a book contract sounds like "Just anything to get my book published, Lord!" you may have received some light from the preceding discussion that will illuminate *your* direction.

But primary in our discussion of agents and agenting has been our intent to de-mystify what they do and what they can contribute to those who write and those who publish the books of import and impact in religious publishing today. We hope that objective has indeed been accomplished.

NOTES

1. Diane Cleaver, "All About Agents," *Writer's Digest* (June 1980), 33.
2. Ibid., 22.
3. William H. Gentz, ed. *Religious Writer's Marketplace* (Philadelphia: Running Press, 1985).

SUGGESTED READING

Appelbaum, Judith, and Nancy Evans. *How to Get Happily Published*. New York: New American Library, 1982.

A writer-friendly guide by two insiders to penetrating the publishing mystique and finding your way in the world of agents, publishers, and book promotion.

Gentz, William H., ed. *Religious Writer's Marketplace* (Philadelphia: Running Press, 1989).

A guide to more than three hundred Christian and Jewish publishing markets along with a wide range of basic information, including working with agents, for every serious writer who wants to reach the religious marketplace.

Mathieu, Aron. *The Book Market*. New York: Andover, 1981.

A readable, basic source for nearly everything a writer needs to know and do to get a pertinent manuscript published. Written by a former editor and publisher with a half-century of experience. Dated, but a useful source of information nevertheless.

Bookstore Journal. Monthly magazine of the Christian Booksellers Association, Inc., 2620 Ventucci Blvd., Colorado Springs, CO 80906-4000.

A current source of information concerning publishers and books every Christian writer should be familiar with for an overview of the trends and topics publishers are marketing.

Publishers Weekly. An international news magazine of book publishing, produced by Cahners Publishing Co., 275 Washington Street, Newton, MA 02158-1630.

The definitive, current source of all book publishing and featuring religious books and the religious publishing scene. Current information on editorial and marketing personnel, interviews with authors, book promotion events, and reviews.

Chapter 12

Some of
My Best Friends
Are Editors
and Publishers

D. Bruce Lockerbie

In 1862, a shy New England woman sent four poems to Thomas Wentworth Higginson, editor of the *Atlantic Monthly*. Her cover letter asked Higginson to tell her "if my verse is alive." She also added, plaintively, "If you please — Sir — to tell me what is true?"

Emily Dickinson's question is the unspoken question every writer asks every editor and publisher every time a completed manuscript is sealed in an envelope and mailed to the editorial office. Subjectively, of course, the writer believes his work is true; else he would not have written it. But limited to the subjective, truth remains locked in a drawer; only by receiving corroboration — affirmation, acceptance, and an opportunity for the writer's voice to be heard from the printed page — can truth be recognized objectively.

So the moral responsibility of editors and publishers is to tell the writer the truth about his work, then publish the best of what is true. Integrity belongs in every aspect of the relationship, from the author's

D. Bruce Lockerbie, formerly Staley Foundation Scholar-in-Residence at the Stony Brook School, is a full-time writer and lecturer and the president of two agencies: Stewardship Consulting Services, offering counsel to schools, and Paideia, working with colleges, seminaries, churches, and other nonprofit organizations. His books include *Take Heart*, co-authored with his wife Lory, *Thinking and Acting Like a Christian*, *Who Educates Your Child?* and *The Cosmic Center*.

proposal and finished manuscript through the publisher's contract, the content editor's careful attention to meaning and style, the proofreader's jot-and-tittle proofreading, the editor's selection of dustjacket blurbs, the printer's and binder's painstaking operations, the advertising department's promotion, the sales representative's pitch, the bookstore owner's display, the reader's fairness.

Writers need publishers if for no other reason than to handle the mechanical problems of producing from a sheaf of pages a bound book. In addition, unless the writer is foolish or desperate enough to subsidize his own undertaking at a vanity press, the publisher assumes all the costs of the project and sometimes offers pin money in advance of royalties to be earned. Which of us private persons could afford to risk our capital on such uncertain ventures?

Since 1965, my three-dozen books have been published by more than a dozen different houses; I have current contracts for forthcoming books with two or three firms with whom I've never worked before. Over the years, I've probably dealt with two score and ten editors I know by name — not counting those faceless drudges with whose grammatical or stylistic scruples I've quarreled and from whose dedication I've benefited. In addition, I've become acquainted with various other essential persons in my publishing experience — art editors, sales managers, publicity directors, and so on.

In most cases, the first meeting takes place over lunch. For you writers just beginning to work your way around the game board, let me warn you about the snare called "Lunch Along Publishers' Row." It sounds rather glamorous and, indeed, it may well be. You send your idea for a book to a publishing company, and a few weeks later a reply by phone or mail expresses interest and asks if you ever get to the city. As it happens you do, and so a date is set for next Wednesday. When the writer shares this coup with his wife, immediately she begins planning a wholesale renovation of the house or a vacation in Pago Pago; the writer considers an appointment with his broker (at least, the broker he intends to need after next Wednesday's lunch!).

With such anticipation, the writer arrives in Manhattan at the publisher's skyscraper address. An elevator ride to dizzying heights seems symbolic. The writer gives his name to the receptionist and sits down to stare in awe at the shelves of best-sellers under the firm's imprint. Ten minutes later, the editor herself or one of her flunkies appears to guide you back through a maze of cubicles to the corner suite. Once while waiting at Doubleday, I shared the waiting time with a most distinguished-looking British gentleman whose face seemed familiar. Both of us were summoned simultaneously by our respective editors: Evy Herr for me, Jacqueline Onassis for the Englishman, who turned out to be Lord Kenneth Clark of Saltwood.

After the editor has greeted the writer in her office, introductions to several editorial colleagues are in order, along with the obligatory cup of coffee. The writer sits uncomfortably on the edge of art deco furniture, looking for somewhere inconspicuous to place his attaché case with its precious contents — perhaps a three-page proposal or a sample chapter or tearsheets from a representative magazine article or maybe even the entire manuscript recently returned from some other editor more heartless and obviously more benighted than your present host.

All the while names are falling like paperclips off the edge of the desk. Billy Graham is being wooed again; Hans Küng is in town; Jerry Falwell insists on a menu at the publisher's dinner that includes no wine in the veal marsala; Isaac Bashevis Singer has a new collection of stories; Henri Nouwen was in the office yesterday to discuss his new meditations on suffering. It's all too breathtaking! The author wonders, *What am I doing here? When do we get around to me and my work?*

At the next pause in conversation, the editor excuses herself to punch the telephone and ask the assistant to notify the Waldorf that her party will be a few minutes late. Be still, my heart! It's lunch in Peacock Alley! Shortly thereafter, joined by yet another editor, a procession makes its way back through the labyrinth. En route to the elevator, we pass editorial functionaries who never leave their desks for power lunches, tunneling their way through mountains of manuscripts and page proofs. Their brown bags and thermos containers bring a momentary pang of recognition to the writer, but his empathy passes by the time the elevator arrives.

A brisk walk around the corner or up the street brings the writer and his companions to a luxury hotel and its sumptuous dining room. The editor is well known to the maitre d', who seats the party at her regular table. The room is crowded with similar entourages. Over there sits a famous novelist; hard by, a rising mystery writer; at an adjoining table, a feminist critic; behind a column, the renowned political essayist; all of them "doing lunch."

The writer feels his gorge rising. Too conspicuously he grabs for a roll and butter to cram into his mouth. Already noonday beverage orders are being taken. Apparently the two-martini lunch is customary. Eventually oversized menus are distributed by a European captain. The writer struggles with dim lighting and middle-aged vision, then settles for the chef's specialty as described in continental dialect by the obliging captain. The dish turns out to be vastly richer than the writer's usual cup-a-soup at home; however, the writer is amazed at how hungrily, how wolfishly, he cleans his platter.

Meanwhile, seemingly random chatter goes on. Someone knows somebody else in the writer's acquaintance. The writer tries to be amusing, engaging, witty, sophisticated. The dishes are cleared, dessert ordered in spite of protests of diet and calorie counting, and coffee is poured all around. The writer catches a glimpse of the American Express charge slip and gulps at the bill for lunch.

So far, not a single word has been said about the writer's purpose in being present, his reason for coming to town, the contents of his attaché case abandoned in the editor's office.

Back in the elevator and ascending to the sky, the writer feels a sudden claustrophobia attack. Has he missed his cue? Was he expected to bring up the subject? What happens now? Is there no handbook on protocol he might have read in advance? The elevator doors separate and the party disperses with "Glad to have met you" and "See you again sometime." Trailing the editor, the writer retraces his steps to her office. Should he sit or stand? Does the editor expect him to accept yet another cup of coffee instantly offered by her assistant, or is it proper to refuse in the interest of finally getting down to business? Who knows?

The editor seats herself, swings her chair around to gaze out upon the skyline and the river glistening in the mid-afternoon sunlight. She seems about to say something and does. She says, "We ought to get together sometime and talk about your book idea."

The writer nods in disbelief, checks his watch, and notices that he still has time to make an early connection for the trip home. He reaches for his case, awkwardly shakes hands with the editor, declines the services of a guide to the men's room and thence to the elevator.

All the way home, the writer wonders and wonders, *What can I tell my wife?*

In time, the writer will learn how to play this game, its rules, its nuances, its etiquette for working with editors and publishers. Among the first is this: *Don't talk about your book, write it.* Talking is a debilitating, enervating exercise, inimical to writing. Talk often and long enough about your work, and when it comes time to put it down on paper, you may discover that the words have all seeped away. Beware of the editor who wants to hear the whole plot or argument before you've set it down. He doesn't know his own business, and he's certainly harming yours.

A first-class editor, however, looks for something else over lunch: congeniality, good will, an absence of taking oneself too seriously, an awareness of other issues besides the writer's central preoccupation. That initial lunch is really a corporate interview, a psychological test, to determine whether or not the writer has any depth of character and intellect. Books are expensive to publish, and few publishers are eager to take on a project by lightweights, even if the raw idea sounds promising.

But writers need editors and publishers for more than economic reasons. *Direction, encouragement,* and *criticism* are three other significant contributions a writer may receive from caring editors and publishers. When these gifts are given, the writer knows that he has found a special friend.

A writer often needs *direction*. Working with intense passion for a particular subject or persuasion, a writer can become oblivious to his own blind-spots; or he can become blocked to the folly of a wrongheaded decision; or stymied by a seemingly impenetrable problem. A caring editor will raise new issues, spell out pitfalls to be avoided, prod the writer toward greater use of anecdotes, help to shape a book out of the tumble of impressions and fragmentary notes. Jon Pott, editor-in-chief at Eerdmans, has been this kind of friend to me.

A writer also needs *encouragement*, even when the work is going well. Writing is such a lonely vocation. The writer wishes it so; thus there's no cause to feel sorry for him. But working in his self-imposed exile from the rest of the human race, a writer sometimes forgets how much he needs the tonic of encouragement to keep on writing. Spouse and family and friends, sometimes colleagues and acquaintances, can all help; but there's nothing quite like a letter or a call from an editor to encourage the fainthearted. Here I must name two editors who have been of particular encouragement to me: Robert Heller, formerly executive editor for Doubleday's religion department, now publisher of Crossway/Continuum Books, and Rodney Morris of Multnomah Press. During the writing of several books with each firm, Bob Heller and Rod Morris have kept in touch, sending an occasional note, a clipping of some news item pertinent to my topic, a humorous cartoon, a word of greeting from a mutual acquaintance, a phone call just to ask, "How's it going?" Neither of them has hovered or threatened or made me feel guilty. Each has kept me assured of his personal interest in my welfare and in my writing — and in that order! I call them friends.

But a writer also needs honest *criticism*. Editors are similar to teachers in many respects. Over the years, as my experience with gifted editors increased, I began to see a parallel between their work and mine as a teacher of writing. For too long, I'd been notorious among my students for little more than the swiftness of my red pen in searching out and exposing dangling participles, such as "Smoking his cigar furiously, the newborn infant was handed to her nervous father." My marginalia consisted almost entirely of cryptic notations about my students' failure to write with greater clarity and effectiveness.

Then I became a student myself in manuscript school with editors as my teachers. I learned from them and their pasted messages attached to my pages the value of asking questions. Their inquiries taught me the value of the pointed question. From their pithy reactions and detailed comments I began to understand the worth of such time-consuming analysis to follow up my misdirected logic, my slippage in tone, my questionable diction. Most of all, I felt for the first time the benefits of criticism, which every writer secretly desires and which only the giants of literature receive. Even if there is no praise as such, the fact of knowing that someone else has read closely and given thought to what I've written is its own reward.

Oh sure, occasionally one encounters an editor with a dyspeptic spirit, jaundiced by disappointment at his or her own failure as a writer. But more often than not, editors are people of goodwill, devoid of jealousy, like athletic coaches who never themselves made it to the Olympics or the major leagues, yet who want the best for those with whom they work.

I honor such large-hearted persons, one of whom I name: Evelyn Bence, who edited my book *Fatherlove: Learning to Give the Best You've Got*. Petite and tough, blessed by an ironic wit and an ear for the English sentence, she nurtured me through the writing of a difficult book. She was unrelenting in disallowing me the excesses of sentimentality. When I submitted too many paragraphs fulminating on the importance of a particular influence in my life, she blue-penciled the whole passage, writing in the margin, "Those who care already know." Enough said.

Some of my best friends are editors and publishers. But as every published writer knows, there are those other editors and publishers who — let's just say — aren't mentioned in my will. These are the publishers who specialize in remaining as aloof as possible from the business of selling books. Why they bother at all beats me! They provide no budget for marketing, no support for publicity, and they whisk books off the shelf and into the remainder bins almost before the author's mother-in-law has finished reading.

Other publishers overwhelm the market with their flood of new titles, but the ebbtide drags into oblivion all but one successful book, wiping out any chance for the rest to find their own audiences in time.

Some publishers apparently pay their employees in Confederate money because the turn-over of editors suggests low morale and fleeting loyalty. A writer signs on with a firm, begins work with an editor, is passed on to a second, winds up with a third who knows little about the origins of the project or its obstacle course on the way to completion. Meanwhile, the writer and his book-in-progress flounder.

Shall I also tell you about the publishing firm that asked me to help begin their list by submitting a manuscript in six weeks, then performing all the editorial, graphics, layout, and design myself, plus serving as the only proofreader. All this on a word-of-mouth agreement and a handshake. The book sold one hundred thousand copies, but I never saw a royalty check. The publisher claims to have sent royalties regularly to someone else who owned the rights. I finally wrote off my losses as a bad debt. Then, years later, I received a bill from the publisher, charging me for corrections I'd made as proofreader! From this I learned the hard way: No more Mr. Nice Guy; no more agreement without legally binding contracts, no more contracts without an appropriate advance — enough, one hopes, to motivate the publisher to get his money back by promotion, advertising, and sales.

There are other horror stories: publishers who lose your manuscript, then claim never to have possessed it; publishers who commission a work, then go backrupt. Or my worst: some years ago, I wrote a biography of an unsung American military hero, a general responsible for major decisions affecting both World War II and the Korean War. I'll spare the minutiae, but everything that could possibly go wrong did: My advance checks were sent to the wrong address, even to the wrong country! The editorial office lost a chapter, then the index, then misplaced the photos. The marketing director declined to serve. The book got stalled in production and missed an important anniversary.

I undertook its promotion, obtaining citations from the subject's classmates at West Point — household names in American history — as well as from the United Nations General Secretary, the United States Senate, the governor of Pennsylvania, the mayor of Philadelphia. Still the publisher did nothing to sell the book, and it went out of print with fewer than one thousand copies sold.

You won't be surprised to learn that I refuse to consider having my work published by any of these disreputable houses. Furthermore, I'm not shy about warning others to avoid my fate. It's not revenge or greed that impels me. Writing is my vocation under God. I expect editors and publishers to hold their work in the same high regard. We're in this work together, and our stewardship of time and talents is important.

When I give my word to an editor, when a publisher and I sign a contract, we commit ourselves to each other; we become morally responsible. I want to live by that commitment, as do the best editors and publishers. That's why some of them are truly among my best friends.

Chapter 13

How Editors Decide What to Publish

and How What They Decide to Publish Gets Published

Andrew T. Le Peau

In book publishing, the job of the editorial department is somewhat equivalent to that of the research and development segment of many industries. It's the responsibility of R & D to come up with new products that the factory can make and that marketing can sell. Generally there are two requirements that each new product from R & D must fulfill. First, it must in some sense be new — either new for that company, better in some new way than a competitor's version, or completely new. Second, it must allow the company to generate a profit — by keeping production costs reasonable and then by either selling a lot at a modest price or selling a few at a high price.

Perhaps this picture is a bit stark compared to the romantic version many of us (including many editors) have in our heads about the world of publishing. We picture a meal in a quiet corner of a fine restaurant. The editor, perhaps pipe in hand, is in sophisticated yet casual conversation with a writer who has a slightly frayed look about him. They discuss art, beauty, and the meaning of life as it is played out in the novels of the day

Andrew T. Le Peau is editorial director of InterVarsity Press, where he has worked since 1975.

and the manuscript the author is working on. With a gentlemen's agreement, sealed by a handshake, the book is accepted for publication in a small, quality edition. The reason? The book is outstanding, or, perhaps a bit more realistically, the editor sees great artistic potential in the author. While this book may not be a literary masterpiece of the highest caliber, the writer shows such promise and skill that the next one just might be his tour de force. The editor believes this artist is worth encouraging and developing.

As much as we may wish it were not so, the second picture is uncommon, except in small, closely held publishing firms that operate more like hobbies than businesses. Christian publishing houses, of course, may be expected to have more of a vision and mission than the typical New York house. Their performance will be measured against their ultimate purposes of spreading the gospel or improving Christian education or the like.

But Christian publishers must also operate in the world of commerce unless they are subsidized by a parent organization (such as a denomination or parachurch organization) or some other benefactor. Even in those cases, however, the ones providing the subsidy will want to know that their money is being well used. They will watch to see if the books they want to publish are actually getting out to the people they want to reach. And one measure of that is economic success. Other Christian publishing houses are publicly owned and are responsible to stockholders or to a parent organization that may not be Christian. Certainly they will be measured by money.

In the following pages I want look more closely at these and other factors that editors must take into consideration as they evaluate potential manuscript ideas. Then I will conclude by outlining the steps a book goes through from acceptance through publication and into the market.

How Books Are Born

First, where do manuscript ideas come from? Not always from authors. Generally publishing houses divide manuscripts or proposals into two groups — solicited and unsolicited. Unsolicited manuscripts are those sent in cold, without any request from the publisher. Some Christian publishers will receive a few hundred of these each year. Others receive as many as five thousand. Only a few of these manuscripts, obviously, ever see the light of publishing day. At InterVarsity Press, some of our best-selling books have been unsolicited. Calvin Miller's *The Singer*, as an example, came in complete without any prior contact with the author. But such a story is rare.

The majority of published manuscripts were originally solicited. They can come from several sources. Most likely someone inside the publishing house came up with an idea for a book. If the idea is evaluated positively, an editor is assigned to find someone to write it.

Or a publishing house may decide it wants to publish a particular person (usually well known, often previously published) and asks that person to submit a proposal or to sign a contract. In a sense, in such a case the book is accepted before it is even thought of because the primary criterion is the author, not the topic.

Literary agents can also be sources for book ideas. They try to match the right book with the right author and then bring the book to the right publisher. While most New York houses publish exclusively through agents, with little contact with the author, agents currently channel only a small but growing percentage of books to Christian publishers.

Second, how are manuscript ideas evaluated (whether the idea originated inside the publishing house or not)? I have identified seven criteria that most editors consciously or unconsciously use in making a decision about publication. There may be others, but I would guess that these seven will cover about 94 percent of the cases. These are also much the same sort of criteria secular publishing houses might use. They will even have some kind of corporate mission statement to help in evaluating how appropriate a given manuscript might be. The criteria are:

1. Format, Genre, and Topic
2. Quality of Writing
3. Quality of Content
4. Potential Market or Audience
5. Financial Feasibility
6. Mission (Mentality, Purpose, Ethos, and Theology)
7. Intangibles

Let's look at each one in turn, and for each I will suggest action that authors might wish to take.

1. FORMAT, GENRE, AND TOPIC

Most publishing houses find by trial and error or by design that certain kinds of books work better for them than others.

Format and Size. The physical characteristics of the finished product can be a key factor in an editor's decision about publishing a given manuscript. Some can make a success of hardbacks (like Word Books) but seldom try paperbacks. Some book publishers don't produce workbook-size pieces (especially if they sell mainly through bookstores where such books are difficult to display adequately) or those that would need to be in a three-ring binder or be spiral bound. Still others don't have a line of small pamphlets or booklets because they don't have suitable display racks available for bookstores or because they can't find appropriate outlets for bulk distribution. Moody, IVP, and Multnomah, however, have successfully produced these smaller pieces.

Length. One Christian book publisher I know will not consider manuscripts of fewer than 120 double-spaced, typewritten pages. For others, the lower limit may be 200 or 100 or 60 or 30. They have found over the years that books of a certain size aren't feasible for them. On the other end of the spectrum, some publishers are reluctant to publish manuscripts of over 400 pages.

Structure. Books are organized in a number of common ways. Some structures tend to work better than others for particular publishers. For example, editors may shy away from manuscripts that are too outline-ish. Or they may be reluctant to take a book that has too many very short pieces.

Another common problem for publishers is the multiple-authored book. Collections of essays by different people — even well-known authors — often receive a cool welcome in the marketplace. Generally publishers find that they may even have more trouble selling a book with two authors than a single-authored work.

One notable exception to this rule are books that have a strong reference character to them. Dictionaries, handbooks, and the like with many expert contributors are often stronger editorially than a similar book by one author who might not have the breadth to provide quality material on a wide range of topics.

Another difficult structure is the collection of essays by one person. One of the most common types of submissions I see as a book editor is a group of sermons by a minister. A collection may also take the form of a number of previously published articles or papers. The basic problem in these cases is the lack of unity in theme, tone, or audience. It makes for somewhat disjointed reading that puts readers off. (These same problems often plague multi-authored books.)

Genre. The category of literature that a manuscript fits in is another factor. Some publishers don't publish any devotionals or poetry or fiction or reference books, for example. Others do wonderfully with nonfiction but terribly with fiction. Again, one publisher may discover that their how-to books on gardening, cooking, and even computers sell quite well but that venturing into biography is almost always a mistake. Of course, the very large houses (such as Zondervan) publish a full spectrum of books. But even there, certain factors of size or structure may limit what an editor will seriously consider.

Topic. Often publishers will tend to gravitate toward certain topics like family issues or evangelism or academic concerns. Denominational publishers will generally be more likely to take on books that deal with issues or people associated with their own church or tradition. At the same time, publishers can sometimes find themselves overpublished in certain areas, even in topics they are known for. This can be true if the market is generally flooded with a particular topic. In that case publishers will either begin pulling back or start looking for new angles on old topics or for books dealing with a smaller slice of the pie.

For example, Christian publishing has seen dozens of books on parenting produced; so most publishers would likely have a bias against doing another general book on the topic. But a writer who takes a narrower piece of what topic, like single-parenting or parenting in blended families, might meet with a more favorable response.

Action for Authors. What can writers do to increase the odds of having the format, genre, and topic of their piece be received favorably? It's actually quite simple. First, request catalogs from the publishers you're interested in. Analyze them for types of books, topics, and physical characteristics. Sometimes catalogs are organized by type of book, or they may have an index in the back that reveals the topics a publisher has emphasized.

You can also go into a local bookstore and see which publishers are doing what. Many stores have organized their shelves by broad typical categories, so your task can be relatively simple (assuming you know what topic you want to write about).

Finally, you can talk to others who know the field. Perhaps you could chat with a published author. Or you could even call a publisher and ask to speak with an editorial assistant who probably knows most of the answers concerning the types of books his or her publisher generally releases.

2. QUALITY OF WRITING

The second factor an editor considers is the quality of writing. It might seem that all editors would give equal weight to this. But as with the format, genre, and topic, it varies from house to house.

Some editors care little about the quality of writing because their interest is primarily in the idea or topic the book covers. They know that if the content is strong enough, they can get a good content editor or copy editor, or perhaps even a ghostwriter, to put the manuscript into publishable shape. This is especially true with books for the popular market.

Perhaps surprisingly, this may also be true for academic or textbooks — which are often written with notoriously unreadable prose, even for scholars. But such books often will not have the benefit of heavy editing or rewriting since the potential audience is limited to a small number of academics who want the content so badly that they will plow their way through the dreariest or most ornate writing to get it.

Usually, however, editors are quite concerned about the writing itself. They look for good use of images and illustrations. They want to see sensitivity to word choice and even to rhythm. Writing cluttered with redundancies or inflated language can be a big problem. Poor grammar or spelling even in a cover letter can be the death knell for an otherwise good idea.

Why is good writing important in the evaluation process? One reason is that the editor expects writers to be able to write well. If they can't write well, they most likely won't get published. Another reason is that the editor usually doesn't have the time or money in the budget to get the manuscript put into acceptable form. The writer has to have the ability to revise adequately, or even good ideas will go unpublished.

The reverse is also true. Outstanding writing can make an editor take a second, third, and fourth look at a topic that has been covered many times in other books. It can make ordinary ideas seem fresh and inviting.

Action for Authors. I am a believer in the theory that good writing is just plain hard work. Sometimes it can come in a flash of inspiration, but generally, I think, moments of inspiration and creative explosions must be preceded by long hours of working at the craft.

Certainly two of the best books on the basics of good writing are William Zinsser's *On Writing Well* and Strunk and White's *Elements of Style*. I especially recommend Zinsser because he practices so well what he preaches. He turns the unlikely topic of how to write well into interesting reading.

Going beyond the mechanics to the art is not as easy to do. Reading good writers from William Shakespeare to Walker Percy is not a bad place to start. G. K. Chesterton, Garrison Keillor, Walter Wangerin, and other writers of their class are also worth careful study, if not imitation.

3. QUALITY OF CONTENT

A book is supposed to have good ideas the way a pizza is supposed to have cheese. You just can't make one without it. A trip to a bookstore might make you question this truism since so many books seem to have so little in them. But good ideas can take many shapes and sizes. For rarely is a totally brand new idea ever generated.

If the ideas are rather ordinary, then editors will look for a spark of freshness or vitality, a new approach to an old problem. C. S. Lewis could have written just another book on personal holiness, and it probably would have sold quite well. But instead he took a backward twist on the whole topic by looking at it from the viewpoint of a senior devil giving advice to a junior demon on how to bring about the downfall of the human he was assigned to. The result was *The Screwtape Letters*, a classic read by millions of Christians and non-Christians alike. (Of course, many subsequent attempts to do the same sort of thing have almost universally failed because once Lewis did it — and did it so well — the technique was no longer fresh.)

Editors will also look at the author's personal experience in the topic area of the book. Likewise, it can be helpful, if the author has a public ministry or significant education related to the manuscript. Such credentials can give credibility to the proposal because they make it more likely that the book itself will bear the stamp of reality. An editor wants to know if the author's ideas have been tested in the furnace of life or if they are just impersonal theory.

The key is to have experiences and a biblical understanding that match the level of the book. Often I have seen manuscripts or talked to authors who wanted to, say, offer a brand new interpretation of the book of Revelation. But if the author is without any formal biblical training, it is hard for a publisher to take such a proposal seriously. The author is unlikely to be aware of the hundreds of interpretations the church has offered throughout the centuries or how this "new" interpretation is likely to be received even among conservative scholars. Book learning is not the greatest prerequisite for generating good ideas. But authors without an awareness of what is going on in the scholarly realm will have an extra hurdle to jump.

Unity is the last element editors look for. Unity actually straddles the line between content and style, and it can take many forms. Does the author consistently address one audience? Do the parts of the structure hang together in a coherent way? Is the writing level consistent throughout? Does the book primarily make one main point, and what is it? The more varying answers there are regarding audience, structure, style, and theme, the more likely the book is to be ill-conceived or ill-executed. The more unity, the more strength. And that can translate into a book with a significant ministry for the kingdom.

Action for Authors. First, read, study, and do background research.

Get to know the potential pitfalls and what has already been said on the topic the book covers. Second, get involved in people's lives, find out what their problems are, what their needs are. That will give an essential vitality and realism to the book. Third, be prepared to work hard.

4. POTENTIAL MARKET OR AUDIENCE

While the task of editors is to think primarily about the kinds of issues we've looked at so far, editors must also consider the potential market. They must do so because often the very nature of much Christian publishing in North America, operating as it does in a commercial environment, requires it. And just as some publishers find from experience or design that they have better results with certain kinds of genres or topics than others, the same is true with types of audience. So editors (as well as book marketers, of course) will ask what a book's potential audience (purchasers) is likely to be and how well that audience profile overlaps with that of the publisher's typical book buyers. So they will look at such factors as the following:

Age. Is the primary intended audience children, youth, young adults, adults, or senior citizens?

Sex. Is the primary intended audience male or female?

Socio-economic Status. Is the primary intended audience, e.g., working class, professional, managerial, middle-income, or low-income?

Marital Status. Is the primary intended audience married, single, divorced, widowed?

Education. Does the primary intended audience require less than a high-school education, a high-school education, a college education, or a graduate education?

Accessibility. Do the channels exist to reach the primary intended audience? Are there organizations or magazines or mailing lists for this group? For example, there may be fifty thousand urban pastors in North America, but if they are not organized or easily accessible, there could be no real market for a book directed to them.

Felt-need. Is the primary intended audience interested? Again, there may be 80 million smokers in America, but the potential audience for a book on how to stop smoking is only the fraction of that figure who actually have a desire to stop.

Because it can take one to three years on average for a book to get published, editors generally try not only to stay on top of trends but to anticipate them. In that way, by the time some new idea or topic or concern hits the public consciousness, a book will be there, ready to meet that need.

The Airport Test. One Christian publishing house asks whether or not a book can pass the airport test. For example, would you be seen in an airport carrying around a book called *How You Can Stop Being a Homosexual* even if that was a felt need of yours?

Niche. Is the topic overpublished (like self-esteem or charismatic gifts) or underpublished? Is there a niche your book can fill even in an overpublished area? For example, while there are many books on marriage and a number on spiritual disciplines, we at IVP were struck by a proposal for a book that would look at how couples could work on spiritual disciplines together instead of as isolated monks. The result was the publication of *Marriage Spirituality*, a book that we thought could find its own way by targeting a narrow niche that was as yet unfilled.

Action for Authors. You can find out what a potential audience might be for a book idea by studying publishers' catalogs and going to bookstores to see what's out. (If little is published on a given topic, it could mean that there is no market for a book on that subject or that there is an empty niche waiting to be filled.) Another help can be talking to bookstore owners about what people are asking for but have trouble finding. Equally important is talking to people who are part of the intended audience you have in mind — pastors, professors, couples, students, or whoever. And as before, being involved with and ministering to people is of key importance. Find out what their needs are, what they care about, and in what areas they are having trouble finding adequate resources.

5. FINANCIAL FEASIBILITY

Editors are not the only ones with a say in what gets published and what doesn't. Marketers have a chance to give sales projections, of course. But the finance department gets to make their own projections, too, based on editorial, royalty, manufacturing, and marketing costs weighed against projected income from sales at various discounts to different channels (distributors, bookstores, bookstore chains, libraries, book clubs) and from subsidiary rights payments (translations, mass-market rights, serial rights). The key is not just to sell lots of books. You can lose money even when you sell hundreds of thousands if, for example, promotion costs are too high or a royalty advance is so large that even healthy sales don't recoup the investment. So financial advisors (and likely the head of the publishing house as well) will want editors to make sure the project will do better than break even.

Occasionally, however, some books will be published even though they won't make money. Sometimes a parent organization (or a benefactor) will subsidize a project because it is felt to be so close to the organization's primary mission that the investment even in a money-losing book is considered worthwhile. A publishing house may choose to do the same thing, using its own profits to subsidize a book. The reasons could be again that it is committed to the message of the book. Or it could see this book as a step in developing a promising author.

Even if a publisher projects that it could do better than break even financially on a project, it might decide not to do it. The reason often has to do with the size of the venture. A multivolume reference project, a Bible translation, a curriculum sequence for churches, or signing up a big-name author can all be calculated to show very adequate profits. But the investment before any income is realized can be hundreds of thousands or even millions of dollars. If a publisher doesn't have a big line of credit or an investor ready to capitalize the project, the decision may be negative. Or, if the cash is available, a project with such an enormous initial investment would probably have to be in the dead center of the publisher's priorities. While the house might frequently do low-investment projects on the fringes of their interests they must reserve the big money for the truly central.

Action for Authors. Authors need to be realistic about the magnitude of a publishing project. Money is limited for most organizations. That is why bringing as many resources and connections as possible to the publisher can help. For example, many books have been published because the author is connected to a Christian organization that is willing to guarantee the purchase of several thousand copies of the book.

6. MENTALITY, ETHOS, AND THEOLOGY

Most publishing houses have very distinct personalities that are affected not only by their work habits but also, and especially, by their commitments and their origins. Obviously, denominational houses like Broadman (Southern Baptist) and Abingdon (Methodist) will have many convictions and traditions (and conflicts) that arise out of their association with their parent churches. Likewise, they will find a significant audience among the members of their denominations. All of these issues enter into how editors make their decisions.

Nondenominational houses also have theological or ecclesiastical biases. They may be charismatic or noncharismatic in orientation. They may be Reformed or dispensational. They may be fundamentalist or liberal. They may be broadly evangelical or narrowly evangelical. If they are associated with a parachurch organization (such as NavPress and the Navigators or Multnomah Press and Multnomah Bible Institute), the traits and mission of the parent will have a strong effect on the audience, theological slant, and mission of the publishing division.

Most publishers, whether owned by a denomination, parachurch organization, private company, or public firm, will have a mission statement, and many will have a statement of faith or beliefs. This will often make explicit what some of the operating assumptions of the editors are. They will all generally converge on each manuscript with the question, "Do the overall assumptions, purposes, and perspectives of the manuscript fit with those of our publishing house?" The closer the answer is to a no, the more likely the decision to publish will also be no.

Action for Authors. Being familiar with the stance of various publishing houses can save authors a lot of unnecessary rejection slips. Many publishers will be quite willing to offer a statement of faith or publishing purpose. But again, just looking at publishers' catalogs or asking bookstore owners who has what theological slant can be just as helpful.

7. INTANGIBLES

Finally, editors are human. And many human, unquantifiable dimensions enter into a decision to publish or not to publish. Sometimes a factor in the decision can be as subtle as the appearance of the cover letter to a manuscript. Is it neatly typed or casually handwritten? Editors may also look for clues in the cover letter to indicate whether the author would be easy to work with. Does he or she express a willingness to take suggestions and revise? Or is there some indication that the author thinks the manuscript is exceptional in its current state and probably doesn't need any help. I prefer the author who is willing to take advice.

Sometimes an intangible can be as personal as whether or not the editor (or publisher) has met the person submitting the proposal. Usually having met the author has a positive impact on making sure the submission is considered seriously. I am sure many good manuscripts have been turned down because the editor had too many other pressing priorities and didn't have enough time to evaluate the manuscript adequately.

Action for Authors. About the best thing to suggest here is that a writer pray for the editor. God's hand is in editorial decisions. And Christian editors consciously want God to lead them in their decisions. I think they would all welcome this spiritual ministry from writers.

From Acceptance to Publication

These, then, are the seven criteria that editors (and the entire publishing house, ultimately) use to decide what to publish. Some factors are more important in some houses than others. Sales can be key in one, whereas quality of writing is very important in another. Of course, a potential book does not have to hit a home run in each category to get accepted for publication, but the higher it rates in each category, the better its chances.

After a book is accepted for publication, what steps does it go through to finally reach bookstore shelves? The figure on pages 155–56 summarizes this process. Unsolicited manuscripts are usually reviewed by one person in the editorial department. If that reviewer sees potential, it will be referred to others; otherwise it is rejected. Solicited manuscripts are usually evaluated by several people, sometimes by an editorial committee, and are either accepted for publication or rejected.

You will notice in the chart, however, that there is an arrow running directly from *Solicited Manuscripts* to *Contract Negotiated*. This is because sometimes an individual is authorized to send a contract to an author without prior approval of the manuscript itself. This might be the editor-in-chief or the publisher.

Contract negotiations will concern advances, rates of royalties, royalties for subsidiary rights (book clubs, periodical excerpts, translations, radio, TV, film, and the like), discounts for purchase of the printed book by the author, the cover, and almost anything else the author and publisher might want to consider. Usually the more prestige an author has or the greater potential sale the publisher sees in the book, the more generous the contract will be for the author.

Ultimately, agreement may not be reached between the two parties, often because the author is negotiating simultaneously with more than one publisher and is able to choose the more satisfactory agreement. There is nothing unethical about submitting a book idea to several publishers at once so long as the author makes it clear at the beginning of the process that he or she is talking to other companies.

If agreement is reached and if the manuscript is not completely written, an editor may help the author develop the book until a draft is finished. Once the manuscript is complete, it may proceed directly to copy editing or it may undergo further evaluation for revision. Outside reviewers with special expertise in topics the book addresses may be employed for such evaluations. For example, a commentary on the book of James may be reviewed by a New Testament scholar. A book on sexual abuse of children may be reviewed by a psychologist.

The Publishing Process

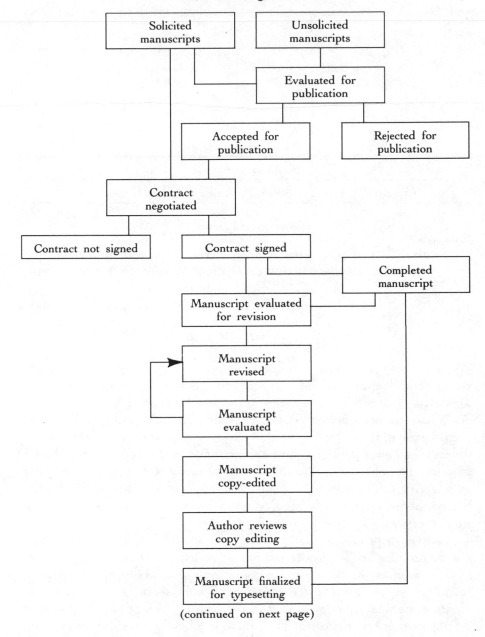

(continued on next page)

The Publishing Process (continued)

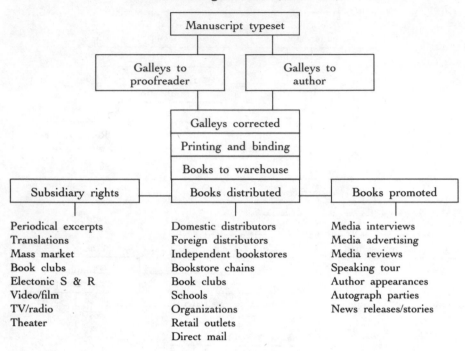

Manuscript typeset	
Galleys to proofreader	Galleys to author

Galleys corrected

Printing and binding

Books to warehouse

Subsidiary rights	Books distributed	Books promoted
Periodical excerpts	Domestic distributors	Media interviews
Translations	Foreign distributors	Media advertising
Mass market	Independent bookstores	Media reviews
Book clubs	Bookstore chains	Speaking tour
Electonic S & R	Book clubs	Author appearances
Video/film	Schools	Autograph parties
TV/radio	Organizations	News releases/stories
Theater	Retail outlets	
	Direct mail	

If reviewers suggest significant changes, their reviews are combined with editorial input and sent to the author. These changes are also usually a matter of negotiation between author and editor.

Once the book is revised, if the revisions are adequate, the book will then be sent to a copy editor, who will conform the piece to the publisher's house style, improve the grammar and prose as needed, and prepare the book for typesetting. Sometimes the author will review the manuscript before it is typeset, and sometimes the author will see what has happened in copy editing only when he or she reviews page proofs. Publishers vary in their standard practices.

After the proofs are proofread by the author and by a proofreader, the corrections are incorporated into a second set of proofs, which are read by another proofreader. A copy of the proofs are sent to the author for preparing an index if one is desired. When all corrections have been made, camera-ready copy is sent to the printer. Most publishing houses do not own printing presses. Each book is jobbed out to the printer that can do the best job at the best cost according to the best schedule.

The chart indicates that once bound books hit the warehouse, the business of seriously marketing the book gets underway. Actually, however, marketing a book generally begins about six months before books are printed. Preliminary copies of the manuscript will be sent out to book reviewers, book clubs, bookstore chains, and the like. Publicity will also be organized, including media interviews and perhaps an author appearance tour or speaking tour. All of this is coordinated to coincide with the release of the book itself. In the matter of publicity, some books get more attention from publishers than others.

One myth about publishing is that a publisher can *make* a book a best-seller. There are many well-documented cases, however, of both Christian and secular publishers pouring hundreds of thousands of dollars into books that did not return their investment or become significant best-sellers. If the public isn't interested or if a book is just poorly done, no amount of marketing expertise can make it succeed.

The spiritual ministry a book has is also largely out of a publisher's control. Some books sell relatively few copies but have great impact in shaping the church. Carl Henry's book from the 1940s *The Uneasy Conscience of Modern Fundamentalism* sold only a few thousand copies but had a decisive influence in awakening the social awareness of many conservative Christians and changing evangelicalism for the entire next generation. Other books also, books that the publisher never suspected would strike a chord, sometimes have a profound effect on many Christians.

The wind blows wherever it pleases, as Jesus said of the Spirit. And those of us in Christian publishing would do well to remember that that is as true of Christian publishing as of any other ministry.

SUGGESTED READING

Coser, Lewis A., Charles Kadushin, and Walter W. Powell. *Books: The Culture and Commerce of Publishing.* New York: Basic Books, 1982.

Markets, authors, networks, and more from the perspective of three sociologists. Especially chapter 5 on how editors make decisions.

Shatzkin, Leonard. *In Cold Type: Overcoming the Book Crisis.* Boston: Houghton Mifflin, 1982.

Strong opinions from a consultant with a long career in publishing, with a focus on sales and marketing and production, but also including two helpful chapters on the editorial process and how authors relate to publishers.

Tebbel, John. *Between Covers: The Rise and Transformation of American Book Publishing.* New York: Oxford University Press, 1987.

A readable history of publishing in America from Columbus to the present, full of information and anecdotes. A tendency to glorify publishing, and a focus on mainstream fiction publishing.

Williams, Joseph. *Style*. Chicago: University of Chicago Press, 1990.

In going beyond the mechanics of Strunk and White includes the ways words, phrases, and sentences are put together to make effective prose. Exercises at the end of each chapter for practicality.

Zinsser, William. *On Writing Well: An Informal Guide to Writing Nonfiction*. 4th ed. New York: Harper & Row, 1991.

In my opinion, the best book on writing — from getting rid of clutter to thinking about your audience. Many helpful chapters on different types of writing — humor, interviewing, and so on.

Chapter 14

What Do Book Editors Do?

Dean Merrill

For a special section on editorial work, *Folio* magazine once featured a dramatic cover photo depicting the back of an orchestra conductor in full tuxedo, his arms raised for the downbeat. Instead of a baton, though, he held a huge yellow pencil.

That captures some of what editors do: we don't create the printed work, we orchestrate it. We pull the many parts together into a whole for the benefit of an audience.

But perhaps the image of the conductor is a bit too dashing. I would suggest that editing — and especially book editing — is more like midwifery. It is assisting in the long, painful process of an author's giving birth. All the attention is on the mother. All the expectation is for the new child. In the end, all the rejoicing surrounds the happy parents. There is little glory for the midwife who stands nearby, whispers words of encouragement, explains things the mother needs to know, acts with force and determination at critical moments, gets the baby ready for public viewing — and then quietly goes home.

"Editing is a very private job," says Ann Harris, longtime senior

Dean Merrill, who has guided book publishing programs at Creation House and David C. Cook Publishing Co., is now vice-president of publications at Focus on the Family. He is also the author or co-author of a dozen books.

editor with Harper & Row and, later, executive editor at Arbor House. "But the product is very public. Editing a book means procuring it in the first place, being the *chief worrier* until it is off the press, getting others to notice it (salespeople, promoters, reviewers), and handling dozens of other things along the way. In short, editing is the job of bridging the gap between an author's intentions and his execution."

An editor's work thus is submitting personal ambition to a greater cause. It is not caring about the limelight. It is the role of John the Baptist, introducing the Greater One with a humility that says, "He must increase, but I must decrease" (John 3:30 RSV).

The work breaks down into four general areas.

Acquiring/Developing/Sifting

Editors in some countries bemoan the flood of mediocre writing that arrives in each day's mail from would-be authors — while editors in other countries yearn for *more* manuscripts by Christians, more options to consider. Both groups dream of enjoying the other's "problem."

The truth is that both are asking the same question: "Where can I find *good* manuscripts?" The editor is on a perpetual hunt for those who have something worthy to say on paper. It is not an easy search, whether digging for articulate writers in Kerala or fending off sentimental poetry from Kentucky. One often grows discouraged. I have often complained, "Why do all the people with something to say have no time to write, while those who have time to write have nothing to say?"

The efficient book editor carries in his or her head a set of criteria, a picture of just what the acceptable manuscript will look like. Here are the questions I consider whenever I evaluate a book prospectus:

1. *Is it true?* Not that I encounter intentional lies very often — but does this person know what he or she is talking about? Is this really the way things are in the world? Or is this wishful thinking? Does this promise that if you treat Problem X with Solution Y, everything will be fine? Well . . . will it?

I think this is an appropriate question even for works of fiction. Does this story reveal God and life or distort them? Pornography is one kind of distortion: it simply isn't how things really work out between men and women. Sticky-sweet utopian Christian fiction is another kind of distortion. It isn't true.

2. *Is it Christian?* Again, this question is harder to answer than you might think. Not every manuscript that mentions God or religion is thoroughly Christian in its outlook. Sometimes, God, church, the clergy,

and so forth, are merely stage props in a book. Some books on family life are essentially pop psychology with a little reverence here and there.

At one point a publishing house where I worked learned that American books being imported into Canada received a smaller duty charge if they were "religious books." How did the customs officials decide? They checked the pages for the number of Bible references and quotations. We actually went back and "doctored" a certain autobiography in order to pass their test!

3. *Is it significant?* In other words, do very many people care about this subject? Does it matter that much?

4. *Is it well written, or at least salvageable?* Here is the journalistic question, and we all, of course, have our opinions. We decide whether readers will be captivated by these paragraphs — or whether we can improve them enough to make them so.

5. *Will enough people pay to read this?* Here is the marketing question. Some things are exceedingly true, Christian, and even significant and well written — but people simply aren't going to lay down hard cash in order to read about them. They should. But they won't.

A current example in the United States (I am ashamed to admit) is books about missions. American Christians are generally in favor of missions and are willing to give their money for such causes. But read a book on the subject? Seldom.

A dangerous statement in a Christian publishing house is: "People really need to know about this." Unfortunately, people don't read what they *need* to know, *ought* to know, *should* know. They only read what they *want* to know. Never forget: Reading is an *optional* activity. People don't *have* to read. Book editors, beware.

6. *Can the publisher afford it?* This question seldom dawns in the mind of the eager author. But publishers know that every time they say yes to a manuscript, they have just committed 10-15,000 dollars of investment, or some such sizable figure. That is why publishers tend to say yes very carefully!

The best manuscript in the world will get nowhere without financial backing.

It is the book editor who, whether meeting someone in a restaurant, listening to a conference speaker, or going through the daily mail, must ask these six questions and make hard decisions.

Shaping/Guiding/Focusing

Dr. Burton Marvin, a Christian under whom I studied at Syracuse University, once said, "Our job is to make significant things interesting." That capsulizes this part of a book editor's task.

It is hard enough to write something unique, let alone write it in proper sequence, moving effectively from A to B to C. Authors are often so consumed with creating individual trees that they are oblivious to the shape of the forest. When an editor says, "You know, maybe chapter 5 should be chapter 1," the author is astounded and even stubborn in many cases.

But the editor has taken an objective look and sees something the author doesn't. Will the editor prevail? It depends upon how good a diplomat he or she is.

Organizing a text for interest and clarity is harder for some than others, but all must strive for it. The goal in book editing is to create a fire hose, not a lawn sprinkler — a work that drives home its point with such force that it is irresistible. Too many manuscripts wave lazily back and forth, sprinkling insights here and there with no impact whatever. The book editor must not let that happen.

The most heated arguments usually are about the book's title. Authors are notorious for marching in with esoteric phrases that struck them in the middle of the night that *absolutely must* go on the cover. I remember contending with one determined woman who insisted upon *The Excellency of Our God*. A verse in Jeremiah had leaped out at her, and that was it.

It took several sessions to persuade her that most customers in a bookstore would not be stopped by such a title. "The point is not to make either you or me happy," I argued. "It's to reach out and grab the casual shopper and say, '*Read me!*'" We finally settled on a compromise.

Says Henry A. Grunwald, editor in chief at Time, Inc., "An editor serves his writer when he, in fact, represents the reader. The editor must ask all the questions that the reader is likely to have and he must ask them with the relentless insistence and single-mindedness of a five-year-old."

. . . All the while serving as a gracious midwife, you understand.

Actual Line-by-Line Editing

Finally, it is time to get to work with a pencil or word processor. The task of cleaning up sentence structure, correcting spelling and punctuation, verifying references, and so forth, are well known. This is the time for the Christian editor to practice Galatians 6:9 (NIV), "Let us not become weary in doing good, for at the proper time we will reap a harvest if we do not give up."

I remember how, after eight years in magazine editing, I tackled my first book manuscript. I was used to wrapping things up in an hour. Here, a week went by, and I hadn't even reached the one-third mark! The idea of spending a *month* or more on one piece of writing overwhelmed me.

Book manuscripts, despite their mass, deserve careful attention and proofreading all the way to the end. Fatigue must not sabotage the message.

"Selling" to the Sellers

Are you surprised? Editing is more than finding and refining good literature. It is also convincing others of its worth.

Here is what I mean. I once wrote a memo to my editorial staff in which I said that any given book has to be sold at least five times:

1. The author must convince us that this book deserves to see the light of day.

2. We must somehow convince the marketing people that this book is worth their time.

3. They must in turn inspire and motivate the field staff.

4. The field staff has to sell the book to the retailer.

5. The retailer has to sell the book to the customer.

Any break in the chain spells defeat for the book. If editors do not accept No. 2 as part of their work — talking about the book, outlining its merits, truthfully but enthusiastically letting people know that this is a book worth working for — its future is doomed.

As John P. Dessauer says in *Book Publishing*, "The true publisher moves with equal comfort in the world of mind and art and in the world of commerce."

The same may be said of good editors. And if we are, as Dessauer puts it, engaged in something as important as "injecting live matter into the cultural bloodstream," we must do it with an eye for both quality and quantity, both excellence and efficiency, serving both the felt needs of people and the high calling of God.

Chapter 15

Marks of a
Creative Editor

Judith E. Markham

Exactly what is it that you do?" Every editor has been asked this question a hundred times. And no matter how articulate we may be on other subjects, such as the use of imagery in prophetic fiction, this simple question sends most of us into mumbling incoherency.

This is not some conspiracy to keep editing a secret craft practiced by elitist, ivory-tower grammarians. While certain editors may guard the details of what they do out of an insecure desire for territorial control, most love to talk about their work — about publishing and editing and authors in general. Yet when asked, they find it difficult, if not downright impossible, to explain the editing process.

There are several reasons for this, but perhaps the simplest explanation is that every editor is different; every writer is different; every book is different. I may work with an author on three books, but each book is on a different topic, with a different focus, and written at a different time in the author's life. How, therefore, can I generalize about how I edit, even for a single author?

Editors pride themselves on their objectivity, but there is a sense in

Judith E. Markham has spent twenty-eight years in publishing. For nineteen years she was an editor at Zondervan, where she managed her own imprint, Judith Markham Books. She is now partner-owner of Blue Water Ink, book producers.

which editing is subjective and highly personal, rooted in each editor's personality, instincts, experience, and knowledge. Let me suggest, however, that at least four qualities stand out as the marks of a truly creative editor.

Editors Are Teachers

Actually, the teaching aspect of editing has been a source of amazement to me, since I originally went into editorial work to avoid teaching, which I hated. Yet looking back over 27 years as an editor, I realize that teaching is exactly what I have been doing, directly or indirectly. Teaching others to care passionately about words; teaching them to listen to the rhythm of the language; teaching them to strive for the clearest communication, even if that means discarding a favorite phrase.

Editors often give direction by example. They don't just suggest restructuring; they show the writer exactly how it will look when chapter 2 is inserted between chapters 6 and 7, or when chapter 8 is divided into two chapters. Editors rewrite paragraphs, changing the focus from first person to third person, or expanding the opening illustration from a pedestrian retelling into a lively anecdote. This is particularly true when working with the beginning writer who shows potential but is unskilled in technique and execution.

I can still recall one author saying to me, "The editing experience was a major lesson for me as a writer" — after I had literally taken her manuscript apart and put it back together again. She added, "On my next book I will use the principles I learned from your editing." And she did. She went on to write several more books, and with each one required increasingly less editorial input.

Editors cannot endow talent, but they can teach writers to be more serious about the talent they have. To see one of them learn from the editing experience, moving on to become a better writer, is one of the greatest satisfactions in an editor's life.

Editors Are Encouragers

This means being available, accessible, and sensitive.

Writers are fragile people — a complicated mixture of insecurity and authority, pride and humility. Editors must learn to read between the lines to discover exactly what form of encouragement a writer needs at any given time. When an author calls, is she looking for help in solving a problem with the ending of her book, or reassurance that she can take a week longer for the deadline?

Skilled writers may not need the direct editorial intervention required by the novice, but they need as much, or more, hand-holding and reassurance; they need a sounding board for their ideas and an editor's willingness to agonize with them through every stage of the writing process.

Encouragement is often indirect. For that reason, *how* editors say something to a writer is as important as *what* they say.

Editors are not professors admonishing foolish students, nor are they superior intellects instructing inferiors. And it doesn't matter how earnest writers are in assuring the editor that they want their work critiqued honestly; when the moment of truth comes, every revision, every mark is excruciatingly painful, like the tiny, almost invisible, paper cuts that are an occupational hazard for editors.

Editors should read their editorial comments back to themselves as if commenting on their own work. Are the criticisms too harsh? Do they sound too arrogant?

While qualifiers may weaken certain types of writing, they are an important part of an editor's working vocabulary. A "probably" here, a "possibly" there, or a "what do you think?" can often determine whether an author will be able to move beyond pride, subjectivity, stubbornness, and weariness with the work to hear and accept an editor's critique. I was fortunate to discover this early in my own career after reading the author-editor correspondence of Maxwell Perkins, that dean of American editors. Any editor who wants to learn the art of editorial diplomacy could benefit from reading Perkins's correspondence with writers such as Hemingway, Fitzgerald, and Wolfe.

Editors Are Visionaries

The editor must be a visionary. Editors must see what the writer is trying to do, even when it isn't there. That way they can inspire writers to draw on resources they never knew they could command.

This does not mean that editors have all the answers. One of my favorite lines is, "I'm not certain what is wrong in this spot, but something doesn't ring true. Would you take another look?"

I don't know why I first began using this device — probably because I just didn't know what to tell the author. However, I have found it very effective in prompting writers to dig into "soft" areas and come up with excellent rewrites. Recently an author I have worked with for years commented, "Very often your 'this sounds funny, but maybe it's just me' notes are the most perceptive ones on the manuscripts."

To be a visionary an editor must trust his or her instincts.

Editors Are Servants

A servant is entrusted to care for property belonging to someone else. Similarly, everything an editor cares about belongs to someone else. Someone else's ideas. Someone else's words. Someone else's book.

With a nudge here and there, the editor urges the writer to strive for perfection. The best writers want this, knowing that good editors have the writer's own interest at heart. Only this desire would prompt an experienced writer, author of numerous books, to respond, "I appreciate your demand for clarity, precision, and conciseness. I have full confidence that you know what I'm trying to express and that you appreciate my desire to find just the right word or phrase."

A concern of editors and authors alike is whether something will be edited too heavily. Actually, "too much editing" has little to do with the number of marks on the manuscript. You'll know you have gone too far not by the ink but by the realization that you are trying to make someone else's work your own. Conscientious and creative editors care passionately about the style and substance of language, but only because they want to bring out the best in the writers they serve.

In his book *On Writing Well*, author William Zinsser sums it up well:

> Editors. Are they friends or enemies — gods who save us from our sins or bums who trample on our poetic sousl? Like the rest of creation, they come in all varieties. I think with gratitude of a half-dozen editors who sharpened my writing by changing its focus or its emphasis, or detecting weaknesses of logic or structure, or suggesting a different lead, or letting me talk a problem through with them when I couldn't decide between several possible routes, or cutting various forms of excess. Twice I threw out an entire chapter of a book because an editor told me it was unnecessary — and both of them were right. But above all I remember those editors for their generosity. They had an enthusiasm for whatever project we were trying to bring off together as writer and editor. Their confidence that I could make it work often kept me going.

Chapter 16

How to Prepare a Nonfiction Book Proposal
A Step-by-Step Guide

Michael S. Hyatt

If there's one thing a publisher hates to see, it's a manuscript.

Surprised? Most authors are. The fact is that most unsolicited manuscripts are returned to the author without *ever* being read. Publishers simply do not have the time or staff to wade through the enormous number of unsolicited manuscripts they receive.

What a publisher really wants is a *Book Proposal*. Once the Publisher has accepted the manuscript for publication, and once the supervising editor has approved the book's basic premise and structure, then it's time to begin drafting the manuscript. Not before.

In our company, Wolgemuth & Hyatt, Publishers, we strongly believe in the creative interaction between author and editor. Out of this process come the very best manuscripts. Consequently, we prefer giving the author as much input as early in the writing process as possible. A book proposal gives us — and other publishers — that opportunity.

So then, how do you prepare a good book proposal? From our experience, it needs to include three distinct elements:

Michael S. Hyatt is president of Wolgemuth & Hyatt, Publishers, Inc. Before founding his own company with Robert D. Wolgemuth, he served as director of marketing at Word Publishing and later as vice-president and publisher of Thomas Nelson Books.

1. The book's *content*.
2. The book's intended *audience*, and
3. The *author's background* and qualifications.

It should be no more than four to six, single-spaced pages in length (not including the cover letter).

This kind of proposal will accomplish two things. First of all, it will help the publisher better evaluate your book idea and decide whether or not he wants to pursue the project further. Second, even if you've previously had a book published, you'll find tremendous value in preparing a formal book proposal. It will go a long way toward helping you to clarify your own thinking about the subject before you begin the actual writing process.

To illustrate these principles, let's create a book proposal. Be sure to keep in mind, though, that this is only a *hypothetical* book proposal, an *example*. It is not an absolute formula to be followed blindly. Though all good proposals mirror its basic content, they each bear their own distinctive flavor as well. Now, with that in mind, let's create the proposal.

For the sake of illustration, let's assume that you are a Christian financial planner. Through the years, you've observed that many of your clients' financial problems are the result of never having received adequate training in money management during childhood. You're convinced that if Christian parents would do a better job of training in this area, it would spare them — and their children — a tremendous amount of grief later in life.

Because of your conviction, you've worked hard to train your own children. You've even developed a seminar around this theme and taught it in a few churches. The response has been overwhelmingly enthusiastic.

Before long, several of your friends encourage you to write a book on the subject. Initially, you're flattered, and soon you begin to give the idea serious consideration. But where do you start? A book is such an *enormous* project! And how do you go about getting it published? The answer to both questions is a written book proposal.

Before you actually begin writing a book, you have to decide two things: What you want to say, and who you want to say it to. In other words, you must determine the book's *content* and identify the book's *audience* (a complete Book Proposal Outline is found in Figure 1).

1. Determine the Book's Content

WORKING TITLE

The first thing you must do is develop a *working title*. The purpose of the working title is to focus your thinking as you develop the book idea.

The working title should either clearly encapsulate the book's premise or state the promise to the reader if he reads the book. It may even state the consequences if he doesn't. Sometimes the title will also include a subtitle.

Figure 1: Book Proposal Outline

Working Title

I. Content
  A. Premise
  B. Annotated outline
  C. Other details
    1. Special features
    2. Number of manuscript pages
    3. Manuscript completion date
II. Audience
  A. Demographic and psychographic description
  B. The competition
III. Author
  A. Background
  B. Previous writing

Let's consider the hypothetical book we introduced above. After a little work, you come up with the following working title:

Helping Your Children Become Financially Responsible

After a little more thought, you add the following subtitle:

What Every Parent Should Know

This title clearly encapsulates the premise and communicates the promise to the reader.

Once you've come up with a title, you need to remember that a working title is just that: a *working* title. It's tentative. You may decide to revise it later. Sometimes, the publisher will want to revise it. In any event, its purpose now is simply to focus the development of your book idea.

PREMISE

The second thing you must do is develop the book's *premise*. The premise is a two or three sentence statement of the book's basic concept or thesis. Usually, it identifies the need and then proposes a solution.

Let's return to the hypothetical book. What's the need you're trying to address? Isn't it the lack of training in money management that children are receiving from their parents? Or, to turn it around a bit, isn't it the failure of parents to teach their children how to become financially responsible that concerns you? After a little work, you come up with the following premise:

> *Most children will leave their homes upon graduation from high school with little if any training in money management. As a result, they are likely to experience years of struggle and frustration. The purpose of this book is to equip parents to teach their children the attitudes, principles, and skills they need in order to enjoy a life free of financial hassle and heartache.*

Not bad. You've identified the problem, and you've said exactly what the book will do to solve it. And, you've done it in three sentences!

Developing a good premise is one of the most difficult challenges of good writing. It is, however, absolutely vital. Without it, your writing will lack clarity and focus. With it, your writing is more likely to be strong and forceful.

ANNOTATED OUTLINE

Once you have a solid premise, you need to amplify it through the development of an *annotated outline*. The purpose of an annotated outline is to give you (and the publisher) an overview of the book's structure. It should include section titles, chapter titles, and a two or three sentence description under each chapter title of what will be covered in that particular chapter.

Don't worry that these things will be set in concrete. Every book changes as it moves from the proposal stage to the manuscript stage. The idea here is simply to provide a tangible and realistic look at your book project.

As a general rule, a nonfiction book should include at least three sections: (1) a description of the *problem* or need, (2) presentation of the *solution*, and (3) an amplification of the solution through concrete *applications*.

As you develop the proposal for *Helping Your Children Become Financially Responsible*, you begin by identifying the major sections. After looking back through your seminar notes you come up with five:

> Part I: *The Road to Frustration and Misery*
> Part II: *Five Attitudes Your Children Must Acquire*
> Part III: *Four Principles Your Children Must Learn*
> Part IV: *Three Skills Your Children Must Master*
> Part V: *The Envelope System of Cash Management*

Of course you'll also need an introduction and a conclusion. But the three basic parts are there: *Part I* will describe the problem or need. *Parts*

II–IV will present the solution, and *Part V* will amplify the solution through a concrete application. Now that you have the major sections, you need to add the chapter titles and supply the annotations. The result is shown in Figure 2.

OTHER DETAILS

Under this section, you also need to cover the *other details* related to the manuscript. These would include the following:

a. Special Features: Are there charts, graphs, tables, illustrations, photographs, etc.?

b. Anticipated Number of Manuscript Pages: Generally speaking, each chapter should run between eighteen and twenty-two double-spaced, manuscript pages and should be typed in a pica (10-pitch) font. In order to arrive at the approximate length of the manuscript, simply multiply the number of chapters by what you think will be your average number of pages per chapter.

c. Anticipated Manuscript Completion Date: When do you anticipate completing the manuscript? In other words, when will it be ready to submit to your editor? You might want to set a goal of so many pages per day, week, or month. Make sure you set a date you can live with.

2. *Identify the Book's Audience*

Once you've determined the book's content, it's time to identify the book's audience. To a large degree, you've already done this, especially in developing the premise. However, in this part of the proposal, you need to get more specific. A good definition of the audience includes both a *demographic* description of the potential reader and a *psychographic* description. Let's look at these one at a time.

DEMOGRAPHIC DESCRIPTION

The term demographics refers to the statistical characteristics of populations as it relates to their distribution, density, and vital statistics. Whew! What a mouthful. In reality, it's a very simple concept. The term simply refers to the *external, objective* characteristics of your audience. It would include such things as gender, age, socioeconomic status, religious affiliations, and so forth. In other words, you must determine if the book is for men, women, or both? Is it for Christians or a more general audience (Christians and non-Christians)? What is the reader's average

age, income, political affiliation, theological orientation, and educational background? Try to describe the characteristics of the typical prospect.

Let's take another look at our hypothetical book, *Helping Your Children Become Financially Responsible*. The first thing you'll want to consider is the kind of people who have already shown an interest in your message. (If you haven't delivered the message orally, you'll have to describe the kind of people you think would be interested.) After jotting a few ideas down on paper, you come up with the following demographic description:

> *The audience for this book will be middle to upper middle-class Christian parents of children ages five through fifteen with at least a high school education.*

So far, so good. All we need now is a psychographic description to put meat on the bones. In other words, we need to make our description three dimensional.

PSYCHOGRAPHICS

The term psychographics refers to the statistical characteristics of populations as it relates to their motivations. While demographics refer to the *external, objective* characteristics of your audience, psychographics refer to the *internal, subjective* characteristics of your audience. Demographics tell us *what* and psychographics tells us *why*. For example, why would the reader want to buy your book? What are his needs? What are his frustrations? What motivates him? What does he expect to get out of the book?

Again, let's look at our hypothetical book. What needs and frustrations are characteristic of our target audience? We've already said that the child has a need to learn money management. But the child is not going to be the one buying the book; his parents are. What are their needs? After a little thought you come up with this:

> *The audience for this book is made up of parents who have experienced frustration in their own lives as it relates to money management and, because they love their children, would like to spare them the same grief.*

Now by combining these two definitions — the demographic and the psychographic — you will give the publisher a concrete idea of the audience you have in mind. But just as important, it will be an immense help as you begin writing the book. Specifically, it will guide you in your selection of appropriate vocabulary and illustrations.

COMPETITION

Before you commit a great deal of time and energy to writing a book, you need to know what else is available. Why waste your time writing a book that has already been written? As Dawson Trotman, the founder of the Navigators used to say, "Don't do anything that others can or will do when there is so much of importance to be done that others cannot or will not do."

Figure 2: Sample Book Proposal

HELPING YOUR CHILDREN
BECOME FINANCIALLY RESPONSIBLE
WHAT EVERY PARENT SHOULD KNOW
A Book Proposal
by Joe Author

I. CONTENT

A. The Premise:

Most children will leave their homes upon graduation from high school with little if any training in money management. As a result, they are likely to experience years of struggle and frustration. The purpose of this book is to equip parents to teach their children the attitudes, principles, and skills they need in order to enjoy a life free of financial frustration and heartache.

B. Annotated Outline:

Introduction

Our country is in financial trouble. We have budget deficits, trade deficits, and massive consumer debt. Americans are saving less and spending more. How did we get in this shape?

If money is such a big part of life, why aren't children taught how to manage it? I grew up in a respectable, Christian home and yet I never received any training in financial management. Most of my clients didn't either.

Part I: The Road to Frustration and Misery

Chapter 1: A Rude Awakening

The chapter will open with the story of Bill, a young Christian and recent college graduate who finds himself in deep trouble because of his inability to manage his money. Bill's not alone; most adults find themselves in the same boat. The inability to manage money leads to all kinds of suffering and frustration. In fact, most Americans are broke by age 65 and dependent on the generosity of their families or the resources of the State. The bottom line is this: our children are headed down the same path unless we do something now.

Chapter 2: Dropping the Baton

The chapter will open with the true story of an Olympic relay race — the team would have won, but the baton was dropped in the pass to the last runner. God gives parents the responsibility to teach and train their children. This responsibility is comprehensive; parents are to equip their children for life (Deut. 6:4–9; Prov. 22:6), and this includes money.

(And so forth through the end of the book.)

C. The Manuscript

1. Manuscript status: I have completed two chapters, which are available on request.
2. Special features: The mansucript will include approximately seven tables and three charts. It will also include questions for discussion at the end of each chapter so the book can be used in a small-group study.
3. Anticipated number of manuscript pages: 240 double-spaced pages.
4. Anticipated manuscript completion date: June 1, 1988.

II. THE AUDIENCE

A. Demographic and psychographic description:

The audience for this book will be middle-to-upper-middle-class Christian parents of children ages five through fifteen with at least a high school education. The audience is made up of parents who have experienced frustration in their lives in regard to money management and, because they love their children, would like to spare them the same grief.

B. Competition:

I have not found a single book on this topic from a secular perspective or a Christian perspective.

III. THE AUTHOR

A. Background:

I have a B.A. in accounting from Michigan State University and an M.B.A. from Vanderbilt. When I graduated from Vanderbilt in 1969, I went to work for Arthur Anderson, where I stayed for ten years (see the attached résumé for further details). In 1979, I started my own business, Joe Author and Associates, which is a financial planning service. I have ten employees and approximately sixty clients.

Recently I have begun teaching a seminar entitled "Helping Your Children Become Financially Responsible." We have held this seminar now in five cities and have ten more planned for this year. Nearly one hundred couples attended my last seminar in Seattle.

B. Previous writing:

I have begun publishing a monthly newsletter as a result of interest expressed at my seminars (copies available upon request). I have never written a book before, but think I would work well with an editor.

You may need to go to a bookstore and simply browse the shelves for books that address your subject or are in some way similar to the one you are proposing. Or, you may want to flip through several current catalogs of the major publishers. It might even be a good idea to scan the subject and title listings in *Books in Print*.

The issue here is twofold:

a. Is there a proven market for this kind of book, and if so

b. How does this book differ from other books like it?

Now that you've described the book and its audience, you need to take a little time and help the publisher get acquainted with you, the author.

3. Give an Overview of Your Background

AUTHOR'S BACKGROUND

Describe your background, particularly as it relates to the subject of your book. Tell the publisher why you feel you are qualified to write the book. You may want to include a brief résumé. Your academic credentials may be important, but you may have other qualifications that are just as relevant. If so, be sure to mention them.

PREVIOUS WRITING

Tell the publisher about your previous writing. Have you written a book or magazine article before? If so, what was it, who published it, and how did it do? Let the publisher know that samples of your written work are available upon request.

If you've never written before, that's fine too; there's a first-time for everyone. Just make sure you detail why you are the person to write the book.

A Few Words of Caution

Remember, your proposal may be the only opportunity you will have to sell yourself and your concept to the publisher. Make every word count. Make certain that you come across well. First impressions make for lasting impressions. Therefore, take careful note of the following do's and don'ts:

- Do be polite, respectful, and friendly; don't make demands or launch into diatribes.
- Do make your proposal stylistically lucid, clear, and direct; don't write with lurid ornateness, showing off your voluminous vocabulary (this is *just* a proposal after all).
- Do make certain that the proposal is neatly typed and systematically organized; don't send the publisher a faded printout from a second-rate dot-matrix printer, a shoebox of scraps, or a collection of random notes you've accumulated over the last ten years.
- Do make sure all your facts and figures, names and dates, people and places, are accurately noted; don't force the publisher to sift the wheat from the chaff.
- Do engage in a little market research, sending your proposal *only* to those publishers whose backlist and editorial objectives match the predisposition of your project; don't simply mail out a query to every book house listed in the latest edition of *Writer's Market*.

Also don't send simultaneous submissions to *any* houses unless you let them know in advance that's what you've done.

Conclusion

Preparing a book proposal like the one outlined above will require a considerable investment of time and thought on your part. However, this kind of investment will pay substantial dividends later when you begin the actual process of writing. More important, perhaps, it will go a long way toward actually improving your chances of getting published. Who knows? The next book you read may be your own!

Chapter 17

Religious Fiction

Brenda Wilbee

Three strikes and you're out when it comes to religious fiction. Strike one, the publishers. Strike two, the readers. Strike three, the writers. It looks bleak from the bleachers — even with Frank Peretti smacking the ball clean over the fence and taking a home run. Why bother? the rest of us are asking. No one seems to appreciate a good story anymore.

But did they ever? In old England few Christians read fiction. *Robinson Crusoe* by Defoe was considered a "lie" because it was "made up," and to read it, the reasoning went, was to sin. Surprisingly, a remnant of this attitude still lingers within the fundamentalist, evangelical world. Despite Christ's use of story, there remains a strong distrust and hesitancy when it comes to fiction. At the very least there is profound confusion. Religious publishers do not understand its import and power. Readers do not understand its purpose. Writers do not understand its function. And so we have an industry that keeps dropping the ball. Yet none of us — publishers, readers, *or* writers — can quite give up the ball

Brenda Wilbee, an award-winning novelist and feature writer, is the author of six books (her latest is *Taming The Dragons*), twelve audio cassette tapes, and dozens of articles, short stories, and radio scripts. She is the owner and director of The Literary (Service) Agency, a facilitating service for writers wanting to break into publication. She has taught at Western Washington University and the University of Washington's Experimental College.

game yet. Instinctively we know the power of story. Jesus certainly did, and so, despite the odds, we keep getting up to bat.

The first strike against us is the religious publisher. Many see no value in story. An editor of a teen magazine made the statement that he did not accept fiction. "We are a publication," he said, "that is interested only in truth."

STRIKE ONE! Publishers Often Do Not Understand What Fiction Is. I teach creative-writing seminars at the University of Washington as well as Freshman Composition at Western Washington University, and before each class begins we have to define our terms. "Just what is fiction?" I ask. "And how does it differ from nonfiction?"

If you're like most of my students (and a certain editor from a religious teen magazine), you'll answer, "One is made up and the other is true." But nothing could be further from the truth. The truth of the matter is that fiction *is* truth — in a way nonfiction can never be.

Do we ever rewrite Homer or the Brontë sisters the way we do our history books? Which is true then, if what is true is changed?

And what literature has been passed down through the ages if it hasn't been fiction stabbing unrelentingly at the undeniable truth of human existence? It's been myth, folklore, and fairy tale — stories and more stories from the beginning of time. Can't you still hear Shakespeare's *Hamlet*? "To be, or not to be — that is the question!" And what of Mark Twain's Tom Sawyer? Who among us hasn't wished to attend our own funeral? Ached to know if we'd be missed when we're gone? And can we not just taste the wicked witch's turkish delight in C. S. Lewis's fantasy *The Lion, the Witch and the Wardrobe?* And feel the tug of disobedience and greed in our own hearts?

Let's take the Bible. Do we know the truth of God's love because of Leviticus and law, or because of Exodus and Moses on the Nile? The crossing of the Red Sea? Joshua and Caleb among the giants? What of the New Testament? Do we best remember Paul's theological treatises in Romans and Hebrews or Christ's parables in the gospels?

We remember stories because they *reflect the truth* of our reality. They mirror back to us our lives — what we *are*, not what we *should* be. Story illuminates for us the *dilemma* of human existence, not the answers. It reflects the things that bind us as well as propel us, that trick as well empower us. We pick up a book and look into its pages, and we see reflected back at us the world, human nature — and ourselves. Who do we see in Hamlet, Tom Sawyer, and selfish Edmund if it is not us? As hesitant as we might be about the value and importance of fiction, and even though we may read more nonfiction and even honor it more, what is it that we remember? Fiction every time. Because fiction *is* truth.

The secular world has long since come to terms with the truth and power of fiction. Catherine Marshall, Eugenia Price, Madeline L'Engle, Marjorie Holmes, Walter Wangerin, Jr., . . . these are just a few of our Christian authors who have had to take their religious fiction to secular presses — in order to be recognized, and read. Because our religious heritage has been one of publishing tracts and sermons,[1] there's been an inbred bias that not even two hundred years can erode. Exhortation, not reflection. Telling, not showing. Preaching, not exploring. These are the valued commodities in the religious marketplace. Publishers have always sold the "Sermon on the Mount" and not "The Prodigal Son," and it's hard to break the swing — unless, of course, they publish "The Prodigal Son" *with* the "Sermon on the Mount." But to just sell the story? Without explanation? Many publishers do not understand that story speaks for itself. But then neither did the disciples. They too were always wanting explanation — much to Christ's irritation and dismay.

It is not all bad news. Some publishers *would* like to take a swing at fiction. In a recent, almost colossal turnabout, fiction dominated the best-seller lists for 1990 and publishers are now lining up at the bat, scrambling to understand and publish fiction at its very best. Bethany House, Harvest House, Tyndale, Zondervan, HarperCollins, and Cross-ways — houses that in the past have approached fiction cautiously, giving those of us in the game a chance to see what we could do — are now taking us very seriously. In the June 1991 issue of *Bookstore Journal* these houses all announced their feature novelists — and their intentions to foster and promote fiction in the future. Bob Hawkins, Jr., of Harvest House says, "Fiction is definitely a growing market, and the market is going to grow in the years ahead if publishers choose the types of high-quality fiction that will keep the demand growing." Ken Peterson says that Tyndale will quadruple its production of fiction by 1993. "But," he adds, "we are saying no to lots of manuscripts. It's not easy to find really good novels." So the publishers are lining up, ready to play ball. There is ample opportunity, but you have to be good. And that's the catch.

Strike two against us is the religious reader. Because many of them do not understand the purpose of fiction, they've set up rigid (and often contradictory) standards and limitations — in order, I think, not to feel threatened by the lives of our characters. A few months ago a woman, incensed at my "profanity" in *Sweetbriar Bride*, wrote my publisher and bookclub quite the letter. "The misuse of God's name," she wrote, "is atrocious! I can't let this creep into my home, I guard against this all the time!" My offense? Page 136. *"God," he moaned, half praying, "what a mess. What a nightmare of a mess."*

STRIKE TWO! Readers Do Not Understand What Fiction Is, and So They

Misread It. This woman, representative of many readers, objected to Doc Maynard because, one, she didn't understand what I was saying through him (that even non-Christians turn to God in times of trouble, albeit hesitantly) and two, she was looking at the story all wrong. Fiction is a mirror, reflecting *what is*, not an *exhortation to ideals* — as is nonfiction. Too many readers, however, simply do not understand this critical difference. They do not understand that fiction is the creation of characters, who, as Roy Carlisle, an editor, publisher, and instructor at U.C. Berkeley, says, "encompass the full embodiment of the human experience." Including the good, the bad, and the ugly — they, the created characters, can illuminate *our* strengths, and weaknesses; reflect *our* ideals, and sins. Fiction is not a sugar-coated tract, a sermon, a ten-step how-to on the Christian lifestyle, yet many readers approach it this way and as a result are easily offended by a character who doesn't "live" the way *they* do, or at the very least, the way they *think* they "should." Like readers in Defoe's time, they read a story as if reading an essay; they interpret a character's actions and words as the author's exhortation. In short, they read fiction as if it were nonfiction, and it can't be done.

Too, readers often *want* illusion, and not the reality that good fiction is. They want to read of sweet characters who always say sweet things and who always smile sweetly and who always do very sweet deeds. Because isn't this what we're supposed to be doing? (Exhortation?) They do not want to read about pain and failure and conflict. Yet isn't this more accurately what we experience? (Reality?) And so this Pollyanna expectation makes it rough on the fiction writer who strives to spin truth out of the tangled threads of struggle and sin in order to demonstrate the offer of ultimate redemption. They want, as Philip Yancey, editor of *Christianity Today*, says, "to hear of only the resurrection without the cross."[2]

So we have two strikes against us if we want to write religious fiction: publishers who often do not understand the truth and power of story and readers who do not understand its purpose. We go up to bat knowing strike three and we're out.

A lot of writers do strike out. Most do, in fact — because they themselves do not understand the function of fiction. The bulk of this chapter, then, is not on how to convince publishers to buy our fiction (because they will if we're good enough), or on how to educate readers to better understand what fiction is (because they will eventually catch on), but on how to write it so we can at least get to first base. After all, there really is nothing we can do about the ball game until we step up to bat. And then, no matter how bleak, the game can still be ours because when all is said and done, the game — and how it is played — is really up to us.

Understanding the Ball Field

Just as there are four bases on the old ball diamond, so are there four key elements when it comes to fiction: conflict, crisis, climax, and resolution. Without these four elements there is no story. Why? Because fiction, remember, mirrors our reality. And who among us does not currently have a problem? (Maybe two?) And are these problems going to get worse before they get better? You bet. But will they still be problems next year? Probably not.

M. Scott Peck says in *The Road Less Traveled* that "life is difficult." A bumper sticker says it more bluntly: *Life's a Bitch, Then You Die*. Conflict, crisis, climax, and resolution — these have been the stuff of life ever since the Fall, and if we're going to write fiction, we have to write of all four.

Getting to First Base–CONFLICT. Lee Roddy, author of *The Life and Times of Grizzly Adams*, as well as the TV series and author of over fifty other novels, teaches: "People come to see the fight, not the arena." Yet most beginning writers make this fatal mistake. They spend page after page describing the arena before ever getting to the conflict. Sometimes they never get to it. All sunshine, no clouds. They slide into home plate without ever getting their knees skinned hugging bases on a few close calls. The umpire blows his whistle and the manuscript comes back REJECTED.

When I was writing *Sweetbriar* in 1980 I took a workshop from Lee. He had us read aloud the first one hundred words of our novels, and after I'd finished my golden prose he crossed his arms and stared at me for ten long seconds. Finally he said, "Pretty words, Brenda. But they don't say a thing. Cut them."

In the end I cut not only those first one hundred words, but seven whole chapters. I'd spent nearly a hundred *pages* describing scene after scene after scene of preparations for going West. How to cure hams, how many pounds of flour a family of four would need, how to splice hemp and pack eggs, what to do if an axle broke, ad nauseum. Not until chapter eight did the people finally get underway — and this is where the story began. This is where the conflict entered. Louisa Boren, leaving her dearest friend to tramp two thousand miles into the unknown, and for what reason? Because David Denny was going, that's why. David Denny who didn't even know she existed — or at least she didn't *think* he did.

Dave Lambert, editor at Zondervan, says that when we write fiction we must "step into lives already full." If a couple is arguing we dare not describe the room, the clothing, what they look like, the incidents that led up to the fight, but we must begin when the neighbor lifts his hand to knock on the front door — in the middle of the quarrel. We must begin when Louisa's heart breaks.

Stealing Second—CRISIS. Lee Roddy puts it succinctly for us: "Put the antagonist and the protagonist up front. Let the black hat win all the battles but let the white hat win the war." There's got to be a skirmish on second base, and in C. S. Lewis's Narnia series there always is. In Narnia the battles are always won by the wrong side, but Aslan's team, in every book, always wins the war. Because isn't this the way it is? Things *do* get worse before they get better, and children, skipping rope on the school playground at recess, know this. "Same song, second verse, a little bit louder and a whole lot worse!" and the rope swings faster and faster and faster, lickety split until someone's legs get slapped with a sting.

Look at the tension and trouble in your own life. The alarm doesn't go off. Your daughter is late. She needs a ride to school, but you've got to get a manuscript out in today's mail. But if you skip breakfast and the morning cup of coffee, you can still get it done. But wait! Your son needs $3.00 for his school picture today, and you forgot to go to the bank yesterday. Does *anybody* in this house have $3.00 cash? No, of course not. So after you take your daughter to school, you run by the bank, but the bank of course isn't open until ten and in your hurry to get out of the parking lot over to the Safeway open twenty-four hours a day (scolding yourself for being such an idiot), you knock over the drive-in teller sign. No problem, just put it in reverse, pick up the sign, check out the dent in your bumper, pop back in, unthinkingly put it in reverse again, and slam right smack dab into the front end of another idiot who hasn't had his morning cup of coffee either and who also forgot that the bank doesn't open until ten. But it doesn't end there, does it? No, no, no. You're in such a hurry by now that you zip out of the parking lot, forgetting that it's a one-way street.

Don't we do this all the time? Don't we always go from bad to worse? As if fate propels us forward, catapulting us into disaster. Sometimes we can even see it coming but are somehow powerless to steer clear. Doesn't even the flu put us to bed before letting us out the door?

Crisis is the *escalation* of conflict. Each event pushes the next until disaster can't help but occur. And if fiction is to mirror reality, conflict has to get bigger and bigger and worse and worse until like a tight balloon —

Sliding into Third—CLIMAX! — it pops! This is when Pudge, the Potato, who's been gobbling up one family member after another in Walter Wangerin's *Thistle*, finally explodes and spews mashed potatoes everywhere. Conflict and crisis *must* explode — and spew. In fiction you must reach a point where "all is lost," when it cannot get any worse. In romance this is when the guy and the girl will never oh never get back together again. In Jerry Jenkins's *Margo Mystery* series this is when the hoodlum is tracking the girl, the moon slides behind a cloud, the car won't start — and the gun isn't in the glove compartment! It's the loss of hope, the face of despair. It's the cross.

Conflict, crisis, and climax. This may be the stuff of life, we say, but do we have to write of such things? Is there not enough pain and misery without our adding to it? Why not write of Pooh and Piglet and picnics with Heffalumps? Because we, as human beings, resist making choices until we hurt bad enough and this is the very essence and function of fiction — choice. The Garden of Eden, and redemption from the Fall.

John Westfall is the pastor of adult ministries at University Presbyterian Church in Seattle, and when single parents come into his office lost and overwhelmed by the conflicts of life, he always asks, "What are you going to do about it?" If they answer "I don't know," he tells them, "Come back when you're hurting bad enough to decide."

The truth of the matter is that we'd really rather not decide — because choice involves risk. Given to us in the Garden of Eden, a gift not given to animals, choice makes us responsible for our lives. And so we resist, even when it generates further conflict, because if we start making choices, then we can no longer blame anyone else for our pain. And it's much easier to "endure" than to do the "wrong" thing; there is something so much more "saintly" about it. And if ever fiction reflects reality, it shimmers here with blinding light: conflict and crisis must accelerate to a climactic point, *forcing* characters to choose — right or wrong, good or bad, wise or foolish — because this very act of choice, this gift of God, is the only defense we have against the enemy philosophy that has dictated ever since the Fall: Life's a Bitch, Then You Die. The right choice releases us from sin and pain.

The heroine must choose bravery. The hero must choose to forgive. Margo must confront the hoodlum. Even Pooh is not without his troubles. He must choose to quit eating honey if ever he is to get through Rabbit's door. And as fiction writers we have to throw our characters into conflict — and if they do nothing, we have to pitch them headlong into crisis and, if they still do nothing, drive them to a point of climax where they see no hope, find no salvation, discover there is no way out. They have to hug third base while we knock them upside the head with raw, ugly, brutal pain. And fear. And doubt. And despair. And all the debilitating human emotions we feel. Because it is *this* sort of dilemma that forces choice — and resolution. In the end we are not writing of conflict and pain at all. We are writing of resolution in a fallen world.

Crossing Home Plate!—RESOLUTION. Conflict exists, but there is usually resolution on some level, and this tumbling of conflict and resolution, occurring simultaneously and on various levels, moves us through life, and so we make choices, reaping the rewards or paying the penalties, and growing stronger in the midst of peril. It is when we live in a world of conflict without resolution, *never making choices*, that we wind up neurotic, in mental institutions, and eventually committing suicide. Too much, too fast, too hard, and it will drive the sanest of sane over the edge. We must have resolution — sooner or later — but have it we must, or we will lose our minds, and this is why fiction carries such import.

At this point we might well ask ourselves why so much conflict in the first place? Why so much suffering? Why the pain that makes resolution even necessary?

Edith Schaeffer wrote a book called *Affliction*. Philip Yancey wrote a book called *Where Is God When It Hurts?* A rabbi wrote the best-seller *When Bad Things Happen to Good People*. C. S. Lewis wrote *The Problem of Pain*. Nonfiction abounds with the "whys" of suffering. But fiction never does. Fiction, like John Westfall, asks not *why*, but *what*. What are you going to do about it?

Life *is* difficult. "Megashit," as another bumpersticker puts it for us, "Does Happen," and so to ask why is useless. It got Job nowhere in a hurry, and as fiction writers we recognize this. It is not our function to analyze for our readers the impossible whys of conflict — as nonfiction writers do. Rather, we accept the fact that conflict, crisis, and climax are inevitable, and we go on to write of resolution. After all, no one can score until he reaches base four — home plate.

The first thing to remember when it comes to resolution is that it can only come about *through choice*. The second thing to remember is that that choice *must* be made by the individual caught within the conflict. No one in the bleachers can move him home — in fiction, no fairy godmothers, or in religious writing, not even God himself. No outside force swooping down and magically eliminating the trouble. Why? Because this doesn't reflect reality. God never removes us from pain. We do.

For example, David Denny in *Sweetbriar Bride* had to come to terms with his accelerating fear. There was nothing he could do about the dangers surrounding early Seattle; this was not something in his control, just as there are many things in life beyond our control. But he, like us, could choose to do something *about* it. He could, if he wanted to, choose to live a normal life despite his fear.

But being male and macho, it was hard to get him to this point. He didn't even *know* he was afraid (although he acted on his fear) and I (like God, at times, must do to us) had to drive him into a corner of absolute despair so that he could no longer deny his conflict.

Would Louisa die?

The question fired, not a jabbing sword anymore, but a ball from a cannon now. There was no dodging, no ducking. It was no new question. It was an old one, one that had haunted David from the beginning, ever since they had married, in one way or another.

Knees drawn, arms wrapped, he looked squarely at the open cannon of his fear. He forced himself to say it out loud, to put name to his fear. "Maybe Louisa will die. Maybe I will lose her."

He remembered the first time he had felt the poke of that jabbing sword: last winter, when John had raised his hatchet against Old Alki. *What if John hadn't come to his senses? Dave, what if you hadn't been there? Louisa, there's no sense in asking those questions.*

But it was all he asked anymore — all those "what ifs"! What if another cougar comes out of the hills? What if more renegades cross the mountains? What if, what if, what if. . . . What if Louisa dies in childbirth?

Will Louisa die?[3]

It wasn't until he was emotionally thrown against the wall and facing the fact that yes, Louisa might die — the very worst of his fears — that he was finally able to admit that yes, he was running scared, and that yes, it was up to him to *do something about it*! David, being the hero that he was, chose to embrace his fear and take Louisa, with all its impending risk, *back* to their isolated claim. And by doing so, he demonstrated — to the reader as well as himself — resolution. No, the dangers did not cease, but his fear did — by facing his fear and in the process naming it, he found his peace, the "peace that passes all understanding," and the conflict was resolved.

But does this mean your character can never have help in the face of conflict? Obviously not, because we all have help from time to time. None of us ever slugs it out alone. But if we look back and analyze some past resolution in our lives, we'll find that while we may not have been directly responsible for the conflict, we were, from earlier choices, responsible for *facilitating* the resolution. In *Sweetbriar Spring* Louisa made the choice early in the winter of 1854 to befriend the city's crazy man when no one else would. So when a fir tree fell on top of Mrs. Holgate's roof in the spring, crushing the cabin and Louisa's four-month-old baby asleep on the bed, it was the crazy man who effected the resolution to the immediate conflict — but it was really Louisa's earlier love and kindness that motivated him to do it. It was really Louisa, by *her* choices, who precipitated the resolution, and in that sense it *was* she who resolved her own difficulty.

This is fiction throwing itself across home plate.

187

Picking Up the Ball

In baseball attention is focused on the ball, and in fiction, it's focused on character. Character is the very life of fiction says John Gardner, and we don't read for conflict as much as we do for the characters involved. Why? Because, as the characters work out their conflict, making choices and reaping the rewards or paying the penalties, readers catch a glimpse of themselves and are affirmed, challenged, cautioned, or warned. "Setting," says Gardner, "exists so that the character has someplace to stand, something that can help define him. . . . Plot exists so the character can discover for himself (and in the process reveal to the reader) what he, the character is really like. . . . Theme exists only to make the character stand up and be somebody."[4]

Characterization *is* the ball game. You can fail at technique, plotting, or any other aspect of writing, but if you have strong characters, if you hang onto the ball, your story will survive. Frank Peretti? Why is he such a success with *This Present Darkness?* Because he's captured the imagination of the reader with character. He hauls the reader with him, turning pages around that battleground of a ball diamond, and he demonstrates — through his characters — choice . . . and redemption. What is going to happen next? the reader asks, focused on Hank. Will he make all the right choices? Or will he, like me, be tempted to slip up?

The opposite is true as well. All the strength of plot and technique is of no avail if you drop the ball and let your characters walk. Who wants to read a whole book about grotesque, ugly little hobgoblins anyway, if that is all it is? Just a bunch of evil spirits hovering around without contest? Without Hank, without strong character, there's not much excitement at the old ball game, and readers will put the book down and go on home.

So how do we develop strong, believable characters that will take a swing at life and keep a reader interested? How do we take a name on a page and make it a man? a woman? Prop them up and send them careening around those bases of conflict, crisis, climax, and resolution! Making choices that snatch a reader, sitting him up to think!

Pitchers spend hours perfecting their pitch, getting to know the swing of their arm, the weight of the ball. Batters spend hours getting to know the strength of their delivery, and the curve and spin of the approaching ball. So too, characterization comes about by spending hours upon hours with our characters and getting to know them very, very well. We get to know what they eat — and how they sound when they eat it.

Whether they sing in the shower.

How they look in the morning when they roll out of bed.

Do they burp when they're tired?

We discover their favorite color and song, their ambitions and failures. Their dreams, their fears, their weaknesses, their triumphs.

We learn their every secret.

Dr. R. D. Brown, award-winning mystery writer and professor at Western Washington University, suggests to his students that they write biographies as a way of learning all about their characters. "Just start writing down everything you know," he says. "The more you write, the more you learn." So Johnny was abandoned as a five-year-old in the mall? Good! We need to know that; it'll affect what he does on page 156.

Carole Gift Page, author of over thirty novels, suggests going through magazines to find out what your characters look like. You like Paul Newman's eyes? Cut them out. Tom Selleck's shoulders? Cut them out. Bruce Springsteen's chin? Cut it out. Paste the composite together and stick it up over your typewriter so that your macho hero can stare dreamily at you while you put him through his paces on paper.

Too, there are various characterization charts available to help us get to know our character as well, and the one I find most helpful is Colleen Reece's, published in *Writers Digest*. After answering her thirty-seven questions you can't help but know your characters very, very well.

What are your characters' main problems? How will they get worse? Who are their friends? Their enemies? When were they born? Where did they live? How did they die? What were their worst experiences? Their best? How do they perceive themselves? How do others perceive them? If you have a heroine who sees herself as incompetent and insecure but a world who sees her as assertive and capable, don't you think this is going to affect her decision whether to go for home plate or ride it out safe at third?

After I read ten years' worth of David Denny's diaries and filling out Colleen's characterization chart, David Denny graduated from being what Colleen calls "just a pile of words." Something magic happened: I fell in love.

I loved what David stood for. I loved how he treated his wife. I loved how he admired and respected the Indians. I loved how he, at sixty-one years of age, sacrificed his three million dollars to keep one hundred men working as long as he could in the Panic of 1893. That love took him from just being a name on a page to being a real live hero.

In *The Velveteen Rabbit* the nursery animals become real when they are loved. And once we get to know our characters, we do fall in love, and this translates itself onto the page. Our characters become, magically enough, very real indeed.

But what of the antagonists? you might well ask. Are we to hate them with just as much intensity? With just as much passion? Does the Velveteen Rabbit principle work in reverse? That we hate our enemies so well they become real?

I don't think so. Hatred never makes anyone real, and if it doesn't work in real life, how can it work in fiction, which mirrors reality? Hatred reduces people to two dimensions, a static construct, a Saturday-morning cartoon, and as such, they fall flat. So how do we then create strong, believable enemies? Because to be sure, in every work of fiction there is an enemy just as in every ball game there are nine other guys out there whose sole purpose is to wipe you out.

We have to become like God. To make the antagonist real and well-rounded we have to rise above our human, petty judgments and limitations — and *love unconditionally everyone* in our books. This means we have to love each and every character, good *and* bad, and come to understand *why* each character does what he does, or is the way he is. And is this not what God does? And are we not, as authors, the creator of our characters as God is the creator of us? And so as "God," we have to love our enemies, because this *is* the only way we'll ever be able to see them as being more than just two-dimensional.

Charles Johnson at the University of Washington, in speaking of characters, says we must "temper those we love with frailty" and "temper those we hate with nobility." "Do not think of yourself more highly than you ought" (Rom. 12:3).

Conflict, crisis, climax, and resolution, played out by strong, believable characters. This is what story is all about, whether it's religious fiction or not. And so we sit on the edge of our seats watching the ball game, watching the ball whizz through the air. Fly. Foul. Fumble. Two strikes and we're out. Then *thwack*! — the ball connects and whizzes between second and third! The bases are loaded! Casey's up to bat! Wait! It's our turn!

It's not the 1600s anymore, and we've all read *Robinson Crusoe*. Harvest House, Bethany House, and Crossways are all publishing fiction now. There are at least 2 million fans of *This Present Darkness* and *Piercing the Darkness*. We *can* score! And if we're lucky (for yes, much of it does revolve on luck), we might even hit a home run. Frank Peretti did. Twice!

NOTES

1. Roy Carlisle, Lecture, Pacific Northwest Writers Conference, 1988.
2. Philip Yancey, Lecture, Seattle Pacific University, 1983.

3. Brenda Wilbee, *Sweetbriar Bride* (Eugene, Oreg.: Harvest House, 1986), 229.

4. John Gardner, *The Art of Fiction* (New York: Knopf, 1984), 52–54.

HELPS AND SUGGESTED READING

Gardner, John. *The Art of Fiction*. New York: Knopf, 1984.

A practical guide to the "art" of fiction as well as detailed discussion on common writing errors.

Klauser, Henriette. *Writing on Both Sides of the Brain*. San Francisco: Harper & Row, 1987.

"Should be required reading for all people who need to write." — Peter Morton, executive, Boeing Commercial Airplane Company. A helpful look at right brain vs. left brain, with ideas on how to break past writer's block in order to tap into unconscious creativity.

Stern, Jerome. *Making Shapely Fiction*. New York: W. W. Norton, 1991.

A guide to the basics; not rules, but encouragement to write spontaneously, with a view to "momentum, tension, and immediacy."

Wilbee, Brenda. *How to Write Best-Selling Romance*. Seattle: The Literary (Service) Agency, 1988.

Six forty-five-minute audio cassette tapes on the craft of genre romance. "The most helpful instruction I have yet seen. Concise, detailed, abounding with everything you need to know, I highly recommend them to *all* my clients, and *insist* upon them for every beginner." — Natasha Kern, literary agent.

Available only through direct mail. Write to CAMS Distributors, P.O. Box 1868, Woodinville, WA 98072 for catalog and further information.

————. *Writing for Publication: Fiction That Sells*. Seattle: The Literary (Service) Agency, 1987.

Six forty-five-minute audio cassette tapes on the craft of fiction. "An innovative approach to fiction, and a must for all serious students of story." — Charles Johnson, head of the English Graduate Program at the University of Washington and a PENFaulkner and 1990 National Book Award recipient.

Available only through direct mail. Write to CAMS Distributors, PO Box 1868, Woodinville, WA 98072 for catalog and further information.

Chapter 18

Writing Children's Books

David R. Collins

It happens every time. Whether it be a meeting of the PTA, the Rotary, or an adult Christian fellowship group, the same question comes up after my formal presentation. The tone of the voice is friendly, almost sympathetic and understanding, and there is usually an accompanying smile.

"Mr. Collins, now that you have written so many books for children, when are you going to write books for adults?"

Actually, what the interrogator is saying is, "Now that you have climbed the first rung of the writing ladder, when are you going to climb higher?"

I am tempted to answer, "Well, when you're already writing for the most important reading audience, why change?"

But I do not yield to the temptation. Why? Because most people do not appreciate the tremendous challenge in trying to write quality children's books. Many individuals, picking up a slim volume containing multicolored illustrations with little text, would probably consider the writing an afternoon's work. Nothing could be further from the truth.

David R. Collins has been a full-time English instructor in Moline, Illinois, since 1962. He is the author of fifty-four children's books published since 1970, including six biographies in the popular Media Mott Sowers Series. He has been awarded a Junior Literary Guild and Cornelia Meigs Prize.

A good children's book should *entertain* and *educate*. A child should grow while reading, perhaps taking a fresh concept from your writing, or maybe a different understanding of himself or herself, or even just one new word. Hopefully, the reader will enjoy that growth process. Whatever the amount and depth of material you give your readers, you must not waste their time. One of the most severe indictments a young reader can offer upon completing your effort is that it was "boring." It is the equivalent of receiving Hawthorne's scarlet letter. On the other hand, if your reader *enjoys* your work and takes something useful away from the reading encounter, you are indeed approaching the top rung of the writing ladder.

There are those who have reached a point of being able to entertain and educate effectively. Their efforts reflect craftsmanship, a few even attain artistry. They know the difference between writing down to a child and writing to a child. They have mastered the skill of gaining maximum effect from a minimum number of words. They recognize the importance of using the senses to hold and retain young readers' interest.

Let me suggest a third *e* as a goal for the Christian writer for youth: in addition to "entertain" or "educate" is the verb *emulate*. To emulate is to strive to equal or excel. Who was the greatest storyteller of all who ever lived (as well as the greatest of everything else)? Jesus Christ. Of course, we will never equal or excel the Master Storyteller, but the key word is *strive*. We must learn all we can about the craft of writing and marketing, search deeply for whatever artistry lies within us, then emulate him who is our example. Youth seeks knowledge, direction, hope, faith, love, endurance, acceptance, and so much more. What more noble calling could we choose than to strive to follow the Lord's example, reaching out to the precious audience of the young? Is this not the top rung of the ladder?

If you become a successful Christian writer for children or young people, what may you hope to achieve? Probably not a Swiss château or a Mercedes-Benz. No, the rewards are seldom tangible. But you can enjoy the inner satisfaction of knowing you made a boy or girl smile for a moment, or cry, or understand, or feel. You may have provided some new language, information, or skill development. If you tap a young reader's mind, you have done well. If you tug at a young reader's heart a bit, good job. And if you have reached into the young reader's soul and drawn the child closer to God, rejoice!

Young readers are the most important readers of all. They are precious and sacred. Their minds are open and receptive, ready to discover and grow. If you simply want to write and don't care for whom, write for adults. If, however, you sense the challenge and excitement of climbing to that top rung, read on. Learning to educate and entertain children and to emulate the Master in doing so demands wholehearted attention. Whether writing can be taught or not remains a constant debate, especially among writers themselves. Yet there seems little argument that writing tips related both to the craft and to the experiences in writing for publication can be shared and can prove useful. During a period of some twenty years, I have enjoyed having fifty of my books for children and youth published, many of them by religious publishers. This is in addition to teaching creative writing for twenty-seven years as a full-time secondary-school teacher. I hope that my experiences will prove of some value to you. Whatever the case, I will give it my best shot!

Writing the Story

Time. Is there ever enough of it? Not for me. Each day I meet approximately 130 high school students, attempting to make them thrill to Shakespeare, Dickens, and Poe — then leading them to clauses, the infinite phrase, and gerunds. Besides the job, there are family responsibilities to meet, a home and car to maintain, friends and neighbors to chat with. Then there is the membership on the library board, speeches to give, deadlines to meet. I am always amazed (and I'll admit somewhat annoyed) at those authors who tell me about their time schedules for writing that are unencumbered by any other responsibilities. I simply do not have two or three hours together each day in which to write. I'm lucky to find such premium writing time on Saturday or Sunday. Summertime is my prime writing time.

But to wait until a writing time period occurs is to get nowhere as a professional writer. *Discipline* is the key word. Each day I can do something to better myself as a writer. It may be to read a chapter in a writer's text, to study market lists, to critically analyze a children's story or book, to attend a critiquing session or lecture — something! Mentally I must set myself to do it faithfully, without fail, before I go to sleep at night.

When I was growing up, my father, who was a health teacher, insisted that the last thing I do each night before going to bed was to brush my teeth. It was also the first thing I was to do after waking up. There were moments when I wondered, *Just what goes on in my mouth during the night that dirties my teeth?* Yet I did exactly as he said, and I still do. That's discipline. If you are serious about becoming a published children's author, you must have discipline. Decide, right here and now, that each day you will do something toward that goal.

Frankly, it is presumptuous for an unknown individual to think he can march right into a book publishing house and expect to have a manuscript accepted. Oh, it happens sometimes that such a person's manuscript is accepted, but that is the exception rather than the rule. Beethoven mastered the keyboard before writing a sonata. So, too, a certain amount of preparation must go into the making of a writing career. In the realm of religious publishing, it's extremely useful to enter via the magazine door. There are so many denominational periodicals, many of them published every week, and they need vast amounts of free-lance material. Staffs are small; a magazine's full-time employees cannot do all the writing. You are needed. Study marketing lists, then write to those magazines that you feel your own manuscripts might stand the best chance of hitting. Request writer's guidelines. (Don't forget to include an SASE — a self-addressed stamped envelope.)

An added thought about submitting your work to children's or youth magazines: there is a misconception that because there is such a constant need for material and because payment rates, particularly at denominational publishing houses, are generally lower, a writer can get by with sloppier work. *Wrong!* Any manuscript you send out should be your very best effort, in content and appearance. Don't rely on an editor to correct your spelling or check your sources; they have too much to do. After studying the writer's guidelines and a few copies of the magazine, send the editor a suitable manuscript, carefully proofread, readable, and with a SASE.

Naturally, the same advice applies to a book manuscript. I once heard a would-be author say, "I heard that F. Scott Fitzgerald was a lousy speller and grammarian. He just let the editor clean up his submissions." Well, those days are long past, if they were ever here. Perhaps if you can write like F. Scott Fitzgerald, you will find editors willing to clean up your material. Not many writers can write like that, however, so let's provide the most finished, error-free manuscripts possible.

Christian book publishing, for both adults and children, is a highly competitive market. It is naïve to think you are immediately going to capture an editor's attention unless you do your homework. A worthy initial plan of attack is to find out what has already been done and what is presently being done. Visits to Christian bookstores will help familiarize you with the major publishing houses, as will studying the latest editions of *Writer's Market* and the *Inspirational Writer's Market*. Browsing can prove most enlightening, and conversations with bookstore people can help you learn what books are popular sellers and what topics customers are currently requesting. Don't be afraid to take notes. You *are* a writer, remember! Just because a particular topic has been covered does not mean the subject is exhausted. One writing friend of mine mentioned, "I was going to do a book about understanding death aimed at young people, but I found there was already such a book on the market." One book on such a broad topic should not discourage anyone. Frankly, I know of several. But if a unique approach can be found, there is always room for another.

In 1975 a man named George Mott approached me about writing youth biographies for his publishing house, Mott Media. He wanted the lives of notable people who had exhibited some degree of Christian influence to be used as role models for youth. His first suggestion was Abraham Lincoln. Upon researching, I found there are more books written about Lincoln than any other person who ever lived. If I would have stopped at that point, there would have been no Lincoln offering in the Mott Sowers Series. But further research revealed there was no book for youth highlighting Lincoln's spiritual faith, and I decided to write such a book. I wrote it in the first person, so the reader could "live" Lincoln's life. Well, the book remains in print after multiple printings, and I have enjoyed similar success with *Johnny Appleseed, George Washington Carver, Francis Scott Key*, and others.

Christian booksellers get together on both a regional and a national level. If time, money, and geography are on your side, try to attend a conference. The national Christian Booksellers Association conclave is exciting indeed. Don't feel self-conscious being a "gawker." Ask questions, snag available handouts, meet guest authors. It may cost you a few bucks, but it's worth the investment.

Many individual churches have their own libraries, and those who operate them are often willing to open their doors and shelves to would-be Christian authors. By making a few telephone calls you can discover which churches have libraries and what times they are available for browsing.

If you are planning to write books for children, the area children's librarian should become a good friend. In smaller communities, the library may not break into adult/youth/children divisions, but in sizable locales, the children's division often boasts a real "pro" in the field. This individual will likely know who is publishing what, what books kids are reading, the latest about reviews and awards — lots of information.

By now you may be sensing there is a great deal of work to be done before the writing process. You're right. When you sit down at the typewriter or word processor, you want to be totally prepared. You want to know what has been written, what has been overwritten, and what needs to be written and who might publish it. Marketing lists suggest general manuscript lengths editors and publishers desire, what topics appear to be most suitable to certain publishers, etc.

What you write is determined by your own interests, your experiences and expertise, and the needs for youth and children. There is a constant need for both nonfiction and fiction offerings for young readers among Christian book publishers. Do not feel you are limited to your own denominational house. Catholics, Methodists, Baptists, Lutherans, and all the rest are interested in a quality story about honesty, courage, and modesty. Every denomination is concerned with how spiritual faith can help the young reader deal with disappointment, grief, and depression.

Every youngster is a unique individual. One boy may be thoroughly fascinated with spiders. Another may find spiders totally repulsive. Girls differ equally in their preferences. You will never write a fiction or nonfiction book that appeals to every young reader. But a conscious awareness of the needs of children and youth may help provide you with direction and inspiration. Time and space do not allow a complete writing course on these pages. Yet a brief overview of what should go into your writing may help.

In writing for young readers, keep in mind that they want to be loved. They do not have complete control over their own lives, therefore, they have faith and trust in those around them to offer deep emotional support. We may hope that as they accept love, they will return it. Some young readers turn to reading when they feel unloved and unwanted. If you can reach them through your words and make them feel vital and necessary, you will be fulfilling a blessed service.

When a young person is loved, he or she can feel out of danger, psychologically and physically. When Maurice Sendak's book *Where the Wild Things Are* was first published, there was an outcry from parents, librarians, and teachers. "It's too scary for kids," declared many, "especially those frightening illustrations." Yet when it reached the kids, they loved it — most of them anyway. Kids enjoy being scared, as long as they feel safe and secure. If you can make young readers feel fearful without feeling in real danger, you will be appreciated. (Sadly enough, we live in a world where children must be suspicious of strangers, wary of any unknown person. My generation was encouraged to be friendly to strangers, not forward, but simply somewhat outgoing. Nothing stays the same.)

Young readers have fertile minds, eager to learn and understand. Keep that in mind. You can plant new words, ideas, and thoughts worth pondering. Keep your fiction and nonfiction simple in vocabulary and sentence structure, but avoid a condescending tone. Make kids reach up.

If you're writing for third graders, recognize that "naïve" is above the vocabulary of the average third grader and offer context clues — for example, "John was very naïve. He would believe anything anybody told him." Help your young reader grow intellectually. Beware of editors and publishers who insist that you rely totally on a second- or third-grade word list for stories at that level. You will develop a vocabulary awareness, a conscious feel of what kids can handle and what they can't. But kids should always reach up.

And with that reaching up, they should reach beyond the mere world in which they live. Imagination thrives in the minds of young readers, and you possess the key to stimulate it. Each day a child exists in a very real world, but that same child is ready to board an "imagination jet" any time. Some editors express a generally negative feeling toward fantasy, but if the story is good enough, if it captures the child's spirited senses and delight, it's a "blast off!"

Kids want to belong — within a family, a group of friends, a neighborhood club. Can you write about how a child finds a special place among those people the child considers important? By developing a talent or skill, a child can win a place on a team or a part in a play. Such accomplishments are important. Or it may be that a little sister can win her big sister's approval. That feeling of belonging and accomplishing something is paramount among young readers, among *all* readers, really.

But it is up to you to do the writing, whether it be a short story, play, poem, or article. That's another beautiful thing about young readers. They are capable of enjoying all forms of writing, regardless of structure — as long as it's quality. So, too, there are book editors hoping to find a quality manuscript as they look over submissions. After a number of rejections, some writers come to think of editors as some sort of monsters, gleefully returning every manuscript they receive. Ridiculous! Editors need quality manuscripts from quality writers. Without them, publishing houses would quickly go out of business. Think positive.

Here are a few craft tips, regardless of what form your manuscript takes:

1. Lure, don't label with your title. You must attract a young reader's attention, tap his or her shoulder, and say "Read me." Kids like words such as *adventure, mystery, secret, surprise.* Lure, don't label.

2. Appeal to the senses. Let your young reader feel, hear, see, touch, and taste everything possible in your manuscript.

3. Show, don't tell. Don't write, "Tommy was nervous." Instead, write, "Tommy wiped his sweaty palms on to his shirt."

4. Use action verbs. They give a feeling of things happening and move the action along. Whether fiction or nonfiction, the reading

experience should be active, exciting. Avoid helping verbs like *had, have* and *has*. Also, don't use adverbs where the verb can carry the action. "Swagger" or "strut" is better than "walk proudly."

5. Encourage your readers to develop a broad vocabulary, but don't use a more complicated word when a simple one will do. A junior in my creative writing class once wrote a sixteen-hundred-word basketball story using much dialogue. No character ever "said" anything, but rather "jeered," "whispered," "laughed," etc. Sometimes people do just "say" things. Find the most appropriate word, then use it.

6. Display sentence variety. Narrative is often the dominant part of both fiction and nonfiction, therefore you will probably use more declarative sentences — sentences of statement. Yet don't overlook imperative (command) interrogative (question) and exclamatory (strong-feeling) sentences.

7. Young readers enjoy dialogue. Learn to use it effectively and punctuate it correctly.

8. Avoid sermonizing. Many writers for children feel a need to pound a moral in at the end or to overstate the information offered within the manuscript. If you have written carefully, with force and clarity, you will have no need to get on a soapbox at the end of your selection.

9. Read your work aloud when you have finished. Much material for young readers is going to be shared orally. Often you will find material that reads well on paper does not real well aloud. Try for a lilt in your writing, a pleasing lyrical flow. Even in nonfiction, gentle pacing can help.

Enough said about the manuscript itself. Don't forget to proofread. A final, careful reading often catches a mistake or two.

Submitting Your Manuscript

So, now the manuscript is ready. It's ready to be submitted for publication. The late Lee Wyndham often said, "The marketing can be even more important than the writing." It can also be more painful.

It is essential that you keep accurate records as you submit your material. Your records should be simple and suited to you. Why simple? You are a writer, not a clerical worker. Establishing an elaborate system of record-keeping will take time and concentration away from your writing. My system uses large index cards. I note the manuscript title at the top, noting the approximate number of words immediately behind in parenthesis. My first column title below is *Sent to.* Under this column, I record the editor to whom I sent my manuscript and the date sent. Directly to the right of that is a column I label *Received from.* In this column, I record the result of my submission; if sold, for how much and date; if rejected, comments, if any, and date. If my manuscript is rejected, I then record under column one where I am resubmitting.

Do not take rejection personally, until you have accumulated ten or twelve rejection slips on the same manuscript. Then look at it again, critically. Maybe some editors have commented. That helps. I have a special place in my heart (and I hope there is a special place in heaven) for editors who make a note or two. But Humbug! to those who send only a form rejection. I know they're busy. So am I. And I am investing money in my work to put it in front of them. Surely they reach a spot where the manuscript fails. Whatever the reason, it would be helpful to know the editor's reaction. "Weak characterization." "Unrealistic plot." "Dull." Any of those would help, and I don't think it's too much to ask. I take in thousands of student papers a year too, and I can tell you those students receive plenty of comments. The comments may be subjective, but I'm supposedly an expert, and my remarks should carry weight. I've never accepted the editorial retort, "We're too busy to reply personally."

I have found that Christian book editors for children and youth are much better about this than secular editors. Not all, but many. My favorite has been David Eller at Brethren Press. Not only did he respond at once to a query on my manuscript *Not Only Dreamers*, he also made concrete suggestions whether or not I should send his smaller publishing house the final manuscript or not. "Undoubtedly, you will place your manuscript," he noted, "and others might market it better through larger distribution channels. But I'll do all I can for you, as will Brethren Press." Yes, I did get other offers, yet none so personal and prompt. I went with Brethren; they put out a fine product. Look for *Not Only Dreamers*, and if you like it, David Eller gets much of the credit.

Although children's picture books are often short, I still recommend multiple queries before sending out the manuscript. Yes, I know it's hard to describe a picture book, but you *are* a writer, you know. Get your manuscript description into a one-page query. Include your credentials for writing the book, any past credits (this is where those juvenile magazines you published in come in handy), the age/grade audience for whom your manuscript is aimed, the approximate number of words, and how soon you can get it to the editor. One page, remember? Editors appreciate brevity. If you can't make every word count in a query letter, you probably won't succeed with your manuscript. If you know a semiprofessional or professional illustrator, mention it. But do *not* include illustrations right off. Editors take a vivid imagination into their reading. Let them think visually at this point.

By all means, make multiple queries. You are under no obligation to any editor through a query. A query is merely an ice-breaker and gives editors a chance to show interest and curiosity, while saving you time and money. How many queries should you send out? It depends on your manuscript. Before you send inquiries, study your potential markets very carefully. (David C. Cook, a major longtime Christian publisher still is sent recipes, just because of the name David C. Cook. Ridiculous? Certainly, and it reflects a writer's shabby investigation of the market.) Writer's Digest Books issues both the general *Writer's Market* and *Children's Writer's and Illustrator's Market* annually, while Sally E. Stuart has more recently joined the ranks by putting out a yearly *Inspirational Writers' Market Guide*. Regular periodicals such as *The Writer, Writer's Digest, Christian Communicator,* Society of Children's Book Writers "Newsletter," and others include marketing news and addresses. Visits to the area bookstores, especially Christian and family, will help. Sending a dozen queries would not be out of line. Hope and pray that half of the answers are positive. Do you include a SASE with your query? It is certainly a kind gesture, but you are likely to get a reply either way. Editors don't want to receive manuscripts that are destined for rejection, yet those same editors are always hoping for a usable offering.

The question of multiple submissions of the same manuscript is a bit sticky. Naturally, an editor would like to enjoy exclusive evaluation of your manuscript at one time. A while back, that was the rule. Personally, I feel that if an editor would be sure to act within a reasonable amount of time, say, four to six weeks, the arrangement would still be fair. Yet all too often the wait for a submitted manuscript can be from four to six months. I once waited sixteen months on a five-page picture-book manuscript, only to receive a form rejection slip. Although I have heard some authors, both those who write for children and those who write for adults, suggest broad multiple submission, I cannot go along with that. I will submit up to three copies of a manuscript at one time. What happens if more than one editor accepts? Well, we all should have such problems! Seriously though, if a publisher accepts his manuscript, the author must immediately inform the other publishers. The time it takes to evaluate a manuscript varies from publishing house to publishing house. Generally, religious publishing houses respond more quickly than others, but not always. One denominational publisher with whom I had done several children's books kept a manuscript of mine four years, always planning to use it, only to return it without apology. (I no longer publish with that publisher, needless to say.)

Once you have submitted your work, you begin a waiting game. But not inactively! Never pin your hopes on one manuscript. Having a work constantly in progress is what makes being a writer exciting. The more manuscripts you have circulating, the more chances you have for acceptance. This is not to imply that producing one manuscript after another is, of and by itself, commendable. The bottom line is quality. That is the ultimate goal of a truly professional writer. But professional writers have more than one idea. Editors are looking for an author who can produce quality material, not one fluke effort. Many publishing houses depend on their backlists for profits. First titles by new writers seldom garner a major audience, but repeat performances add up. Certainly, if you have an idea for a series, let the editor know in your initial query. Then hit that editor with a fantastic piece of work that *can't* be turned down.

Some writers aiming at Christian publishing houses and writing for youth may not appreciate the emphasis on commercialism. "I have a message," one might offer; "the financial return is a minor consideration." That is certainly noble, and if you're writing for a young people's market, it's a good way to feel. But Christian publishing houses are very aware of the thriving young audience in the marketplace. Competition is fierce, and no book is published without hopes of making a profit.

Chances are, your book is going to be rejected. That isn't meant to sound pessimistic, just realistic. I always anticipate rejection; it makes acceptance that much more exciting. But although I know my chances of placing my book manuscript are small, I know they do exist. I have done my best to couple artistry with craft and studied the market carefully. This is where faith really takes hold.

If and when a manuscript is returned, I am ready to send it out again — immediately. I try to get it out within twenty-four hours. Somehow the pain is lessened that way.

But if, by some marvelous stroke — not of luck, because I don't have much faith in luck — I feel God has seen fit to allow me to be accepted, I know my work is not done. The contract must be analyzed with care. Some authors consult attorneys, but I have found numerous articles in books and magazines that are able to answer my questions.

A quick word about agents: there are some very good agents who handle authors who write for juveniles. But they cannot sell a manuscript that lacks merit. Once you have placed one good book manuscript on your own, you are in a far better position to team up with a good agent. Not every agent is interested in handling those who write solely for the juvenile market. Study the markets on your own, submit your work, and try to establish good contacts among editors.

Should your book be accepted and on its way to being published, do not sit back. As I mentioned previously, constantly be working on new ideas. But also plan to help the publishing house in whatever way you can. Most book publishers have a staff of people who handle promotion and marketing. Let them know any of your own ideas about selling your book. Maybe you can speak to groups and organizations. Can you line up any autograph parties? What about area media? A first-time author makes a good feature story. You are in a position to know what opportunities exist in your locale better than a distant publisher does. Initiate and cooperate.

Finally, when your book comes out, enjoy it. You've earned the right. So many people say, "Oh, I could write a book." Few ever do. Don't feel guilty flipping through the pages time after time. However, never feel satisfied. You can always do better. Your readers will be counting on it. So will God, who has helped you through the initial ordeal. What more do you need for motivation?

Summary

A letter hangs near my writing table. In it is this sentence: "Please keep writing books Mr Colens because you write good and make me a better boy." The letter is signed "Franklin Hamilton." Franklin hails from New York City. I don't know him, and yet I do know him. He read my book about George Washington Carver and liked it. Then he wrote me a letter. It doesn't matter that he misspelled my name. What matters is that I touched him in a positive way, with my words, and he was grateful. Now it may be that his teacher required everyone in the class to write letters to an author, and Franklin had to do the assignment. The bottom line is that he chose me. I reached him. I wrote "good" enough for him to select me.

If the preceding pages have been of any value to you, I am glad. If there is too much of me in this brief personal essay, it is simply because I know my own experiences best. Writing for publication is a roller-coaster ride, full of dips and glides and turns and climbs. There are times when I wonder why I ever got into this business. But you'd have to pull me out!

Just remember, as you write for young people, they deserve the best. Entertain them by giving them words and thoughts to help them love, to make them think, to make them grow — in mind, heart, and soul. Educate them to the beauty and glory of God's world, help them understand. Emulate the Greatest Storyteller of all — you will never reach the goal, but there is much joy in the striving.

And someday, God willing, you will have your own Franklin Hamilton.

SUGGESTED READING

Aycock, Don M., and Leonard George Goss. *Writing Religiously*. Grand Rapids: Baker, 1984.

> A step-by-step procedure for getting a nonfiction book written and published; consistent with what should be done, even though not designed specifically for juvenile authors.

Gates, Frieda. *How to Write, Illustrate, and Design Children's Books*. New York: Lloyd-Simone, 1986.

> An emphasis on the visual by a well-known juvenile author, teacher, and lecturer. Much technical information.

Roberts, Ellen E. *The Children's Picture Book*. Cincinnati: Writer's Digest, 1981.

> A fine job of tracing the steps needed in writing and marketing the children's picture book, with a bibliography containing many titles worth studying before even getting started.

Shulevitz, Uri. *Writing with Pictures*. New York: Watson-Gupill, 1985.

> An informative and inspiring volume that was ten years in the making.

Whitney, Phyllis. *Writing Juvenile Fiction*. Boston: The Writer, 1960.

> Everything you wanted to know about writing fiction for young readers, presented by an artist and craftsmaster of both adult and juvenile literature.

Wyndham, Lee. *Writing for Children and Teen-agers*. Cincinnati: Writer's Digest, 1968.

> Wise direction that is conversational in tone and wide-sweeping in scope, from a now deceased writer who probably gave "wings" to more juvenile writers than anyone else.

Yolen, Jane. *Writing Books for Children*. Boston: The Writer, 1973.

> Information for both the beginner and the polished professional from a major force in juvenile literature.

Chapter 19

Religious Academic Publishing

Ed M. van der Maas

Many academicians consider "religious academic publishing" an oxymoron: if it is religious it cannot be academic, and if it is academic it should not be religious. This points up a curious phenomenon. It is entirely acceptable to write, for example, history from an ideological perspective such as Marxism. But it is not academically acceptable to allow religious convictions to intrude into academic writing, especially when the subject matter is religion. Witness the change from "departments of religion" at our universities to "departments of religious studies." This leads to a preliminary distinction we must make when talking about religious academic publishing — the distinction between *religion* books and *religious* books.

Religion books are books that deal with religion from an "objective" perspective. They are books *about* religion that bracket any religious commitment and avoid the question of the truth value of religion. They ask of the religious reader to suspend belief and of the nonreligious reader to suspend disbelief.

Religious books, by contrast, reflect a religious commitment on the part of the author. We might say that religion books are written "from the

Ed M. van der Maas is editor for reference books at Zondervan Publishing House. He has taught Bible, theology, and Greek and is the translator of several books.

outside," religious books "from the inside." It is important to note that the former category is essentially limited to books that have religion as its subject matter, while the latter can include books about virtually any discipline in which religious commitments may affect the understanding of the subject. Thus, for example, "religious books" include books about sociology, history, or even biology. (Some subjects such as accounting would obviously be very difficult to approach from a Christian perspective — although undoubtedly someone has tried.)

But even if we grant the legitimacy of religious commitments in academic publishing, the wide variety of specific religious commitments still leaves us with very different perceptions of what can legitimately be called religious academic publishing — in other words, the publishing of books that are legitimate from both a religious and an academic standpoint. By and large, we tend to question the academic legitimacy of those who are more conservative than we are in their religious commitments and the religious legitimacy of those who are less conservative. Thus, for example, nonevangelicals by and large would seriously question the academic validity (and certainly the academic respectability) of most evangelical academic books, while evangelicals would have severe doubts about the religion that is represented in nonevangelical academic books (as well as about the academic validity of books from the "fundamentalist" camp). And both sides could point to a good number of examples of justify their claims.

For our purposes it is sufficient to note that religious academic publishing covers the religious spectrum as well as the academic spectrum. Religious academic books, then, are books that are written for the academic market (postsecondary through postgraduate) from a more or less explicitly religious perspective.

Before moving on to the actual publishing process as seen from the inside, we should ask the question, Why is academic writing and publishing important? Authors who write academic books in the hope of receiving large royalty checks usually know better after their first book. (There are exceptions — authors who keep on hoping and a few authors who do indeed make a great deal of money from their books. As A. A. Milne said, "Almost anyone can be an author; the business is to collect money and fame from this state of being.") One main impetus for writing academic books is, unfortunately, the publish-or-perish syndrome, which has resulted in unprecedented numbers of academic books being published — many of them mediocre and some strictly for the benefit of the author's ego, job, or résumé.

Yet, in spite of the pressure to write and publish and, in the process, to adhere to rather strict canons of academic respectability, good and outstanding academic books are being written and published — books that expand the frontiers of knowledge and understanding as well as books that communicate excitement and enthusiasm for a given discipline.

The latter — communicating enthusiasm and excitement — may well be in the long run the most important aspect of academic publishing. The only time most people are required to read is in a formal educational setting. The textbook, in conjunction with the teacher, is the one chance many people have to either fall in love with a subject (or at least be convinced of its value) or to be convinced forever that Alice was right and that "a book without pictures or conversations" is useless, especially in the academic Wonderland — in other words, they will read strictly for entertainment because they have never learned the joy of reading for knowledge and the pleasure of browsing. (On the other hand, they will save a lot of money because of the books they won't buy.)

Religious Academic Publishers

Religious academic publishing to a large extent follows the pattern of nonreligious academic publishing. The spectrum embraces on one end textbooks for college freshmen and, on the other, monographs for specialists of such a technical nature that few people understand them. A distinction needs to be made between "academic publishing" (mostly textbooks and supplemental texts) and "scholarly publishing" (more specialized and advanced works).

In nonreligious publishing, college textbooks for undergraduate and graduate courses are published by textbook publishers such as John Wiley and Macmillan. Monographs and scholarly books of a more specialized nature are published by university presses (which are generally subsidized or at least do not have to make profitability a prime concern) or by "short-run" publishers such as Scarecrow Press or the University Press of America, which specialize in books that have a limited market and thus require small (or "short") printruns. These short-run publishers may or may not pay the author a royalty. Some of these short-run publishers publish specifically for the library market (e.g., the Edwin Mellen Press, which does not pay royalties, publishes in specialized areas and breaks even on sales of a few hundred copies). Finally, there are the vanity presses, which the author pays to get his or her book published. (Some academic presses ask the author to pay a subvention to partially offset the cost of publishing his or her book. This is very different from payments made to vanity presses, who have neither the editorial expertise nor the prestige nor the marketing capabilities of the legitimate academic presses.) An excellent source for information on the various kinds of academic publishing is Beth Luey, *Handbook for Academic Authors.*[1]

Publishers have to specialize to some degree. Some publishers will focus on the humanities or one or more of its subdivisions, others on the natural sciences, etc. A publisher who does not set priorities and has no publishing program or plan will never be able to create an identity in the marketplace and will probably not last very long.

Religious academic publishers have fairly distinct identities. They are distinguished, first of all, by their position on the theological spectrum. At one end are publishers like Beacon, whose list consists largely of books that fall virtually outside orthodox Christianity. Then, moving from "left" to "right," are publishers like Crossroad/Continuum, John Knox/Westminster and Fortress, HarperCollins San Francisco, Eerdmans, Zondervan, InterVarsity, Baker, Moody. Some of these also publish trade books for the more general reader (e.g., HarperCollins), while others are strictly academic publishers (e.g., Fortress).

Before approaching a publisher, the author should first take time to determine which publishers would be most likely to be interested in a book like the one he or she is writing, taking into account the subject matter, approach, theological orientation, and intended readership of the book. The best way to do this is to consult publishers' catalogs or visit a local bookstore.

Query Letters, Proposals, and Manuscripts

Sometimes a publisher will ask an author to write a book for publication. Although some of what follows applies in such an event, the main hurdle — getting the foot in the door — has been overcome. The solicited manuscript will still be reviewed (and if unsatisfactory may be returned to the author for revision or may even be rejected), but the chances that it will be published are excellent.

Most academic authors, however, are not asked to write a book. They have an idea for a book and may not yet have a complete or even a partial manuscript. Once the author has narrowed the field to the most promising publishers, he or she should select one and approach that publisher in one of three ways.

The first approach is to write a query letter, asking whether the publisher is interested in a book on a given subject that takes such-and-such an approach. Included should be essential information about both the proposed book and the author. The query letter should be straightforward and to the point.

The second approach is sending a proposal. This includes at least an outline of the book, perhaps with a sample chapter, as well as the author's vita, his or her reasons for writing the book, an explanation as to how the book will differ from other books on the same subject, what the intended readership is, what the author believes the market for the book to be, and any other information that may be relevant, including (if the proposal does not include a sample chapter and the author is not well known) a sample or samples of the author's writing. (Incidentally, many authors feel that their book will have a large market among "educated laypeople." Unfortunately, the educated layperson who has the time and interest to buy and read academically oriented books, while certainly not altogether mythical, is an endangered species, and many authors mistakenly assume that because the educated lay people *should* be interested in the book they actually will be.)

The third approach is sending a complete manuscript. A manuscript is rarely self-explanatory and should be accompanied by the same information that is included in a proposal. Editors dread receiving a 500-page manuscript with nothing but a brief letter saying, "Here is a manuscript on topic X. I think you'll like it." The editor has already noticed the former and isn't too excited about the prospect of determining the latter without any help from the author. Editors receive a large number of queries, proposals, and manuscripts, and editors who receive an unsolicited manuscript for an academic book need all the help they can get to make an intelligent preliminary decision: whether to return it to the author without further review or to look at it more carefully and to have it assessed in greater depth. Few editors have the time to read unsolicited 500-page manuscripts from start to finish, and the option to have a book reviewed in-depth is expensive — the cost of having a single manuscript reviewed may run into hundreds of dollars, and the majority of the manuscripts reviewed are still not accepted for publication.

To get an idea of how likely it is that a query letter or manuscript sent to a publisher will result in a publishing contract, consider the following figures from a recent study of university presses. A mere 10 percent of all query letters resulted in a request from the publisher for a manuscript, of which 18 percent were published — an overall success rate of 2 percent for query letters. The numbers for unsolicited manuscripts were about the same: 9 percent of all unsolicited manuscripts were sent out for review, and 21 percent of those sent out were eventually published — again an overall success rate of 2 percent. By comparison, 22 percent of all manuscripts actively solicited by editors were published. These percentages may be somewhat higher for academic publishers other than university presses, but probably not much.[2]

Let me make a brief comment on "multiple submissions," in other words, manuscripts that are submitted to more than one publisher simultaneously. Multiple submission of a manuscript is generally not a good idea. For one thing, many publishers will not consider manuscripts that have been sent to other publishers at the same time. To invest money and time in in-depth reviews and in the decision-making process, only to find that the book has already been accepted by another publisher is an unpleasant experience and does not create goodwill toward the author. If there is nevertheless a compelling reason for making a multiple submission, the fact that a manuscript is simultaneously submitted to other publishers should be communicated clearly to all publishers involved.

Reaching the Publishing Decision

It would be reassuring to know that the decision to publish (or, much more often, not to publish) is strictly objective. Unfortunately, by its very nature it never quite is nor can be. This is true both in general publishing and in academic publishing. Except in small publishing houses where one person wears several hats, a number of people are involved in the process: the acquiring editor, the publisher, the in-house or outside reviewers, the marketing and sales department, production people, and others. Each of these has a different area of expertise and responsibility, and the contribution of each to the decision-making process of necessity involves judgments, estimates, and informed "best guesses." Often the combined efforts produce good decisions, but at times the decision to publish a given book turns out to have been a poor decision. Conversely, every publisher looks back with regret on books that were rejected and in retrospect should have been accepted.

Next, I will indicate in broad outline what happens to a religious academic manuscript after it is sent to the publisher. (For convenience' sake I will use "manuscript" to refer to all three initial approaches — query letters, proposals, and partial or complete manuscripts — since all of these are evaluated by the same criteria.)

The decision to publish or not to publish generally involves three steps: evaluation, review, and decision. The sequence and the number of people involved in the process vary from publisher to publisher. Also, there are exceptions to the usual process. Occasionally a manuscript comes in that is so obviously worth publishing that the normal process is bypassed and the decision to publish is made virtually on the spot. But this is the rare exception. What follows are usually the main ingredients of the decision-making process.

A. EVALUATION

As already indicated, the first person to see the manuscript is an editor (often the editor who will be responsible for the book if it is accepted), who makes the initial decision whether to take the proposal through the review and decision-making process or to reject it without going through the process. The initial evaluation revolves around the following issues:

1. The topic or subject matter of the proposal.

Does the topic fit into the general publishing program of the publishing house? Each publisher can publish only a limited number of books in a given year and consequently has to decide both what to publish and what to ignore. Sometimes the statement "Your proposal does not fit into our publishing program" will be used in rejection letters. Occasionally this statement is used to avoid having to tell the author that his or her book is simply awful, but usually it is indeed the reason why a manuscript is not accepted. A well-defined publishing program is necessary if a publisher wants to have any kind of identity in the marketplace.

Is the topic timely? Many topics are in vogue for a few years, and usually a large number of books on these topics are published. But eventually interest wanes, and a new book on a topic once in vogue is bound to fail in the marketplace — even if it is a good book. The number of proposals a publisher receives on a given topic after interest in the topic has crested is remarkable.

Is the topic significant? It is possible to get so involved in a subject that it becomes a filter through which the rest of a discipline is viewed. This happens on occasion, for example, when a person spends years researching and writing a dissertation on a relatively minor topic that then tends to become in the eyes of the writer a microcosm of crucial issues. Next, some unsuspecting editor finds in the mail a 500-page manuscript propounding the crucial significance and ramifications of an obscure point of theology with a cover letter describing the pivotal importance of this hitherto overlooked facet of theological studies. Now, occasionally the writer of this kind of cover letter is right — the book is significant and merits publication. But more likely the editor's initial reaction to this kind of introduction — a suspicion that the topic has not been overlooked in the past but merely given its proper place in the larger scheme of things — proves correct.

2. The readability and structure of the manuscript.

Is the manuscript well written? Unfortunately, there is no sure correlation between earned degrees and the ability to write readable (let alone interesting) English. The editor, at least when reviewing a manuscript, represents the reader for whom the book is ultimately intended.

Style and readability are of lesser concern if the book is intended for a scholarly, specialist audience. But if the book is intended for use in the classroom, especially for undergraduates, style and readability become very important. In that case, even though the topic may be timely and would fit in well with the publisher's list, if the manuscript is poorly written — or worse, boring — chances are good that the manuscript will not get beyond the editor's desk.

Let me make a brief digression here. Academicians live with and for ideas. Ideas in and of themselves are exciting to the scholar, who would rather read a poorly written book with stimulating ideas than a well-written book that says nothing new or stimulating (although academicians too have limits to their tolerance of poor writing). It is often all too easy for the academician to write about ideas he or she finds exciting without realizing that many of his or her readers (especially undergraduates!) must be convinced first that these ideas are indeed worth getting excited about. To them, these ideas and concepts are just one more thing to learn for the next exam. The *form* in which ideas are presented is not merely incidental — the less sophisticated the intended reader, the more care the form requires and the more creativity is needed in the writing to stimulate interest and even excitement on the part of the reader.

Neil Postman's *Amusing Ourselves to Death* may overstate the case, but there can be no doubt that he is correct in his observation that we are rapidly moving from a society that was taught to think linearly by means of the printed word to a society that is visually oriented and thinks in images and consequently fails to learn the discipline and skill to read. Much as we may expostulate that it *should* be otherwise and that academia *should* preserve the preeminence of the printed word, the reality is that the academic books we are now writing and publishing, especially those for undergraduates, are written and published for students who are different from the students of past generations.

We cannot very well demolish the ivory tower altogether, but there is a crying need in academic writing and publishing for scholarly Rapunzels who will let their academic hair down and write skillfully and creatively, yet with full academic integrity. The problem is that this may mean risking academic respectability. Academic *integrity* means dealing with the subject at hand with honesty, consistency, and a clear awareness of one's assumptions and presuppositions, without glossing over problems and unresolved issues. Academic *respectability* is something rather different: it is based on an acceptance of the assumptions, presuppositions, and expectations of the academy, of one's peers in the discipline. This includes (perhaps especially) the proper form in which academic material must be presented. Deviation from the accepted form (including simplification without endless strings of qualifying clauses) means that the material is academically suspect, and every editor who has ever found young scholars who would be eminently qualified to write exciting, creative textbooks is familiar with the objection, "I can't afford to do that yet. I must first establish credibility in the academic community."

Some prospective authors will object, considering it the editor's responsibility to make the book a better book. This is only partially true. An editor can help improve a reasonably well-written manuscript by looking at it from the standpoint of the reader and asking for clarification or suggesting ways to make some statements clearer, but no editor can afford the time (and no publishing house can afford the expense) needed to rewrite a poorly written manuscript.

Is the book structured well? Problems in the structure of a manuscript that is otherwise well written can often be remedied relatively easily by moving portions and/or adding transitions. Unfortunately, the model for much academic writing (regardless of whether the intended market is the trained specialist or the freshman student) is the dissertation — one of the least exciting models from the standpoint of the reader.

Invariably, a lot of pages are spent discussing the parameters and significance of the topic (a logical but exceedingly unexciting beginning), followed by a lengthy discourse on the history of the topic and a detailed treatment of the latest scholarship. Finally, the reader who has persisted through all this is rewarded with a discussion of the topic itself — which was what he or she was looking for in the first place. Editors get excited when they find an author who looks at his or her topic from the standpoint of the reader and has the creativity (and courage) to approach the subject from an unexpected angle, drawing the reader into the subject from the start.

Does the book stimulate thought and inquiry or does it merely present information or indoctrinate? Authors of academic books, especially authors of books for undergraduates, should adopt the motto "The real purpose of books is to trap the mind into doing its own thinking."[3] All too often textbooks lay out a topic for the student in greater or lesser detail and stop there. They give students *information about* the topic. Others (too few by far) present the same information in such a way that the reader is forced to think about the issue because it either raises real-life questions or builds on questions the reader already has. For example, a book on Christology may present a well-written outline of the doctrine and its historical development without ever touching on the real intellectual and

personal issues raised for the reader who lives in a religiously pluralistic society — the question of the uniqueness of Christ and his finality.

"Trapping the mind into doing its own thinking" can be risky because the author has no control over the reader's thinking process and the directions it may take — but the author who wants to indoctrinate or guide students' thinking step by step underestimates the compulsion of the mind to do its own thinking anyway.

3. Other Considerations.

Is this an economically viable book? Whether or not publishing a book makes economic sense is an issue that is all too often frustrating for both editor and author. How much editorial investment will this book require to make it marketable? Is the market for this book large enough (i.e., will it sell enough copies) to at least break even? Some publishers will not accept a book for publication unless they are virtually certain that the book will sell a given number of copies in its first year (in some cases as many as 20,000 copies!).

Sometimes a publisher will accept a book for publication that is almost sure to lose money, simply because it is an outstanding book that deserves to be published. But publishing too many of these will jeopardize the financial viability of the publisher. (Statements like "We are afraid that this book is not economically viable" will occasionally be used as a "cop-out" in rejection letters, but more often than not it is based on actual projections and careful consideration.)

Economic considerations can be extremely frustrating for the editor as well. Sometimes when an editor feels very strongly about a book and wants to see it published, no measure of playing with the numbers (increasing sales projections, projecting a lower editorial investment, adjusting the projected retail price of the book) will make it viable.

Is this an author the editor can work with? This may seem a rather petty question on the part of the editor, but the fact of the matter is that the editor will spend a good deal of time working with the book and with the author, and if the author has a reputation for being difficult to work with, the editor may either avoid problems and reject the manuscript or pass it on to another editor who is more likely to work well with this particular author.

B. REVIEW

Editors are generalists. They are not and cannot be experts on most of the subjects the manuscripts they review deal with* (though they may have a special interest in certain topics). As someone has said, "Editors have a knowledge as wide as the Nile — and about an inch deep." Editors are very much aware of this, and an editor reviewing a manuscript may consult initially with his colleagues, especially if a fellow-editor has a special interest or background in a given topic.

If the editor's initial response to the manuscript is favorable, he or she will enlist the help of outside reviewers to read the manuscript and give an opinion. The outside reviewers are chosen for their expertise in the subject matter of the manuscript.

Sometimes, especially if the manuscript deals with a viewpoint or position that is controversial or on which a number of distinct views exist, the editor will send the manuscript to several reviewers, one or more of whom the editor knows to be in general agreement with the author's viewpoint and one or more who disagree with it. The purpose of this is to find any possible weaknesses in the author's position or presentation. Given the plurality of viewpoints on many issues, the editor's primary concern is that the manuscript must present the author's position clearly and with integrity and any opposing viewpoints fairly and accurately. Also, it is all too easy for an author to smuggle hidden assumptions into a manuscript — to jump from point A to point C without examining or stating point B, simply because to the author it is self-evident and does not need to be stated. And it is exactly the omission of point B that may weaken the author's case and make it unconvincing to those who do not agree with his viewpoint.

When the editor receives the reviews, he or she must weigh them. If the reviews are unanimously positive or negative, the conclusion is fairly easy. If the reviews are mixed, however, the editor must take into consideration the perspective from which each reviewer wrote and the significance of the specific criticisms. A review complaining about inaccuracies in the manuscript is one thing, but a review pointing out a fatal flaw in the argument, logic, or integrity of the manuscript is something entirely different.

---

*Contrary to popular wisdom, a preposition is a perfectly acceptable part of speech to end a sentence with, just as it is necessary to occasionally split an infinitive.

C. DECISION

If the reviews are all negative, the editor will most likely return the manuscript to the author at this point, usually with an indication of the criticisms received from the reviewers. (Generally the names of the reviewers are not given to the author.) If, by contrast, the reviews are positive or mixed (or if the editor for some reason feels so positive about a manuscript that he or she does not consider reviews necessary), the manuscript will be brought before the editorial committee — a group of people that may include the publisher, other editors, and sales and marketing people. To this group the editor presents a summary of the manuscript and the author's credentials, a summary of the reviews, a statement of the editor's own evaluation, and financial projections.

The financial projections for the book include (1) projected sales figures — a "best guess" as to how well the book will sell, based on experience with other books of a similar nature and an evaluation of the market for this particular book (Is there a need for a book of this kind? Is this book unique is some way? How have other books of this type done for us or for other publishers?); (2) an evaluation of the estimated cost of producing the book (Does this book require a lot of editing or is the manuscript "clean"? Is there anything about this book — such as illustrations, charts, etc. — that will add significantly to its cost?); and finally (3) an analysis of projected cost versus projected sales.

In some cases these projections turn out to be way off the mark. Projected sales may never materialize or the editorial cost may skyrocket because of unforeseen problems. Of course, there are occasionally pleasant surprises when the sales of a book exceed even the most optimistic projections. But by and large the projections for academic books tend to be more accurate than those for nonacademic books, since the market is more clearly defined and it is easier to determine specific areas of current academic interest or courses for which a textbook is needed. On the other hand, the editorial investment in an academic book tends to be higher than the investment needed for a nonacademic book, and the chance of its becoming a surprise best-seller is considerably less.

The main reason why publishing academic books makes economic sense is that academic books generally have a much longer life than general books. The economic strength of a publishing house depends to a large extent on its "backlist" — books that have been in print for more than one year and continue to sell (newly published books are "frontlist" books). Given a strong backlist, a publisher has a stable source of income and is not totally dependent on a strong frontlist. No publisher can publish only highly successful books year after year. There are always disappointments; some frontlist books go out of print after a year or so simply because they don't sell or because of the topic. Thus an important consideration in the publishing decision is the backlist potential for a book. Will it sell steadily (even if in relatively small numbers) for the next four years or more?

Incidentally, this is why it takes quite a few years of investment on the part of a general publisher who wants to enter the academic market. Until a fairly strong backlist has been built, the publisher entering the academic field will have to invest a great deal more money than can be earned back from sales.

After the available information (reviews, projections, and the editor's conclusions) is discussed and weighed, the decision is made whether to publish or not (or, in not a few cases, to request the author to make certain changes and modifications and submit these before a final decision can be made).

As stated before, the decision is always to some extent subjective. If totally objective publishing decisions could be made, only best-sellers would be published, most editors would be out of work, and many academic résumés would look rather bare.

The Contract

Under the current copyright law, the author owns the *copyright* of a book by virtue of his or her creating the work. This copyright exists whether or not it is formally registered with the U.S. Copyright Office. By signing a publisher's contract the author assigns to the publisher the *publishing rights* (but *not* necessarily the copyright). An exception is a work that was written for the publisher as a "work-for-hire," generally initiated by the publisher. (Note that under a work-for-hire agreement a publisher may pay the author a lump sum for his work without future royalties, or give the author royalties only, or a combination of the two: an initial lump-sum payment and reduced royalties.)

It is surprising that many authors (especially new authors) sign the publisher's contract without carefully reading or understanding it. A 10-percent-of-retail royalty sounds good, but if the fine print includes a clause that says that the author will receive only 5 percent of net sales (i.e., 5 percent of the money the publisher actually receives for the book after discounts) of any books sold at discounts over 50 percent, the author may be in for a rude awakening when the first royalty statement is received — especially if the publisher's discount to the bookstores averages 52 percent.

An author should never sign a publisher's contract without fully understanding it. It may be a good idea to have an attorney read and explain it before signing it. If the author has any questions, he or she should call the publisher and ask for clarification. This does not show distrust of the publisher, but rather good sense. It is also a good idea, especially with an author's first contract, to check with colleagues and see what their publishing contracts are like.

Also, a contract is not necessarily a case of all or nothing at all. Most publishers issue a standard contract, and if an author is not comfortable with a particular clause, he or she can always approach the publisher with an alternative for discussion.

Two questions that come up frequently concern advances and accelerated royalties. Many — if not most — academic publishers are fairly stingy with advances against royalties. Exceptions may be made for major, long-term projects such as reference books, which often require major advances simply because no scholar can afford to spend one or more years of his or her life on a project without a source of income during that time. Besides, major reference books tend to have a fairly high retail price and a long life, and this means that the publisher can expect relatively high revenues and the author can expect significant royalties. But the expectations for the average academic book are much more modest. A rule of thumb used by some publishers is that an advance against royalties (if given at all) should not exceed the amount of royalties the book is expected to generate in the first year after publication.

Another question is that of accelerated royalties. Under this arrangement the author's initial royalty rate is the publisher's standard rate, but this rate increases after a certain number of copies of the book have been sold. For example, an author might receive 14 percent of net for the first 20,000 copies, 14.5 percent for the next 20,000 copies, and 15 percent for any copies sold after that.

Most academic publishers are very reluctant to agree to accelerated royalties. True, the more copies the publisher sells, the more revenue is generated. But the catch is that generally sales follow a predictable curve: after the first year or two, sales begin to decline until they reach a plateau. Since under the current tax law publishers are taxed on their year-end inventory, it is generally most economical to reprint books once or even twice a year, rather than to print enough copies for several years. But here an economy of scale takes over. The per-copy printing cost of a book is much lower when 20,000 copies are printed at one time than when, say, 2,000 copies are printed.

Thus, when sales of a book decline or have reached a plateau, the per-copy printing cost of the book is higher than when the book was first published. Under an accelerated royalty arrangement, the publisher is then faced with both higher printing costs and increased royalty expenses — a situation that could, if the book has become economically marginal, lead to its being put out of print earlier than would otherwise be the case.

An alternative adopted by some publishers is to allow for an accelerated royalty for any year in which a book sells more than a specified number of copies, thus passing on part of the savings on printing to the author.

The Editorial Process

When the contract has been issued and the final manuscript is in the hands of the publisher, the editing process begins, and the editor assumes a somewhat ambivalent role. During the publishing process an editor must switch allegiance several times. In the initial evaluation of a manuscript, the editor represents the reader and looks at the material from the reader's perspective. The editor also represents the publishing house in making a preliminary assessment of the economic viability of the book.

Once the editor has determined that the manuscript merits taking to the editorial committee for a publishing decision, he or she becomes the in-house champion for the book and the author and tries to make the best case possible for publishing the book. Once the book has been accepted for publication, the editor will again represent the author in contract discussions.

But when the actual editing begins, the editor must have a dual allegiance. His or her primary responsibility is to the reader. The editor will go through the author's manuscript in detail, looking for ways the overall structure of the manuscript can be improved to make it easier for the reader to grasp the author's argument, for any statements or arguments that need further support or clarification, and for any other possible flaws and weaknesses in the content of the manuscript. This aspect of the editing process is, not surprisingly, called content editing. In addition, the editor looks for infelicitous sentences, for statements that may not be immediately clear to the reader, for sentences that can be made more readable, and, of course, for grammatical problems. This is known as copy-editing and is sometimes done by copy-editors who specialize in stylistic and grammatical matters.

But the editor also has a secondary allegiance to the author. It is the editor's responsibility to make sure that the author's ideas and concepts are not violated in the editing process and that the efforts to make the manuscript more readable do not change the author's intent and content in the process.

A good editor will be sensitive to the author's intent and style and will be careful to change wording without changing meaning. Any time the editor is not sure whether he or she has correctly interpreted the author's intent behind a statement that needs rewriting, or whether a suggested change affects the author's meaning, the editor will send the author an "author query," usually a note written on the manuscript or attached to the printout of the edited manuscript if the editing is done on computer.

A mediocre editor will have a tendency to conform a manuscript to his or her own preconceived stylistic standards without much sensitivity to either the author's intent or the author's style. A poor editor (who should not be in the business in the first place) will try consciously or subconsciously to smuggle his or her own ideas and convictions into an author's manuscript.

Nevertheless, every editor has had experiences with authors who are so convinced of their stylistic superiority (in some cases, near-infallibility) that they are unwilling to consider any but the most minor changes suggested by the editor. Ideally, the working relationship between author and editor should be a cooperative effort to make the manuscript into the best book it can be. This involves discussion and negotiation based on mutual professional respect.

In the final analysis, of course, it is the author's book, and (unless it involves matters of incorrect grammar or house style) the editor will grant the author the right to make the final decisions about the book. In most cases, the publishing house will decide on cover design, book design, and advertising, but a good editor will certainly ask for the author's input on these matters.

From a purely practical standpoint, any questions about the manuscript and any changes in the content should be settled after the author has received the edited manuscript and before the book goes to page proofs, since the cost of making changes in later proofs is considerable.

By the way, two things that will unnecessarily frustrate an editor are lack of complete documentation and inaccurate quotes. Some academic authors are surprisingly sloppy about providing complete documentation for bibliographies and footnotes. Editors generally do not have research libraries at their disposal (nor the time to locate missing information if they did), and the editor will have to go back to the author with a request for the missing information. Similarly, the author should make sure that any direct quotes in the manuscript are copied *exactly* from the original.

Editors cannot verify the accuracy of most quotes, and sloppy quotes that find their way into the published book will be embarrassing for the author.

Once the book has been edited, the editor switches his or her full allegiance again back to the author when it comes to marketing and advertising.

Marketing and Advertising

No author is ever totally satisfied with the marketing and advertising efforts the publisher puts behind his or her book. Generally, the editor who acquired the book fully agrees with the author (as do, surprisingly, the marketing and advertising people).

But whereas in the review and decision-making process the editor represents the intended reader and the author, he or she is put in the unenviable position of having to represent the publishing house to the author when it comes to the question of advertising and to explain to the author why his or her book does not get more publicity.

The total marketing and advertising budget is usually a percentage of the overall budget for the year. This means that a finite amount of money is available for all books published during that year and for all backlist books. Each new book is allocated a portion of the available money, based on the book's potential. This is at least in part a subjective, "best-guess" process. And in a sense it has an element of self-fulfilling prophecy: a book that is perceived as having modest potential will receive a relatively small share, thus in some cases virtually ensuring that it will only live up to its perceived modest potential.

When marketing plans are drawn up, the editor will make every effort to get the best marketing and advertising efforts (in short, as much advertising money as possible) for the book. But once the money has been allocated, the editor must try to explain to the author why there isn't more money available for the book.

I would like to make several observations on this point. First, for academic books, the most effective means of advertising may not be the print ad, the highly visible half- or full-page ad in the major magazines. These ads are very expensive; designing and preparing a print ad costs several thousand dollars, and a single insertion of a half-page ad in a major magazine can cost anywhere from $2,500 to $4,500. And the effectiveness of these ads is still a matter of debate. Often the only print ad in which an academic book will appear is a so-called list ad, which combines several books in a single ad.

Given the reality of limited funds for advertising, *targeted* advertising is the most cost-effective means to get an academic book known to its intended readership. This means, first of all, including the book in the publisher's academic catalogs, which are sent to a large mailing list. Second, review copies of the book (or notices with the offer of a complimentary review copy) are sent to journals and magazines. Third, a letter announcing the book is sent to all schools and/or professors who might be interested in the book, either personally or for adoption in a class, offering a complimentary review copy. In addition, the book is usually displayed at major professional conventions such as the annual combined convention of the American Academy of Religion and the Society for Biblical Literature (AAR/SBL). Also, for some books it is appropriate to place smaller ads in one or more professional journals, which not only have relatively low advertising rates but also reach a highly targeted audience.

The author, incidentally, can be of great help in the targeted marketing of his or her book by sending the editor a list of journals, magazines, and individuals who should receive a complimentary copy of the book for review, as well as suggestions for any other specific means of making the book known.

Conclusion

In true academic fashion, let me conclude with some quotes. Three hundred years ago Voltaire had, to put it mildly, a rather low opinion of publishers and editors:

> I could show you all society poisoned by this class of person — a class unknown to the ancients — who, not being able to find any honest occupation, be it manual labor or service, and unluckily knowing how to read and write, become the brokers of literature, live on our works, steal our manuscripts, falsify them, and sell them.

Times (as well as publishers and editors and, perhaps, authors' opinions of them) have changed. Jacques Barzun has a somewhat less vitriolic view of the relationship between authors and publishers: "In spite of good will, and frequently of true friendship, Author and Publisher are natural antagonists. Authors, as everybody knows, are difficult — they are unreliable, arrogant, and grasping. But publishers are impossible — grasping, arrogant, and unreliable." He concludes that "many publishing tangles come from the fact that authors and publishers are far too much alike."

Whether he is right or not, religious academic publishing, like all publishing, is a balancing act between idealism and realism, between what an author would like a publisher to do and what a publisher can actually do, between what a publisher would like to do and what he is limited to by economic realities.

NOTES

1. New York: Cambridge University Press, 1987.

2. Paul Parsons, *Getting Published: The Acquisition Process at University Presses* (Knoxville: University of Tennessee Press, 1989), 50–61.

3. This quote by Christopher Morley is from a delightfully nonacademic book, *The Peter Prescription* (New York: Morrow, 1972, 13), by Laurence J. Peter, who, incidentally, also said, "Before publishers' blurbs were invented, authors had to make their reputations by writing."

SUGGESTED READING

Aycock, Don M., and Leonard George Goss. *Writing Religiously: A Guide to Writing Nonfiction Religious Books*. Grand Rapids: Baker, 1984.

A resource guide and reference book covering the whole range of writing and publishing questions.

Harman, Eleanor, and Ian Montagnes, eds. *The Thesis and the Book*. Toronto: University of Toronto Press, 1983.

A small but important book for anyone considering reworking a dissertation for publication.

Luey, Beth. *Handbook for Academic Authors*. Cambridge: Cambridge University Press, 1987.

An excellent source for general information about scholarly and textbook publishing, with a helpful bibliography.

Mills, C. Wright. "On Intellectual Craftsmanship." In *The Sociological Imagination*. New York: Oxford University Press, 1959, 195–226.

A fascinating essay to be read especially by those who ask publishers, "Is there any topic you need a book on?"

Parsons, Paul. *Getting Published: The Acquisition Process at University Presses*. Knoxville: University of Tennessee Press, 1989.

A look inside the world of university press publishing that traces the steps in the acquisition process.

Powell, Walter W. *Getting into Print: The Decision-Making Process in Scholarly Publishing*. Chicago: University of Chicago Press, 1985.

Zinsser, William. *On Writing Well*. 3d ed. New York: Harper & Row, 1985.

> The first fifty pages recommended as required reading for all nonfiction authors, academic and otherwise; to be read together with Strunk & White's famous *Elements of Style*. 3d ed. New York: Macmillan, 1979.

Chapter 20

How to Handle Rejections
Without Feeling Rejected

James E. Ruark

P ity Snoopy, the lovable, big-nosed beagle in the "Peanuts" comic
strip. Charlie Brown delivers a letter to Snoopy with the report, "Here,
this is for you. I think it's a note from one of the magazines you sent your
stories to." Snoopy reads:

> Dear Contributor:
> Thank you for not sending us anything lately. It suits our present
> needs.

Over the years Snoopy has received a host of rejection slips like that one.
In 1982:

> Dear Contributor:
> Thank you for submitting your story. We regret that it does not suit
> our present needs. If it ever does, we're in trouble.

How about this one?

> Dear Contributor:
> Thank you for considering us with your manuscript. Has it ever

James E. Ruark is managing senior editor of Academic and Professional Books at
Zondervan Publishing House. He has held editorial positions at David C. Cook
Publishing Co. and the Bucks County (Pa.) *Courier Times*. He is the author of *The House of
Zondervan*.

occurred to you that you may be the worst writer in the history of the world?

(Snoopy muses, "I have a unique collection of rejection slips.")

In 1987, Snoopy was still trying:

Dear Contributor:
We are returning your worthless story. It is the dumbest story we have ever read.
Please don't send us any more. Please, please, please!

(Snoopy: "I love to hear an editor beg.")[1]

Snoopy seems to take rejection with more grace than most of us would. Undaunted and undismayed, he keeps trying and hoping. And well he might. Perhaps Snoopy read novelist Kit Reed's maxim for writers: "We feed on possibilities."

Sometimes hope is the only motivation to keep a writer going. "A great many writers," Reed says, "keep working through rejection, struggling for years with little to go on. . . . We don't always know whether we are working well, whether we will be paid, whether our work will be published. . . . Like the actor who said, with exquisite accuracy, 'at any moment *the phone can ring,*' we subsist on hope."[2]

Are you waiting for a phone to ring? Any successful writer (in this context, "published") will tell you that rejection slips are a fact of life, an occupational hazard, a tool of the trade. Unwelcomed and intrusive. And not just one or two rejection slips — lots of them.

Snoopy uses his rejection slips to get laughs. S. S. Hanna turned a pile of his into a book: *The Gypsy Scholar: A Writer's Comic Search for a Publisher.*[3] But with those options foreclosed, you'll just have to live with yours — and try to learn from them.

I could cite numerous examples of famous writers who collected their share of rejections, but let's consider Irving Stone's experience. Seventeen times Stone was turned away and asked how he could expect to sell a novel about an unknown Dutch painter to Americans in the middle of the Great Depression. "I was convinced I could sell *Lust for Life,* but I knew it was going to take a long and difficult time," Stone said of his biographical novel about Vincent Van Gogh. "So while I was teaching at Berkeley, I wrote another book — straight fiction about life at Berkeley, which I considered to be a very poor book. The book was titled *Pageant of Youth,* and it sold immediately to a small publisher. Right then I knew there was something incredibly crazy about the publishing world."[4]

Here is another "crazy" example: Robert Olen Butler wrote a novel inspired by his military service in Vietnam in the early seventies. Twelve publishers rejected the book, doubting the "marketability" of a story about an American army deserter who brings a Vietnamese prostitute home with him to a small town in Illinois. Then Methuen accepted the book, called *The Alleys of Eden*, only to cancel it because of budget cutbacks when the book was already in the galley stage. "Butler took the decision with a healthy measure of outrage but continued sending the book on its rounds," reports Stella Dong.[5] There were seven more rejections, making twenty in all, before Horizon Press finally published the book. And that's not all: Butler still had five other unpublished novels sitting at home.

Irving Stone and Robert Olen Butler would be called by some courageous, by others stubborn, perhaps even foolish. With far fewer rejections than Stone and Butler had, writers can easily find their stubbornness giving way to self-doubt, their courage shriveling to despair. Why go on? *Maybe I'm deluding myself, and this isn't worth publishing no matter how good I think it is.*

Perhaps it isn't. But if you are convinced that you are intended to publish (and if there are some objective reasons for that confidence), there are ways to deal with rejection slips without getting neurotic about feelings of rejection. If after the latest curt rejection letter you are uncharacteristically talking to yourself or mumbling minced oaths, it's time to take stock. Let's give it another try. In fact, you have already taken the first step in my just-devised, newly unveiled four-step plan for responding to rejection slips.

Ask Questions

The first step is asking questions. All the questions you can ask yourself begin with the single word "why." Why was my work rejected? Why didn't it catch on when it seemed to be just what the editor/agent/publisher was looking for? There are at least four responses to these questions:

1. It's a hopeless cause; the manuscript isn't worth publishing.
2. The publisher made a mistake; they'll rue the day they passed it up.
3. I sent the manuscript to the wrong place.
4. The manuscript needs some work or even a total rewriting.

Let's throw out the first response right away. We are talking about courage, stubbornness, determination. Our desire to write is based on more than whim. We are certain we have something to say and are developing the skills to say it effectively. We have the three qualities that

John Irving's Garp says are necessary for every writer: "stamina, patience, and passion." Remember Kit Reed: "We feed on possibilities."

Don't put too much stock in response number two, the idea that the publisher made a mistake. Publishers and editors are in business to print. They are always looking for new authors and fresh material, or even old ideas packaged in new, imaginative ways. (The Orpheus myth has been used countless times for two thousand years and as recently as Tennessee Williams's twentieth-century play *The Fugitive Kind*. Shakespeare's *Romeo and Juliet* reappeared in the 1950s in the musical *West Side Story*. Indeed, the Bard himself achieved great success in recycling old stories as Elizabethan drama.)

We don't always know the various reasons for a rejection, and it may be that the editor has relied on that important commodity developed and relied on over time: instinct. We might not like or agree with all the criteria for judgment if we knew the reasons for a rejection; but publishers and editors are paid to make those decisions. They know what they want, and if we don't give it to them, someone else will.

Naturally a publisher's judgment can be faulty. Richard Bach's manuscript bounced around from one children's book department to another until someone finally recognized it as a book for adults. Then Macmillan published it as *Jonathan Livingston Seagull* — to great acclaim. But remember that editors and publishers seldom get criticized for what they *don't* publish. Instead, they are prone to be faulted for publishing something that the world could just as well do without. When we consider that there are more than forty thousand new books published in the United States every year, we can be certain that some of them shouldn't have seen the light of day.

Realistically we are down to two responses: we have sent the manuscript to the wrong places, or it needs revising. And at this point we can turn to the second point of the four-step plan for turning rejection into acceptance.

Consider Your Options

Step number two: Consider your options.

If we are not going to quit, and if we have already been through a half-dozen or more publishers and editors, we have a choice of sticking with the manuscript as it is or looking to see how we can alter the work to make it more palatable.

The experiences of Stone, Butler, and Bach show that sometimes the manuscript is perfectly okay and simply needs to make the right connection.

Have we been sending the manuscript to the wrong places? We may need to do some homework to reevaluate the best prospects, especially in the case of magazines. We must be familiar with the publication's purpose, philosophy, statement of faith, audience, and tone. Is the focus of the article too broad, too narrow? Has the periodical covered the subject recently? I once sent a query and outline to a monthly periodical that I had subscribed to for a number of years; I very quickly received a curt rejection letter with a tearsheet showing that the magazine had published an article on my subject less than two years earlier. I had completely overlooked it in my planning.

In book publishing we must be sure that the market isn't saturated with books on the same subject or having the same angle. "Me too" publishing satisfies neither the publisher nor the readers. The first book on a trendy subject — let's say, codependency — will not necessarily be the best, but it has a selling and promotional edge on those that follow.

There may be room for several books on a particular subject if each has a different focus and contributes something different to the reader's understanding. Marriage and family issues are a case in point. Ed Wheat, James Dobson, and Mike Mason have all published books on the marital relationship in recent years, and all their approaches are distinctive. There will surely be more "marriage and family" books published in the future; some will be redundant, but there is always room for originality.

It goes without saying that publishers or editors need to be persuaded that we are qualified to write about our subject. I remember one well-published author with a multibook contract who submitted a list of twenty-five topics to his publisher and asked which one they would like him to write about in his next book. He apparently thought he could be an expert on anything, given enough time and research. That kind of *chutzpah* makes an editor shudder.

How many manuscripts on the book of Revelation or biblical prophecy have been submitted to religious publishers that are subjective, redundant, scholastically inept — and written by laypeople who have nothing more than a soapbox to stand on?

We must ask ourselves, What will make the reader want to buy my book or read my article? Unless we can articulate a clear, honest answer in one short statement, we will not persuade an editor or publisher, and our work will never see print.

If we have been turned down by an editor or publisher, we may wonder whether that door is still open to us for a different submission. There are several clues to look for in discerning whether this is an option.

Most rejection letters are generic and impersonal, perhaps even curt. It may not seem fair to be treated impersonally, but that is a publisher's common response, especially if the manuscript was unsolicited. It is unreasonable to expect a large publisher to give personal replies to the hundreds of unsolicited manuscripts it receives every year. If the editor tagged a handwritten P.S. onto the letter, it may mean that he or she at least took a second look and feels we may have some potential for publication. If the editor in a rare fit of generosity has taken the time to write a personalized letter, giving some general criticisms or suggestions among the rejection clichés, our hopes should soar. Fantastic! I have written a few such letters when I wanted to encourage a writer who seems to have a developing talent.

Giving encouragement or specific criticism to a writer whose work is being rejected entails risks for editors. Unless there is a clear indication of wanting to see your work again, don't resubmit it after revising, whether a little or a lot. It is not unusual for beginning writers to ask for criticism when what they really want is affirmation. For example, several times I have received letters like the following:

Dear Mr. Ruark:

You may remember that about a year ago I submitted a manuscript entitled _____. It was an imagined correspondence concerning _____. You returned the manuscript because you felt it was too short and the format wouldn't work.

To say that I was upset would be too mild. I was furious! I knew it was good, for another major publisher had already shown interest in it. (I sent it to you [Zondervan] because I felt you were more apt to reach the audience I had in mind.) Well, in the midst of my ranting and raving, my wife quietly remarked that she thought you were right. That bombshell was enough to stop my tirade and send me back to the typewriter.

I have rewritten the book. It is now in the form of a novel and is 106 typewritten pages long. I estimate it will be about 125 pages in print — still short, but to make it longer would be to put in a lot of fluff.

In its present form, my wife likes the book. I think you will too. May I resubmit it?

I do not recall my response, but I know I did not ask to see the manuscript. I commend this writer (a doctor) for listening to his wife. I think he learned a vital truth the hard way.

Sometimes an editor will withhold specific criticism to spare a writer the kind of pain the doctor suffered. Cynthia Ozick relates, "I submitted my first novel, 'Trust,' to an editor when it was three-quarters done and she declined it cuttingly. I lost six months in despair before I could get back to it. I was nothing and nobody and working in the dark and old already, and the amount of destruction was volcanic."[6]

So accept a rejection letter at face value. You might be better off not knowing what went through the editor's mind. (You might hear Snoopy's editor begging, too.) Publishers rely on their editors to make good judgments and, like it or not, good editors usually know what action a particular situation requires.

Accepting that rejection, however, leaves you with a crucial decision. We're at step three of the four-step plan for handling rejections profitably.

Decide What to Do Next

If we rule out further submissions of the manuscript in its existing form, there is only one option left: the awesome, fearful task of revising or rewriting the manuscript to arouse persuasive interest where there has been none.

The decision is more difficult if you already went through several drafts before beginning your submissions. I was horrified to hear a published author tell a writer's workshop, "I never revise. I submit manuscripts just the way they come out of the typewriter." If that is true, the woman had a very rare gift or she left it to a patient editor to whip the book into publishable form.

The most famous and gifted writers, including F. Scott Fitzgerald and Ernest Hemingway, always revised. Often they were still rewriting as they read the galley proofs. The Associated Press reported recently that in writing *A Farewell to Arms*, "Hemingway went through 44 different, often sappy or verbose, endings . . . before he settled on a last line."[7]

Let us hope that we attain perfection in our work long before we write forty-four endings. We have the will to revise. If ever we were vulnerable to writer's block, this is the time. What do we do now?

An editor has given at best only the slightest counsel. There are limits to our self-understanding. Do we turn to friends? Most likely some friends saw our work before we ever submitted it to a publisher. But they had nothing to lose in affirming our work and, if they were qualified to evaluate our writing at all, everything to gain by not telling you what was wrong with it. If friends serve any valuable service at this stage of our career, it is not evaluation, but inspiration.

Cynthia Ozick says, "Writers have a little holy light within, like a pilot light, which fear is always blowing out. . . . At the moment of greatest vulnerability, that's the moment for friends to help get the little holy light lit again."[8]

If there is a writer's group in your community, this may be a good place to get some objective and knowledgeable evaluation of your work (as long as others aren't praising your writing in exchange for your giving praise to theirs). Perhaps a local professor of literature would be willing to critique your work for a small sum. Possibilities are endless, but not all will work for you. You have to find the right situation — one that will not damage a marriage or friendship.

The basic ingredient for a useful and helpful critique is trust between writer and reader.

Gail Godwin and John Irving have been exchanging their works chapter by chapter for years. "We've been doing this for so long," Irving says, "that our work has, by no design, sort of paralleled each other's. We've written, I think, exactly the same number of books, and we tend to be at the same point in a book at the same time. And we're so different from each other as writers that we suffer no fear of influence. Gail's the only person I show my work to for feedback now, except that I always read it to my children."[9]

Other writers find it more helpful to have nonwriters as readers. Alice Adams relates that her reader is "an absolutely nonliterary person. He's an interior designer, and his overall aesthetic judgment I value greatly. He doesn't give me the line-by-line criticism that a literary person would, but I can do that myself. He reacts to the story as a whole."[10]

Sometimes helpful criticism will be hard to come by when it's needed, no matter how hard you search for it. I wrote to Joe Bayly, a mentor and former colleague who wrote a number of successful nonfiction books, after his novel *Winterflight* was published in 1981. I was quite critical and expressed my disappointment at the flaws I perceived in the futuristic story: "too didactic . . . dialogue very stilted and unnatural . . . needed a heavy editorial hand."

Joe's response was as disturbing as the book: "Four years ago, hearing . . . criticisms from . . . , I said, 'Help me.' Nobody moved to suggest ways I could change the MS. or (as I requested) took a particular section and rewrote it to give me the help I desperately wanted. Perhaps this wasn't possible. But I got the impression I should throw the MS. away."

He acknowledged that the book publisher's editor who worked with him "offered good suggestions," yet he added, "Christian publishers lack Maxwell Perkins-type editors. You're almost totally on your own as a writer."[11]

I felt deep regret upon reading Joe's letter. Help was not there when he wanted it and needed it most.

If good criticism generally is hard to get, specific guidance is rarer still. I learned many years ago to be as specific as possible when trying to help a writer under contract get from first draft to the final form of a book. In these instances, the author will very likely get the manuscript back with all kinds of suggestions in the margins, whole sentences or even paragraphs rewritten, and a rationale for the changes. The authors have usually received the criticism with courage and grace, and some felt they became better writers as a result of the process. Only one time do I recall a writer's resenting this kind of treatment and refusing to take it to heart. Zondervan never did receive an "acceptable manuscript" and eventually canceled the contract. If *Books in Print* provides a clue, no other commercial publisher ever did the book, either.

If you are not under contract, if you don't have realistic possibilities for a writer's club or other knowledgeable feedback — if you're on your own to make the revisions — what do you do?

The wisest way to start may be to set the manuscript aside. Don't look at it, don't fret about it, don't mess with it. Let it grow cold. Especially if you have been working intently with it for some time, put yourself at some distance from it.

If you can't afford not to be writing during this interim, start on something else — a different subject, a different audience. By turning your mind in a new direction temporarily, you may stimulate the freshness and creative spirit you will need when you return to your literary problem child. After two or three weeks — longer if necessary — you may feel that you are ready to renew the struggle and once again take up the task of revising.

Review the essential characteristics of your project:

Audience: To whom am I writing? Who is going to be most interested in this book or article?

Theme: What is my main point? What is it that I want the reader to learn?

Format and structure: Is my subject appropriate for an article or a book? Do I have a rational outline with a beginning, an ending, and a discernible route to take the reader from one to the other? Is my focus narrow enough for the article, or specific enough for the book — that is, can the subject be treated adequately in the space allotted to it?

Style and tone: Am I communicating effectively with the audience I have in mind? Is the tone too humorous and light-hearted? Too stodgy and dull?

Cecil Murphey sums up "the big picture" this way: (1) Asking what is the purpose (and being able to state it in one sentence), (2) deciding on the market (the group of readers who would be most interested and benefit most), and (3) determining what the piece will be saying (what hasn't been said before or in the same way)."[12]

An article in *The Editorial Eye* states that "a good magazine article has three qualities: thorough research and reporting, a writing style appropriate to the material, and the writer's ability to fit the material together and give it meaning and focus. The third quality is the one that separates very good articles from adequate ones."[13]

Until we can answer the essential questions decisively, we will be treading water, and our writing will float no better than it did before. Only as the big picture becomes clear will the details begin to fall into place satisfactorily.

In the hands of a good writer, those details can be distinct and plain no matter how deep the subject. I have sometimes heard preachers justify a lack of depth in their preaching with the excuse that they want the ordinary person in the pew to understand what they are saying. That confuses being simple with being simplistic. Clarity is just as essential and attainable in quantum mechanics as in a daily devotional. William Zinsser, who emphasizes this point in his book *Writing to Learn*, relates one extraordinary example:

> Albert Einstein gazes out at me from the cover of a small paperback book called *Relativity: The Special and the General Theory*, looking not at all scary — looking, in fact, like a benign uncle who is about to tell me a story. The blurb on the cover says: A CLEAR EXPLANATION THAT ANYONE CAN UNDERSTAND. Albert Einstein is going to explain the theory of relativity to me. To *me*? That's what it says.
>
> I've wanted to get the book ever since two science professors at Gustavus Adolphus College mentioned that it was a model of clear linear writing. At first that surprised me; I hadn't expected Einstein's theory to be reducible to plain English. But on second thought it made sense. *If clear writing is clear thinking, a mind clear enough to think of the theory of relativity would be likely to express itself simply and well* (italics mine).[14]

There are several other factors to keep in mind in striving for clarity in details. Even though this chapter is not intended to be a manual of style, it seems in order to give a few reminders that will help you make a good impression on editors while helping you revise your writing.

- Use good grammar and punctuate properly. There is no excuse for the comma that splices a compound predicate, an apostrophe that changes the possessive pronoun "its" to "it's," the word "irregardless," or the expression "could care less." All are wrong.

- Avoid jargon and current fad phrases. One delights in the way Southwest Airlines ticket-counter signs translate the jargon on ticket stubs: "We overbook. You may get bumped. We will pay you."[15]
- Put the major ideas in logical order and use good transitions to link one with another.
- Use "that" instead of "which" in restrictive clauses.
- Avoid clichés — dare I say it? — like the plague. Peter Lubin calls clichés "that outward sign of inward mental lassitude."[16]
- Beware mixed metaphors. Casting your bread upon the waters won't necessarily bring home the bacon.
- Be precise. Is "continually," "constantly," or "continuously" the word you want to use? Mark Twain said that "the difference between the right word and the almost right word is the difference between lightning and the lightning bug." James Russell Lowell put it this way: "Precision of thought is not only exemplified by precision of language, but is largely dependent on the habit of it."
- Don't write the way you talk. Speech tends to be less precise, more verbose, less grammatical, and more impressionistic than good writing.
- Don't overwrite. Nothing is gained when we send, in W. G. McAdoo's words, "an army of pompous phrases . . . over the landscape in search of an idea."
- Heed William Strunk: "Rule Seventeen. Omit needless words! Omit needless words! Omit needless words!"[17] The disposable words may be a result of poor usage, imprecision, laziness, obscurity, ambiguity, or diffuseness.

Strunk's Rule Seventeen is perhaps my Rule One. If editors were paid just for every word they took out, they would all be millionaires. Two examples will emphasize the point.

Avodah K. Offit had little good to say in his review of James C. Neely's book *Gender* (Simon & Schuster, 1981). Among Neely's "more readable excesses," Offit wrote that "frequently he repeats himself. Occasionally he loses the point." Offit continued:

> Neely tells us he is in his 50s and at last writing the book that he "always wanted to write." He observes: "As a surgeon I can use half the number of stitches I had to use 20 years ago and get twice as good results. The trick is knowing the crucial sutures that need to be placed and wasting no time on excess energy expenditure. It is a matter of the selection of the detail, the particulars that are most important, most necessary to the occasion." Perhaps if this surgeon had begun to write

20 years ago, he might now feel toward words and ideas as he does toward sutures.[18]

By contrast, having faulted Hemingway earlier on his plethora of tentative endings, let us give credit where it is due. Actor Charlton Heston, upon reading *The Old Man and the Sea* aloud for an audio recording, remarked, "Hemingway was such a joy because there was not one extra word; it was all so beautifully constructed."[19]

To help you ferret out the unnecessary language, I suggest that you also read loud and listen to the sound of the words you write. Repetitious vocabulary, sameness of sentence structure, and lack of clarity become more obvious when we hear the words. Reading our work aloud may prove to be one of the best instructors for the task of revising.

That brings us to the last part of the four-step plan for handling rejections without feeling rejected. The first three steps have been intended to help make the pain of rejections, though unavoidable, at least bearable and to suggest a cure for the rejection malady. In summary:

- Step one: Ask yourself questions.
- Step two: Consider your options.
- Step three: Decide what to do next. (And in doing so, reevaluate your audience, theme, structure, and style. Then brace yourself to revise, revise, revise.)

Get Going

Let me present step four with as few of those expansive words as possible:

- Step four: Get going.

Remember Kit Reed: "We feed on possibilities."

NOTES

1. United Features Syndicate, © 1982, 1983, 1987.
2. "What Writers Live On," My Say, *Publishers Weekly* (27 September 1987), 5.
3. Ames, Iowa: Iowa State University Press, 1987.
4. "Five Bestselling Writers Recall Their First Novels," *Publishers Weekly* (10 October 1980), 47.
5. "The Cinderella Story of 'The Alleys of Eden,'" *Publishers Weekly* (1 January 1982), 25.
6. Helen Benedict, "A Writer's First Readers," *New York Times Book Review* (6 February 1983), 11.

7. "A Protracted Goodbye for 'A Farewell to Arms,'" *Grand Rapids Press* (28 September 1989).

8. Benedict, "A Writer's First Readers," 11.

9. Ibid., 12.

10. Ibid.

11. Correspondence, 2 October 1981.

12. Adapted from "Christian Scripts," Seventh-day Adventist newsletter for writers (Fall 1980).

13. December 1989.

14. William Zinsser, *Writing to Learn* (New York: Harper & Row, 1988), 192. Physicists will catch the irony in this anecdote, since Einstein was exasperated by quantum mechanics and never was able to figure out how the concept could coexist with his theories of relativity — a problem scientists still haven't solved.

15. Quoted by Martin E. Marty, *Context* newsletter (15 October 1981), 5.

16. Peter Lubin, "An 'Edgewise' Manifesto," *National Review* (13 October 1989), 53.

17. William Strunk, Jr., and E. B. White, *The Elements of Style*, 3d ed. (New York: Macmillan, 1979), xiii.

18. "A Surgeon's Anatomy of Sexual Identity," *Los Angeles Times Book Review* (27 December 1981).

19. Keith Love, "Simple Dignity for 'The Old Man,'" Classics on Cassette, *Los Angeles Times Book Review* (21 January 1990).

SUGGESTED READING

The Chicago Manual of Style. 13th ed. Chicago: University of Chicago Press, 1982.

The bible on style for most writers and editors.

Flesch, Rudolf. *The Art of Readable Writing*. Rev. ed. New York: Harper & Row, 1974.

A little heftier than Strunk and White and almost as valuable. Includes a helpful formula (something like Robert Gunning's Fog Index) to gauge levels of reading ease and interest in a piece of writing, for people who like that sort of thing.

Gordon, Karen Elizabeth. *The Transitive Vampire: A Handbook of Grammar for the Innocent, the Eager, and the Doomed*. New York: Times Books, 1984.

Strong evidence supporting the idea that good usage and grammar account for half of style.

Hudson, Bob, and Shelley Townsend, eds. *A Christian Writer's Manual of Style*. Grand Rapids: Zondervan, 1988.

A complement to *The Chicago Manual of Style* that is especially helpful to persons writing for the religious marketplace.

Johnson, Edward D. *The Handbook of Good English.* New York: Facts on File, 1982.

Good sections on grammar, style, diction, and composition.

Strunk, William, Jr., and E. B. White. *The Elements of Style.* 3d ed. New York: Macmillan, 1979.

Still the one book on writing that a person would most want to be stranded on a desert island with.

Zinsser, William. *Writing to Learn: How to Write—and Think—Clearly About Any Subject at All.* New York: Harper & Row, 1988.

If it is possible, an even better book than Zinsser's *On Writing Well.* Especially helpful for writing on difficult subjects.

Chapter 21

Searching for the Great Commission
Evangelical Book Publishing Since the 1970s

John P. Ferré

At the end of the nineteenth century, when formerly genteel American book publishers began using aggressive publicity and promotion techniques to carve out large middle-class markets, essayist Samuel Butler proclaimed the elusiveness of successful bookselling.

> There are some things which it is madness not to try to know but which it is almost as much madness to try to know. Sometimes publishers, hoping to buy the Holy Ghost with a price, fee a man to read for them and advise them. This is but as the vain tossing of insomnia. God will not have any human being know what will sell. . . .[1]

During the 1970s, evangelical publishers defied Butler's observation by issuing six books that each sold over two million copies, one of each to at least every one hundred Americans. Those remarkable best-sellers were *Prison to Praise* and *Power in Praise* by Merlin Carothers, *The Late Great Planet Earth* and *Satan is Alive and Well on Planet Earth* by Hal Lindsey, *Angels: God's Secret Agents* by Billy Graham, and *Joni* by Joni Earekson. In fact, *The Late Great Planet Earth* sold over ten million copies, breaking the

John P. Ferré is associate professor of communication at the University of Louisville. He is the author of *A Social Gospel for Millions: The Religious Bestsellers of Charles Sheldon, Charles Gordon, and Harold Bell Wright* and other books.

religious book sales record that Charles Sheldon's *In His Steps* had held for almost seventy-five years.

These best-sellers signified a boom in evangelical book publishing that was part of the rise of popular evangelicalism, which followed a growing disillusionment with the social activism of the 1960s. While Harvard theologian Harvey Cox demythologized the kingdom of God and prophesied its realization in secular institutions, the endurance of the Vietnam War into the second term of Richard Nixon's law-and-order presidency, which ended in the shame of one too many executive privileges, eroded faith in Cox's secular city.[2] Many Americans, especially the so-called baby-boomers, turned from liberal politics, social ethics, and moral ambiguity to social conservatism, individual piety, and biblical authority. And the new evangelical best-sellers reflected the changing American culture. Like their secular counterparts, evangelicals acquired a voracious appetite for answers to practical questions about living successful lives. To help them make sense of the world, they purchased millions of evangelical books, thrusting religious titles into the social mainstream and making the good fortune of evangelical book publishing seem limitless.

But as *Joni*, the last of the 1970s blockbusters, was selling its millions, Martin Marty of the University of Chicago Divinity School foresaw the end of the era.

> It is unrealistic to picture the present prosperity continuing. Revivals usually breed reactions. Flows imply ebbs. The "free ride" the culture has given all religion is not apt to last too long. The public finds many religious promises unfulfilled, and turns away.[3]

Since Marty's prediction, no religious book has sold to one percent of the population. Moreover, as the accompanying table illustrates, total religious book sales have slowed in the 1980s to half the annual growth rate of the 1970s. The prosperity that evangelical publishers enjoyed in the 1970s, like the burgeoning of popular evangelicalism, has abated.

Logos International Fellowship exemplifies the recent rise and decline of evangelical publishing. A former jeweler without publishing experience, Dan Malachuk established Logos in 1967 as an Assemblies of God church, naming himself president, pastor, and elder. Logos's first book, *Run Baby Run* by Nicky Cruz, sold over eight million copies. Logos followed this blockbuster by selling more than four million copies of *Prison to Praise* by Merlin Carothers. Along with other popular titles by the likes of media revivalists Pat Robertson and Kathryn Kuhlman, Logos published a monthly magazine, *Logos Journal*, which gained more than

Religious Book Sales in United States, 1967–1986

	Religious Book Sales (Million $)	1967 $	Average Annual Growth for Previous Decade (1967 $)
1967	108	108	
1977	304	168	5.5%
1986	685	209	2.7%

Based on John P. Dessauer, ed., *Christian Book Publishing and Distribution in the United States and Canada* (Tempe, Ariz.: CBA/ECPA/PCPA Joint Research Project, 1987), 127.

fourteen hundred subscribers. Malachuk, seemed to have the Midas touch.

But his reach eventually exceeded his grasp. In 1975, Logos bought a printing plant, hired 135 experienced Christian journalists at competative wages, and began publishing the *National Courier*, a biweekly religious newspaper that gained a paid circulation of 110,000. In 1976, Malachuk directed the *National Courier* to drop its traditional news coverage and to focus exclusively on charismatic and other religious news. (Apparently Malachuk was concerned about the Internal Revenue Service's ongoing investigation of Assemblies of God churches.) With only a 25 percent renewal rate on subscriptions, the *National Courier* folded a year later. Logos continued publishing books and its magazine, but it never recovered the $5.5 million debt that the newspaper owed to eight hundred creditors. Eventually newspaper debts consumed book profits, and in 1981, Logos filed for bankruptcy. The publisher sold its copyrights to Bridge Publishing, a British and Canadian company, and its magazine subscription list to *Charisma* magazine.[4]

The rise and fall of Logos International Fellowship illustrates the shifting fortunes of evangelical publishing in the 1970s and 1980s. The absence of recent evangelical blockbusters, the decline in growth of religious book sales, and the failure of prominent publishers like Logos reflect an industry in recession. Although evangelical book publishing is still a significant American industry, many of its resources are now devoted to maintaining the market strength it won in the 1970s. The boom years are over. From the publishers to the wholesalers and the booksellers, evangelical book publishing is increasingly run like a business instead of a jubilant ministry. It has made great strides in the last decade toward more efficient operations and market research, but the quality of its products and its ability to penetrate the broader culture are less assured.

The Publishers

In a sense, contemporary religious publishing is a schizophrenic industry. Its employees and trade magazines speak of the industry as a ministry, but the major publishers are now owned by public corporations whose primary "mission" is to generate profits for stockholders. This Janus-headed industry is unique in publishing history. In the early twentieth century, a tiny mail order outfit like the Book Supply Company could sell religious blockbusters like Harold Bell Wright's *Shepherd of the Hills* and *The Calling of Dan Matthews*. Today, however, religious book publishing is dominated by denominational houses like Broadman Press (Southern Baptist) and Abingdon Press (United Methodist), and especially by Harper & Row and two publicly owned corporations established by evangelicals: Thomas Nelson Publishers (Nashville) and Word, Inc. (Waco). In 1988 the Zondervan Corporation (Grand Rapids, Michigan), formerly one of the largest evangelical independents, became part of the Harper & Row (now HarperCollins) empire.

HarperCollins is the only major trade company to maintain an aggressive religious division. General trade houses and university presses publish about one-fifth of all religious titles in the United States, and the annual output of about sixty-five titles from HarperCollins's religious publishing division, called HarperCollins San Francisco, comprises a significant portion of them.[5] HarperCollins is an ecumenical publisher — it produces Catholic, academic, mainline Protestant, evangelical Protestant, and new age books — so it sometimes encounters resistance by evangelical bookstores looking for doctrinally pure publishers and titles. However, the corporation's purchase of Zondervan gave it access to Family Bookstores, the largest chain of religious bookstores in the world. Moreover, its access to other bookstores is enviable: B. Dalton, for instance, buys 90 percent of HarperCollins's religious titles.[6] A far cry from the mail-order ministries of the early 1900s, HarperCollins is part of a multinational media conglomeration, having been bought by Rupert Murdoch's News Corporation Limited in 1987.[7]

Like HarperCollins, Word and Thomas Nelson are public companies that began as small, private businesses. They grew steadily until they became predominant in the religious book industry. Despite their strength, though, each has faced financial trials common to companies in vicissitudinous industries.

Word, Inc. is a case in point. Word was founded in 1951 as a religious record company by twenty-two-year-old Jarrell McCracken who recorded a song about a football scrimmage between good and evil called "The Game of Life." For thirty-five years, McCracken directed

Word's remarkable program of recording profitable singers like Amy Grant and Evie and publishing successful writers such as psychologist James Dobson and evangelist Billy Graham. McCracken's success attracted the attention of media conglomerate ABC, which bought Word in 1974, keeping McCracken as president. However, in 1986, Capital Cities/ABC, facing its own financial crisis, pressured McCracken to resign. The changing of the corporate guard signified the plight of many evangelical entrepreneurs from an earlier era of independent publishing. According to the president of ABC publishing, the company had "to do a better job running [its] business from a profit standpoint." The house that McCracken built no longer had room for him.[8]

Thomas Nelson Publishers is another Horatio Alger story, but without the unhappy corporate ending. Although Nelson was established in the United States as a branch of its British parent in the mid-nineteenth century, its prominence in Bible publishing has more recent roots. Arriving in South Carolina from Lebanon in 1950 with only $600, Sam Moore paid for his education by selling Bibles door to door. In 1957, Moore borrowed $2000 to establish the National Book Company, a sales organization based in Nashville. In 1961, Moore founded the Royal Publishing Company, which went public the following year. Royal Publishing bought Nelson in 1969 for $2.6 million. Nelson had exclusive rights to publish the profitable Revised Standard Version of the Bible. The company also enlisted one hundred evangelical scholars, editors, and church leaders to produce the New King James Bible, an updated King James Version for which Nelson has exclusive publishing rights. Most of Nelson's income comes from five hundred varieties of Bibles in six translations.[9]

In the early 1980s, Nelson tried to expand its operations to Christian romance novels, archaeology books, academic books, teaching cassettes, and films. The company even bought Dodd-Mead in order to enhance its position in secular publishing. The expansion failed, however, and Nelson lost $5.3 million in 1985. It soon sold Dodd-Mead and other operations and laid off dozens of employees, including over half of the book division. Nelson found itself back in the business of selling its staples of Bibles and reference, trade, and children's books.[10]

Like Nelson, HarperCollins's evangelical subsidiary, the Zondervan Corporation, climbed the industry ladder through aggressive Bible publishing. Started by P. J. (Pat) and Bernard Zondervan in the back bedroom of a farmhouse near Grand Rapids in 1931, the company was already a Bible publisher at the time it acquired the rights to one of the most profitable Bible versions of all time — the New International Version (NIV). Because Zondervan provided the seed money, it secured a thirty-year exclusive publishing agreement with the New York International Bible Society to publish the NIV. Meanwhile, books like *Halley's Bible Handbook*, Cowman's *Streams in the Desert*, and Lindsey's *Late Great Planet Earth* gave Zondervan reason to call itself "The House of the Million Sellers."[11] Zondervan's status as a family-controlled and then publicly owned corporation changed again in 1988 when Harper & Row purchased it for $57 million. This purchase made Harper & Row the largest publisher of religious books in the United States, and perhaps the world.

Corporate success seems to have led evangelical publishers naturally into the world of public ownership, but not without an expensive price in limited editorial freedom. By selling stock on the open market, companies such as Word and Zondervan raised needed cash for expansion and acquisition. But public ownership also shifted the primary responsibility from the production of books to the enhancement of shareholders' investments. The shift was sometimes subtle, given that these publishers still produced evangelical books. Still, ministry gave way to marketing as management's goals changed. For a publicly owned evangelical publisher and bookseller, observance of the Sabbath might prove irresponsible, as would the publication of a book the editorial board believes is valuable but limited in appeal. In a growing number of situations, such a publisher would defy the interests of the shareholders only at great peril. Moreover, public ownership made evangelical publishers exceedingly vulnerable to takeovers by semi-friendly corporations hoping to gain a foothold in the evangelical market and to skim some of the financial cream from rights to Bible translations.

HarperCollins, Zondervan, Word, and Nelson may control a sizeable portion of the religious book market, but they face stiff competition from denominational presses, which enjoy the benefits of tax-exemption, as well as from a number of smaller publishers. The most notable newcomer is Multnomah Press of Portland, Oregon, established in 1969 under the auspices of Multnomah School of the Bible. Multnomah publishes thirty to forty new books a year and has 240 titles in its backlist, the bread and butter of religious book publishers. Multnomah signed such popular authors as Charles Swindoll and James Dobson. It has earned the respect of other evangelical publishers, winning several Gold Medallion awards from the Evangelical Christian Publishers Association[12] and being named in 1987 with Augsburg, Harper & Row, Zondervan, and Abingdon as one of the most highly regarded evangelical publishers in an industry survey.[13]

Regardless of the size or ownership of evangelical publishers, they are widely criticized within evangelicalism for their growing business mentality. To some observers of evangelical publishing, the decline in growth is just deserts for an industry long on the bottom line and short on literary and intellectual integrity. According to *Wittenburg Door* editor Mike Yaconelli, "the focus of Christian publishing has changed from providing resources for the church to making money." He contends that the phenomenal sales of *The Late Great Planet Earth,* in which a former riverboat captain linked contemporary world history to the imminent return of Christ, prompted Christian publishers and booksellers to focus on profits. "Why else would Zondervan publish the autobiography of former automobile industry executive John DeLorean?" Yaconelli asks. "Surely not because of the great theological insights gained from over one year of being a Christian."[14] John H. Timmerman of Calvin College likewise decries the growth of commercialism, charging that religious publishers are usually more interested in whether a book will sell than in whether the book is worth selling in the first place. Publishers, he says, want books that are short and zippy, and they willingly sacrifice nuance and rhetorical flair to that end. "In the commercial approach to publishing," Timmerman says, "writing is not unlike commercial advertising, selling ideas in neat little packages."[15]

Many other writers who bemoan the poor quality of evangelical books blame the evangelical market more than the evangelical publishers. These writers indict contemporary evangelical books, first, for their parochialism. They question the books' evangelistic power given the fact that nearly all of them are written of, by, and for evangelicals. They say such books offer piety for the pious, and often in jargon or a dialect of Bible babble.[16] These critics indict evangelical books, second, for being simplistic. Floyd Thatcher, former editor-in-chief of Word Books, complains about what he calls the "hype of electronic Elmer-Gantry types" with their "ill-conceived razzle-dazzle, a series of sin-suffer-repent exposés, poured out passionately and hysterically, but failing to deal responsibly with the complexities and spiritual needs of life."[17] Similarly, Philip Yancey of *Christianity Today* argues that evangelical authors who gloss over ambiguous realities may find tolerance from true believers, but they will surely be rejected by the formerly curious.

> The Christian public will applaud books in which every prayer is answered and every disease is healed, but to the degree those books do not reflect reality, they will become meaningless to a skeptical audience. Too often our evangelical literature appears to a larger world as strange and unconvincing as a Moonie tract or *Daily Worker* newspaper.[18]

Critics like Yancey call for honesty and complexity, for books that discover instead of rationalize, for authors who understand doubt and disbelief before they dispense their faith. Critics argue, third, that evangelical books are mediocre. With the exception of classics from previous eras — books by G. K. Chesterton, C. S. Lewis, George MacDonald, J. R. R. Tolkien, and Dorothy Sayers — Christian fiction of the twentieth century is notorious for its heroes-and-villains plots and lobotomized characters. "Among the books produced by evangelical authors today, good fiction is as rare as a snowflake in Florida," Yancey says.[19] These critics view evangelical nonfiction with equal dismay. Thatcher complains of drabness and irrelevance; rare is the quality of *Pilgrim at Tinker Creek* by Annie Dillard or *Celebration of Discipline* by Richard J. Foster.[20]

Book Distributors

Until recently, the plethora of small evangelical bookstores bought their stock directly from a myriad of publishers. Book ordering and shipping was a clerical and logistical nightmare that rendered the industry almost inescapably inefficient and costly. Without the standard Bibles and celebrity authors, such a system would have died long ago. Even after publishers computerized shipping and billing in the 1970s and 1980s, the myriad of publishers made it inefficient for bookstores to maintain their inventory and to serve the growing number of customers placing special orders for unstocked titles. Perhaps the most revolutionary development in evangelical book distribution is the growing dominance of influential wholesalers.[21] Bookstores generally place their initial orders with publishers and restock their shelves with books from the wholesalers.[22]

The first national wholesaler of religious books was short-lived. Ingram Book Company of Nashville launched Reedwood House in 1976, but by the end of the following year it had only three hundred subscribers. Unable to penetrate the religious bookstore market, Reedwood was phased into Ingram, whose microfiches now list both religious and secular titles. Today Ingram targets religious departments in secular stores, foregoing religious bookstores altogether.

A year after Reedwood House folded, Spring Arbor Distributors was founded in Belleville, Michigan. Unlike Reedwood House, which had difficulty deciding what to stock and which never penetrated the religious bookstore market, Spring Arbor succeeded on both counts almost immediately. Perhaps Spring Arbor's success was the result of the experience of James E. Carlson, its founder, who attended Gordon-

Conwell Seminary near Boston, served for several years as a counselor with InterVarsity Christian Fellowship, and founded the Association of Logos Bookstores. Carlson understood the evangelical book world.

Spring Arbor serves three thousand trade stores, including the B. Dalton and Walden chains, and has captured the religious bookstore business. This wholesale supermarket of religious products stocks 50,000 different items including 20,000 book titles and 3700 types of the Bible. It ships orders within twenty-four hours from its warehouses located around the country. Publishers sell Spring Arbor books at a "long" discount (50–55 percent), which enables the distributor to sell them at up to a 40 percent discount to stores. Spring Arbor's twenty-item or $100 retail minimum drives away few stores because it can be met with products from some five hundred vendors. Besides offering numerous titles and quick shipping, Spring Arbor has two other services for bookstores. One is an inventory list with a semimonthly report on which books are selling and which authors are scheduled for television appearances so that stores can do promotional tie-ins. The other service is a model inventory, a report geared to an individual store's size that recommends what titles to stock and in what quantity, based on figures of current and perennial best-sellers. Despite resistance from both publishers and booksellers who believe that wholesaling diminishes their profits and from authors who worry that wholesaling reduces their royalties, Spring Arbor's product sales for 1988–89 totaled $95 million, a twelvefold increase over 1980.[23]

Another growing area of evangelical wholesaling is remainders, unsold books that can sell briskly when marked down as much as 80 percent on bargain tables. The remainder market enables publishers to clear valuable warehouse space rapidly and recoup some of the costs of printing, promoting, and editing. Remainders also help bookstores attract bargain-hunters and they save buyers money on books, some of which are notable titles by known authors. Religious remainders will never be a large market, however, because the rate of return for religious books is only 11 percent. As Ted Andrews, former executive director of the Evangelical Christian Publishers Association, says, "Booksellers feel that if they can't sell a book today, they'll sell it tomorrow."[24]

The major wholesaler of evangelical remainders is Book Bargains of Westwood, New Jersey, which began in 1981 and regularly stocks over seven hundred titles. Book Bargains not only sells remainders to bookstores, but through its parent, Barbour and Company, Inc., it also republishes remaindered titles that have received a second life on the bargain table, some of which sell better as remainders than they did initially. Barbour and Company also issues inexpensive hardbound editions of such perennial titles as *Pilgrim's Progress* and *In His Steps*.[25] Other companies in the religious remainder business are Baker Book House of Grand Rapids and Cokesbury, the United Methodist chain, which sells remainders through mail order catalogs.[26] Zondervan operates one factory outlet in Grand Rapids, where its own titles returned by stores outside the Family Bookstore chain are sold at discount prices. Within the chain, slow-moving Zondervan titles are discounted in individual stores.[27]

Evangelical Bookstores and Markets

Most of the sixty-five hundred religious bookstores in the United States are small, independent outlets that make much of their profit on knickknacks and cards. But like the family publishers that were transformed into public corporations, bookstores are slowly becoming bureaucratized and centralized. Southern Baptist Bookstores' sixty-two outlets constitute the largest denominational chain. The largest nondenominational chain is Family Bookstores, begun (though not under that name) in 1932, one year after the Zondervan brothers went into business. With more than a hundred outlets, including two in Great Britain, Family Bookstores is the fourth largest bookstore chain in the country, behind only Waldenbooks, B. Dalton Booksellers, and Crown. Zondervan sells more than just its own products; in 1984, only 18 percent of its sales were Zondervan's own books and records.[28] Family Bookstores' sole independent religious rival is the Association of Logos Bookstores. Begun in Ann Arbor, Michigan, as part of InterVarsity Christian Fellowship, Logos also publishes its own titles. In the 1970s, Logos expanded into an association of over eighty member-owned stores in the United States and Canada; two decades later the Association included less than half as many. Most of the Logos stores are for-profit, some are not-for-profit.[29]

The increasing centralization of the industry is problematic because booksellers and publishers are idea brokers who decide which ideas can be presented to the public and in what form. Media researchers refer to this role as gatekeeping, harking back to a study of a Peoria newspaper editor in the 1950s who refused to publish information flattering to the Roman Catholic Church or the Soviet Union. Although a potentially endless variety of religious ideas may be conceived, they must pass muster with publishers and booksellers alike before the reading public can entertain them. Ideas can stop at the "in" box of an editor's desk or at the briefcase of a publisher's representative. For evangelical publishing, which has always been sensitive to the demands of what Nathan Hatch calls the "sovereign audience," this keeping has been both a blessing and a curse.

A religious publisher's initial approval of a manuscript does not guarantee a book's availability to readers, however. Such was InterVarsity's recent experience with *Brave New People*, a book on biomedical ethics by D. Gareth Jones, an evangelical who teaches anatomy at Otago University in New Zealand. In *Brave New People*, Jones said that therapeutic abortion may sometimes be "the least tragic of a number of tragic options." His ambivalence concerning cases such as Lesch-Nyhan syndrome, a genetic disorder that leads to uncontrollable self-mutilation, vomiting, screaming, and childhood death, was enough to raise the ire of a few very vocal pro-life groups. The Christian Action Council claimed that *Brave New People* "lent Christian respectability to the 'pro-choice' position" and urged subscribers to write to InterVarsity Press. The Pro-Life Action League of Chicago picketed InterVarsity Press headquarters in Downers Grove, Illinois, with placards reading "IVP Revives Eugenics" and "Unborn Babies Feel Pain."[30] And fundamentalist author Franky Schaeffer circulated a letter at the Christian Booksellers Association convention in which he called *Brave New People* "coercive, leftist, and pro-abortion," and advocated a boycott of all InterVarsity Press books.[31] InterVarsity withdrew the book from sale, complaining that abortion was no longer a debatable issue among evangelicals. The author, too, complained of unfair treatment:

> Many evangelicals and fundamentalists complain bitterly about the humanist bias of the media in America and also of the difficulty of getting a fair hearing for the evangelical point-of-view. Unfortunately, these same people do not appear to be worried about stifling freedom of expression when it suits their own purposes. Neither do they worry about unfair bias when it works in favor of their cause. It should not surprise us, then, that those outside evangelicalism look with suspicion on our claims to revere freedom of expression and opinion.[32]

Usually publishers avoid public offense by rejecting manuscripts; the above-mentioned case of gatekeeping is notable because it occurred after publication. Although Eerdmans subsequently published *Brave New People*, evangelical publishers may have learned to toe the evangelical hard line. As a letter to InterVarsity asked, "So where does it stop? Whose book is next? What effect does this decision have on the editors of the press in their attempts to secure relevant manuscripts? What are the new criteria by which writers for IVP are to be judged?"[33] Prudence is central to gatekeeping.

Bookstores can keep the gate of ideas closed just as effectively as can publishers. Nathan and An Keats founded Keats Publishing, Inc. in New Canaan, Connecticut, in 1971 as a publisher of religion and health books. "We're not a religious house," Nathan Keats says, "but we publish religious books." Among their first titles was *Prophet of Destiny* by Ellen G. White, a Seventh-day Adventist. They managed to sell sixty thousand copies, but Nathan Keats learned a lesson in the process: "I wanted to start a line of religious books — Jewish, Unitarian, evangelical, whatever. But I learned fast that your religious line has to be evangelical or related in order to gain acceptance in most Christian bookstores."[34] Keats eventually found its religious niche with the Shepherd Illustrated Classics and Large Type Christian Classics. By publishing acceptable books such as James Stalker's *The Example of Jesus Christ* and Thomas à Kempis's *Imitation of Christ*, Keats avoided the disfavor of evangelical bookstores.[35]

Evangelical publishers and bookstores have every right to select what they will sell and to refuse titles antithetical to their professed mission. A pluralistic democracy requires not that all publishers issue variety, but that there be other avenues for the circulation of ideas that any one group may reject. If the world of religious books becomes dominated by any particular faith or group, then what the public is allowed to choose from becomes narrow and safe because little that lacks an imprimatur can reach it. Evangelicals have repeatedly shown that despite their diversity, they are often suspicious of the ideas of other faiths.

Nevertheless, in recent years evangelicals have expressed far greater concern with secular gatekeepers than with gatekeepers within their own ranks. Besides complaining about the secular books used in public schools, they have groused frequently and provocatively about the news media's inattention to their own books. Even when sales of evangelical books are brisk and voluminous, the most popular titles rarely appear on the prestigious and influential best-seller lists of the *New York Times* and *Washington Post*. The exceptions to this rule are notable: Robert Schuller's *Tough Times Never Last, but Tough People Do!* and *Tough-Minded Faith for Tenderhearted People*, Billy Graham's *Approaching Hoofbeats: The Four Horsemen of the Apocalypse*, and Peter and Barbara Jenkins' *Walk West*. Usually, though, religious titles are conspicuously absent, which leads some evangelicals to complain that the press either ignores or censors them. And it leads religious bookstores to wonder about lost revenues, since best-seller lists undoubtedly affect sales.

According to the *Times*, however, the rarity of religious titles on its list has to do with their marketing, not their message. In an article on religious publishing, *Times* reporter Edwin McDowell explained.

Most of the 100 or so religious book publishers are private, denominational firms that sell their wares by direct mail, through religious book clubs, in discount stores and convenience markets and in some 5,000 religious bookstores, which tend to be small "mom-and-pop" operations. All these marketing techniques help religious books reach wider audiences than they would otherwise, but they also explain why even runaway religious best sellers rarely show up on the best-seller lists of the *New York Times Book Review* and other publications, which report only the sales of trade or "general interest" books.[36]

In other words, only when religious titles sell rapidly in general-interest bookstores like Waldenbooks or Kroch's and Brentano's, the types of stores that newspapers survey, will they appear on the best-seller lists in Sunday newspapers.

Evangelical best-seller lists are just as exclusive as their secular counterparts; they too survey sales at their own outlets, including stores and Spring Arbor Distributors, which publishes its own list. In fact, *Bookstore Journal*, the monthly publication of the Christian Booksellers Association, did not list Robert Schuller's *Tough Times Never Last, but Tough People Do!* as a best-seller because most of the copies sold through general-interest, and not evangelical, stores. Of course, religious best-seller lists never include general-interest best-sellers. No list reflects what books have sold the most in the United States during the past week; instead, there are religious lists and general-interest lists, a sacred-secular split.

Evangelical authors and book outlets have criticized this sacred-secular dichotomy. Millionaire businessman Jerry Nims invested substantially in the promotion of Francis Schaeffer's *Christian Manifesto*, which sold some 300,000 copies. Angered because it never appeared on the best-seller list of the *Washington Post*, Nims asked *Post* editor Ben Bradlee for an explanation. Predictably, Bradlee explained that the book was not selling in general-interest stores. Nims, however, says that it did not sell in general-interest stores because general-interest publications like the *Post* would not review the book, following a policy that keeps evangelical viewpoints off of the public agenda.[37] Cal Thomas, former vice-president for communications of the Moral Majority, put the point bluntly. "The *New York Times* list," he said, "is a phony best-seller list. It does not deal with total sales in all stores. It is a gerrymandered system that routinely excludes the Christian sales."[38]

Such arguments about best-seller lists seem curiously self-contradictory. On the one hand is the desire for general-interest stores to stock evangelical titles, for general-interest publications to review these books, and then for general-interest publications to acknowledge evangelical best-sellers. This desire makes perfect sense because its fulfillment would presumably boost sales and open new channels for evangelism. On the other hand, evangelical separatism is evidenced in publishers who produce only "Bible-based" books, bookstores that carry only narrowly defined "Christian" titles, and the Christian Booksellers Association, an organization for the advancement of evangelical publishers and book-stores. Although in a pluralistic society it is expected that subgroups will maintain a strong sense of self-identity, evangelicals who complain that the *New York Times* and *Time* magazine routinely ignore them are asking for something more. They are asking for recognition and legitimation by the very culture that they reject. To paraphrase H. Richard Niebuhr, they want their Christ against culture and Christ of culture, too.[39]

The Future of Evangelical Book Publishing

Despite improvements in wholesaling and the expansion of book-store chains, a $75,000 study commissioned jointly by the Christian Booksellers Association, the Evangelical Christian Publishers Association, and the Protestant Church-Owned Publishers Association criticized the industry for ignoring religious book readers. The report asks,

> What could be more beneficial than to learn more about book customers, their identities, similarities, differences, lifestyles, back-grounds, spiritual commitments, reading habits, buying habits, inter-ests, likes and dislikes, reactions to books read in the past, requests for new titles, etc., etc.? What could be more logical than to use a panel of readers as a sounding board before deciding to publish a title, adopt a cover design, or choose an advertising approach?[40]

The report urged publishers to base their publication schedule on audience research and involvement rather than waiting for manuscripts to arrive over the transom. Likewise, the report encouraged booksellers to broaden their local markets with tailored direct-mail campaigns designed to increase store traffic. Finally, the report optimistically claimed that publishers and booksellers can revitalize sales with aggressive marketing, finding an additional fifteen million people to buy between two and four religious books every year throughout the 1990s.[41] Finding fifteen million buyers of evangelical books will be difficult, however, because a small percentage of people buy the majority of books. At the very most, only 15 percent of adults regularly read religious books. The typical reader is a married evangelical woman, twenty-five to forty-nine, who lives in the Sun Belt from California to Georgia. She earns a moderate income, is at least high school educated, and attends church regularly. Evangelical book buyers are a committed, but relatively small, group of people.[42]

According to the report, evangelical publishers needed a concerted "outreach program" to tide them over until the next period of prosperity, which will occur on schedule during the decade of 2000–2010. These years, predicted the report, will see "one or several religious revivals" that occur cyclically in American history. The first part of the cycle is what the report called "seeding," an era in which new religious groups and heavy immigration introduce a challenge to the religious establishment. The challenge becomes an "upheaval," a period usually noted by the growth of evangelicalism. As institutions absorb the challenges of evangelicalism, upheaval subsides, and the churches enter a period of "consolidation." The report concluded that the upheaval stage was ending and consolidation was beginning in the late 1980s. Because the momentum that spurred the growth of evangelical publishing during the 1970s had subsided, the industry needed shrewd marketing to maintain its strength.[43] The advice of the report resembled that of the rabbi in *Fiddler on the Roof* who is asked whether forced emigration is a signal of the Messiah's coming. "We'll have to wait someplace else," the rabbi says. "In the meantime, let's start packing." The report hedged, "We'll have to wait for another revival. In the meantime, let's start marketing."

The report itself was a remarkable testimony to the state of the American evangelical book-publishing industry. Optimistic in the face of obvious industry decline, the report reflected evangelicalism's long-standing optimism about its own future. And placing such hope in the hands of marketing and promotional techniques, the report echoed evangelicalism's close affinity to mass persuasion and free-enterprise capitalism. The report revealed an optimistic but worried industry in search of solutions, an industry, as Butler said, "hoping to buy the Holy Ghost with a price."

Although it comes as no consolation for publishers and booksellers who have budgets to meet, downturns in religious book sales do occur occasionally. There was no reason to believe that the boom of sales in the 1970s would continue. Indeed, only a few years before, religious publishers had been predicting their own demise! In 1970, Doubleday editor John J. Delaney said, "We are in the most critical situation religious publishing has ever experienced in the United States,"[44] and Werner M. Linz, executive vice-president of Herder and Herder concurred: "It seems to have been generally proven that no publisher can live by publishing religious books alone."[45] The circumstances, in retrospect, were no more dire than those of the late 1980s, but they were sufficient cause for caution. At least for the time being, the public has stopped buying evangelical books by the bushel even though marketing and distribution are better coordinated and more efficient than ever. Apparently, much of the audience has turned to other books or to new video technologies. Perhaps evangelicalism itself is experiencing a general decline.

Nevertheless, not all of the readers are gone. Christian book publishing is a billion-dollar industry, still selling a lot of books. Only now it is selling almost exclusively to the evangelical subculture, hardly penetrating the broader culture. The evangelical publishing industry — from writers and publishers to wholesalers and bookstores — defines its audience as the already devout; it rarely includes doubters and disbelievers. Perhaps the plethora of Christian bookstores and publishers has robbed writers of the incentive to produce works compelling to those outside the fold. Whatever the reason, evangelical book publishing serves more of a pastoral than an evangelistic role — an irony, clearly, but one with benefits, as Martin Marty noted: "Tribalism . . . can . . . be a creative deterrent to totalitarian Bigness in church as in world. It helps give value to group life in a day when super-individualism often drives people into do-it-yourself religion and utterly private world views."[46] Indeed, evangelical books do not have to reach beyond their devotees to perform a service.

Throughout the twentieth century, religious titles have accounted for about 5 percent of all books published in the United States. Despite the recent cooling of sales, this figure still holds true, indicating an enduring industry. Evangelicalism may have faded somewhat from the cultural limelight, but it remains a dominant force in religious book sales and a subcultural mainstay. Evangelical publishing, for all of its problems, is testimony to the endurance of that subculture.

NOTES

1. Henry Festing Jones, ed., *The Note-Books of Samuel Butler* (New York: Dutton, 1912), 160.

2. Harvey Cox, *The Secular City*, rev. ed. (New York: Macmillan, 1966).

3. Martin E. Marty, "A Spiritual Revival, a Commercial Boom, and Yet . . . ," *Publishers Weekly* (13 February 1978), 84.

4. Rodney Clapp and J. Alan Youngren, "Logos Publishing, High-Flier in the '70s, Files Bankruptcy," *Christianity Today* (6 November 1981), 69, 88; "Publisher Bankrupt," *Christian Century* (16 December 1981), 1305.

5. Stella Dong, "Faith in the Trade Houses," *New York Times Book Review* (11 April 1987), 12.

6. Jerome P. Frank, "Harper's 'Bishop' Reflects on 50+ Years of Religious Bookselling," *Publishers Weekly* (4 March 1983), 66.

7. Lisa See, "Harper, San Francisco: Experienced at Weathering Change," *Publishers Weekly* (31 July 1987), 49.

8. "McCracken Leaves Word, Publishing House He Started," *Christianity Today* (17 October 1986), 48.

9. Madalynne Reuter, "Nelson, Bible Publisher, to Acquire Dodd, Mead," *Publishers Weekly* (1 January 1982), 12; Edwin McDowell, "Publishers: A Matter of Faith," *New York Times Book Review* (6 April 1980), 8.

10. Dale D. Buss, "The Problems at the 'Big Three,'" *Christianity Today* (17 October 1986), 60–61.

11. LeRoy Koopman, "The Netherlands Quartet," *Publishers Weekly* (26 September 1980), 63–64; Charles Storch, "Murdoch Faces Battle for Evangelical Publisher," *Chicago Tribune* (19 July 1988), sec. 3, p. 4; telephone interview with Mark Rice, Supervisor of Market Research for Books and Bibles, Zondervan Publishing House, 12 September 1988.

12. Roy Paul Nelson, "The Multnomah Formula," *Publishers Weekly* (6 March 1987), 41–42.

13. John P. Dessauer, Paul D. Doebler, and Hendrik Edelman, *Christian Book Publishing & Distribution in the United States and Canada* (Tempe, Ariz.: CBA/ECPA/PCPA Joint Research Project, 1987), 72.

14. "Religious Flea Market," *Christian Century* (30 October 1985), 967–68.

15. John H. Timmerman, "Train of Robes, Plume of Feathers: Rhetoric in the Religious Publishing House," *The Cresset* (October 1986), 12.

16. Philip Yancey, *Open Windows* (Westchester, Ill.: Crossway, 1982), 176–78.

17. Floyd Thatcher, "Welcome to a New Breed of Religious Writers (And About Time, Too)," *Publishers Weekly* (4 March 1986), 46.

18. Yancey, *Open Windows*, 182.

19. Ibid., 204.

20. Thatcher, "Welcome," 46.

21. Dessauer, Doebler, and Edelman, *Christian Book Publishing*, 108–9.

22. Judith S. Duke, *Religious Publishing and Communications* (White Plains, N.Y.: Knowledge Industry Publications, 1981), 104.

23. Bill Dunn, "Spreading the Word by Discount and Computer," *Publishers Weekly* (9 March 1984), 39–41. Telephone interview with David B. Dykhouse, vice-president for marketing development, Spring Arbor Distributors, 8 March 1990.

24. Lisa See, "Speaking for the Evangelical Publishers," *Publishers Weekly* (30 September 1983), 59.

25. Hugh R. Barbour and Bruce R. Barbour, "Born Again Books," *Publishers Weekly* (28 September 1984), 52–53.

26. Gerald N. Battle, "The Unexploited Part of the Remainder Explosion," *Publishers Weekly* (24 September 1979), 42–43.

27. Chris Meehan, "Carrying the Christian Message: Zondervan's Mission and Marketing Goals Translate into Retail Expansion," *Publishers Weekly* (9 March 1984), 90–93.

28. Ibid., 90–93.

29. Stanley P. Shank, "A Word about Logos," *Publishers Weekly* (26 September 1980), 60–61.

30. Randy Frame, "InterVarsity Withdraws a Book Opposed by Pro-lifers," *Christianity Today* (21 September 1984), 63, 66.

31. Franky Schaeffer, "An Open Letter to the Christian Booksellers Association and Christian Bookstore Owners and Buyers in America," 1984.

32. D. Gareth Jones, "A View from a Censored Corner," *Journal of the American Scientific Affiliation* 37 (September 1985): 175.

33. James W. Sire, "Brave New Publishers: Should They Be Censored?" in *Evangelicalism: Surviving Its Success*, ed. The Evangelical Round Table (St. Davids, Pa.: Eastern College and the Eastern Baptist Theological Seminary, 1987), 142.

34. Judd P. Anderson, "Soul and Body Catered to at Keats," *Publishers Weekly* (1 October 1982), 49.

35. Anderson, "Soul and Body," 48–49.

36. McDowell, "Publishers," 8.

37. Randy Frame, "Jerry Nims: Backing Books from the Religious Right," *Christianity Today* (26 November 1982), 38–40.

38. Steve Rabey, "Despite Recent Breakthroughs, Most Christian Books Don't Make Best-Seller Lists," *Christianity Today* (17 February 1984), 45.

39. H. Richard Niebuhr, *Christ and Culture* (New York: Harper & Row, 1951).

40. Dessauer, Doebler, and Edelman, *Christian Book Publishing*, 85–86. The College of Arts and Sciences at the University of Louisville provided funding for the purchase of this report.

41. Ibid., 140–41.

42. Duke, *Religious Publishing*, 13; Dessauer, Doebler, and Edelman, *Christian Book Publishing*, 102, 125.

43. Dessauer, Doebler, and Edelman, *Christian Book Publishing*, 97–98.

44. "Publishers Comment on Problems and Opportunities of Religious Publishing Today," *Religious Book Guide for Booksellers and Libraries*, (January-February 1970): 13.

45. Werner Linz, "Surviving: A Report on the Present and Future of Religious Publishing," *Religious Book Guide for Booksellers and Libraries* (May-June 1970): 10, 12.

46. Marty, "A Spiritual Revival," 84.

Chapter 22

Bookselling in the Religious Marketplace

Lee Gessner

Like the tree falling in the woods with no ear to hear, a book written but not read produces no sound. The passion and efforts of the writer, the craftsmanship of the editor, and the costs and labor of the printing and binding all bear fruit when the book is read. While it seems so obvious as to be silly for anyone to say it, in order to be read, a book must first be sold. Knowing how, where, and to whom a book can be sold will determine its success.

I want to describe ten areas in which religious books are commonly sold. While this is not an exhaustive presentation of all markets, it is my feeling that the vast majority of all religious books sold go through one or more of these ten areas. I will make an effort to describe the way books are placed into these outlets and how they reach out to consumers. The role of the publisher's sales and distribution staff in the process will be described in part. Opportunities unique to a particular kind of bookselling operation and tensions that exist within a given type of operation will be mentioned as they ultimately make an impact on sales.

Lee Gessner is vice-president of sales and distribution at Word, Inc.

Independent Christian Bookstores

The vast majority of religious books sold in America are sold off the shelves of Christian bookstores. Estimates provided by the Christian Booksellers Association (C.B.A.) indicate that there are more than seven thousand Christian bookstores in America. Stores range in size from small side-porch operations to aggressive regional chains that are independently owned, to national chains such as Family Bookstores (owned by the Zondervan Corporation) and Baptist Bookstores (operated by the Southern Baptist Sunday School Convention).

Before describing details of how books are sold to and through these stores, it is important to discuss the sense of mission that drives their owners and employees. The same desire to serve God, the church, and needy people that leads individuals to enter the pastorate or the mission field motivates these fine people to open and operate Christian bookstores. Extreme care is exercised in selecting products for sale. Those with the authority to buy are concerned about the contents of the books on their shelves. Although they cannot read all that they sell, bookstore buyers expect Christian publishers and their representatives to be considerate of their desire to serve and please God by the sale of Christian books. In some cases this passion may lead to a limited range of products, i.e., those the bookstore buyer agrees with, but, in most situations, such buyers are open to purchasing a wide range of books that they feel are within the confines of Christian orthodoxy. The general view of the owner and staff of a Christian bookstore is that every person who walks into the store has a need. The need may be for books that provide Bible study, inspiration, counseling, or entertainment, to name just a few. The role of the store and its staff is to identify that need and satisfy it with a product that does not violate God's word or purpose.

The challenges and tensions that independent store owners face are not unlike those of other retailers. Many of the stores have very low capital resources. Start-up capital often comes from personal savings or private borrowing. Limited capital restricts floor and shelf space, making it difficult to stock and feature products for sale. The sheer volume of books available for sale from religious publishers has increased dramatically in recent years, forcing buyers to make more decisions and making shelf space all the more competitive. Growth in the sale of music, gifts, and stationery items crowds the store's space. In addition, because so many people have entered the business as a means of service, the entrepreneurial risk-taking and promotion-mindedness important to commercial success are sometimes lacking.

Given these tensions, it is important for each book to have a champion. This is the role of the publisher's sales team. Whether by phone or personal visit, or at a bookselling convention, the likelihood of a book selling well is enhanced when it is described and presented to the bookstore buyer. Knowing the audience for whom the book is written, what the book will do for the reader, and what the author and publisher are doing to tell the public about the book will influence the buying decision. Knowledge of a store's customer base and selling history, coupled with content and promotional information, allows the representative to lead the buyer through the list of books intelligently. Buyers schedule appointments regularly with their publishers' sales reps to learn of new products and discuss promotional opportunities. In addition, buyers are reminded to continue to stock books that are selling.

Each July representatives from most Christian bookstores attend the Christian Booksellers Association Convention. There they visit the booths of hundreds of publishers and suppliers to see what's new and what's available. Authors attend at the invitation of their publishers to autograph their books and occasionally to speak. Classes and instruction are offered, covering an array of topics to assist in bookstore operations. Publishers go to great expense to feature high-profile books and to make their sales staff available to attendees.

Between conventions and sales visits, bookstore buyers read the *Bookstore Journal, Christian Retailing,* and other trade periodicals to learn about new products and opportunities. Buying decisions are being made continually during this process of information assimilation; however, there is a strong seasonal emphasis in the industry. In-store customer traffic is highest in the weeks and months prior to Christmas, and bookstore buying intensity precedes that. Products especially suited for gift-giving, such as inspirational-devotional books and children's books, are often featured during this time. It is interesting, though, that popular reference books and Bibles sell well in the fall. One positive characteristic of the Christian bookselling industry is the long life span of many titles. It may take months for a book to begin to sell well, but once it begins to sell, its success often continues far longer than a comparable book in the nonreligious market. A higher percentage of religious books will sell successfully for many years than their secular counterparts.

Bookstore Chains

Of growing significance in the religious bookselling market are corporate or independently owned chains. The Family Bookstore chain owned by the Zondervan Corporation operates over 130 stores throughout much of the United States. Joshua's Bookstores, owned by

Tandycraft, operates over twenty stores in the southern United States and is expanding. The fifteen Berean Christian stores, owned by Stander throughout the United States, fall into this category, as do the independently owned Lemstone and Logos bookstores.

There are a number of common characteristics found among these stores. They aim for high customer traffic locations, usually in or near shopping malls. They often develop mailing lists of customers and create attractive catalogs and sale flyers to promote products. They are very promotion-minded and are aggressively working to attract walk-by shoppers who would not normally shop in Christian bookstores. A drawback for many of these stores is limited space. Costs per square foot are high in or near malls, so product and services may be limited. Many of these stores rely on in-store signs and posters and well-defined floor plans to create a self-service atmosphere. The large, full-service Berean stores are an exception, as they seek to provide a wide range of products and services to customers and churches.

Many of these chains buy from a central office. The role of a publisher's rep is to present new products, negotiate the buying of advertising space in flyers and catalogs, suggest products and terms for in-store promotions, and keep bookstore buyers informed of product availability.

Denominational Chains

Several denominations support bookstore chains, such as the Baptist Bookstores (S.B.S.C.), the Cokesbury stores of the United Methodist Church, and Provident Bookstores, owned by the Mennonite Church.

Although owned by a parent denomination, all of these chains seek to reach beyond denominational boundaries. Buying decisions are usually made on the local-store level with some central buying control. Publishers' reps who visit these stores to present products are mindful of denominational interests. Although these chains strive for a measure of diversity, their product selection is usually influenced by a guiding theology or philosophy. You probably won't find a book on praying with icons in a Baptist bookstore. Similarly, because the Mennonite church is historically pacifist and has strong interests in social justice, the buyers of Mennonite church-owned Provident Bookstores will be guided by those principles.

The role of the denominationally owned stores is largely to serve their local churches. Therefore curriculum sales and church supplies take a higher profile, as do books written by denominational authors or to denominational interests. Publishers' reps do well to keep this in mind

and take advantage of an opportunity to promote a book to a niche market.

Beyond the ability to serve their constituents through denominationally owned bookstores, many church denominations maintain lists of pastors, youth directors, Sunday school teachers, and alumni of church-owned schools. Publishers' reps, often national account reps, work with decision makers to offer books for sale via church-sponsored mailings. This is a good way to raise money, to support a ministry emphasis, or to feature a denominational author.

Church conventions and meetings offer a forum to sell books, as many denominations either operate temporary bookstores on site or allow publishers to set up booths. Given the number of conventions held, it is not possible for publishers to attend most of them; however, a publishing sales rep can often arrange to have books present to support an author. Sales are usually made on consignment. This is a good time to mention how important it is for an author to provide an accurate itinerary well in advance of speaking engagements where books may be sold.

Secular Bookstores and Bookstore Chains (American Booksellers Association — A.B.A. Stores)

In general the owners and operators of A.B.A. stores view religious publishing as niche publishing. Although they are interested in stocking what sells, they are reluctant to carry a wide range of religious books. If you have ever visited the "Religion" section of most A.B.A. stores, you have probably seen a wide array of books on all varieties of religious thought. This stems from a lack of sophistication on the part of bookstore buyers and from the inability of many religious publishers to adequately create products suitable for the A.B.A. stores or to cultivate the relationships necessary to forcefully present their products.

There is a reluctance to place books published by religious publishers outside the religion category for several reasons. One is the fear of customer complaints that a book may offend the reader who unknowingly buys a book appealing to Scripture. Another claim by buyers is that their customers for such books are "religious" and expect to find the titles in the Religion section. It is true that store staff, especially in the A.B.A. chains such as Waldenbooks and B. Dalton Booksellers, will place books from religious publishers in the Religion section out of habit, despite the urgings of the publisher's rep to the contrary.

Despite the hurdles, the A.B.A. is a large market for religious books. Many publishers such as Word, Zondervan, Thomas Nelson, and Tyndale have national account representatives who focus on the large

A.B.A. outlets. Opportunities to present books to multiple buyers responsible for various sections of the store do exist. Often religious books are introduced to test sales in regional markets where the author resides or is appearing. While dealing with A.B.A. stores is extremely expensive and riskier than dealing with C.B.A. stores, opportunities to promote religious books in A.B.A. stores are present. It is important for publishers' reps to know their product well and to be persistent if they believe a book will sell well in the A.B.A. market. Bookstore buyers will often put off buying until a book has been presented several times. After that, a very efficient computerized inventory system reports sales, and the A.B.A. stores are quick to return to the publisher books that are not selling. Obviously, credibility is at stake, and a rep cannot insist on selling a product that is not likely to succeed.

Book buyers in A.B.A. stores are especially interested in the size of the first print run and the advertising and publicity support a book receives. Publishers who have enjoyed success in the A.B.A. market — such as Tyndale with the "Living Bible," Thomas Nelson with Minirth-Meier books, and Word with Robert Schuller and Billy Graham books — have been most successful with products having large advertising and promotional budgets and authors with a high profile. This does not exempt other books, but usually new books are introduced on a regional basis.

Catalog/Mail-Order Sales

Publishers are able to reach customers directly through catalog and mail-order sales. "Christian Book Distributors" in Peabody, Massachusetts, is the largest religious mail-order business with regular mailings to over a million readers. Others in the same business include "Great Christian Books," T & D Books, Baker Books, and Scripture Truth.

While usually offering a varied range of books, many of these businesses mail to a more academic market. Often students at seminaries will be targeted, and they will continue to buy directly from the mail order house for years. Books on theology and biblical studies, commentaries, reference books, and books on academic disciplines may enjoy their greatest sale through the mail.

The theological leanings of a particular catalog/mail-order business may provide an opportunity to feature a book with a photograph, detailed review, and discount price to a targeted market. Most catalog/mail-order businesses rely heavily on discount prices to motivate customers to buy through the mail. They achieve lower prices by keeping overhead costs low and buying in large quantities, often on a nonreturnable basis.

Publishers' reps work closely with these buyers to select products appropriate for their constituents. The frequency, size, and timing of mailings are considered as products are recommended. Catalog/mail-order mailings may be structured to promote a theme or a season, creating a window of opportunity to feature a new or previously released book. Decisions are made months in advance and only when the buyers are convinced that inventory will be available. It is costly and destructive to customers' goodwill to include in a mailing a book that does not arrive at the warehouse on time.

While catalog/mail-order sales are an irritation to bookstore operators, there is good evidence to suggest they do not impede bookstore sales. For one thing, many of the core books sold by catalog/mail-order business are not carried in many bookstores. They may be viewed as too academic or they may be targeted to a limited audience, such as church leaders. It is also interesting to note that response rates (sales) usually are around 2 percent of the list mailed. This means that 98 out of 100 people who received the mailing did not buy, but the product was in fact advertised. Given the fact that many decisions to buy come only after repeated exposure to a product, many stores can benefit from this promotional exposure given to a book.

Ministry — Institutional Sales

The rise of many popular parachurch ministries, evangelistic associations, and counseling or other service organizations outside the church has created opportunities to sell religious books.

It is important to recognize that the primary purpose of these organizations in selling books is to further their mission and to raise funds so that the work may continue. Leaders of these organizations may use book-selling opportunities as a forum for themselves and others who share a similar vision.

Newsletters and magazines from the organizations promote books to listeners and supporters. The ability of an organization to use its public voice can have a marked effect on the sale of books, both through their own distribution channel and through bookstores. In religious bookselling, when an author is interviewed, for example, on the "Focus on the Family" radio program, awareness goes up markedly, as do the sales of that author's books. When Dr. Dobson and the "Focus on the Family" staff think enough of an author and his or her book to devote their time to it, a sense of credibility is conferred to the listeners.

When Billy Graham holds up a book and recommends it, people respond. Recent best-selling titles by Drs. Minirth and Meier testify to the powerful influence such media exposure brings. I have been impressed by how keenly aware these leaders are of the need to protect this public trust. Despite the public's cynicism regarding radio preachers or Christians with a highly public profile, these leaders and their staff are extremely cautious and careful to protect the public trust they enjoy.

Publisher representatives who focus on ministry and institutional sales work with ministry buyers and decision-makers. They recommend books suitable for the particular needs of the ministry. Review copies, often in manuscript form, are submitted for consideration. When an organization makes a decision to use a book, it may follow one of several options:

1. The book offered may be purchased from the inventory of the publisher. Thus it is identical to the edition being sold through bookstores.

2. The organization may pay a licensing fee and royalties to publish its own edition, perhaps in softcover or with prefacing comments from the ministry. If a decision is made to offer a book for sale prior to printing, a Special Edition may be tagged onto the print run. This may involve some special cover treatment, perhaps even a bonded leather for large donors.

3. A ministry may copublish with a publisher in order to achieve the greatest results. Rapha Counseling and Treatment Centers copublish with Word. While retaining rights to sell books through their own network, this organization sells books through Christian bookstores as well, creating the widest possible market.

Some ministries have started their own publishing divisions to satisfy the ongoing need to have products appropriate for their constituents. While primarily useful for the services of such ministries, many of these books are now being distributed to bookstores. Focus on the Family Publishing produces numerous books sold in Christian and general bookstores by a wide range of Christian authors. Worldwide Publishing has published and distributed books for years to help support the work of the Billy Graham Evangelistic Association.

Book Clubs

Another method of selling directly to demonstrated regular book buyers is through book clubs. Unlike a catalog/mail-order business, which mails flyers offering a wide array of products to a broad list, book clubs offer a very limited selection to a smaller membership. When a book is offered as a main selection, success on that book is often near 40 percent.

Book clubs are highly selective in choosing titles because they recognize their need to be very specific. A club with pastoral and scholarly members such as the Ministers Personal Library will offer primarily those books felt to be consistent with members' interests in study and counsel. Book clubs such as those of *Guideposts* and *Christian Herald* draw their membership from Christian laypeople, many of them women, and will often lean toward inspirational books or those dealing with practical Christian living. The Word Kids Book Club, as one would expect, features children's books or some outstanding books on parenting.

Book-club managers select from books submitted for review often in manuscript form. They work closely with publishers' representatives who understand the specific audience of the club. At times seasonal books will be featured, or the club may promote a theme such as marriage and family. Some clubs, such as those of *Christian Herald* and *Guideposts*, will print their own edition of a featured main selection. Alternate selections will often be purchased from a publisher's inventory.

Because of the incredible number of books to be considered and the limited needs of book clubs, only a small percentage of the religious books published are adopted by book clubs. When they are selected, success rates are good and many books can be sold.

Rack Jobbers

Have you ever stood at the cash register of a restaurant or pharmacy and seen a wire-stand of books for sale? It was probably put there with the owner's consent by a rack jobber. A rack jobber is someone who seeks out high walk-by locations in businesses not primarily in the business of bookselling and requests space for his book stand in order to stimulate impulse sales. Parent companies, such as Successful Living in Minneapolis, serve as buyer/distributors to a network of independent rack jobbers. Local jobbers fill their cars and vans with books purchased from their distributor and service the racks periodically.

Popular fiction and Christian-living books with the broadest appeal are usually most successful. Periodically, when there is widespread interest in a theme such as Bible prophecy, you will find an assortment of titles seeking to capitalize on that interest. Hal Lindsey's *Late Great Planet Earth* sold extremely well off the rack, as do the Janette Oke fiction books from Bethany House.

There are limitations to selling through rack jobbers because of their particular nature. Beyond the fact that only books with a broad, popular appeal are appropriate, price and format are also an issue. Rack jobbers prefer the small mass-market paperbacks that sell for $4.95 and $5.95. Many of the larger, more expensive trade paperback books are sometimes sold, but hardcover books are too expensive to be sold on racks.

Because of the number of people in the chain between publisher and customer, rack jobbers require higher discounts. This puts a strain on publisher and author revenues and may further limit rack-jobber sales. Preferably a title is selected prior to a print run, enabling the publisher to tag on a sizable additional quantity of nonreturnable books. This can provide for economies of scale, lowering overall production costs per book.

Publisher representatives work with rack jobbers in recommending books, with the hope that just the right choice will result in the sale of many thousands of books to customers who often do not buy from bookstores. This is a way of presenting a selection of religious books to a public largely ignorant of what is available. Publishers hope that some of these customers will become motivated to shop in Christian bookstores once they get a taste of what is available.

Sale of Rights

Once a book has been published, an opportunity to generate additional revenue and public exposure for the author may come from the sale of rights. For an agreed-upon sum of money, and perhaps future royalties, a clause in the author's contract may permit a party other than the original publisher to use all or some of the book for a specified purpose. The length of time this may be done, when it may begin, and specifically what is permissible are all agreed to in the contract.

There are many options available in the sale of rights. Usually softcover or paperback rights are sold, perhaps to an A.B.A. mass-market publisher. Rights sales for foreign-language editions are very popular. Occasionally, a television or movie studio will express interest in a book and negotiate the rights to treat the contents on film or video.

The sale-of-rights procedure may involve a bidding process between several paperback publishers when interest is strong. A floor or entry level amount is determined by the publisher holding the copyright and interested parties bid for the right to publish a new edition. Revenues from a successful sale are shared with the author according to stipulations in his or her contract with the publisher.

The consideration for rights sales is usually initiated by the original publisher or its agent. Books are submitted for review along with sales histories of current editions. Interest is usually shown only in those religious books that have enjoyed a best-selling status in the religious market and are viewed as having broad secular audience appeal.

The sale of rights to publish foreign-language editions is usually accomplished when a representative of the foreign-language publisher learns that a book has been or will be released that might have appeal in the representative's country or language. Individuals looking to buy foreign-language rights attend the C.B.A. convention annually. They receive new-announcement catalogs from publishers regularly and copies of books and manuscripts from publishers' representatives who work in this area. A number of Spanish publishers, some in the United States, maintain very close ties with many publishing companies so that the growing Spanish-speaking community at home and abroad may read a variety of religious books in Spanish shortly after they appear in English.

International Sales

There is a market for English-language religious books outside of the U.S. Most publishers seek to sell to this market by entering into distribution agreements with foreign distributors. The Canadian market is sold to by companies such as R. G. Mitchell, G. R. Welch, and Word Canada. Recently Spring Arbor, a U. S. distributor, has made inroads into the Canadian market.

The bookstores of the United Kingdom buy books published in the United States from Marshall-Pickering, Word U.K., and others. Many of the foreign distributors are publishers themselves. They may publish works of authors from their own country and sell books or rights to the U.S. market as well as to their home market.

Because of foreign-exchange-rate obstacles, shipping costs, and time factors, these publishers will often buy the rights to publish English-language editions in their home country. Without this option, a $15.95 hardcover book might sell for $22.95 or more in the U.K. or Australia.

Foreign distributors make their decisions on what books or rights to buy on the basis of books regularly submitted for review by the publisher. The C.B.A. convention is another active marketplace for this, and representatives from distributors and publishers outside the U.S. often schedule appointments across the country to consider books from many publishers during the weeks prior to and following the convention.

Summary

Given the variety of opportunities to sell religious books, one might think the publisher of Christian books reaches most customers on a regular basis. Unfortunately, this is nowhere near the truth. Actually, fewer than one in ten church-attending, proclaimed Christians shop in any Christian bookstore with any degree of regularity. As I have pointed out, there are numerous ways to sell books, but given the vast number of people who should be reading our books, we seem to address the potential only superficially. A select few religious books, probably fewer than 1 percent, will sell two hundred thousand copies in a year, and they will be revered as best-sellers. Even a low-interest, box-office flop of a movie will reach more people than these books.

Many good books go unpublished because the writer lacks a public forum or name recognition, while at the same time the marketplace suffers from having too many products and too few customers. Ironically, many of the religious books that enjoy best-seller status appeal to consumer curiosity and eccentric opinion but seem to have little literary or theological value.

In spite of the shortcomings, ultimately we publish as we live — by faith. We stretch our advertising budgets beyond the limit, and we urge our dealers to be creative and aggressive in reaching out. We toil over covers and titles and subtitles and jacket copy and catalog copy and every other controllable factor. We mail review copies by the thousands each year in search of favorable reviews and author publicity appearances. And then we find out how successful we have been in this enterprise of faith.

Chapter 23

Religious Book Distributors

Jim Carlson

Religious book distributors have come to play a vital role in the religious book industry. Typically, distributors purchase new and existing titles from the publishers and sell them to all the retail bookstores. This provides low-cost distribution of the product for the publishers and cost-effective, one-stop shopping for the bookstores. The publishers can thereby reduce their costs of fulfilling small orders and increase their sales. Their sales go up because the stores are able to order more often from a distributor than they can from each publisher. Therefore, because the product is in stock more consistently, both the stores and the publishers sell more.

When distributors fulfill their role creatively and professionally, the results can be dramatic for everyone. The authors sell more books to the consumer. The publishers increase their sales and efficiencies. The stores increase their sales and decrease their operating expenses, and the ultimate consumer finds the books on the shelves more consistently and receives special orders more promptly.

Some confusion exists within the book industry over the issue of

Jim Carlson is vice-chairman and founder of Spring Arbor Distributors, the world's largest distributor of religious books. He was also the founder of the Logos bookstore chain.

who is a distributor. In this chapter, I am describing distributors who sell primarily to retail bookstores. However, there is one retail catalog house that calls itself Christian Book Distributors. Despite this name, they sell primarily to individuals, not to retail stores.

Every distributor to retail stores is continually faced with the issue of who qualifies for an account. Most distributors believe in the value of strong Christian bookstores; therefore, they will try to avoid selling to any account that will weaken the viability of the local Christian bookstore. They will not sell to churches or to individuals unless these qualify as authentic retail outlets.

In the days before electronic communications and UPS, there were about a dozen regional religious book distributors in the United States. One by one most of these distributors have either closed or been acquired. Today most of the distribution of printed material is done by three companies.

The smallest of the three is Appalachian Bible Distributors, which operates out of Johnson City, Tennessee. Riverside, another distributor, was founded by Earle Fitz about forty years ago. He recently sold this business, which was grossing under $40,000,000 per year, to a conglomerate out of New York City. They have recently added some Christian books to supplement their Bible inventory and operate out of Iowa Falls, Iowa. As the founder of Spring Arbor Distributors, I am obviously most familiar with its philosophy and operations. It was formed in 1978 and since then has grown to be the largest distributor of religious books in the world, with annual sales in excess of $100,000,000.

There are also several Spanish distributing companies operating out of Miami, Florida. They serve the Spanish communities in the United States as well as in Central and South America.

Although hard statistics are not easy to come by within our industry, I believe it is safe to say that around 25 percent of all religious books and Bibles now reach the consumer through distributors. Whether or not that percentage has been increasing is debated within the industry. If it represents an increase, as I believe it does, that increase has largely been caused by the aggressive utilization of electronic technology and the obvious advantages of one-stop shopping. The enthusiastic response of the stores to this creative use of technology and the excellent service that this provides for the retail stores has been dramatic.

The single most important ingredient in the enthusiastic use of distributors by retailers is the opportunity to consolidate orders. There are several advantages to the stores in consolidating their orders:

1. They can save from 1 to 3 percent on their freight costs by getting larger quantities shipped from one source. Formerly, the stores were in a

bind. They either had to order infrequently from each publisher to get their order quantities high enough to save freight and handling costs or, to increase turnover, they had to order quite often from each publisher, thereby incurring high freight costs. Now, by consolidating orders, they are able to order frequently from one source, thereby replenishing what is selling rather than be out of stock while waiting to accumulate orders from the various publishers.

2. Handling costs, which include the placing and processing of orders and their accompanying invoices, have similarly been greatly reduced by the stores that aggressively consolidate their orders.

3. By ordering more frequently, the stores can more easily have the product in stock, available for sale to their customers, thereby increasing their revenue stream as well as their ministry.

4. Through consolidated ordering, the stores can increase their turnover of inventory. If stores order large quantities from publishers less frequently, their inventory levels are high and the return on their investment is low. By ordering more frequently, they can keep their inventory levels lower per title, thereby increasing the frequency of the sale of each item they have in stock. They are then able to reinvest their capital in broader inventory selections, thereby increasing the quantity of titles available in each market area.

5. Returns of defective merchandise and overstock is more efficient if the product came from one source rather than from multiple sources, saving the stores time and money.

All these advantages of consolidated buying give the stores a better chance for survival within an increasingly difficult and costly environment for retail stores. With the increase in rent, labor, and other expenses, the stores must operate more and more efficiently while at the same time increasing their sales and marketing to their communities. Many stores would not exist in today's environment were it not for the opportunity to consolidate their orders from distributors. This is especially true for medium and smaller stores — stores that are providing a genuine service in many smaller communities or niche markets.

When distributors were primarily regional, they were also narrower in their product selection. They primarily stocked the best-sellers, with a view to quickly restocking those titles. Now, however, because inventories can be controlled by computer, distributors are able to control very broad inventory selections. Because of this, even large bookstores are increasingly using the services of distributors for most of their special-order business. This has decreased the hassles in special ordering for almost all Christian bookstores and has also made these books available to the consumer within days instead of weeks. Spring Arbor, for example, stocks approximately 46,000 different products for the retail stores.

These factors have caused a significant shift in the buying patterns of retail stores and have made it possible for the stores to flourish and better serve the consumer.

There are disadvantages, however, in a store's buying from distributors. The primary disadvantage is the inability of the distributor to offer a higher discount for larger orders. If retail stores buy in larger quantity from a publisher, they are given quantity discounts that can run as high as what the distributor receives from the publisher. Therefore, stores must evaluate the relative value of getting higher discounts or increasing their turnover and their sales and decreasing the obsolescence of their stock. Many stores, upon evaluating these issues, have recognized the value of service and turnover and have foregone the higher discounts.

Another disadvantage for the stores is that, for one reason or another, publishers are occasionally slow in shipping new titles to distributors. Therefore, the bookstores that depend on the distributor to have new titles often wait in frustration. So far there has been no creative solution to this chronic problem; however, it is encouraging that some effort is being made by some publishers to correct this bottleneck in distribution.

These disadvantages are more than offset by the advantages the distributor offers. In addition to those mentioned earlier, there are valuable services that distributors provide the Christian book industry. One of these is supplying information. With an enormous selection of product all in one place, product information is organized and transmitted to the stores in two ways. The first of these is, of course, printed catalogs for each product grouping; the other is microfiche, carrying the same information. Since each microfiche can be reproduced inexpensively, the distributors are able to provide new microfiche for the stores as often as every week. Furthermore, not only can these listings be made by title, they can also be offered and sorted by author, subject, and publisher. Stores that subscribe to these programs can thereby research and find titles in four different ways. This enables the store to find titles for their customers more efficiently and effectively even if the customer doesn't remember the title of a given book. This alone has significantly increased the service levels for the consumer and has increased the sale of books.

Another service that distributors can provide is computerized inventory-control systems. There are now distributors who provide cost-effective inventory-control systems for retail stores, from the smallest to the largest. All of these systems utilize the capability of the computers to print inventory-control tickets and to receive electronic transmissions of orders from the stores directly into the computer at the distributor. These systems again have enabled the stores to control a larger selection of inventory at the store level and increase their efficiency of ordering to make them more viable as bookstores. It is interesting to note that over 2,500 of a total of probably 6,000 Christian bookstores are using some level of computerized inventory-control systems. This percentage of stores using computers in the Christian industry is much higher than in the secular bookstore industry. That difference is a testimony to the aggressive application of technology to our particular segment of the book industry as well as to the willingness on the part of the retailers to use the services made available by the distributors.

Yet another service that the distributors are able to make available to both the publishers and the retailers is the various consumer marketing promotions. Monthly four-color flyers are produced and sold to the retail stores for distribution to their customers. An example of this is the Pure Gold flyer from Spring Arbor. This flyer contains thirty-two new items displayed each month in a four-color presentation. The most successful and widely used marketing vehicle has been the Christmas catalog. Here, once again, because the distributors are in a unique position of being able to carry a broad range of product and to sell to the entire breadth of Christian bookstores, they are able to produce catalogs with a wide selection and sell most of them to the bookstores. Spring Arbor has sold approximately 3 million copies of its Christmas catalog each year to the retail stores. There are also spring consumer catalogs and children's consumer catalogs available. Some other catalogs deal with specific market groups, such as the Catholic market; Spring Arbor produces the Catholic Gold each quarter. Catholic bookstores buy this to give to their customers; in addition, some Protestant-oriented stores buy it for their customers who are from the Catholic tradition.

Still another service that the distributors provide the retail stores is educational seminars. Each year dozens of seminars are conducted throughout the country by Spring Arbor to help the booksellers become aware of more efficient ways of management and more effective procedures in their marketing and other operations. These seminars are generally offered free of charge to the stores, so managers and staff from even the smallest stores can afford to attend them.

Overall, these services have enabled the retail stores to operate more efficiently and effectively in their respective markets. Each of the services also creates a better climate for increased sales through the distributor, thus insuring the long-range viability of Christian book distributors.

The use of distributors by retailers has, of course, had an impact on the publishers. In some cases it has even caused some publishers to reevaluate the necessity of their maintaining their own warehouses and accounts-receivable departments. Some of these publishers have signed contract-distribution agreements with various distributors and then look to the distributor for handling 100 percent of their products. This enables the publishers to focus all of their resources and management energies in the area of acquisitions of new titles, editing, and marketing. The availability of the strong distributors of today has enabled new publishing houses to ask the important question, "What is our business?" The obvious answer has been "Our business is to produce and sell the product, not to run warehouses."

There are several specific services that the distributors provide all publishers in their effort to form a good commercial partnership.

Publishers increase their sales by selling through distributors. Today the booksellers can aggressively offer special-order services to their customers because they can get the product so quickly and easily from distributors. Therefore, the publishers sell more of those books that formerly the retail stores dreaded to order if they didn't have them in their own inventory. Also, the stores used to run out of many products between their sporadic orders placed with the publishers. These titles were often the fastest-selling product; therefore, what were theoretically the hottest items in each community were often out of stock at the bookstore level. Now, however, the stores can reorder quickly from the distributors and get these items in stock again to be sold to their customers. Also, because the stores are now on good inventory-management systems, they are replenishing stock regularly and keeping a good level of inventory in their stores; this not only increases sales but also increases the health and viability of these retail outlets. On the short-term basis this has reduced the number of bankruptcies, and on the long-term basis it has created an environment of stronger stores with good survivability and increased market penetration in their community.

The consumer-marketing promotions and point-of-purchase displays have further increased the ability of the stores to present a wide range of products in a professional manner. These marketing vehicles are themselves glorifying God by their creativity and design and layout as well as communicating effectively the content and desirability of the products on display. No one publisher can produce the kind of marketing promotions that are cost effective for the stores to carry and handle. And, finally, when the distributor opens new accounts with small new stores and with religious departments in secular bookstores, the publisher thereby increases its own distribution through these additional outlets. Most publishers market their products in from three to four thousand retail stores, whereas a distributor may sell to as many as nine thousand.

The publisher's operating expenses are thus also reduced. This can be seen, for example, in the size of bookstore orders. Spring Arbor receives an average order of only seventeen lines (probably from seventeen publishers) and only 1.97 items per line. If this order went to each publisher, it would be very costly for both the publisher and the bookstore.

Publishers also reduce their expenses by having the distributors absorb all the losses from uncollectible accounts. Many bookstores get into financial difficulty and therefore go out of business or go bankrupt. These uncollectible accounts must be written off by someone. They are a considerable expense for the distributor but a total savings on expense on the part of the publishers. The publishers also save the expense of processing all the returns from the booksellers of the products that are returned to the distributors.

Because some distributors use computers, they are able to provide important statistical information to the publishers. One type of information is a quarterly listing of all sales by the distributor of the product from that publisher listed by state or zip code. This provides valuable information to the publishers for the effectiveness of their respective salespeople. Some publishers, therefore, are giving a commission to their sales personnel on products sold through the distributor as well as on what has been shipped from the publisher. They give the commission because the salesperson is the one who introduced the product into the store and the publisher wants to reward him or her, regardless of where the stores buy the product on successive orders. This practice by some publishers has gone a long way toward reducing the subtle pressure salespeople give to the stores to "save up" orders for them and to buy in larger quantities than good economics would dictate.

On most sales publishers give distributors a higher discount than they give to the stores. Therefore, the gross margins for the publisher are somewhat less on the products sold to the distributor. The publishers' gross margins have been further eroded by the publishers themselves as they increase discounts to stores in order to continue to attract their business. These two reasons for the reduction of gross margins must be weighed against the increase of sales and the decreased cost of operations in dealing with distributors. The economics involved in these changing environments is causing some reevaluation of operations. This is why some companies are turning over 100 percent of their sales to distributors.

It is interesting to note that the distributors in the general book industry account for more than 50 percent of the sales of general books as opposed to the 25 percent in the Christian market. The future of the distributors is good as long as the publishers view the distributors as allies in getting the product from the author to the consumer.

This chapter would not be complete unless I also addressed the issue of how publishers affect distributors and booksellers. Obviously, they affect them most by the quality of the products they produce. Having good, salable products is the biggest single service that the publishers can provide the industry. Publishers also must provide an adequate discount so the distributors can provide services to both the publishers and the retailers. Publishers also need to provide timely shipment of new and existing products to the distributors so the flow is not interrupted. Finally, the publishers who see distributors as true partners in their own distribution of their products will continue to think of ways that the industry can work together to accomplish the good we are called to do.

Distributors also have an indirect impact on authors by increasing the sales of their products through more efficient availability and more effective distribution. In some cases, author contracts need to be reworded so they do not work to the detriment of the author when sales are increased through distributors. Perhaps the contracts of the future should provide a percentage of net sales regardless of where the product is sold, rather than a percentage of retail sales with exceptions made for sales through distributors and rack jobbers.

What does the future look like for distribution in the United States? The future depends on the changes that have occurred and the changes that will occur. One of these changes is in the area of economics. Obviously, personnel costs keep going up; therefore, both publishers and retailers must continually look at the high cost of the paperwork involved in each shipment. Also freight costs keep rising; therefore, every means needs to be used to reduce this expense. The cost of financing is now a consideration for any business, running as high as 10 percent or more today; therefore, inventory control is highly important for both publishers and retailers. To have good inventory management, one must have a good control over receivables. Publishers must have good and fairly large computers and personnel to manage them. The cost of this type of operation is already being borne by distributors. Therefore, there is a significant savings to publishers who use the facilities and services of a distributor. The effective application of these new tools has created a whole new opportunity for a sophisticated management never thought possible by most Christian bookstores fifteen years ago. Consumer marketing vehicles are now available and cost effective for both the publishers and the booksellers. From all indications, the need for strong national distributors will continue to exist and undoubtedly increase.

One final thought may also influence the nature of the relationships that distributors and publishers have with retail stores and the ultimate consumer. The customer of the publisher is the consumer of the product that they are publishing. Therefore, when the publisher is making decisions regarding what to publish and how to package it, the publisher must be thinking of the ultimate consumer. All the research, focus, and attention needs to be given to that consumer. The distributor and the retailer are channels of distribution and not the customer of the publisher. The customer of the distributor on the other hand is the retail store. The only thing the distributor has to sell is its service to the retail store. Because of that, the distributor does not control in any way what is published or how many of an item are published or sold. However, large chains of stores do control what is published and how much of each item is published because they are controlling the direct linkage to the consumer. In the secular marketplace, the large chains of B. Dalton and Waldenbooks are, therefore, feared by the industry as having a dominant control over the product. Those who want to make a comparison between the large chains and the distributors are not considering the nature of their respective businesses and who their customers are. Since the customer of the distributor is the retail store, it is natural that the distributor's total focus is on how best to serve that retail store. Therefore, the successful distributor's strategic question is, "What are the needs of retail stores and how best can we meet these needs?"

I believe the underlying purpose of Christian book distributors should be to reflect and radiate the nature and character of God in everything they do. They should try to reflect the love, kindness, patience, truthfulness, justice, and mercy of Christ as these qualities relate to all of the policies, actions, and attitudes of the company and the individuals within the company.

The mission of the distributor should then be to carry out its purpose by serving both the publishers and the retailers in whatever ways are helpful and commercially viable. The vision of a distributor needs to be broad enough to see the industry from all vantage points. A distributor who accepts the truism that "reality always prevails" will try hard to understand all realities such as the economics and environments of both publishers and booksellers. Then, armed with this understanding, the management of that distributor will make all decisions, policies, and plans accordingly. If realities change, the distributor, along with everyone else involved, needs to adjust to those changes. However, at the present time it appears that the realities of economics and the environment have created an opportunity to communicate the word of God and the words of authors through the new, highly efficient and effective methods of national religious book distributors.

Part 3
Specialty Areas in Religious Publishing and Writing

Chapter 24

Religious
Journalism

Robert Walker

Today communications, that generic term for print and audio journalism, is hot. In the religious sector, the art and craft of reporting what God is doing in the affairs of people and organizations also is being regarded with a new respect.

With no fewer than five major associations (Evangelical Press Association, Religious Publishers Association, Christian Booksellers Association, Christian Broadcasters Association, and Evangelical Christian Book Publishers Association) directly or indirectly related to the profession, religious journalism has matured enormously since a turning point in the late 1930s. I know from experience.

After graduating in 1936 from the Medill School of Journalism at Northwestern University, I served stints on two daily newspapers. Then as a result of a deeply moving spiritual experience, I sent letters to the editors of half a dozen religious magazines with the largest circulations.

"I have just become a Christian, and I believe the Lord is leading me to switch from secular to Christian journalism," I wrote. "Do you have an

Robert Walker is a journalist, author, editor, and publisher. He is retired as editor and publisher of *Christian Life* and *Christian Bookseller* magazines and Creation House Books. At present he is editor emeritus of *Charisma & Christian Life* magazine and chairman of the board of Christian Life Missions and Christian Life Institute.

opening on your staff or can you advise me how I can prepare to serve the Lord in your field?"

Only one responded. "You need to get a seminary degree and then serve as a pastor," he replied.

I was puzzled. Later, when I had met these men personally, I discovered none had received journalistic training of any kind. Their education had been in theology. To them writing or editing was not simply ancillary to their "call from the Lord," but actually an encumbrance to it. Most of them considered that time taken for editorial activity kept them from the more meaningful occupation of "preaching the Gospel." Indeed, one ruefully confessed he felt his journalistic assignment might have been given to him as some sort of discipline from the Lord.

Religious journalism not only has come of age in the 1990s, but many observers believe it may be poised on the threshold of its most useful contribution to the Christian scene. To them religious journalism — both print and audio — may emerge as the most significant factor in the upcoming religious awakening they predict will usher in the twenty-first century.

For instance, beginning in the 1950s the number of Christian magazines has proliferated enormously, with new titles emerging almost monthly. Only a few years ago those of us involved in religious publishing could name most of the then viable periodicals. Today a computer print-out of the membership of the Evangelical Press Association alone reveals more than three hundred periodicals extant. Meanwhile, the whole ministry of Christian radio and TV has burgeoned from little more than inconsequential to the most colorful and perhaps most significant in the entire Christian communication picture.

Also, most Christian colleges and seminaries now offer one or more courses in journalism. Moreover, with the increasing number of Christian magazines, Christian radio and TV stations another group of journalist has emerged. These are free-lance writers to meet the demands of the new breed of skilled religious communications technicians. Their need for help and encouragement has led to another level of preparation for religious journalism — the development of scores of religious writers conferences and seminars.

At the same time, few religious publishing houses today welcome editorial personnel who have not had some training in journalism or writing. And virtually no top-flight religious magazine will consider an applicant for editorial activity without such training. Christian radio and TV, although still emerging from the ad-lib stage, are not far behind in looking for trained religious journalists and writers.

Does this mean the millennium has come to religious journalism? Not quite.

The most vexing situation involves the quality of training available for religious journalism. At many Christian colleges journalism subjects are taught by teachers with neither journalistic education nor hands-on newspaper, magazine, or radio/TV experience. As a result, students emerge from the classroom with little concept of what will be expected of them in the real world of deadline discipline.

Equally disturbing has been the assumption, too often apparent in Christian communication circles, that the media should not be expected to finance their own existence. Rather, by virtue of their message, they should receive funding from outside sources.

Clearly, however, the picture is changing. Not only are young men and women discovering the ministry open to them in religious journalism — but they are coming to it better prepared. Moreover, in a growing number of publishing houses and radio and TV installations — both denominational and institutional as well as independent — greater emphasis is being placed on improved management techniques comparable to the industry at large.

How does this current concept of religious journalism impact on our world today? It is hoped that the following fictitious scenario will shed some light on the possibilities.

A Special Meeting

It's 9:55 A.M. Tuesday. "JD," as he is known by his associates at Evergreen Publishing House, has called a special meeting of his editorial staff. JD is in his mid-forties with tinges of gray in his hair and looks the take-charge sort of person he is as editorial director of Evergreen, a successful publishing house primarily serving the Protestant religious market with a book-publishing division and a magazine or periodical division producing multiple magazines. Five editors report to JD; the editor of the book-publishing division and the editors of each of the house's four magazines.

Pete, the youthful editor of *Gangle*, Evergreen's teenage bimonthly, has just turned twenty-five and is the first to arrive. "Good morning, Pete," JD greets him. "It's good to see *Gangle* leading the pack again."

"Good morning, JD. Please don't hold me to it. Next time I might be last. Besides the others are right behind me now."

The office fills quickly. Jill, editor of *Priscilla*, the house's woman's magazine, and Todd, editor of *Christian Jock*, the sports magazine, take seats at a round table in the corner of the office. In their early thirties, they continue their conversation begun in the corridor. The subject is how to meet their next deadline with a shortage in both of their editorial departments.

Frank, editor of *Bible Study*, Evergreen's only quarterly publication, is in his fifties and the oldest of the group. He sits down opposite them with a nod and a smile.

There's a rush at the door as Bill, editor of *Christian News*, Evergreen's only weekly magazine, and George, editor of the house's flagship magazine *Hosanna*, jostle to see who can make it to the table first. They are both thirty-seven and considered by the others as the top journalists of the group. Both came to Evergreen with several years of newspaper reporting and editing experience.

Last to slide into a chair next to JD is Evelyn, editorial chief of the book-publishing division, which operates under the house name as Evergreen Books. Clearly, the most composed of the group, Evelyn carries her forty years well. She looks exactly how a successful woman executive should look. But there is a softness in her manner that identifies her as a warm-hearted believer in Jesus Christ. This she demonstrates to her staff and the authors with whom she personally works in rewriting their manuscripts.

At 10 A.M. JD looks up from the yellow notepad on the table before him. "Thank you for responding so promptly to this special meeting. I'm calling it because I will be out of town at the time of our regular monthly meeting."

He pauses and makes several notes on his pad. "I apologize for failing to provide you with the usual agenda in advance. But it's important that we all be brought up to date on one another's activities. So I am going to ask each of you to give us an impromptu report on progress in your department. Then I would like to ask you, Todd, to have your secretary, Mary, join us for a final wrap-up on the next issue of *Christian Jock*, after we conclude this meeting."

All nod their agreement. Each details several projects coming up in his department. George is enthusiastic about a report he has just received from the circulation department with news of a major mailing that has netted twenty thousand new subscribers. "They're coming on just in time to catch our two-part series on the massive spiritual renewal that is sweeping the continent of Africa. This is a real breakthrough for us — we'll be the first magazine to report on what God is doing there." The others are quick with their questions.

"Have you heard of conversions of any top athletes in the revival?" queries Todd. "*Christian Jock* would like to profile them. . . . So let me know."

Jill injects, "I'd like to know about outstanding African women who have been born again."

"That's an encouraging report," JD interrupts. "I'll leave it to you, George, to share your information with the others. . . . And I'm sure Evelyn will be eager to hear if you turn up some good Christian writers who have been involved in the revival. And Evelyn, the material that George has come up with might be considered for a 'quickie' book for Evergreen."

Evelyn is not waiting, but is passing a note to George: "Please let me see stats of your manuscript material before you go to press."

With pertinent suggestions to each of his editors, JD dismisses the group. "I'll be out of the office a couple of weeks on a combined vacation and visits with possible new editorial personnel. Each of you needs help, I know. My hope is that we can locate a couple of people you can share between you. I've got a line on a couple of men in the east, top journalists, who also have a real witness for Christ."

JD looks around at his people. "Meanwhile, I'm asking George and Todd to sit in for me in my absence. If you have any questions go to them. I'll be talking with them every two or three days."

Todd and George nod.

"George and I will hold the fort," says Todd. "And I hope you have a good trip just so long as I get 50 percent of the good journalists you bag."

"Oh no you don't," interjects Jill. "Ever since Eve got only one rib we women have been left with too small a piece of the action. You want *Priscilla* out on time, don't you?"

By the time the others have left, Mary, a recent college graduate joins Todd and JD. "I brought along the schedules for the next three issues," she says, handing them to Todd who passes copies on to JD.

"I've asked Bud, the assistant editor, to join us also," Todd says. "He's working with a young free-lance writer you may want to talk with on your trip. He has done only two pieces for us, but I'm impressed. Whether or not he'll make a good desk man, I don't know, but Bud says he has taken some journalism courses at the Christian college he graduated from."

"Let's look at the schedules first, then I'd like to hear about your writer, Bud," says JD.

Todd passes out copies of the editorial schedules for the next three issues of *Christian Jock*. He explains that the next issue will be the first anniversary of *Jock*. "Recalling attention to the fact, but being modest about it at the same time . . . We're following our formula with one big story for cover treatment. This time it's a profile of the number-one NFL draft pick — a fine Christian who captained USC's championship football team last year. It's a good piece, and we've got great pictures."

JD nods, "Sounds good. Have you double-checked his spiritual credentials? We don't want to make another mistake like the one we did in the first issue."

"I know," Todd shakes his head. "We thought we could depend on the writer. He apologized afterwards, but it was my fault for not asking for more background. That's all different this time. We've not only checked with the boy's pastor, but also several other evangelical ministers in his hometown. They all claim he's not only a genuine believer, but also a great witness for Christ in the community."

Todd reviews the editorial formula for *Christian Jock*. "In addition to profiles of athletes — and we're trying to cover all the major sports — our schedule calls for an analysis of one sport each issue from a Christian athlete's point of view. This will be a real in-depth treatment. We're also trying to do a short piece each issue on one of the less popular sports such as lacrosse, archery, badminton, and that sort of thing. Then there are the statistics for as many sports as we can cover — that is, the major ones. We're trying to come up with ways to get these for the more successful athletes in each sport."

JD looks up from the pad on which he had been taking notes. "What progress are you making on that?"

Todd shakes his head. "It's slow. We're getting good cooperation from athletic directors and coaches at Christian schools. But it's difficult finding responsible stringers to keep us informed on Christian athletes at the secular universities. . . . But I'm encouraged at the progress we're making."

He goes on to relate how he's working with circulation director Tom and advertising/marketing director Fred to get *Christian Jock* into the black.

"This is my first experience with a start-up magazine and it's exciting," he says.

They talk more about the problems of launching a new publication. They agree to let the first anniversary pass without undue attention. "I'd rather wait until I'm satisfied the product is meeting the expectations of the reader. Also, we need to have a solid circulation of a hundred thousand or more. That's what Fred says it will take for him to sell enough ad space to have *Christian Jock* operating in the black."

JD pushes back his chair, "I appreciate the job you're doing, Todd. I also know that the inner office is satisfied with the progress. Your regular reports to me I pass on to them."

Bud is assistant editor of *Christian Jock*. He has been with Evergreen for a year after graduating from a university department of journalism. He began at *Christian Jock* as a first reader — that is, reviewing all manuscripts and recording them by author, title, and date. Under Todd's close supervision he learned the requirements of the formula established for *Christian Jock*. Todd had seen that notices of the editorial needs of the new publication were sent to all instructors of journalism at Christian colleges and also to the departments of journalism of the major universities. *Christian Author*, newsletter of the Christian Writers Institute, had carried an article on the new publication. *Writers Digest* also noted it, as had the Evangelical Press Association's publication *Liaison*. A flurry of manuscripts had followed. Only a few proved publishable, but Bud had discovered several writers who he thought could be developed.

"That's good," JD responds. "Work closely with them. Give them the opportunity of taking assignments. But be sure to impress on them that we want good writing as well as usable ideas. And above all, accurate reporting. *Christian Jock* is a new magazine. We want to get off on the right foot by producing a publication that is not only a bright idea but also one that honors the Lord by being well written and well edited."

Todd nods. "I believe Bud has the idea, JD. But he does need some help. You know, we've got only one other person as a typist besides Mary. That means Bud and I are often pretty well snowed under."

By eleven o'clock all are back at their desks. JD is putting the last of a stack of papers into his briefcase before heading for the airport. He has already given his secretary her last instructions when the telephone rings.

"Yes, Mr. Carter," he says, "I'm just getting ready to leave."

Carter, president and publisher of Evergreen was in his early sixties. He had inherited his position from his father-in-law, now deceased, who had started Evergreen after his conversion to Christ as a young newspaper editor. His father-in-law had always said that his objective was to bring to the Christian community the same type of informative, timely, and well-written publications that the secular public enjoyed. The way had not been easy. He had discovered the Christian public slow to be willing to pay the same price for its Christian magazines and books that it paid for the secular material it so readily accepted. But he had persevered, and the publishing house had prospered under him. Then his daughter had married young Carter, an enterprising editor of a small daily newspaper. After watching him a few years, the old man invited Carter to join the staff of Evergreen Publishing House. As Carter often said later, "That was the smartest move I ever made in my life — next to accepting Christ as my Savior and marrying my beautiful wife."

Now Carter is speaking to JD. "I know you're joining your wife on the Cape for a vacation. You'll have a good time, and I trust you'll enjoy good weather also. At the same time you mentioned you will be talking to several prospects for our editorial staff. I'm glad. I encourage you to encourage them with the possibilities in Christian journalism. You know as well as I do, JD, that the possibilities in Christian journalism are unlimited — that is, for good Christian journalists. It's too bad that so many of the publications in the Christian marketplace have had to accept men and women with little training and no experience. But by holding our standards high, perhaps we can encourage more of these young people to realize how important it is — not just to be Christian writers, but capable and professional Christian journalists. . . . Now have a good trip. Greet your good wife for me, and blessings on you and your family."

JD smiles as he puts down the phone. *What a great Christian publisher Carter is*, he thinks. *No wonder the Lord put his blessing on the books and magazines that Evergreen produces.*

A Fast-Breaking Story

It's three o'clock on Friday afternoon. Bill slams the receiver down. "Wow!" he exclaims to nobody in particular. Then he calls to his secretary, "Betty, the biggest story the Christian public has ever heard is in the making. I'll tell you about it later. Call George and Todd and tell them I've got to see them immediately."

Moments later Bill rushed into George's office where Todd had already joined him.

"You won't believe it," Bill begins. "I just got a tip on the biggest news that has hit evangelical Christianity since Luther nailed his theses to the Wittenberg door."

"And I've never seen you so excited, Bill." Todd says, "Tell us about it."

Bill explains that he has just received a tip from a very reliable source that two of the wealthiest young men in Christian circles have gotten together on a plan to bring together a consortium of independent Christian colleges and one of the most prestigious evangelical seminaries to form a Christian university complete with a seminary. The schools have already agreed to sell their campuses and move to a beautiful site of fifteen hundred acres in the rolling hills of Brown County in southern Indiana. So impressive is the plan that four smaller evangelical denominations have tentatively agreed to close down their schools and name the new university as the choice for their denominations.

"I've heard of similar plans like this before," George cautions. "What makes you think this has any more possibilities for success, Bill?"

"I don't blame you for being skeptical. But this sounds for real. You both know these two men. They are not novices. My source says they have already committed themselves to more than a billion dollars to launch this project. With their brains and money — and the remarkable cooperation they appear to have gotten already — I don't see how it can fail."

Todd looks up from the pad on which he was writing quickly, "Certainly sounds interesting, Bill, but what are we supposed to do about it?"

"That's why I've asked you two to tell me what I should do. My source says that if I will come to Los Angeles, he will give me the complete scoop. He and his firm have been named to head up public relations for the project. I could get a plane out of here tonight and be in Los Angeles to meet with my source the first thing tomorrow morning. We would have a whole day for me to get all the details and still be back in the office to meet my Monday-morning deadline."

George's response is immediate. "It sounds good to me, and I like your idea of getting on it quickly."

Todd looks up from the pad on which he is now doodling. "It certainly is a remarkable development. And I agree with you, George, that Bill is to be commended for having gotten an inside track on the story. However, I can't believe the source won't talk with anyone else before he arrives. Probably he has already tipped off the Los Angeles Times religion writer as well as a dozen other newspapers around the country. Not to mention Christian TV and radio stations."

Bill replies slowly, "I suppose that's so. But we'd still have the jump in the religious print media."

"That's true," Todd says. "But it seems to me on a story like this that the real impact you could make would be with an in-depth treatment of the subject including interviews with some of the principles involved."

"Todd is probably right," George interjects. "Why wouldn't it be better to call your source back and get the basic information to run a short article now. Later you could give it the in-depth treatment Todd suggests."

After further discussion the three agree that this would be the best policy. As the conference breaks up, Bill stops at the door.

"Thanks for your counsel. It was good. As a matter of fact, I realize now, this is the same counsel I give my stringers when they send in news items. Often it is better for them — and for me — if, rather than rushing an item to me, they take another day and get the necessary background material to make the item worthwhile. After all, *Christian News* is on a weekly schedule. We just can't compete with television, radio, or even the daily newspapers."

Choices Can Be Difficult

True to his word, JD called in several days after his departure. George and Todd joined him on a conference line, and they talked about one of the prospects JD had interviewed. He was graduating from a Christian college the coming June and wanted to enter the field of Christian publications . His education and experience were unique. He had taken all of the courses in writing and journalism that the college had to offer. In addition, during the summer he had enrolled in journalism classes at the state university. In high school he had edited the school newspaper and done the same at college. Moreover, his grades in college were excellent.

"This fellow sounds as if he has just about everything we want," said George. "What's more, his father is the pastor of one of the largest evangelical churches in the state."

George and Todd went to the company cafeteria after their telephone conversation with JD. I'll admit it all sounds great," agreed Todd. "The only thing that bothers me is JD had nothing to say about the young man's commitment to Jesus Christ." They had fallen silent over their coffee cups when Jill stopped at their table.

"Is the Evergreen Company's think tank in action, or is it possible for a mere plebeian to intrude?"

"We were just waiting for some real inspiration to come along," responded Todd. "Sit down and unload on us."

Jill explained her problem. In the morning's mail she had received invitations to speak at two different schools to groups interested in journalism. One was a Christian college with a long history of developing graduates in music, art, and education. However, despite Mr. Carter's efforts to encourage an interest in writing and journalism, no courses were available.

Now the picture appeared to be changing. The dean, in response to the demands of a number of senior women on campus, was throwing his weight behind a three-day seminar on Christian journalism. Two other speakers were well-known authors. He was asking Jill to represent a Christian publisher with special emphasis on the opportunity in Christian journalism for women.

"That certainly is encouraging," said Todd. "We've already got several young people in our editorial division who have graduated from the school. But they came with no classroom training in journalism. It's been a long pull to bring them to the point where they're making the contribution we need."

"Where did the other invitation come from," asked George?

Jill held out an impressive looking letter from the state university. "I'm a little bit overwhelmed at this," she said. "It's from the head of the department of journalism inviting me to participate in a round-table discussion on women in journalism. As you can see, I'm only one of a number of women. But the others are better known than I — and probably far better speakers than I will ever be."

"Orchids to you!" exclaimed George. "Not everyone gets an invitation like that. Seems to me there's little question of which invitation to accept."

"That's the problem," ruefully admitted Jill. "I'd like to do both, but they come at the same time."

Todd returned from the dispenser with a cup of coffee for Jill, "Calm your nerves with this," he said, "and let's consider all the possibilities."

In the discussion that followed, the three considered the merits of the invitation from the university. Clearly, it would be an opportunity to represent Evergreen Publishing House and other Christian publishers as well. And there would be the possibility that some of the young people present would be potential candidates for staff positions at Evergreen. They also recognized that these young peple would probably be some of the best-prepared candidates for such positions. The temptation to respond to this invitation was real.

On the other hand, although the Christian college campus was certainly not as prestigious, if the number present at the sessions were the same, there would likely be more true believers at the Christian college. Also, the long-range effect of being able to encourage the administration to offer classes in journalism and writing would certainly be beneficial for the entire Christian community. Evergreen was only one of many Christian publishers that today needed committed young people trained in the field of Christian journalism. And the fact that Jill had been selected to represent the Christian publishing field was significant in itself.

In the end, they agreed that while the state university assignment might be more exciting at the present, for the benefit of all concerned the opportunity to encourage a Christian college to become involved in preparing young people for the ministry of Christian writing would have a more long-range significance.

"Thank you, gentlemen," said Jill rising. "You've helped me resolve a difficult decision in the way I believe is most pleasing to the Lord."

Getting the Most Out of an Idea

It was 9:30 Wednesday morning. George had just told his secretary to take all of the incoming phone calls. "I want to concentrate on thinking through how to handle our upcoming feature on the revival movement in Africa," he explained. "And I need to do it without interruption."

"But I've just had calls from Jerry in circulation and Tom in advertising. Both of them want to talk to you about the African series."

"Well, OK, I might as well get their thoughts on it as well," responded George, "It may help me in planning the series from their perspective."

When the men got together, they discussed George's two-part serial from every possible angle. Jerry explained that he did not contemplate another large mailing like the one that had brought in twenty thousand new subscribers. But he did want his promotional people to get out notices of the upcoming series to some of the more missionary-minded churches on their lists. Also, he felt it was important to publicize the series with posters and fliers at the top seminaries, Christian colleges, and Christian bookstores.

"In fact," said Jerry, "if you can get me photocopies of the pages from the first installment I would like to send them out with a letter to some of the top leaders in the evangelical community. Perhaps we could get comments from them as to what they see as the world-wide significance of this renewal."

"I like that idea," responded George. "In fact, if their comments are significant enough, perhaps we could use them as a sidebar with the second installment."

Up to this point Tom had remained silent. "It's great to see how you fellows can coordinate your activities between circulation and editorial," he said. "As you know, we sell advertising on the basis of each issue and try not to depend on special editorial emphasis. But this series seems so significant to me that I've been trying to think of some way we could contribute to it without appearing to take advantage from a financial point of view."

In the discussion that followed, the three men discussed the merits of Tom's policy and agreed it was good. At the same time, George pointed out it was important for the mission agencies with work in Africa to identify themselves with the renewal in every way possible. Hence he wondered if there was some way that Tom could inform them of the upcoming series with the suggestion that their mission boards acknowledge the revival and report their participation in it with institutional advertising. It was decided to leave the matter up to Tom.

At the same session it was noted that the company policy called for 50 percent of the content of *Hosanna* to be advertising, and 50 percent editorial. Tom pointed out that this was possible largely because *Hosanna* was a monthly magazine, and the same proportion applied to Evergreen's two other monthlies: *Priscilla* and *Christian Jock.* Admittedly though, *Christian Jock* as a new publication hadn't yet been able to reach its budget in this respect. As a result, editorial was getting more like 60 percent of the space because advertising hadn't yet been able to clearly define the market.

By contrast, Pete's bimonthly *Gangle* and Bill's weekly *Christian News* were pretty much locked in to a 40 percent advertising and 60 percent editorial formula because of their higher frequency of publication. Meanwhile, Frank's quarterly *Bible Study* sometimes carried as much as 80 percent advertising. But it was all positioned at the opening and closing of the book so that the Bible study material editorial carried through uninterrupted.

They also acknowledged the fact that Evergreen's aggressive advertising sales program was necessary because Evergreen was an independent publishing house and depended altogether on financing its program directly from the publications themselves. By contrast, denominational publishing houses operated on far less a percentage of advertising — often only 15 to 20 percent. The difference in the cost of operation was made up by the denomination itself.

"I know some people object to advertising," observed Tom. "But I don't understand why. The products and services presented on our pages provide helpful service to our readers. They should be happy to know about them and appreciate the service that suppliers, publishers, colleges, and so forth, provide through their advertising. We're careful, as are most Christian publications, to screen out objectionable ads. Yet I have to admit that we often print advertisements that are in poor taste because we don't have time to check on them adequately.

Turning to Jerry, Tom said, "This may sound like a naïve question, but approximately what percentage of the income necessary to operate *Hosanna* comes from circulation?"

"Of course, it varies, Tom," replied Jerry, "but with our five paid-circulation publications, rule of thumb says circulation income should pay the cost of printing the magazine. All other costs — overhead, salaries, insurance, mailing costs, and so on, plus whatever profits we can make — must come from advertising income. But with our semicontrolled circulation magazine *Bible Study* it will amount to 20 percent or less."

(By controlled circulation, Jerry meant that the magazine was sent without charge to a list of pastors, key seminary professors, and denominational executives — a highly specialized market. Persons not included in that list could subscribe to a magazine if they wished. As a result, the big burden for financing the publication fell on advertising to provide income to finance the editorial pages.)

A Word from the Inner Office

One morning about a week after JD had left, both George and Todd received a call from Mr. Carter's secretary. "Mr. Carter would like to see you in his office at ten this morning. Nothing serious, he simply wants to know how you are getting along."

When the two men appeared, Mr. Carter welcomed them warmly. "I have your coffee here," he said, motioning to two cups at either end of his desk. "Will you have cream and sugar?"

With his coffee cup in hand, Mr. Carter began. "JD tells me he has left you two men in charge of the editorial division. And from everything I hear, you are doing well in handling it. I appreciate that. Because of the key positions you hold at Evergreen, I want you well informed on what is happening here. I don't know whether you've heard the rumor or not, but I understand that it has gotten around the industry that we are branching out from print journalism. . . ."

Putting his cup down quickly, Todd interposed, "You mean, Mr. Carter. . . ."

Mr. Carter laughed easily, "Not so fast, Todd. My answer is yes and no. Yes, to the extent that you already know production has experimented with several Evergreen books on tape. The latest development is that production is working on three children's titles on video cassettes. But no more than that — at least for the present."

"That's great news," said Todd. "I'm sure we'll be successful in it. But I'd also like to see us do something with the other editorial material we also are producing. Like a Christian news television program featuring all the great stuff Bill is digging up for *Christian News* magazine. Also I believe the format Jill has created with *Priscilla* magazine would make an excellent woman's TV program. . . ."

"You may be right, and we don't want to ignore anything the Lord is saying to us," said Mr. Carter. "These are exciting days in the Christian world. The Lord is using many ways and means by which to communicate the good news of Jesus Christ. And He expects us to be alert to every opportunity he opens to us."

After a few words of encouragement Mr. Carter dismissed the two men. On their way back to their offices Todd observed, "I sure appreciate

Mr. Carter's vision. He may be a print-media man at heart, but he certainly keeps up-to-date with what's happening in other areas."

A Publicist in Action

One day after lunch George received a call from Evelyn, "George," she said, "I appreciate your sending me those proof sheets on the first installment of your African feature. In fact, I'm very much interested in the possibility of doing a book — a quickie I would call it — incorporating the two-part series with a more lengthy than usual introduction and perhaps an epilogue by some authorities on the mission situation there. Would you be good enough to join me and our publicist, Marge, to discuss those possibilities. . . . Let's say at three this afternoon?"

"I'll be glad to, Evelyn. Count on me at three."

When they met in Evelyn's office, George brought along the original manuscript pages from part two. "Sorry about these. They are in a pretty rough state. But I thought you would like to see them now, before they go to the word processor for the final draft."

As the discussion proceeded it became apparent they were faced with a problem. George had scheduled the two-part series on African revival for the June and July issues of *Hosanna* magazine. Normally a book taken from a publication or periodical would not appear until after the editorial had first appeared in the magazine. That would mean Evelyn's book could not be announced until after the annual convention of the Christian Booksellers Association the second week in July. To miss having her book at the Evergreen booth at the convention could mean a loss of many thousands of copies of sales.

Then the publicist, Marge, spoke up. "I have an idea, George. Suppose you were to announce in the July issue that this book is in production and will be exhibited at the Christian Booksellers Association convention. That would give us the opportunity of getting into the marketplace at the proper time but would not make it available to the retail trade until August when book stores would have had the opportunity to stock it."

"I like that idea," said George. "This would not take any of the luster off our series. Indeed, it might even enhance it with the idea that the book will be available later with some additional information — as Evelyn suggests — with her longer introduction and epilogue. I think that might work. . . . What else did you have in mind, Marge?"

"Well, I'd like to have the names of the men I have heard you are going to send advance copies of the first installment to. I would like to contact them for permission to use pertinent extracts from their comments in our advertising and promotion of the book."

"That's good thinking," observed Evelyn. "We can also use some of those quotes on the book jacket itself. We've not done very many quickies, so this will give us a good idea on how to handle such a production."

"Then there's radio and TV," continued Marge. "Spots are easy to produce, and we'll do them for Christian radio stations. But I'm not so sure we can do very much with TV. If we had a single author who was well known in the Christian community and enjoyed some exposure in the secular marketplace it might work, but. . . ."

"Hold on," exclaimed George. "Apparently you don't recognize the name of our author. Not only is he a well-known missionary and an authority on Africa, but recently he was named by the president of the United States to head up a commission to study the needs of African nations desiring to make their governments more democratic in nature."

"Wow!" said Marge. "That's all I need. We're off to the races. . . ."

The Importance of Free-lance Writers

At home one evening after the children were in bed, Todd sat down in the living room with his wife, Betty. "When we were first married, you used to do free-lance writing. With Evergreen's new magazine *Christian Jock* I'm struggling to find good free-lance writers. Do you have any suggestions on how I might attract them?"

"Yes I do, but you don't want to hear them."

"What do you mean, I don't want to hear them? I'm so short of good free-lance writers I need to listen to anybody — even my wife," replied Todd with a laugh.

"Well, my answer is too simple. Just pay them more money. . . . But seriously, writers appreciate being recognized for their ability. Money, or more of it, is one way to do that. But it isn't the only way. I know that you operate on an editorial budget, so there's a limit to what you can pay."

"That's true," said Todd. "And I know I can't expect the editorial budget to be increased until we get the magazine on a solid basis with more advertising and a larger circulation base."

Betty continued, "But there are other ways to show appreciation to authors, Todd. One of them is to report promptly on their manuscripts. Every free-lance writer goes from one idea to another. Seldom does he or she work on more than two manuscripts at the same time. And if he has to wait four or five months for a response from an editor, he's inclined to become discouraged and critical of that editor."

"I see what you mean. And I certainly can agree with you. We try to report now within a month. But maybe we can step that up and report in a week or two. We have some writers who are good enough to make it worth the extra effort. In fact, I'll make that a policy tomorrow. Thanks, Betty."

"Another thing you might do would to be inform them of your needs in the months ahead so that they would have something to be thinking about. Remember, free-lance writers often think of an editor as an ogre intent only on sending them rejection slips. But when they discover you are an ordinary person and have needs that they can supply, you might be surprised how much more productive they could become."

Before Betty and Todd had finished their discussion Todd had brought out his indispensable yellow pad and filled a page with ideas on how to increase the interest of free-lance writers in his publication.

Important in his list was an item in photography. He would encourage his free-lancers to get a good camera and learn how to operate it. Then he would encourage them to take pictures whenever they went after a story. An interviewee, for instance, should be photographed not only sitting in a chair, but also doing the things he would do as a part of his everyday life. Here, as well as in the writing itself, he would encourage quality of production. Photographs are simply not acceptable if they are fuzzy or poorly exposed. The best way to overcome this, he would point out, would be to practice taking pictures of family members or friends. Experiment in posing them in different positions to evoke interest in the photograph itself. Look through photograph magazines to see how experts do it — also in general-circulation publications that use photographs.

He would also encourage his free-lance writers to concentrate on improving their writing. They could do this either by attending seminars or by reading books on writing. Probably even more helpful would be to encourage them to take courses in writing practice such as the Christian Writers Institute, where their manuscripts would be critiqued by instructors who themselves were successful authors or editors.

"That's great," concluded Todd. "I never did very much free-lance writing in my early days, as you know. Right out of the university I went to work for a newspaper. I was kept so busy there that only once in a while did I adapt an article I had written for a magazine. And usually the subject was so hot that the other publication was quick to pick it up. I simply didn't have the experience of rejection slips."

Betty laughed. "You sure missed out on a very important aspect of the life of a writer. But don't worry. Rejection slips are what every free-lance writer would like to forget were invented."

"What most free-lance writers need to remember is that we editors are dependent on what they produce," said Todd. "In fact, we can't exist unless we have manuscripts. And few magazines can afford a large enough staff to produce their own manuscripts. The trouble is, most free-lance writers don't seem to realize that the quickest way to get their material accepted is to read their target publications over and over again. By doing so they can slant their material to meet the needs and desires of the editor."

"And to that I say amen," said Betty. 'It wasn't until I discovered that little secret that I began to sell regularly."

Art for the Readers' Sake

At coffee break one morning George sat down at a table with Jack, head of the art and production department. "I know your department is up to its neck working on the next issue of all of the publications," he said. "But I've got a project that needs some long range thinking."

"Do you mean your upcoming two-part series on spiritual renewal in Africa that I've been hearing about?" replied Jack.

"Yes, that's part of it. The other part is the possibility that Evelyn will want to tie in with a book, picking up the articles themselves and adding a bit with a longer introduction and a postscript."

"I don't usually get this much advance notice, George. Normally, we're supposed to come up at the last minute with the greatest designs and the most fantastic photographs when they are really not in evidence. What do you have in hand now?"

"We have some fair pictures of the author on location talking with several ambassadors of African nations, meeting with nationals in church or evangelistic-type meetings. But that's about all."

"Then let's get a top photographer assigned to coming up with a character-style photograph of the author. I hope he's available in this country for such a picture."

"Yes, but we'll have to catch him on the run. He moves about a great deal."

"That's okay. If you'll let me see the other pictures you have on hand, I'll be able to tell whether or not we need more on location. Do you have anything that sets the mood for Africa or revival?"

"I'm not exactly sure I know what you mean, but I doubt it. I take it you're thinking of some sort of art to create a setting for the articles."

"Exactly. Often we have writers sending art work that either they or some friend has done, which they think will provide illustrative material for their article. It almost never does. In other words, only as we sit down with the editorial material and the photographs can we as artists decide what is needed to really bring the reader into the article."

"I'm glad you're taking responsibility for that," said George. "This is completely out of my ken."

While they were at it, George and Jack talked about photographs. George admitted that often his writers provided poor-quality photographs with their manuscript material. Jack had some suggestions that he thought might be helpful. He pointed out that commissioning professional photographers to take their pictures is far too expensive for a free-lancer. Most editors, including Evergreen editors, he explained, expected their writers to provide photographs. The only way a free-lancer can do that is to take his own. But he does not need to become a professional photographer in the sense that he develops his own pictures. If he gives attention to posing and to the mechanical operation of his camera — you know, exposure, distance, and so forth — he can come up with good enough pictures for reproduction. Jack also pointed out that free-lancers can often get professional-quality photographs from subjects they are interviewing or organizations whom they query or write about. These photographs usually are free of charge with the simple stipulation that they be returned after they have been used. Evergreen, of course, he said, is always glad to return photographs to an author when he requests them. He also added that whenever a writer sends in photographs with a manuscript, he should put his name and address on the back of the photograph just as he puts it on the pages of his manuscript.

"One other question I need to ask," said Jack. "Do you want a resemblance of some sort between your two-part series and the book Evelyn is producing for Evergreen books?"

"That would be an excellent idea," said George. "I believe it would help especially with the sale of the book. We know that more than a million people will be reading the issues of the magazine in which the series appears. So when they see the book, by its similarity in design to the series of articles, they may be persuaded to purchase the book also. Great idea, Jack!"

New Opportunities

It was 10 A.M. Tuesday morning again. The same morning that JD was expected to return to the office, each member of the editorial division received a call from Mr. Carter's office to report promptly for an important meeting. Now they sat uneasily, hardly knowing what to expect.

Mr. Carter began slowly, "You all know the fine job JD has done these past ten years in heading up the editorial division of Evergreen. Each of you has benefited from his training and experience. Now he is moving on to an area of greater opportunity. Over the past several days he and I have talked about an offer he recently received to become manager of his denominational publishing house. He is reluctant to leave Evergreen but believes this is what God wants him to do. I cannot disagree, for it will give him the opportunity of using his training and experience in an area where it is greatly needed. He wanted me to tell you this so that I could explain also that his successor will be picked from this group — not from the outside. JD will be in tomorrow to discuss the matters affecting your publications and to conduct your regular monthly meeting. He believes matters are well enough in order so that he will be able to leave within a month. Meanwhile, he and I will be discussing the matter of his successor," Mr. Carter said, looking around at the group before him.

"I want to commend each of you again for the fine work you have been doing in JD's absence. This is additional evidence of the fine job JD has done in training you for the important job you hold. Unless you have some questions, that's all. Thank you."

During the next two weeks speculations ran high. Many on the staff at Evergreen believed that George would be selected as JD's successor. After all, he was the editor of *Hosanna*, flagship of the publishing house.

The New Editorial Chief Is . . . .

Again it was the usual 10 A.M. meeting time of Evergreen Publishing. When Mr. Carter's voice came on the intercom, everyone knew the big announcement would be made. After a few opening remarks, Mr. Carter said, "I realize many of you have been speculating as to who the new head of the editorial division will be. Therefore, I'll not keep you waiting. He is . . .

Analysis

The foregoing scenario applies to a well-organized and well-administered independent periodical publishing house. It is probably not typical of all Christian publishing houses today, especially the smaller denominational houses. But it does provide goals toward which many should work. It also can offer a model for young men and women now entering the world of Christian periodical publishing. Their time eventually will come. When they find themselves in positions of influence and authority, the procedures outlined here may make the difference between a mediocre performance — mediocre for them and for the publishing house — and the excellence to which God calls all of us.

SUGGESTED READING

General

The Bookmakers Glossary. Compiled by Jean Peters. New York: R. R. Bowker, 1975.

Magazine Publishing Management: Practical Guide to Modern Magazine Publishing. Compiled by editors of *Folio: The Magazine for Magazine Management.* Stamford, Conn.: Folio Magazine Publishing Company, 1976.

Mogel, Leonard. *The Magazines: Everything You Need to Know to Make It in the Magazine Business.* Chester, Conn.: Globe Pequot Press, 1985.

Religious

Eaton, June, and Robert Walker. *New Guidebook to Successful Christian Writing.* Carol Stream, Ill.: Christian Writers Institute, 1990.

Franzen, Janice Gosnell. *The Adventures of Interviewing.* Carol Stream, Ill.: Christian Writers Institute, 1989.

Schultze, Quentin J., ed. *American Evangelicals and the Mass Media.* Grand Rapids: Zondervan, 1990.

Especially chapter 5, "Moving the World with Magazines: A Survey of Evangelical Periodicals," by Stephen Board, which is reprinted as chapter 25 in *Inside Religious Publishing.*

Walker, Robert. *Leads and Story Openings.* Carol Stream, Ill.: Christian Writers Institute, 1985.

Chapter 25

Moving the World with Magazines
A Survey of Evangelical Periodicals

Stephen Board

If magazines are "the interior dialogue of a society," as John F. Kennedy declared, the conversation is indeed rich and noisy. There are 111,000 periodicals around the world[1] and almost exactly one-tenth of these are in the United States.[2] While very few may be "storehouses," as the etymology of the word "magazine" implies, all promise reading of timely interest in accessible format for their audiences. Most of them benefit from preferential postage rates, a centuries-old bias in favor of keeping the interior dialogue going.

To factor by tenths once more, it appears about one-tenth of the magazines in the United States can be categorized as "religious."[3] From *Christian History*, a 1741 magazine that lasted two years, to *Christian Parenting*, which began in 1988 with higher hopes for longevity, the Protestant press has never lacked for publishing ideas.[4]

Since World War II, the evangelical scene has flourished with parachurch organizations, missions, broadcasts, and schools. Periodicals have been a major part of the growth of this venture in Christian free enterprise, breaking down old denominational barriers, introducing new leaders and ideas, and providing access by mail to numerous homes for

Stephen Board is vice-president and general manager of Harold Shaw Publishers. He has been editor of several major evangelical magazines, including *His* and *Eternity*.

ideas that the pulpit alone would never broach. The 315 current members of the Evangelical Press Association, a professional society begun in 1949, range from little more than advertising pieces to journals of record.

A Typology of Religious Magazines

Only dates, paper, and ink are necessary to call reading matter a magazine, and some taxonomy will be useful to classify the variety. If we arrange the variety of periodicals around two characteristics, we discover a matrix (fig. 1) into which, without too large a shoehorn, most of the periodicals seem to fit. The two principles are (1) the degree of sensitivity to the readership, and (2) the degree of control by an establishment, such as a denomination.

———— **From less official to more** ————▶

	Independence	Official Body	
C a u s e	The agenda is that of the vision or cause of the owner or chief supporters. I.	The agenda is that of the organization and its promotional program. II.	
D r i v e n			Increasing degree of control by readers
M a r k e t	The agenda is regulated by the subscribers or target market. IV.	The agenda is that of a constituency sharing a common membership. III.	▼

Figure 1

A position left to right charts the publication's attachment to an established body, such as a denomination or parachurch institution. An entrepreneur would be in the left corner; a church body in the right.

Up-and-down, the matrix illustrates a lesser or greater degree of deference to an audience. Toward the top are those fortunate publications that consult only their own owners, charters and passions; those toward the bottom attend more to the tastes and interests of readers. These may be consumers (left quadrant) or members (right quadrant).[5]

Now let us look at the Christian magazine world with this device (fig. 2), using examples from present and past, and see whence and whither the journalist comes.

	Independence	Official Body	
C a u s e D r i v e n M a r k e t	Examples: *The Liberator, The Presbyterian Layman, Sojourners, The Other Side,* the early *Christianity Today, Good News, Christian Beacon*	Examples: Publications that go to donors such as mission magazines — *World Vision, Possibilities, Decision, Focus on the Family, ABS Record, Abundant Life*	Increasing degree of control by readers
	Examples: The later *Christianity Today, Charisma,* the later *His (U), Christian Life, Eternity, The Christian Century, Moody Monthly, Christian Herald*	Examples: Denominational organs and alumni or scholarly magazines — *The Banner, The Church Herald, The Evangelical Beacon, CMS Journal, Journal of the American Scientific Affiliation, United Evangelical Action*	

Figure 2

Tracts for the Times: Publishing for a Cause

The independently owned advocacy publishers promote and combat ideas. This is propaganda in the best and worst senses of the word. They face the world with a message, pay for its dissemination, and submit gladly to the abuse that has fallen on prophets throughout history. William Lloyd Garrison's *Public Liberator and Journal of the Times,* begun in 1831, announced the tradition:

> I will be as harsh as truth, and as uncompromising as justice. On this subject [of slavery] I do not wish to think, or speak, or write, with moderation . . . I am in earnest — I will not equivocate — I will not excuse — I will not retreat a single inch — AND I *WILL* BE HEARD.[6]

The "cause" may be antiabortion, antialcohol, anticommunism, antislavery. Less commonly has there been a cause promoting a positive message, even evangelism.[7]

Among modern publications in evangelical circles, I would surely put here the now-defunct *Moral Majority Report* (Jerry Falwell) with eight hundred thousand free circulation at its peak, and *Focus on the Family* (James Dobson) with 1.1 million. Likewise the *Christian Beacon*, Carl McIntire's weekly, has crusaded for separatism and anticommunism.

A number of conservative protest publications within denominations have left their marks. *The Presbyterian Journal* (1941–1987) advocated conservative theology in the Southern Presbyterian Church and was finally instrumental in the founding of a secessionist body, the Presbyterian Church in America (1973). A similar Methodist voice, *Good News*, has given a monthly "forum for biblical Christianity" to the nation's second largest Protestant denomination. *The New Oxford Review* began as a voice for conservative Episcopalians, evolving later into a de facto Roman Catholic voice. The early *Christianity Today* was very much an advocacy publication.

Billy Graham was the organizing force behind *Christianity Today*, drawing in a number of evangelical leaders in the mid-fifties. And its first editor, as early as 1946, voiced the tones of the publisher-with-a-cause in a letter to Wilbur Smith.

> The hour is ripe for an evangelical magazine. My hope is that when such a magazine is launched, it will center attention on the great essentials that we may be hammering away at the main enemy fortresses and not at our own outposts which some extremists of conservative convictions themselves may be holding. Perhaps it could display enough editorial acumen to permit reprinting of certain articles each year in book form by appropriate assignment of contributions.[8]

The Presbyterian Layman, one of at least two efforts funded by J. Howard Pew, the chairman of Sun Oil, with a free circulation as high as four hundred thousand, has been a monthly for exposure and complaint in the United Presbyterian denomination (now Presbyterian Church, USA). The same benefactor contributed heavily to the early years of *Christianity Today*. Mr. Pew felt that a publication for the nation's clergy could persuade and restore them to a conservative view, theologically and socially, and that as the clergy went, so went the church. Consequently, the early years of this "fortnightly of evangelical conviction" (C.T.) were heavily subsidized to enable the publication to go to well over two hundred thousand Protestant clergyman free from 1956 to the early sixties.

Sojourners (1968) and *The Other Side* (1965) were born out of the sixties' peace and civil rights movements, respectively. While never heavily funded or widely promoted, they enjoyed a de facto subsidy through very modestly compensated staff and some donations from sympathetic subscribers. In the seventies they turned more toward antinuclear and feminist messages.

In this category also are the periodicals that grow up around personalities. John R. Rice's *Sword of the Lord* and Donald Grey Barnhouse's *Revelation*[9] and his early *Eternity*[10] were personality cult products dealing with subjects in each man's range of interests. The cause was the man. Circulation was welcomed but the magazines ignored the ups and downs.[11]

Advocacy publications tend to have short life spans — usually related to their cause or their editor — but their public recognition and even secular acclaim are far beyond their paid circulations. "Hammering away at enemy fortresses," focusing on a common foe, these are magazines of noble effort, like Garrison's *Liberator*. They also can become publications of demagoguery, sectarianism, and character assassination. They represent the best and worst of the first amendment.

Official Promotion: From Hype to Ministry

Moving across the matrix, we come to officially sponsored publications that advocate an organization, a mission, or a charity. There is still a cause but it is more the growth and survival of a program than a set of ideas. Some of these publications are a species of advertising; others are almost consumer magazines. All have in common the absence of a clear marketplace test of their readers' loyalty, since they tend to be free, or virtually free, to the readers. They accept no advertising and are not available in normal subscription channels.

The most ready examples are the mission magazines, sent monthly to remind donors of the ongoing activity of the mission. Fund raisers have learned that voluntary support of a charity requires frequent reminders of that organization's continuing need and existence. The oldest mission magazine still published is surely the *American Bible Society Record*, begun in 1865. *World Vision*, with a million circulation, is a more recent example.

Closer to consumer magazines are *Decision*, the monthly magazine of evangelism and Christian living from the Billy Graham organization, with two million in circulation, and *Possibilities*, a bi-monthly of the Robert Schuller organization with a circulation of eight hundred thousand. Both are sent free to donors (*Decision* has a nominal five-dollar subscription price) and both contain editorial content that supports the theology and ministry of the sponsors. Oral Roberts' *Abundant Life* is another magazine. Promotional of their organizations, all these magazines regard their role as an extension of a total ministry.

Nonprofit organizations, including colleges, missions, and para-church agencies, have invariably felt they needed a regular vehicle of communication for their constituency. But such publications have rarely enjoyed a shared sense of dialogue and community like the paid-for magazines in the lower half of the matrix. They rarely permit letters to the editor critical of the institution or publication; consequently the readers feel little ownership in the publication and may treat it like any other promotional mailing.[12]

Members and Their Friends: House Organs

Moving down the chart, we arrive at official publications that give their readers more of a vote in the product. This is the lower right quadrant. An alumni or fraternity magazine would be the perfect example. In the religious field, denominational magazines usually function as official communication with a membership, even if they sell subscriptions and even if they propagandize for the home office. Glenn Arnold reports that before the Civil War each major Protestant denomination had at least twenty periodicals; the Congregationalists had twenty-five.[13]

Church house organs and denominational vehicles are somewhat akin to officially sponsored donor magazines, but they demonstrate a greater deference to a reading audience. They usually require formal subscriptions, but sometimes those subscriptions are garnered in anonymous collectivities like "every home" programs for churches to give every family a subscription for a flat fee. This tends to diminish the quality of readership and discounts the size of circulation accordingly.[14] Advertising has never been a significant part of the income of this category of publication. None of the denominational magazines has existed without some subsidy from its sponsors.

Among the largest of the official denominational magazines in the Evangelical Press Association are *The Lutheran Standard*, the voice of the former American Lutheran Church (now a part of the Evangelical Lutheran Church), with a circulation of 550,000. The Assemblies of God's *Pentecostal Evangel*, with 287,000, and the Church of the Nazarene's *Herald of Holiness* (170,000) follow. Most in the category report circulation in the range of a few thousand (*Conservative Baptist*, 7,000) to well under a hundred thousand (*The Banner* of the Christian Reformed Church, 48,000).

This is a day of rather small, narrowly focused magazines. As recent as the 1950s, the denominational organs of the Methodists and Presbyterians boasted circulations in the vicinity of one million. But the Methodist *Together* (1956–1975) went from 900,000 and ceased. *Presbyterian Life* has also gone through some evolution, first as *A.D.* and now as a much smaller *Presbyterian Survey*. The American Baptist *Crusader* went from 375,000 in the early 1970s to a new format, *The American Baptist*, with about 150,000 in circulation.

The nation's two largest Protestant denominations presently have no single periodical. Neither the Southern Baptist Convention nor the United Methodist Church, among their numerous periodicals from numerous church agencies, speaks in print with a single voice. The independent *United Methodist Reporter*, published from Dallas as a news weekly for the Methodist communion, functions for many congregations as their church paper; but it has maintained an uneasy independence toward the church agencies and takes no consistent theological stand.

A semi-independent periodical from the past was the *Watchman-Examiner* (1819–1964).[15] A professed Baptist weekly, it nonetheless was not the official voice for any one denomination and should be regarded as close to a consumer magazine. Its most notable contribution was to coin the term "fundamentalist" in 1920, referring to those who sided with the ideas in *The Fundamentals*. In 1964, when the *Watchman-Examiner* folded, its remaining ten thousand subscribers merged with *Eternity*. (As for *Eternity*, not a denominational magazine, its own circulation in the 1980s declined from some fifty thousand to some twenty thousand, and it ceased publication in January 1989).[16]

Church house organs are the magazines of obituaries, conventions, and anniversaries. They love nostalgia, old school ties, in language, pillars of the church, sacred cows, and taboos. In earlier sectarian days, church organs were known for strident cross denominational attacks. Today, in a more ecumenical age, many still engage in lively debate within the rules of the club. Their editorial quality varies with their editors and the support of their sponsors.[17]

Another kind of membership periodical deserves attention: the scholarly or professional journal. Although these have been few in the Christian field, several stand out as remarkably influential. *The Princeton Theological Review* during its history (1829–1931)[18] rendered profound leadership in the field of academic theology. Almost all of what we now esteem from the pen of B. B. Warfield appeared first in that journal. It never exceeded a few thousand in circulation,[19] but it interacted with the intellectual ferments of the day and was regarded by one contemporary as "the most powerful organ in America."[20] Its readership was chiefly among the educated clergy, first of whom were the alumni of "old Princeton."

Among modern evangelical periodicals of a scholarly nature, we could mention *The Journal of the American Scientific Affiliation* (a membership publication of Christians in science), *The Journal of The Evangelical Theological Society*, *The Christian Scholar's Review*, and the journals of seminaries — *Concordia*, *Westminster*, *Asbury Theological Journal*, and *Bibliotheca Sacra*. The last, published by Dallas Theological Seminary since 1934, traces its history to 1844. None of these has a circulation that exceeds ten thousand, but each serves a crucial role for its constituency.

Consumer Magazines

Most of us find the consumer magazines the most interesting of all, in part, perhaps, because they seem to be an instant readout of public opinion. Their subscribers are voluntary. To know the circulation of *Playboy*, *National Review*, or *Charisma* is to know something about the interest and values of our society. These readers have chosen and paid for a distinct periodic visitor to their homes, identifying themselves with social movements and styles of life.

When we identify a publication as "market driven" we do not mean it defers to all potential subscribers everywhere; rather, it attends to the interests of those subscribers within its chosen market. *Moody Monthly* is sensitive to the Moody market, *The Wittenburg Door* (now *The Door*) to *The Wittenburg Door* market, and so on. The editorial goals of a magazine thus link with a defined group of magazine readers. Those publications we are calling "consumer" are those that function in a commercial relationship with their defined market. And if their chosen market is not pleased with their product, the magazine is shortly out of business. This is not the case with the publications higher on the chart that are more promotional in purpose. The period following World War II has been especially rich with consumer magazines, including a variety of new religious ones. I begin, however, with three that trace their ancestry to the nineteenth century.

The Sunday School Times (1859–1967) carried the torch for popular evangelical piety throughout the Protestant denominations. It was a voice for both premillennial interpretation of the Bible and the "Keswick" or victorious life approach to sanctification.[21] A weekly, the Philadelphia-based *Times* offered teacher aids for the Uniform Lesson series used by many of the larger denominations. Its teaching aids created for it a certain necessity in the lives of its subscribers — an element rarely present in religious magazines. It also gave it an audience in church circles that would otherwise have been closed to its distinctive theology. Though the *Sunday School Times* began with the American Sunday School Union, it was purchased by John Wanamaker, the Philadelphia department store entrepreneur, in 1871. By 1876 it had a circulation of one hundred thousand.[22] By comparison, *The Atlantic* had a circulation during that era of no more than fifty thousand,[23] and even the *Saturday Evening Post*, the various *Harpers*, and other periodicals did not exceed the circulation of the *Times*.

The editors of the *Times* were widely esteemed: H. Clay Trumbull (editor from 1875–1903), his son Charles G. Trumbull,[24] Charles's nephew Philip Howard, Sr., and his successor, Philip Howard, Jr.[25]

A strategic blunder occurred in the history of the *Times* in the late 1940s. Under criticism from the fundamentalist right, chiefly Carl McIntire, the *Times* was pushed into dropping the Uniform Lesson series, which was tainted by its Federal Council of Churches sponsorship. Following great subscriber protest, the magazine resumed these lessons a short time later. But the confidence in the Uniform Lessons among conservatives was shaken, while Scripture Press lessons and other alternatives were gaining ground in the curriculum field. The key selling point for this century-old weekly was thus mortally wounded. Its circulation, which had exceeded one hundred thousand, declined in the 1960s to fifty thousand. Advertising income had never been significant, and after an abortive effort to merge with *Eternity*, the prestigious name of the *Sunday School Times* was sold to Union Gospel Press, where it lost its identity in a merger with their *Gospel Herald*, a Sunday school devotional magazine.

Another general audience weekly, the *Christian Herald*, began in 1878 as a branch of the English evangelical scene. Early leadership and articles were from Charles Spurgeon, A. J. Gordon, and A. T. Pierson. Among its distinctives at the turn of the century were its editorial commitment to progressive social legislation, such as labor and immigration laws, and its emphasis on world peace. Circulation exceeded 250,000[26] in 1910. The charities of the organization, including a rescue mission in the Bowery and an orphanage, early gave the magazine a humanitarian, trustworthy image.

The *Christian Herald* decreased its emphasis on prophetic themes and refused to side with the fundamentalists during the 1920s when Charles M. Sheldon, author of *In His Steps*, was the editor. Jesus, Sheldon declared, would not have participated in the fundamentalist debates.[27] The peak years for New York-based *Christian Herald* came during the editorship of Daniel Poling, in the 1930s through the 1950s. Circulation reportedly hit a half million[28] with a regularly claimed advertising base of four hundred thousand. Newsstand and "agency" services generated the vast subscription flow.[29] A weekly until 1930, the magazine was frequently mentioned in the same company with other mass audience general magazines like *Life*.

Dan Poling, who ran for mayor of Philadelphia in the early 1950s, was an institution in himself. He embodied a mainline, mildly conservative Protestantism, without a doctrinaire style. His magazine sometimes had a "Church in the Wildwood" generality to it; it honored few of the taboos of the fundamentalist movement (in the 1950s it carried movie reviews but always sided with the temperance movement) and was not regarded as a champion of the evangelical cause by the conservatives of post-World War II. Some called it liberal.

Today the magazine survives with a chastened circulation of under 150,000, considered its "natural level" by the present management, whose evangelical credentials cannot be doubted. It now considers its closest competitor to be *Moody Monthly*.

That magazine of Chicago's Moody Bible Institute dates from 1900, when it evolved from *The Institute Tie*, an alumni magazine. It grew to a circulation of 19,431 by 1921 in its search for a ministry among lay Christians in the Moody circle of influence. Advertising, including promotion of competing schools, aromatic toothpicks, and fountain pens, gave it the consumer magazine appearance.[30] The editorial emphasis of this periodical has always been Christian living for the laity, with the boundaries defined largely by the constituency of the Moody organization. As an announced "family" magazine, it has included some fare for children, youth, and homemakers.

The *Moody Monthly* of the 1970s became a formidable competitor for advertising and subscribers. With a heavy investment on the part of the school, plus the use of direct mail solicitations offering a subscription with a premium book, the circulation hit three hundred thousand. There was talk of possibly reaching five hundred thousand subscriptions. Today the magazine has a list of two hundred thousand subscribers and is considered one of the few profitable Christian periodicals.[31] Like Moody Press, it earns a profit for the school.

Though *Moody Monthly* is a consumer magazine, it carries its institutional sponsorship as a visible blessing and burden. Not strictly promotional of Moody Bible Institute, it nonetheless observes the school's taboos, cultivates its image, and attends to its market. On the matrix chart, *Moody Monthly* is close to the center — just inside the market-driven, consumer quadrant, but within sight of the publications that promote something official.

The most aggressive growth since World War II has been among the smaller publications that have brought journalism school expertise to the Christian press. In the period of the forties and fifties, a variety of magazine experiments were tried, such as the *Christian Digest*, the *Christian Newsette*, and the *Christian Life and Times*. The last of these came under the control of a Northwestern journalism graduate named Robert Walker. A recent convert himself, he saw no reason why the Christian community could not have a commercially successful magazine, sold by subscription and supported up to 50 percent by advertising. In 1948 he turned a digest-sized Sunday school publication into a contemporary format and began promoting it in the parachurch markets of the evangelicals. "We had no economic model for what we were doing," Walker recalls.[32] He aimed for a fifty-fifty split of advertising and circulation, settling for thirty-seventy. His entrepreneurial ambitions, if not business necessity, generated a family of related magazines such as the *Christian Bookseller* (1955) for retail bookstores, *Choice* (an advertising vehicle for bookstores, 1957–59), and a magazine for camps and conferences.

A number of organizational publications grew beyond their borders to become significant players in the larger picture. Chief among these was *Youth for Christ Magazine* (1944), which became *Campus Life* (1965). Originally a house organ for the organization, "YFC Magazine" was promoted in the Saturday night rallies of the teen evangelism movement. By the late sixties it had evolved into an influential independent product for youth and those concerned about them. Its role as a promoter of Christian colleges is unmeasurable. On a smaller scale, *His* (1941) grew from a house organ of InterVarsity Christian Fellowship to an independent monthly for college students and alumni. As a source of lay-level apologetics it filled a niche unfilled elsewhere. With never more than thirty or forty thousand subscribers, the magazine struggled to an end in 1988, after attempting a name change to *U* in a final marketing move.

The launch of *Christianity Today* in 1956 marked an audacious and remarkably successful experiment in religious magazines. As noted previously, it grew out of Billy Graham's vision for "nothing else but the finest journal in the Western world, comparable to what *Time* is in current events."[33] *Christianity Today's* founding editor, theologian Carl F. H. Henry, valued journalistic reporting, scholarly credentials, and, most of all, serious debate.[34]

However, we must observe several key turning points in the history of this periodical. In the late fifties and early sixties, the magazine converted from a free circulation to a paid circulation. This meant it had to make a transition from a "cause" publication to a market-driven one.

Therefore it started down the road of aggressive promotion, including book premiums and direct-mail programs.[35] Carl Henry's departure in 1968, whether by his initiative or that of Harold Ockenga, the chairman of the board,[36] proved tumultuous. His successor, Harold Lindsell, brought a more parochial agenda to the magazine at a time when its economic fortunes were increasingly tenuous. In the early seventies, the magazine entered an ill fated book publishing venture, Canon Press, and teetered on bankruptcy.[37] Harold Myra, whose successful tenure at *Campus Life* was highly regarded, joined the magazine in 1975 as president and chief executive. He supervised the magazine's move from Washington to Wheaton and weaned the magazine from subsidies. By 1978 the economic corner had been turned and black ink began to appear on the financial reports. Circulation is now in the 170,000s, which is considered by its management to be "optimum."

Myra was widely criticized for the evolution of the magazine from one that spoke for evangelicals to one that spoke to them, from one that published across the street from the White House to one that published across the street from the National Association of Evangelicals, and from one for intellectuals to one for a popular audience.[38] Yet the reader research for the magazine shows its clergy-laity proportions have not greatly changed — about half and half; and the percentage of professional scholars has always been in Myra's words, "around one or two percent."[39]

Two strategic moves in the late seventies have put the magazine on a firmer footing. One was Myra's view that a "family" of magazines, more than just one, was needed to disperse overheads. *Leadership*, a quarterly for clergy, was the first (1980) to join the family and has proved dramatically successful and profitable with a circulation of close to one hundred thousand. Shortly after, *Campus Life*, *Marriage Partnership*, and *Today's Christian Woman* joined the family. *Leadership 100* for lay church leaders and the earlier *Partnership* for clergy wives were not successful, however. A second strategic turn has been the use of readership surveys by Christianity Today, Inc., to determine reader interest for specific features. Since 1980, they have conducted a semiscientific survey to detect the extent of readership for various articles and features. For example, a survey might show that a column on the arts may attract only ten percent of the readers, and an article by Billy Graham may garner well over half. "If we're going to get them to pay, we have to know what they think," says Myra. "The magazine's survival is at stake."[40] This is the nearest to an actual show of hands among the buyers for any publication we have discussed.

The seventies and eighties proved quite fertile for new consumer magazines. Every year a significant new one hit the evangelical market. Among the best known are *Virtue, Today's Christian Woman, Charisma, The Fundamentalist Journal* (now defunct), *The Wittenburg Door, Kindred Spirit, The Journal of Christian Nursing,* and *Discipleship Journal.* The fall of 1988 witnessed a new, aggressively capitalized publication, *Christian Parenting.*[41] Common elements among all these seem to be specialization and an issue frequency of less than monthly.[42] However, not all efforts have succeeded. An ambitious biweekly newspaper, the *National Courier,* went through several million dollars beginning in 1975, seeking a mass audience acceptance for news.[43] In 1978 two newsstand attempts by secular concerns attracted meteoric interest — *Inspiration* and *Faith and Inspiration.* Both hit the newsstands in large numbers with Billy Graham on their first covers.

Probably *Charisma* (1975) has been the most numerically successful of the newer magazines. Begun by a recent journalism graduate from the University of Florida, Stephen Strang, it was sponsored first by a Florida Assembly of God congregation. As it grew, *Logos,* an earlier charismatic bimonthly declined; Strang bought *Charisma* and proceeded to build a small conglomerate, Strang Communications, publishing *Christian Retailing, Ministry Today,* and Creation House books.

Charisma, by 1988, had tied or topped *Moody Monthly* as the largest subscription-based magazine in the evangelical marketplace, with over two hundred thousand subscriptions. It retains its old Pentecostal culture, adding the newer charismatic population and, since merging with Robert Walker's *Christian Life,* the traditional midwestern evangelicals. The Pentecostal movement now appears established and prosperous.

Before leaving this simple four-element typology, we might note that the history of magazines is marked by an effort of a publication to leave its box. House organs seek to move into market-oriented magazines; likewise, cause-oriented tracts become consumer products. And within the staff and management of a publication, most of the problems and conflicts arise over what kind of publication theirs actually is — "Are we representing an organization or meeting a market?" is a commonly heard question.

The Means and the Ends

Evangelical consumer publications survive as businesses and, like other periodicals, they must create a product that will be in demand by a particular market. This pragmatic necessity, combined with religious idealism and mission, imposes numerous paradoxes and constraints on the "business." Among these are economics, circulation, and cultural impact.

"It is so easy to fail with a magazine. Editorial, circulation, and advertising must hit like three pistons in an engine — perfectly — for success." That comment from Harold Myra, president of Christianity Today Incorporated, carries extra credibility because of the history of his flagship publication. *Christianity Today* began in 1956 and did not break even until 1978. Initially it was entirely subsidized; later, subsidies from key donors covered the last half of its expenses — hundreds of thousands of dollars every year.

The three pistons — or the three-legged stool — of editorial, circulation, and advertising have baffled many an accountant and traditional business person. This is a business in which the customer pays in advance. At least two streams of income — circulation and advertising — seem independent yet they are interdependent, for the decline of circulation will jeopardize the sale of advertising. And is circulation an asset or a liability? The accountants will call it a liability, because it is an obligation incurred. The advertising manager will regard it as his chief asset. The bank will side with the accountants as they wince at the balance sheet: all that obligation with only intangible future editorial product to offset it!

To cast the magazine industry in traditional business terms, the key elements are quantity of units (circulation), price of the units (subscription price), ancillary income (mainly advertising, but also list rentals, books, and services), and repeat business (renewals). Blending these requires very delicate fine tuning. Indeed, the formula varies with each magazine; there are few industry-wide norms, either for religious or general magazines. Renewals, for example, must be sufficient for a stable circulation, especially for those magazines that have assured advertisers of a guaranteed circulation (rate base). If the renewal rate is poor, a promotion campaign for replacement subscriptions will prove so costly that red ink is inevitable.

"We had to struggle to keep renewals above 50 percent," says Robert Walker of his *Christian Life* days. *Virtue* reported a renewal rate of 72 percent in 1987. *Guideposts* has claimed a renewal rate of 75 percent.[44] Most experts would say 70 percent is good; 50 percent is adequate if promotion is inexpensive. *The New Yorker* and *National Geographic* have long enjoyed renewal rates well above 80 percent, the envy of the industry. Most of the consumer Christian magazines will not disclose their renewal rates, but the consensus prevails that any periodical that must replace over half its list each year will find profitability elusive. Renewals are widely regarded as the single best evidence of reader satisfaction — not letters to the editor, citation in public, or praise from journalistic experts. Salability among those who know the product best, the current subscribers, defines editorial and (usually) economic success.

Smaller magazines, such as those with under thirty thousand in circulation, cannot win much space advertising except from highly specialized products targeted for their unique audience. Less than twenty thousand in circulation will mean advertising is negligible or even more trouble than it is worth.[45] A valuable mailing list, however, even for a tiny publication, can generate substantial income currently in the range of $50 to $100 per thousand names per rental.

In the religious media, advertising has evolved and shifted in this century. In the 1920s and 1930s, the mix of advertisers in the *Christian Herald* or *Moody Monthly* included a wide variety of consumer products. The *Herald* of the 1930s had ads from Ipana toothpaste, Olson Rugs, and Burpee seeds. Later, with specialization, these magazines found such "secular" advertising harder to get; commercial religious products became the chief category. Robert Walker, the *Christian Life* editor, recalls the 1940s: "We found mission organizations, parachurch organizations, travel agencies, and Bible publishers would advertise. The book publishers were not dominant in the early days." By the 1960s, book publishers were the key category of advertisers in Christian media. And the period of the mid-seventies to early eighties was the golden age for the Christian book publishing industry. After those heyday years, however, the magazines that took advertising found they could not count on ever increasing space sales. The book industry had turned flat, notable indeed among the three largest publishers.[46] *Christianity Today* enjoyed a peak of $1.9 million in space advertising in 1983, but saw a drop the following year to $1.6 million. In 1989 it anticipated $1.8 million.[47] *The Christian Herald*, with somewhat less circulation, anticipated $500,000 to $700,000 in advertising per year.[48]

A final economic element foreign for outsiders to this industry is the art and science of subscription promotion. Circulation must be bought, like office supplies or any other purchase, and it can be bought cheaply or expensively. (Either way the risk is poor renewals.) Through the science of computerized direct mail, however, a vast number of people can be wooed to subscribe. A tiny portion, perhaps 1 or 2 percent, will agree to purchase, some on trial (a "soft" offer) and some with actual payment (a "hard" offer). These new subscribers thus become the growing edge for a consumer magazine.

The larger Christian magazines will commit hundreds of thousands — perhaps millions — of dollars to this quest for new subscribers. This is why a magazine start-up turns out to be capital intensive. The "up-front" money creates the audience, and the payback, several years away, will depend on renewals and advertising. Only a handful of Christian magazines are known to be profitable, for these very practical reasons.[49]

Circulation

The 315 member publications of the Evangelical Press Association range in circulation from two hundred to two million. Approximately one out of ten has a circulation over one hundred thousand and of the thirty-four that go above one hundred thousand, twenty-two arrived in that coveted company by giving their product away.[50] The median circulation is only twelve thousand.[51] Why is this, in a nation where evangelicals number somewhere between fifteen and forty million? A 1980 study by researcher George Barna showed that only 12.7 percent of "Christians" subscribe to a Christian magazine (compared with 62.2 percent who subscribe to nonreligious magazines). Even among a group in that survey called "committed Christians," only 18.8 percent take a Christian magazine.[52]

Granted, magazines lend themselves to small, tight definitions of special audience and special interest. None of the religious magazines — Catholic, Protestant, or Jewish — soar to vast numbers. *Christian Century,* an influential weekly from the more liberal Protestant tradition, has a circulation of thirty-five thousand, of which 25 percent are libraries and institutions. Nevertheless it is clear that evangelicals do not read religious periodicals any more than they listen to religious radio stations. All of the rhetoric in recent years about the booming evangelical "business" has been overdrawn. Evangelicals, like the wider American society, consume a variety of media, only a few of which are specifically religious.

Given the advertising base and the subscription price ceilings open to Christian magazines, it requires great faith to see how any magazine will rise above the two hundred thousand to three hundred thousand subscription level in the present market. It could be done but the formula would have to be: (1) a subscription price high enough to compensate for a reduction in advertising revenue (an increase in circulation equals an increase in ad rates. An increase in ad rates usually causes a reduction in ad revenues, thus higher subscription rates) and (2) a product in such demand that renewal rates could remain high. (The replacement of expired subscriptions would then not be seen as being overly expensive.)

Some might hope that larger advertisers would be attracted to a Christian magazine of larger circulation. Might automobiles, appliances, cosmetics, or clothing turn up in *Charisma* or *Christianity Today?* The consensus among present publishers is that this will not happen. A number of attempts have been made, from the 1960s to the 1980s, but with no real progress.[53] Today the advertising community usually favors highly targeted media placement, for example, cat food in *Cat Fancy*, and for more general products the inexpensive general media. In addition, there are some nonrational considerations involved in advertising. Many advertisers are loathe to entangle themselves in anything religious, regardless of the audience size. It is therefore doubtful that secular advertisers would be attracted to large religious magazines, and it is certain that smaller religious advertisers could not afford them.

Equally daunting in larger circulation ventures is the quest for an audience. Out of a highly segmented divided church scene, an audience would have to be drawn to some common interests or beliefs. They would have to feel an urgency or even a necessity about timely contact; yet even among militant fundamentalists and evangelicals, religion has typically not been propelled by day-to-day events but by timeless truths. Christian magazines that have proffered news, whether secular events or sacred, have not been successful. The evangelical periodicals now on the market are compelled to use premiums, reduced prices, and sweepstakes to keep their advertising base. Competition for readers, including that from free publications and secular media, is keen.

Do evangelical magazines make a difference, either within or without their boundaries? Looking outside evangelicalism's "interior dialogue," it appears that only two or three evangelical periodicals ever turn up in a typical public library. For serious research, only about 35 of the 425 periodicals of the American Theological Librarians' *Religion Index* are distinctly evangelical. Most telling of all, for a mass movement, there are no newsstand success stories. Potential readers are culled almost entirely from internal networking — chiefly direct mail. A Gallup study in the last decade found that among American clergy, *Christianity Today* was first of the ten most widely read magazines. Yet national, public impact cannot be claimed for even the largest evangelical magazines.

At the same time, the traditional newspapers and magazines in the general market have largely given up their own role as disseminators of religious ideas and events. The secular press in previous generations devoted much more space to Christian themes and exposition than they do today. For example, the Philadelphia newspapers published complete transcripts of Billy Sunday's sermons during his 1914 crusade. That was an age that did not feel religious themes were out-of-bounds. Today secular media, though swift and usually accurate in their religious reporting, focus more on conflict and institutional change than on ideas.[54]

Martin Marty puts the problem into the mouth of a fictional religion reporter.

> We cover other dimensions of life and interests in more ways than just to deal with conflict. Our paper talks about athletic games and not just about athletic scandals. We report on financial trends and not just on "insider trading" sleaze. . . . Will you [the secular editor] let me dig up and focus on analogues to these in religion?[55]

As a result, evangelical magazines contribute primarily to the internal dialogue of the religious community and to the economic health of some religious businesses. "Magazines become a part of the family, they take on a familiarity that people relate to, perhaps more even than books" (Harold Myra). Every magazine subscriber feels supported by a larger community and therefore less isolated, less provincial, more a part of the "great conversation," whatever it may be.

"Magazines have supported the book industry, discovering authors and subjects that later became best-sellers," adds William Carmichael. Numerous authors discovered they could write while working on an article for a magazine. Magazines respond swiftly to hot topics; books may take a year or two to develop. "An alert press can expose situations that, with public exposure, will be corrected," suggests William Petersen.[56] The parachurch, independent religious enterprises will only be monitored by the Christian or secular media. They fear publicity and take it seriously;[57] they can be held accountable, in part, through responsible coverage in the media. The examples of this are few, however.

Investigative journalism within the Christian press has probed a number of allegations or problems for its readers. In the last twenty years, these include the organization Underground Evangelism, the Bill Gothard ministry and staff, Robert Schuller's theology, and the charges of heresy directed at Tony Campolo. It is fair to say, however, that numerous moral eyesores, the PTL and Swaggart scandals among them, have been left for the secular media to expose.

Less dramatic, but equally valid, is the published discovery of any previously obscure ministry or method that works well in the life of the church. But good news or bad requires a huge investment of time, money, and a measure of risk; most of the Christian press has not pursued it.

Magazines sometimes cast themselves in an admirable "prophetic" role.[58] But the ineluctable canons of marketing throw doubt on so noble a function. Voluntary subscribers have bought the publication because they essentially agree with it. If it differs radically from their opinions, they simply fail to renew.[59] It is arguable that Harriet Beecher Stowe's *Uncle Tom's Cabin* had more impact than Garrison's *Liberator*.

But might magazines change minds with new facts or daring leadership? They can at least inform. However, studies of crucial turning points in American life have not been reassuring about the magazines' role of leadership.[60] A survey of general Christian magazines in the 1960s would not inspire the word "prophetic" about the racial issue. Yet this turned out to be one of the key social changes from 1954 to 1964 — and one with a clear ethical element.

We all can remember the experience of reading an analysis that articulated and captured our own best instincts and values, as only language can do. We looked up from the page and knew what we thought on a given subject. We were emboldened then to follow our better, more mature judgment. This rhetorical mystery occurs rarely for it requires writers of depth and substance.[61] We magazine readers chiefly want publications and credibility. We want good writing, clever packaging, interesting layouts, titles, and graphics. But we first want credibility. Having that moral and intellectual credibility, we will find in magazines a measure of leadership. Where are these strong editors — not just journalistic craftsmen — who will bring such credibility? Or is an internal dialogue the best that can be achieved?

NOTES

1. *Ulrich's Periodical Directory*, 1988.

2. The *1986 Ayer Directory of Publications* lists 11,328 periodicals in the United States.

3. *The Magazine Industry Newsletter* estimated there were twelve hundred religious publications plus an unknown number for which no information was available, according to William H. Taft, *American Magazines for the 1980s* (New York: Hastings House, 1982), 216.

4. Two recent historical studies are worth reading: Nathan O. Hatch, *The Democratization of American Christianity* (New Haven: Yale University Press, 1988), chapter 4. And Mark Noll, "Mainliners and Evangelicals," *The Reformed Journal* (June 1988): 14–19. Noll draws on Hatch's research in this speech to the Evangelical Press Association and the Associated Church Press.

5. *Folio*, the magazine of the magazine industry, has divided periodicals into "special interest" and "special audience" publications (*Solving Publishing's Toughest Problems*, 1984). Using that division, the consumer magazines on the left tend to be special interest; they are oriented to a subject area. Those on the right are special audience; they are delimited by some demographic boundary. If this seems a bit pedantic, remember that journalism doesn't have many chances at it.

6. Quoted in Sydney E. Ahlstrom, *A Religious History of the American People* (Yale University Press, 1972), 651.

7. The only real magazine that I know currently to be evangelistic is *These Times*, a pre-evangelistic tool of Seventh-day Adventists. It is used to interest friends and neighbors in topics that can lead to serious questions about that faith.

During the Jesus movement of the late 1960s, a number of handout publications had an evangelistic purpose. The *Hollywood Free Paper* hit a circulation of 425,000 (free) and claimed over two thousand conversions. See Ronald Enroth et al., *The Jesus People* (Grand Rapids: Eerdmans, 1972), 74.

8. Wilbur Smith, *Before I Forget* (Chicago: Moody Press, 1971), 177.

9. This publication, begun by the Philadelphia Presbyterian in the 1920s, failed after a board of directors conflict with Dr. Barnhouse over control precipitated his resignation as editor (1949). Within the year he began a new one, *Eternity* (1950), and an ailing *Revelation* soon merged back into it.

10. From 1950 until Barnhouse's death in 1960. The magazine repositioned as a general consumer magazine in 1961.

11. "They dragged in the subscription cancellations in mailbags," was the description of older *Eternity* staff who recalled the month that magazine under Barnhouse dropped from thirty-three thousand to twenty-nine thousand. The protest was over a series of articles on Seventh-day Adventism, considered the "last straw" of a series of disquieting trends in the magazine. (Personal conversation, William J. Petersen, July 1988.)

12. The readership studies introduced most notably by Professor James Engel at Wheaton College Graduate School of Communications have stimulated a healthy scrutiny and pragmatism on the part of the organizations that have used them.

13. *Writing Award Winning Articles* (Nashville: Thomas Nelson, 1983), 19. The opening chapter is a helpful overview of the history of Christian magazines, drawing on the authoritative 1957 study by Frank Luther Mott, *A History of American Magazines*.

14. Denominational periodicals, for example, have had difficulty selling advertising because the advertisers suspected the circulation numbers were artificially enlarged.

15. With that life span it competes with *The Church Herald* of the Reformed Church in America (originating in 1826) as one of the longest continuously published church magazines.

16. The circulation was taken over by *World*.

17. "Denominational publications are, in fact, beholden to the church bodies and the constituencies they serve. No publication, of course, succeeds with an unwilling constituency, but a special factor is introduced in Denominational publishing." Dennis Shoemaker, "The Ministry of the Church Journalist," *The Church Herald* (April 2, 1976): 12.

18. It had a number of names, beginning with *Biblical Repertory and Princeton Review*.

19. Princeton Seminary, with 110 students in 1905, was among the largest of the Protestant seminaries.

20. The editor of the *Autobiography of Lyman Beecher*, cited in Mark Noll, *The Princeton Theology* (Grand Rapids: Baker, 1983), 22.

21. For an explanation of these distinctives see Douglas Frank, *Less Than Conquerors* (Grand Rapids: Eerdmans, 1986), 22.

22. The information here on the *Sunday School Times* has been secured from Herbert Fryling, the last surviving officer; James Reapsome, the concluding editor; and Russell T. Hitt.

23. Roland Wolseley, *Understanding Magazines*, 2d ed. (Ames: Iowa State University Press, 1972), 32.

24. "The greatest editor of any Christian journal in America," according to Wilbur Smith, *Before I Forget*, 77.

25. Technically, Philip Sr. was "president" and Philip Jr. was both editor and president for part of the time.

26. George Marsden, *Fundamentalism and American Culture* (New York: Oxford University Press, 1980), 84.

27. Ibid., 270.

28. Robert Metcalf, currently on the staff of the *Herald*.

29. As with *Saturday Evening Post* and other mass audience magazines, agents or sales people in towns across the land took orders from friends and neighbors for subscriptions. A small commission was earned.

30. Robert Flood, "Moody Monthly: Yesterday and Today," *Moody Monthly* (February 1986): 62.

31. Much of the statistical data on *Moody Monthly* I secured from Robert Flood, currently on its staff. Flood was responsible for the program that gave *Moody Monthly* the circulation boost from about 110,000 to 250,000 in the early 1970s. For subscription premiums he used Moody Press books, such as the *Wycliffe Commentary* in a special edition. He credits "mass mailing, large premiums," and low postal rates as the components of his effort from 1972 to 1978.

32. Private conversation, July 1988.

33. Notes from Wilbur Smith, an early compatriot with Graham and L. Nelson Bell, in the founding of the magazine. *Before I Forget*, 178.

34. Henry's autobiography, *Confessions of a Theologian* (Waco: Word Books, 1986), details his philosophy and experience with the magazine.

35. The Iverson-Ford agency of New York introduced one of the first modern premiums among Christian magazines, the *Four Version New Testament*, in 1963. In later years, numerous other book premiums were tried, a venture that current president Harold Myra considers counterproductive. Myra tells of a parishioner in his church in the early seventies who told him she was returning two copies of *The Living Bible* to her bookstore. She had discovered she could buy two subscriptions to *Christianity Today* and get two free *Living Bibles* for less money than if she would purchase the books alone. Such premium offers thus created a subscriber base that lacked affinity for the magazine itself, and renewals suffered.

36. The two men differed regarding what actually happened. Henry insists he was fired (see *Confessions*), but Ockenga insisted the editor resigned.

37. Heavy subsidies from J. Howard Pew, industrialist Maxey Jarman, and the Billy Graham organization enabled the publication to survive.

38. See Henry, *Confessions*, especially the final chapter.

39. Conversation, August 11, 1988. A Gallup poll has shown *Christianity Today* to be the magazine subscribed to by more of America's clergy than any other, a fulfillment of the original dream of Billy Graham, J. Howard Pew, and Carl Henry.

40. Myra notes that the Carl Henry column was dropped after reader research showed it was the least read of any of their features.

41. The sponsors are the David C. Cook Publishing Co. and William Carmichael, publisher of *Virtue*.

42. Higher subscription prices plus reduced number of issues per subscription term have become commonplace. The fortnightly *Christianity Today* now serves only 18 issues per year. The conventional wisdom among their publishers (my paraphrase): "People don't really notice if you come every month. But they do notice the gross price."

43. William J. Petersen, formerly with *Eternity*, recalls an initial ambiguity in the editorial purpose of the *Courier*. He notes that a presentation at the EPA convention in May 1975 by the publication's first editor and sponsor implied two different editorial philosophies. Robert Slosser, formerly with the *New York Times*, hoped the future periodical would be an evangelical version of the *Christian Science Monitor*. Dan Malachuk, owner of Logos International, a book publishing firm that funded the venture, seemed to imply that it would be more like a Christian *National Enquirer*, sold in supermarkets. As it progressed, Malachuk prevailed, and the publication emphasized charismatic reporting.

44. Taft, *American Magazines*, 219.

45. The conventional wisdom has been that only half the revenue from a page of advertising is kept as profit. About 25 percent is consumed in selling expenses and an equal amount in extra printing costs.

46. Word, Zondervan, and Thomas Nelson.

47. I am indebted to Roy Coffman, CTi executive, for disclosure of these and other statistics on the magazine.

48. Robert Metcalf, advertising manager, August 1988 conversation.

49. Many of these observations about the business side of magazines I owe to Russell T. Hitt, a veteran editor and publisher, who managed *Eternity* through a number of difficult transitions.

50. Although a price is put on many of these that are given away, and money will be accepted, the product is basically free to all who contribute to an organization or who support a ministry.

51. Based on the reported circulation figures of the 1987–88 *Membership Directory*. This does not include publications that did not report circulation, almost all of which are Sunday school curriculum products.

52. The study was called *The Christian Marketplace* and was carried out by Barna's organization, then called the American Research Bureau. A private project of supporting corporations, it was not made available to the general public.

53. The most recent was by CTi in the mid 1980s, an effort to secure "secular" advertising for *Today's Christian Woman,* under the direction of Kenneth Johnson and Dale Hanson Bourke. In the 1960s, an effort was made to form a consortium of large-circulation denominational magazines, led by A. D. In the 1960s Daniel Poling sought large general advertising and met with nominal success.

54. See Roderick P. Hart et al., "Religion and the Rhetoric of the Mass Media," *Review of Religious Research* (Summer 1980), 256–75. This is a study of the religion coverage in *Time* magazine from 1947 to 1976. They argue that the magazine depicts religion as a "conflict-ridden human enterprise."

55. *Context* (1 June 1987), 1.

56. William J. Petersen and Stephen Board, "Our Non Prophet Press," *Eternity* (March 1977), 43–46.

57. An illustration shared with me by a former editor of *Christianity Today:* During a series of news articles exposing a scandal in the Bill Gothard Basic Youth Conflicts organization, Gothard called the magazine and asked the staff not to publish an article. When told the magazine had gone to press and was about to be mailed, Gothard offered to pay for the entire printing and fund the reprinting of the magazine without the embarrassing news story. *Christianity Today* did not accept Gothard's offer.

58. For a nuanced statement of purpose for *Christianity Today,* see "The Difference CT Means to Make," *Christianity Today* (2 January 1981), 12.

59. I have argued in "Jeremiah Monthly: That's No Prophet, It's a Magazine" (*Spectrum,* 1979) that *Sojourners* is no more prophetic, to its own audience, than *Moody Monthly.* All have their own stable of sacred cows. The apparent difference may be in the tolerance that various magazines have for criticism.

60. One study can be mentioned: Robert W. Ross's *So It Was True: The American Protestant Press and the Nazi Persecution of the Jews* (Minneapolis: University of Minnesota Press, 1980).

61. This was part of Joseph Bayly's appeal in *Eternity's* "Out of My Mind" column, which appeared from 1961 to 1986.

Chapter 26

Writing the Religious Article

David Lambert

O n my bookshelf sits a book on writing and selling nonfiction. Prominent on the cover is a large dollar sign. Every time I see that cover, I smile at the irony.

In the world of Christian periodicals, the dollar sign is an inappropriate symbol — at least for the writers. I suspect that my experience is about average. The most I've been paid for any article from a Christian magazine is $500, and that was for a fairly long and difficult piece — several thousand words, counting the sidebars. I suspect that fee came to about $5 an hour. Not much above minimum wage.

I'm paid more, at least per hour, for a column I do for a different magazine — but only because I am listed as a contributing editor and am therefore paid at a higher rate than most free-lancers. And even the income from that magazine, coming regularly as it does, makes up only about 5 percent of the money I need to keep food on the table and a roof over my head.

This isn't a complaint. I just didn't want to make the same mistake

Currently editor of youth books at Zondervan Publishing House, David Lambert has served as a managing editor of *TQ* (*TeenQuest*) magazine and as a publications bureau chief in state government. He is a contributing editor to *Faith 'n' Stuff*, a children's magazine published by Guideposts, Inc., and has published many articles and short stories. His first book will be published by Zondervan in 1992.

here that the cover designer of that book did, and give you the impression that there's a lot of money to be made in writing articles for Christian magazines. In my entire life, I've met only one free-lancer who claimed to be making a living solely by writing for Christian periodicals, and I suspect that her ability to live on very little income had a lot to do with it.

It's also true that most people who are writing for Christian periodicals aren't doing so merely for the money — obviously. There's a definite sense of mission, of wanting to make a contribution. My first Christian articles appeared in magazines for teenagers. I was working with Young Life at the time and wanted to see the material I was developing for my local club kids more widely distributed. I'd have been willing to accept less payment than I actually received just for the sake of seeing those articles in print and knowing they were getting into the hands of some kids.

It's also true that for those creative and dedicated writers willing to scramble, stay up late meeting ridiculous deadlines, and look for article ideas in everything they do and see and read there's enough money in writing for Christian periodicals to provide a healthy chunk in a budget that also derives income from other writing-related activities (such as teaching and book royalties).

So if you're willing to accept the limitations and are still excited about the opportunities, read on. We'll take a look at the ways to find your special subject matter, at the importance of craftsmanship and research, and at a very practical matter: how best to organize your article. We'll also look at the importance of studying your markets and at the difficulties of getting published and then conclude with an exhortation to make yourself marketable.

Finding Your Subject Matter

Years ago, teaching composition at the University of Montana, I found that students (usually freshmen) had a nearly universal question when I would assign a paper: "What shall I write about?" And no matter how many times I was asked that question, I would always stare back at them in something like amazement.

Why amazement? Because I was a writer, and as a writer it was inconceivable to me that someone would face a blank page with not a clue in the world of something to write about. *I* certainly had no shortage of things I wanted to write about. Sitting down to my typewriter, I was often struck by the same vague panic that I feel when I walk into a good library and realize that there are so many wonderful books in the world that I'll never find time to read. In the same way, there are so many things

I'd love to write, and I'll never be able to write them all. Perhaps the greatest despair a writer faces is seeing five good ideas slip away from him unwritten for every one he has time to write.

How do you choose from that tantalizing menu of possible subjects? And don't fool yourself — choose you must. Even though you may have several unfinished projects awaiting your attention on any given day, you can work on only one of them at a time. But there's an even greater constraint: few writers are successful in establishing themselves as a credible voice in more than one genre, in more than one subject. And if you are successful in establishing a reputation as a writer, it's very likely that the same will be true of you — people will not only know who you are, they'll also know what you write about.

John Steinbeck? Novelist. Ray Bradbury? Science fiction. John Gunther? Travel books. Oswald Chambers? Devotional material. Chuck Swindoll? Encouraging, warm, inspirational nonfiction. Hal Lindsey? Popular books on biblical prophecy. Art Buchwald? Politically oriented humor. Erma Bombeck? Domestically oriented humor. James Dobson? Nonfiction on the psychology of marriage and family life.

Continue the list on your own, and you'll see that nearly every well-known writer has a single, narrowly defined area of writing that has made his or her reputation. Do these authors write in other areas as well? Sometimes. James Michener, besides writing best-selling novels, also writes books on Japanese art. William F. Buckley, Jr., besides writing witty political nonfiction, writes spy novels. And you'll be able to think of a few authors who are successful and well-known in more than one area. C. S. Lewis, besides writing fantasy novels, also wrote essays in apologetics (such as *Mere Christianity*). But the principle holds nevertheless, and you can assume that it will hold for you.

So — what's *your* subject matter?

For most of you, that's a trick question. Writers often write for years, writing whatever they think they can get published, before they stumble across, by accident, the genre or the subject that strikes a chord both in them and in their readers, so that they begin coming back to a genre or subject again and again. But I have a suggestion: Don't wait for that accident. Begin to consciously search for your niche, and begin developing credibility in it now.

Don't know where to start looking? Ask yourself a few questions. Do you have a special knack — fiction, for instance, or humor, or biography, or inspirational writing? Do you have a burning concern about something, so that besides writing about it you also find yourself becoming an activist in other ways — serving on committees, joining organizations, donating money, attending conferences? What do you most like to read? If you discover a strong answer or two to any of those questions, then you have a place to start looking for your own niche in writing.

Should you concentrate on that area and ignore everything else? No — I recommend that all writers try their hand at a variety of types of writing. You might always find something you're better at, or that finds a greater readership. And the discipline of attempting different genres will make you a better writer; your nonfiction, for instance, will be improved by your dabbling in fiction and poetry.

Finding your subject matter will to some extent also define the forms you'll find it most helpful to write in, but it's also worth considering that some people have a greater gift for one format than another. One writer may have a great gift for humor, for instance, and another a gift for the journalistic article, another for first-person narrative.

Explore the forms. Try your hand at all of them. Ever done an interview? How about an opinion piece? There are many magazines that print short devotional and inspirational articles; is that a strength of yours? How about the how-to? Book reviews?

In fact, don't restrict yourself to the established forms. When you get an idea for a totally off-the-wall, creative piece that defies classification, follow it up. Its uniqueness will make it all the more memorable — and more likely to catch the adventurous editor's attention in the fist place.

If it's well crafted.

Craftsmanship

Just before the turn of the century, Herbert Spencer wrote a book entitled *The Philosophy of Style*. In it, he pointed out that each reader who picks up something you have written has three tasks: First, to understand the words you use. Second, to understand the relationships between those words. Third, to understand the ideas you're trying to communicate. And the reader brings to these three tasks a limited amount of mental energy and ability (and, one might add, patience).

The implication should be clear: If that reader expends most of his energy on understanding the words you're trying to use (because of inappropriate or inexact word choice) or in trying to understand the relationships between those words (because you've put them together sloppily), then he has little or no energy left for understanding the thing you most wanted him to grasp — your ideas.

"But I'm writing for *intelligent* readers, who are willing to exert a little effort for the sake of my ideas," you say. You might be writing for them, but there are few of them out there, and the few there are may be too intelligent to waste their effort on poor writing when there is excellent writing waiting to be read.

Even intelligent readers have little patience with poor writing. Listen to the words of Montaigne, the sixteenth-century French judge and essayist:

> If in reading I fortune to meet with any difficult points, I fret not my selfe about them, but after I have given them a charge or two, I leave them as I found them. Should I earnestly plod upon them I should lose both time and my selfe; for I have a skipping wit. What I see not at the first view, I shall lesse see it, if I opinionate my selfe upon it. . . . If one booke seeme tedious unto me, I take another, which I follow not with any earnestnesse, except it be at such houres as I am idle, or that I am weary with doing nothing.

Four hundred years have passed since Montaigne, and a hundred years since Herbert Spencer, but readers, even intelligent ones, haven't changed. If you want your writing to be read and understood, you'll have to become a craftsman; you'll have to learn to make your words as transparent as glass.

How does a writer improve his or her craftsmanship? By diligence. There is no shortcut. In *The Elements of Style* E. B. White insists that writing is "a matter of ear."[1] You develop that ear by reading the best writing, by studying books like Strunk and White's, and by analyzing, critiquing, and in general tearing apart everything you read. Even poor writing can inspire you to write better — if you're aware of just how poor it is, and why.

As a writer for an agency of state government years ago, I was subjected daily to some of the most convoluted and obtuse writing in the history of the pencil. The other staff writers and I were appalled by the failure to communicate of much of the writing we were asked to edit, but we also noticed that, with time, our ears became used to stumbling rhythms. Rather than lose the sharp clarity of our writers' ears, we began a process we called "fueling our outrage." We flagged the worst examples of writing each day to discuss among ourselves in contemptuous tones, we read examples of the best writing to provide our ears with sterling models, and we read and passed around books on craftsmanship and style.

Fuel your outrage. Don't let your ear be blunted and made useless by the barrage of poorly crafted writing you're exposed to. Find the sections of your local library where the books on the craft of writing are kept (start looking in 800.1 and 808.3) and begin to read the best of the books you find there. Diligently.

Your writer's ear is one of the greatest weapons in your arsenal. Treat it with care.

Do Your Research

Most articles written for Christian magazines are merely inspirational; they are based almost solely on the author's experience. Few Christian writers are doing the type of writing that would prepare them for a staff writer's job on, say, *Newsweek* or *Time*.

Be a journalist! Do your research! *Any* article, even an inspirational one, is helped by diligent research. What the writer often finds in the course of his research is that his original plan was uninformed and provincial, and thus he saves himself some embarrassment.

Since the topic of research is discussed elsewhere in this book, I won't discuss it further, except to encourage you to make research a vital part of every writing project you undertake. Lack of research is one of the great failings of the Christian writing world; don't contribute to it. And when editors offer you an assignment that pays too little money to cover your research time, explain the problem and ask for additional money for research. The worst that can happen is that the editor says no.

Organizing Your Article

Any magazine editor will tell you that one of the most common errors in rejected manuscripts — as well as one of the most perplexing editorial tasks in the accepted ones — is poor organization. *Where is this piece going?* we often find ourselves asking. In a well-organized article, the reader has the feeling of moving definitely in a well-thought-out direction toward a justifiable conclusion. The reader has a sense of where he is in the article. Those sensations are lacking in a poorly organized piece.

The organization is the *shape* of the thoughts in your article — or, better yet, the *movement* of ideas through your article. As a figure skater begins the movements leading to a difficult jump, every movement must be perfectly timed, perfectly executed, in its proper sequence, or the jump will be a failure. The organization of your article is just as crucial. If you don't understand the parts of your article and the relationship they bear to each other, if you're not sure what order they should be in, if you're not capable of confidently and professionally performing each of the steps you've set out for yourself, then you're likely to fail in your attempt.

What do you gain by a rigorous attention to organization? For one thing, you *discover what your article should contain*. As you've thought about your article, your brainstorming (if you're doing it right) has been wide-ranging, creative and undisciplined. You've probably written down a list of things you think might go into the article; perhaps you've already drafted some of the paragraphs. But remember: it's extremely unlikely that all of those ideas are going to fit into your final article. Some ideas take the reader in one direction, some take him in another. It's in the process of organizing your article that you discover what your most important points are, and which ones support your conclusion — and even whether your conclusion *can* be supported by the work you've done so far, or whether you need to gather more ammunition. (Research! Research!) You will discover all of those things when you sit down and begin to outline your article, trying different organizations to see what works best.

Try to organize your next article according to the following eight principles:

1. *Organize for the reader.* Know your audience and their reading habits. Are you writing for a professional journal, such as *Leadership* or *Youthworker Journal?* Then you can assume that your readers will be motivated differently and will probably have different reading habits from those who read mainly for "inspirational entertainment," such as the readers of *Guideposts* or *The Christian Reader.* The former readers will at least skim most of the journal, will read anything labeled Summary, and will read with great interest those things that promise to help them professionally; the latter will read nothing that isn't entertaining by the end of the first paragraph or two.

Remember, too, that your elaborate system of organization will be lost on your reader. You envision your article as a detailed network of major, minor, and subordinate points:

I.
  A.
  B.
    1.
    2.
    3.
  C.
II.
  A.
    1.
      a.
      b.
    2.

And so on. But your reader is unlikely to gasp the complexity of those relationships; your reader will read your article as a series of points, one after another, giving equal weight to each:

1.

2.

3.

4.

5.

6.

7.

The obvious implication is that, if the point you're trying to make is a major one, something that your reader must not fail to grasp, you'll have to flag it for him.

2. *Group like points; watch for overlap; eliminate repetition.* Those seem like simple principles. Why, then, are they too seldom accomplished? It's a common headache for editors to see an article in which the same subject occurs three or four times in different places. Why wasn't all of that material gathered in just one place in the article, treated thoroughly, and then dispensed with? If you find yourself saying much the same thing in two or three places in an article, there's a problem with your organization. Come up with an outline that allows you to eliminate the overlap and repetition.

3. *Consider the transitions.* Do you remember the story of the canary that coal miners used to take into the mines with them? A canary can't live without high levels of oxygen; therefore, if the canary died, the miners knew that oxygen in the mine was getting low and they had better get out.

Transitions function much the same way as you write your article. They have a hard time surviving if the organization is poor. So if the transition from part *B* to part *C* of your article is hard to write, consider the possibility that maybe the relationship between those parts (and perhaps others in your article as well) is shaky. The Rolling Stones and rutabagas both start with *R*, but if that's your organizing principle, you're going to have a hard time with transitions.

4. *Make your organization clear.* Five-hundred-word inspirational articles, of course, usually have only one point, illustrated by an anecdote. It isn't necessary to explain much about your organization. But the longer and more complex your article, the more you need to help your reader understand where you're going and how to recognize the signposts along the way. By the time he finishes your introduction, your reader should understand

1. What the subject of the article is,

2. How many parts your discussion will have,

3. What the general content of each part will be, and

4. The order of presentation of those parts

Often the best way to convey that information to your reader is by use of a *map paragraph*. Simply put, that's a paragraph that points out, in some detail, what the shape of the article or the next part of the article will be. There's one in this chapter, for instance, just before the subhead "Finding Your Subject Matter."

It's also possible to use the layout itself as a means of making your organization clear to your reader. Subheads, for instance, are a clear means of signaling to your reader that you're moving on to another section. Beginning a new paragraph signals your reader that there's a subtle shift in thought. Lists can help, too.

5. *Emphasize the significant.* There's a reason that managers and executives often read only the summary of the many reports and articles they're given — they don't have time to read everything, and they assume that anything significant in the article will be in the summary.

A willing reader *wants* to get as much meaning out of your article as he can, but you've got to help him. You can't give every sentence in your article equal weight. You have to flag for your reader the things that are important. And how do you do that? By placement.

What are the places of emphasis in a paragraph, in a subsection, in an article? That's easy — the beginning and the end. And which is the stronger of the two? Usually the ending, because that's what's ringing in your ears when you've finished.

Obviously, then, if there's something you want to emphasize in a sentence or in a paragraph or in an article because it's especially significant, you'll put it at the beginning or the ending. That way, its significance will be emphasized. And there's a fringe benefit, too — your prose will be stronger and more dramatic.

Read, for instance, this sentence:

> The greatest fear of most teenagers in the survey was losing their parents, not unpopularity or violent crime, as Dr. Miller had suspected.

Weak. The significant fact in that sentence is buried in the middle. This weakens the rhythm and obscures the significance of the survey's findings. Here's a stronger sentence structure.

> Despite Dr. Miller's expectations, the greatest fear of most teenagers in the survey was not unpopularity, nor was it violent crime — it was losing their parents.

It's also possible to emphasize the significant by eliminating everything else and isolating in its own paragraph the thing you want to emphasize. One way to handle the preceding example, for instance, (somewhat melodramatic, I'll admit, but effective), would be this:

> Despite Dr. Miller's expectations, the greatest fear of most teenagers in the survey was not unpopularity. Nor was it violent crime.
>
> Their greatest fear was losing their parents.

An aside: Don't be afraid to use one-sentence — or even one-word — paragraphs. You were taught not to do so, but the most important purpose for such rules is to allow us to occasionally break them in order to emphasize something by our unexpected use of language. If that thought bothers you, pick up a copy of Theodore Bernstein's excellent book, *Miss Thistlebottom's Hobgoblins*,[2] about superstitions of writing.

Another way of emphasizing the significant — a way commonly found in Scripture, in fact — is repetition. (Check out Romans 7, for instance.) Let's try our example again:

> Despite Dr. Miller's expectations, the greatest fear of most teenagers in the survey was not unpopularity, nor was it violent crime — it was losing their parents.
>
> Teenagers are *afraid* of losing their parents? Don't they want to be free of them?
>
> Yes, someday — but not yet. Losing their parents is, in fact, the greatest fear of *over half* of today's teenagers.

In context, that won't sound repetitive, and no one who reads it will miss the point.

6. *Consider alternative plans of organization.* One reason so many writers submit weakly organized articles to magazines — only to have them rejected, of course — is that they latched onto the first organizational plan that presented itself to their minds. Always remember, as you begin to pull your notes and thoughts together into an outline, that there are at least three thousand possible ways to organize that article. The odds that the first one you come up with is the best one are about the same as the odds of winning the lottery. And yet how many writers stubbornly stick with the first outline that comes to mind? *Always* consider alternatives.

Coming up with alternatives to consider should be fairly simple as soon as you free your mind to look for new possibilities. Understand that there are two main types of organization for articles: natural and logical. Natural outlines are those based on relationships in space or time. An article describing early missions activities among Native Americans, for instance, could begin on the West Coast and work toward the East Coast. It could just as easily be written in chronological order. Either of those organizations would be natural — based on space or time. The two principles could also be combined — dividing the country into five regions, for instance, and within each of those five sections of the article describing events in chronological order.

Logical outlines are those based on the logical, rather than natural, relationships of the parts to each other and to the whole. The possibilities for logical outlines are endless. You can first state the cause, for example, and then describe the effects — or you can examine the effects and then "search" for the cause. You can work from specific to general, or from general to specific. There are many different ways to organize the parts of your article in order of importance. Or complexity. Or function.

Presenting a difficult idea to a conservative audience? Begin with the points that are most familiar to them, or most acceptable, and work toward the less familiar or less acceptable.

Our article on missions among Native Americans could be organized by effectiveness, for instance. Which denominations took root, and why? Or it could begin with three generalizations about the preconceptions missionaries brought to the tribes, and then trace the effects of those preconceptions through specific tribes or reservations or movements.

With a wealth of possible ways to organize the material, how do you choose? By identifying the purpose or point of your article and choosing the organization that best accomplishes that purpose. If the point of our Native American missions article is to demonstrate that there were no effective, long-lasting missions efforts that did not include attention to education and social concerns, then it should be fairly simple to identify a half-dozen outlines that would emphasize that point and settle on one that accomplishes that purpose best for the audience and the publication you're writing for.

7. Don't be married to your outline. Don't be afraid to change outlines in midstream if, as you write, you begin to be uncomfortable with the one you're using. Remember: writing is the process of finding out what you want to say. As you write your first draft (and second draft, and third draft, and fourth draft, and . . .), and even as you scribble your notes and ideas in the early stages of building an article, you're finding out things you didn't know you knew, or thought. Your writing *leads* your thinking. It's completely natural and acceptable, then, for you to discover, halfway through, that the outline you started with just doesn't work anymore. Your overall point may have changed subtly (or not so subtly), or your understanding of the relationships of the parts may have become clearer.

Your big climax may not look so exciting anymore, and how could you have missed the importance of this point over here?

And isn't that when writing gets fun? *Serendipity* is a good word — the unexpected and joyful sense of discovery you feel when suddenly, in mid-sentence, everything becomes clear to you. The missing puzzle piece simply materializes in your brain and slips into place; lights go on; you smile and gasp, and your children give you odd looks. And suddenly that outline you began with just won't work anymore.

So what? Chuck it and come up with a new one. So you have to rewrite most of what you've done so far; so what? That's what writers are for — they write.

One of the saddest things for an editor is to discuss with a writer a book or article that's already half-written and see the writer discover a new thread of logic, a new concept, that would vastly improve that piece, and then to hear him say, "Oh, yeah, it would be *great* — but it would just be too much work. I've got it mostly done already. I'll just stick with plan A."

8. *Write first; outline later.* What? Isn't that against the whole idea of outlining? You come up with an outline to tell yourself what you want to write, so that you will write succinctly and to the point. Don't you?

Yes and no. If you believe in the writing process, then you believe that you don't really know what you want to say until you've said it. In writing. And if that's true, then how do you come up with an outline before you even start writing?

I don't think you can. Not a good one. I think the writing comes first, the outline second, and then more writing and rewriting. If that sounds odd, here's a plan that may make it more clear.

    a. Write your initial ideas about the article. Write pages and pages. This is "shotgun" or "free" writing — you're merely getting it onto the page (or the screen) as quickly as you can. Your creative function is in operation now, and your critical function is not; you're not editing your words or thoughts, not correcting (not even typos or spelling errors). You're simply getting your ideas recorded as quickly as you can. If that takes the form of a list, fine. If as you write that list you suddenly get an idea for a few paragraphs that you think might even make up part of your first draft, fine, go ahead and write them down. *Write pages and pages.* You're limited by nothing. The more you write at this point, the better your eventual article will be.

    b. After you've exhausted that initial creative impulse, state what you think is the core idea, or point, of the article *as you see it now.*

Don't worry if you're not confident that you've captured it accurately.

c. Now go through your pages of free writing and make a long list of all of the separate points you've made. This is a list, not an outline; don't begin grouping yet.

d. Go through the completed list and eliminate those that are irrelevant to the core idea.

e. Reexamine your core idea. Need adjustment yet?

f. Now begin grouping related items on your list. Do several of them have to do with step-parenting? Put them all together. Four are about Billy Graham? Group them. You may decide later, depending on what plan of organization you adopt, that some of these groups need to be broken up, but don't worry about that now. Simply group the things you see as similar.

g. Now — try making an outline of those groups of ideas. Does a logical or a natural order of presentation occur to you? Try it out. Write headings for your groups. If there are holes in your presentation — if you realize, for example, that you've got ideas about Protestant missions to the Indians but you've forgotten to write about the Catholic missions in early California — then write those missing pieces into the plan; you can research and write about them later.

h. When you've got a somewhat complete outline, look at your core idea once more and see whether it needs adjustment in the light of your tentative outline.

i. Arrange your outline one last time. Consider alternative plans, consider the relationships of the parts to each other and to the whole, and settle on an outline you're comfortable with — keeping in mind that you may change it later.

Use those eight principles of organization; they will make a great difference in your writing.

Know Your Markets

The writer of articles, perhaps more than any other type of writer — more than the novelist, for instance — must know his market. Each magazine has its own editorial slant, its own taboos. An article for *Charisma* must be written with the assumption that the "miracle gifts" are legitimate and are in operation today. That assumption will guarantee rejection at *Moody Monthly*.

And, since a personal knowledge of editors is helpful, the writer of articles has the additional task of keeping up with personnel changes at the magazines he's interested in writing for. That's no small task, since magazines seem to trade editors the way baseball teams trade players.

These are the reasons that most successful writers of articles write for just a handful of magazines. They have more success writing for the ones they know well, whose editors they know by first name. And how many magazines can you know that well? Editors always tell you to study their periodical first, to learn its approach, its subject matter, its audience. And those editors are correct. To an editor, a good free-lance writer is the one who knows the magazine almost as well as if he were a staff writer, and who can be counted on to write knowledgeably and authoritatively to that magazine's readership.

Elsewhere in this book, you'll find a description of the best sources of information about the Christian magazine market — how to keep up with current editorial needs, themes for future issues, changes in ownership or approach, and changing personnel. Study those sources. Be constantly on the lookout for new markets opening up for your writing. But be aware, as well, that you'll have the most success with no more than a handful of those markets, and when you've found a magazine whose editor likes your work, commit yourself to learning that magazine's needs as completely as if you were a staff member, and to attempting *lots* of articles for that editor. You might be a contributing editor before long.

Does that sound like good news? I'm afraid the next section will sound like bad news — but you need to hear it.

Marketing Yourself

The next few paragraphs are not for the faint-hearted. They tell you how difficult it is to get published. I know they'll be unpopular — who wants to hear bad news? And, indeed, when I've spoken on this material at writers' conferences, I have often had students get up and walk out during this part of the lecture.

A couple of months ago, one of those students called me at the office. "I was the tall guy in the back wearing a red sweater," he said. "You must have seen me — I walked out after about ten minutes."

"I do remember you," I said. "Tell me — why did you walk out?"

"You were telling us how hard it is to get published, and all the hoops we have to jump through to give our manuscripts the best chance. I was getting discouraged. I need encouragement, not discouragement," he said.

Well, we all need encouragement. I believe in encouragement. But I also believe that the true professional writer wants to know what his chances are and what he can do to improve them. Not a line of meaningless pep talk, but the truth. The real truth.

And the real truth about getting published is: Almost always, it's who you know.

Competition is fierce. The average magazine editor sees hundreds of manuscripts and query letters a week. From those he must choose just a few — a very few — to put in his magazine, usually those that best fit his list of predetermined topics. And if that editor finds three acceptable manuscripts on one of those topics, two from writers he has never heard of and one from a writer he knows and trusts, which will he buy?

"That's not fair," you might be saying. "I don't know any editors, and I'm not likely to get to meet any." Why not? Editors teach at writers' conferences all the time. They go to those conferences expressly for the purpose of meeting writers, examining manuscripts, finding new talent.

Go to those conferences, even if it involves some sacrifice and expense. If you're serious about publishing your articles in Christian magazines, you can't afford not to. Starting out as a writer, I managed to get a few articles in Sunday school take-home papers just on the strength of my query, but I didn't get any acceptances from magazines like *Moody Monthly* and *Virtue* until I saved up some money and went to a writers' conference several states away to meet the editors face to face.

They were friendly, to my surprise. And they still are. They *want* to find promising new writers. But as long as you remain merely an unfamiliar name on a SASE, your query is much less likely to make an impression. Is it *possible* to publish without knowing any editors? Of course. Writers do it all the time. But I'm talking about the way to give your query the *best* chance, and its best chance will come when the editor knows who you are.

Regardless of which part of the country you live in, there's bound to be at least a small magazine published near you, and probably several within a day's drive. Ask for appointments with those editors (you'll probably have to wait awhile); spend two or three days driving around and meeting them. Show them what you've done; explain why you have something to offer them (make sure you do; editors are not fooled by snow jobs); show a willingness to take on even minor assignments, to work on spec, to do research, to work hard on that magazine's behalf.

When you come home from your meeting with an editor, study your notes and decide on an article that you can write for that magazine based on the editor's stated needs. Then, within a month of the time of your meeting so that the editor won't have forgotten you, submit the best query you've ever written. If it's rejected, try again within a month.

Do you know anyone well-known in the world of Christian

literature — the president or bishop of your denomination, perhaps, or an established author, or the president of a seminary? Enlist that person's aid; ask him or her to write you a letter of introduction to the editor of your choice, championing your work. I assure you that editors pay attention to such letters, if only because they don't want to offend the well-known Christians who write them.

This may seem like an impractical solution to many of you, but it's probably the most practical suggestion in this chapter: If you want to write for the Christian publishing world, find a job in the industry. Somebody has to be an editor; why not you? And once you've joined a magazine's staff, you'll meet the editors of many other magazines; you'll share the podium with them at conferences, eat lunch with them, talk with them on the phone. And when those editors need an article on a subject you've discussed with them, they'll trust you to do the job. After all — you, if anybody, know what they need. I can truthfully say that I have more invitations and opportunities to write for Christian publishers than I have time to accept — not because I'm a great writer, but simply because they know me.

If you're young and not yet tied down by responsibilities, take that suggestion very seriously. But, because most of you have commitments to family and church and community that make that suggestion unattractive to you (and because the number of openings for Christian magazine editors is limited), here's another suggestion that's just as effective. Become an expert. Choose your subject matter and make yourself a credible spokesman in that area.

At writers' conferences, I often find myself saying to writers, "I can see that you really care about this subject — but what makes you a credible voice? You have no background in this field."

Understand that writing is a lifetime commitment. And by that I don't mean merely that you'll be doing it for the rest of your life. I mean also that if you are to be successful as a writer, other decisions about activities and commitments often have to be subjugated to your aspirations as a writer. For instance: You want to write on the subject of addictive behavior. You have an opportunity to moderate a panel on that subject at a denominational conference, but it comes at a bad time — you have several other obligations. What do you do? If you want to develop a reputation as an authority on addictive behavior, so that your voice will carry weight with editors (as well as readers) when you write on that subject, the answer is simple. You moderate the panel.

I'm writing in 1990. By 1995, if you want to publish in a certain field, you'll have to be recognized as a professional or at least a paraprofessional in that field. You'll have to have credibility; you'll have to have a voice. Just as in all other areas of our lives, we're seeing a trend toward specialization in writing. If editors don't see degrees after your name, they'll at least want to see some evidence of professional activity in your chosen field; they'll want a pedigree. Or you'll need a coauthor who's a recognized authority.

So begin building a résumé that includes more than your list of publications. Wrangle speaking dates at churches and conferences in your special subject matter; get interviews on talk shows; *manage* your career rather than simply trying to get published.

I've offered these suggestions not to discourage you, but rather to enable you to give your ideas the best chance of seeing publication. It's sad but true that an unsolicited query by an unknown writer has little chance of acceptance. Become a *professional* writer; improve your odds by developing a reputation for yourself and by making yourself known to editors. By the consistently high quality of your work, show editors that your articles are carefully organized, painstakingly crafted, and diligently researched.

Do these things, and the odds are good that I'll see your name in print. Often.

NOTES

1. William Strunk, Jr., and E. B. White, *The Elements of Style*, 3d ed. (New York: Macmillan, 1979), 77.
2. Theodore Bernstein, *Miss Thistlebottom's Hobgoblins* (New York: Farrar, Straus, and Giroux, 1971).

SUGGESTED READING

Barzun, Jacques. *On Writing, Editing, and Publishing: Essays Explicative and Hortatory.* Chicago: University of Chicago Press, 1971.

A classic by one of the most respected voices in American letters; a rather random collection of eleven essays, including four on the relationship between writer and editor.

Evans, Glen, ed. *The Complete Guide to Writing Non-Fiction.* Cincinnati: Writer's Digest Books, 1983.

An anthology of 108 essays compiled by the American Society of Journalists and Authors, which, though uneven in quality, still contains occasional gems and extensive sections on style, the writing process, getting published, and distinct areas of nonfiction writing, such as sports, hobbies, technology, medicine, and so on.

Gunning, Robert. *The Technique of Clear Writing*. Rev. ed. New York: McGraw, 1968.

Jacobs, Hayes B. *A Complete Guide to Writing and Selling Non-Fiction*. Cincinnati: Writer's Digest Books, 1967.

A practical guide from a longtime pro, often used as a textbook in article-writing courses. More a guide to selling than to writing.

Lanham, Richard A. *Revising Prose*. New York: Scribner, 1979.

Mitchell, Richard. *Less Than Words Can Say*. Boston: Little, Brown, 1979.

A brilliant and hilarious indictment of America's misuse of language, from the publisher of *The Underground Grammarian*, an irreverent and irregular newsletter.

Orwell, George. "Politics and the English Language." In *Shooting an Elephant*. New York: Harcourt Brace, 1950.

A discussion of the use of language to conceal meaning rather than convey it; the rationale behind the "newspeak" of Orwell's *1984*.

Ricks, Chip, and Marilyn Marsh. *How to Write for Christian Magazines*. Nashville: Broadman, 1985.

Probably the only book strictly on writing for Christian magazines, aimed mostly at writing rather than getting published. Twenty-five sample articles.

Rivers, William L. *Free-Lancer and Staff Writer: Newspaper Features and Magazine Articles*. Second edition. Belmont, Calif.: Wadsworth, 1976.

An excellent textbook covering both newspaper and magazine journalism.

Trimble, John R. *Writing with Style: Conversations on the Art of Writing*. Englewood Cliffs, N.J.: Prentice-Hall, 1975.

Chapter 27

The Local Muse
Christian Poetry in the Nineties

Bob Hudson

Perhaps no beginning poet ever received better advice than, "Don't give up your day job." It doesn't take long to discover that publishers, usually not known for their generosity, rarely throw more than a few crumbs to even their best songbirds. Although some poets manage to scrape a living from such peripheral activities as lecturing, reviewing, public reading, and being general characters, you can probably count the number of full-time professionals on your thumb. The fact is, poetry doesn't pay.

Nor does it lead to recognition. Ask anyone, by way of experiment, to name a famous living poet (Rod McKuen and Jimmy Stewart don't count). Most people have to think hard before answering, and many can't even name one. Don Marquis, a former living poet himself, once said, "Publishing a volume of verse is like dropping a rose petal down the Grand Canyon and waiting for the echo." In spite of Emily Dickinson and Gerard Manley Hopkins, even posthumous fame is rare. For those hungry for adulation, poetry can be a long road in the wrong direction.

Bob Hudson is a senior editor of General Trade Books at Zondervan Publishing House. He and his wife, Shelley Townsend-Hudson, operate a private letterpress shop, and together they edited and revised *A Christian Writer's Manual of Style* for Zondervan. Bob has published poetry in a variety of "little" and literary magazines.

For these reasons, poetry is self-regulating: only those who truly love it are crazy enough to do it — a crucial starting point for understanding the current state of Christian poetry publishing. We should resist the romantic notion, however, that the Golden Age is past and that we now live in leaden times. There is a reverse egotism in such sentiments, as if the only thing preventing our being recognized as great poets is having to live among philistines. No, the death of modern poetry has been greatly exaggerated.

Poverty and neglect have always been the bane of the bards. Their great survival secret is this: they usually do something else for a living. In mythic times they were shepherds. Chaucer, Milton, and Marvell held government jobs; Donne, Herbert, and Hopkins were ministers. While the romantics fared better at the profession of poetry, living as they did in one of the few ages when volumes of verse regularly reached the best-seller lists, even then many of them depended on patronage, independent wealth, or creative sponging. In our century, William Carlos Williams was a doctor; Wallace Stevens, an insurance executive; T. S. Eliot, an editor. Such great poets as Robert Graves and Thomas Hardy wrote potboilers to support their habit. Many contemporary poets are professors of literature, an occupation that because of the shepherding instinct at its core strangely aspires to the mythic past.

The nineties, I am convinced, will be one of the best decades ever for poets — for at least four reasons. First, just as a vow of poverty frees monks to devote their lives to God, so the slim poetry market frees poets to explore their art. There's a comfort in knowing that hungry mouths don't depend on the next couplet. There is purity in obscurity, and poets are rarely corrupted by success.

Second, our age enforces a humbling equality among poets, because all of them, no matter how widely published, are minor. Even our major poets are minor when you consider that a major novelist, on a bad day, can outsell the major poet fifty to one.

Third, you meet the nicest people. Because the reading public largely ignores poetry, poets are forced to seek out other poets with whom to share their work; in fact, poets are not only the best but also the primary readers of poetry. For a handful of good poets to recognize you as a colleague is a satisfaction that only a three-month stint on the best-seller list could match.

Finally, poets have more fun. Obscurity imposes the need for creativity in reaching the readership. Never has self-publishing been easier. With the proliferation of desk-top systems, it is as simple to declare oneself a publisher as to declare oneself a poet. Furthermore, there is a wide array of guerrilla tactics at the poet's disposal, at least until the traditional market kicks in and takes notice.

In the rest of this chapter I plan to look briefly at what poetry is and then define the present market and its alternatives — all of which may help the person who wants to know how to get a poem published.

What Is Poetry?

Two types of poetry are common in Christian publishing: devotional verse and what might be called "literary" poetry, both of which have their place, the difference between them being what they demand of the reader. Devotional verse, often derived from older and hackneyed forms and styles, offers readers, in a sense, what they already know. At its best, it affirms the tried-and-true, tells a joke or an anecdote, or highlights the obvious — all with a certain amount of panache. With wit or elegance or earnest conviction, it demands either laughter or simple recognition from the reader.

By contrast, literary poetry runs to the unexpected, offering new and sometimes unsettling insights. A wheelbarrow may always be a wheelbarrow, but a good poet will give you a wheelbarrow such as you've never experienced before. Poetry expects readers to stretch themselves, to forfeit their preconceived ideas, and to see the world through alien eyes — which may explain its lack of popularity.

The reason some Christians feel threatened by poetry may be that it is deeply revolutionary at heart. People satisfied with the status quo, be it social or psychological, generally don't like contemporary poetry. Oh, the old poems are okay because our mothers read them to us and we learned them in school, but modern poetry is scary. Like a revolutionary tract, it incites the reader to something higher, different, and sometimes earth-shattering. Like nothing short of the parables of Jesus, it attacks our presumption and pride, our denials of reality, our mental ruts, all the deathly prejudices of the soul. A daily diet of it might even convince us that the world and God are not as easy or as tame or as sentimental as we would like to believe.

Poetry is nothing if not new. It is said we live in an age of novelty — and this has probably been said of every age since the discovery of fire — but I doubt whether we really experience much that is new. Technology tends to recycle the outdated — at a faster pace, maybe, or in a different form, but always as old as original sin. Malcolm Muggeridge somewhere notes that we can generate words faster than people of any previous age, just when it seems we have least to say. Technology itself is not evil, for it has had remarkable triumphs; it has saved lives and fed millions. But it engenders bad attitudes. It flatters us and preys on our myths of self-sufficiency. It may even have some primal connection to the fruit in the Garden of Eden in that it promises us godlikeness and immortality. Anyone who writes on a word processor knows the remendous feeling of power it offers.

But poetry refuses such falsehoods. It appeals to something so invariable, so archaic and everlasting that it is constantly new. The good poet is always attuned to the eerie newness of everything, like a child discovering light and sound and taste and touch, like Columbus expecting any moment to sail off the edge of the world or discover exotic lands. Unlike technology, which lulls us into an artificial dream, poetry expects us to wake up, to change, to experience real joy and real pain, to lay ourselves bare.

Allow me an extended metaphor. We are like passengers on a train roaring past a beautiful medieval cathedral. With each click of the rails the perspective changes, the light outside alters, fades, and rekindles, though few people notice it. The poet describes those fugitive visions, hoping to encourage others — who are too busy eating in the club car, tending their children, or discussing religion and politics — to look out the window. The poet's themes are rock solid, ancient and invariable as the marble of the cathedral but, in the shifting light of daily life, always fresh and new and unknown. For the Christian, poetry is nothing short of prophetic.

The Current Market

"Unsolicited" is redundant before "poetry" — let's face it, nobody solicits that stuff. The traditional publishing market is passive, depending on referrals and the U.S. mail for what little poetry it publishes, and any poet who has undergone the humiliation of repeated rejection understands why the process is called "submission." Poets, who as a race are reputed to be the most sensitive of creatures, usually develop thick skins — artistic calluses — as a result of such rejection. Most combine their hypersensitivity with a sort of rough-and-tumble realism. While Shelley romantically defined poets as the "antennae of the race," Dylan Thomas may have been more accurate; he said the poet was "a dog among the fairies."

Make no mistake — by "traditional publishing market" I mean primarily periodicals. No new poet should even think of sending a collection of poems to a book publisher before most of those poems have appeared in magazines first. Period. A recent survey reported that editors spend about three minutes reviewing the average unsolicited manuscript, at which rate, I imagine a volume of unpublished verse gets about three seconds. The poet's best chance of snagging attention is to present a solid list of magazine credits.

Modern Christian poets face another problem: few Christian magazines publish poetry — or devotional verse either, for that matter. New Christian literary journals spring up as fast as dragons' teeth. Some succeed; most have the life span of a lightning bug. Still, the poet needs to watch for those magazines as they arise, for they are numerous and hunting for good poetry. Denominational magazines are also a good market for poetry, publishing, as they do, a fair amount of excellent poetry.

Without a doubt, the poet's most valuable resource is Judson Jerome's *Poet's Market*,[1] which is available in most bookstores. No poet who hopes to publish can survive without it. Jerome, who is the closest thing the aspiring poet has to a guardian angel, lists many religious periodicals that publish poetry. There is no better place to start.

Jack Leax, a poet and professor at Houghton College, also says that Christians too often neglect the college and university "little" literary magazines. These journals often reach a ready audience for poetry, and some even pay a modest (that is, immodestly skimpy) sum upon publication. Others pay in contributors' copies. The point is not to make poetry pay, but to reach the widest possible audience, and no magazine with a circulation even as small as five hundred should be sneezed at. The so-called "cutting-edge" of contemporary poetry is found in these magazines, and they have established more than one poet's reputation.

Professor Leax's comment suggests another point. Most creditable Christian poets publish in the secular magazine market. While writers of purely devotional verse are largely excluded from secular magazines, serious Christian poets cannot ignore them. Many writers believe that the Christian market is an easier nut to crack than the secular, that religious publishers have different and often less-demanding standards than their secular counterparts. For some genres, unfortunately, this perception may be true. For the poet, however, the narrowness of the Christian market necessitates competition in the larger arena. Serious Christian poets who expect to publish need to write poetry every bit as good as that of the best secular poets. There is no middle ground.

Some beginning poets fear the religious content of their poetry will exclude them from secular journals, though the quality of the poetry, not its content, is most often the problem. Good poetry gets published. The market may be small, but it seldom fails to recognize talent. Furthermore, a look at recent literary journals will reveal that religious themes, Christian or otherwise, are as prevalent as ever. A look at the copyright pages in books by most Christian poets reveals that those poets are active in secular poetry circles. (Speaking of copyright pages, they are a great source of names of periodicals, since many of them list the magazines where the poems first appeared.)

Competing in the secular market, of course, means that Christian poets must read contemporary poetry — and a lot of it — which, I am always puzzled to find, comes as an unpleasant chore for many. But there's no alternative. Poetry has no room for reactionaries who think modernism is trash. The idea that all modern art is somehow anti-Christian and that contemporary poetry is obscure, formless, and self-indulgent is simply chuckle-headed. Some art is bad, of course. Some of it is insincere. But much of it rivals the classics, and let's face it, other than dead poets, only modern ones get published.

I once knew a poet who said no good poetry had been written after Wordsworth; this must be why his own poetry read like bad Wordsworth imitations. There have been those, C. S. Lewis and Francis Schaeffer among them, who criticized T. S. Eliot for being in the vanguard of modernism — a curious attitude, because few poets have been more deeply rooted in tradition and as critical of the loss of human values as Eliot. Furthermore, Eliot was one of the most deeply Christian poets of this century.

My suspicion is that those who claim to hate contemporary poetry haven't read much of it. They need help. I always advise such people to begin slowly with some of the more formal, older living poets like former U. S. laureates Richard Wilbur and Robert Penn Warren. Their themes are classic and often as profoundly religious as the prayers of Anselm. Then the reader can move on to the next generation of poets like Galway Kinnell, W. S. Merwin, Wendell Berry, A. R. Ammons, and countless others — all insightful, disturbing, and tremendously rewarding. Finally, seek out the emerging poets. The little literary journals are full of exciting and engaging new writers, and the aspiring poet who doesn't read them is unlikely ever to appear beside them.

After a long periodical apprenticeship, most poets approach a book publisher, the second phase of traditional publishing. Among such publishers, large is not necessarily better. The last four decades have seen the proliferation of small poetry presses, as well as university presses that specialize in poetry, and these have done more than any large company to shape contemporary taste. Such secular companies as New Directions, City Lights, Black Sparrow, Atheneum, to name only a few, should already be familiar to lovers of modern poetry. Today, new and innovative presses continue to spring up. Not only are they more effective in reaching the poetry reader, they are generally more willing to take risks on good writers. Again, Jerome's *Poet's Market* is an excellent resource.

The bad news for the Christian is that few religious book companies publish poetry of any kind. The Christian bookstores would sell very little of it even if more were published, and what does get sold tends to be either by classic (which means dead) authors, like C. S. Lewis or George MacDonald, or the highly devotional gift-book kind, like Helen Steiner Rice. It is futile to urge publishers to publish more poetry, because the demand must come from readers first. If every poet who has ever sent a poem to a magazine were to buy one book of good Christian poetry (yes, there are a few), it would create a phenomenal overnight demand. Publishers would respond with more and newer and better volumes. My suspicion, however, is that Christian poets buy very little poetry by their brothers and sisters, which is discouraging; to paraphrase Samuel Johnson, "Don't trust any poet who has written more than he has read."

The Local Muse

Current poetry, however, more than any written medium, has a rich life apart from commercial interests. No survey would be complete if it failed to mention the alternatives to traditional publishing that are presently being pursued. "Vanity" publishing is one such alternative. It should be distinguished from self-publishing, which is the most common alternative. An author pays a vanity publisher to print the book, after which the author and publisher split the copies and try to sell as many as possible, although most of the burden lies with the author. For the poet with no interest in self-publishing and who has entirely given up hope of being published in any other format, vanity publishing offers some moderate satisfaction. If nothing else, it provides gift copies for friends and family. Caution, however, is advised, for such books can be expensive and hard to unload.

Self-publication, by comparison, leaves production in the hands of the author. The poet acts as writer, editor, and contractor for the typesetting, artwork, layout, printing, collating, binding, promotion, and distribution. For each task the author is willing to tackle, the cost decreases and the sense of artistic control increases. Printer, poet, and general Renaissance man Clifford Burke has written two books that will help the poet find a path through the production process: *Printing It: A Guide to Graphic Techniques for the Impecunious*[2] and *Printing Poetry*.[3]

Everyone knows someone who operates a desk-top publishing system. These are small computer-driven editing, layout, and typesetting systems that can be easily adapted to the setting of poetry. Some free-lance companies will even set type and produce booklets for a fee. The technology is changing fast. Setting type and having it printed has become easier with each passing year.

Many poets experiment with hand typesetting and printing, a time-consuming but satisfying method of producing small booklets and broadsides. As electronic publishing dominates the industry, old-fashioned printing and typesetting equipment can often be purchased at relatively low cost. My wife and I, as hand-printers ourselves, can testify to its attractions, but it is a long and demanding commitment, not to be considered half-heartedly.

There is a hitch to all forms of self-publishing, however: making books is easy — selling them is hard. Many independent bookstores sell local authors' self-published books on consignment, but almost no such books make their way into the major chains. Don't even try to talk to chain-store managers; most often, a central office in another city has already dictated their stock. Only after a self-published book has become a phenomenal success through mail-order or other markets will it even be considered by the chain stores. For poetry, such high sales are an impossibility.

Nor do self-published poets fare well with the dealers who sell small-press books to public and academic libraries. What little poetry they sell on consignment must not only be of unusually high quality, but it must also be extremely well packaged. Even then sales will be very low: fifty to a hundred copies would be outstanding. Libraries are almost never the primary market for any book, least of all for poetry.

Some self-publishers achieve success through the mail. The concept is called "direct target marketing." The self-publisher of a model-train book, for instance, can buy a mailing list from a hobby magazine, which provides access to a ready-made audience. After an announcement of the new book is mailed, a number of them may be sold — with luck. The major problems, notably the high cost of mailing and low response rate, are often ameliorated by teaming up and sharing expenses with other self-publishers in the same field to offer several books in any one mailing. Still, such tactics are risky for the poet because targeting the market can be difficult at best.

The best comprehensive guide for self-publishers, not surprisingly, is a self-published one: *The Self-Publishing Manual: How to Write, Print and Sell Your Own Book* (now in its fourth edition) by Dan Poynter. The author's own Para Publishing is a model of successful self-publishing. To order the manual or to receive a list of Dan Poynter's many other helpful books write: Para Publishing, P.O. Box 4232-607, Santa Barbara, CA 93140-4232.

So how do poets reach their audience? That question brings us back to the fundamental fact discussed at the beginning of this essay: poetry is not a career, it's a lifestyle. Unless it is an almost sacred commitment, the poet will find neither audience nor satisfaction. The apprenticeship is long, and in a sense, it never ends. Poet Judith Depree once said that poets are called by God to exercise their craft. She wrote in a letter to me:

> Keep on trying. Don't give up because of the paucity of markets. For the time being, hone and prune what you do until it is an awesome testimony to Grace — profoundly, exquisitely simple and original and relevant. When others who *know* what is excellent find *you* excellent, send it out. Here and there, now and then, your words will echo back to you. There is no other reward beyond God's "Well done, good and faithful servant."

As with so much in the Christian life, poetry, whether published or not, is a means of loving those around us, a way of serving God and our neighbor. The poet should never forget that God and our neighbor make up the richest audience any poet could hope for, and this commitment takes many forms:

Poets are involved with other poets. They read to each other, encourage each other, organize public readings. Some even self-publish anthologies of their works for local distribution and gift-giving. They share information and sharpen each other's skills.

Public readings are common. Poetry is as much a spoken as a written art form. Someone once said, "Poetry is singing without music; reciting it is like reading with the eyes closed." Nothing can match the immediacy of poetry when it is read well. Though not always well attended, privately sponsored readings can offer local poets a platform from which to speak.

Christian poets take advantage of the worship potential of poetry. Many poets pursue such questions as: Would the worship committee allow poetry to be read during regular services, perhaps in place of a musical solo or as a prayer? If not, would they allow a special poetry worship on an off-night? How about a special "arts-in-worship" celebration to get the painters and dancers and actors and musicians involved?

Many poets write in other genres and incorporate their poetry. Writer Latayne Scott advises poets to remember that poetry can be an attractive garnish to other forms of writing, like illuminated letters in a medieval manuscript. She recently published a book on the subject of crisis in the Christian life; in her book she was able to use her own relevant poems as epigraphs to the chapters. Poets commonly include their own poems in their articles and books; and as long as they are relevant, such poems can be most effective.

355

Much good poetry is published in church newsletters. This reaches the people closest to the poet. I have received more recognition for three poems I published in my church's newsletter than for all my other credits combined. To this day people tell me that they saved the newsletters just for my poems.

Poets take a broad view of publication. Often churches allow their poets to place free copies of poems on the information table in the lobby. Some nice booklets have been produced on a Xerox machine or at the local copy shop. Typewritten sheets of poetry are often passed from friend to friend.

Most Christian poets make poetry part of their devotional lives. They often keep a pen handy as they read the Bible and pray. They let their spiritual growth become the stuff of their poetry. In that way they let God in on the process.

Finally, good poets meet real needs. Even unpublished poetry can be a ministry. It can empathize with the ill, encourage a church in crisis, bid farewell or welcome, and communicate important messages. Although the audience of a poem may be only one person, it can act like a healing balm. I have seen exhortative poems tacked to bulletin boards, joyful poems passed out after church, and loving poems shared at family gatherings. My late uncle, who wrote light verse about flowers and months of the year, used to read them with great tenderness at the supper table. When my grandfather said, "Oh, John, that's just old doggerel," my uncle would reply, with a wink at me, "But us dogs don't mind, do we, Bob?"

Many beginning poets are afraid of being oddballs. Sensitivity and appropriateness are important, of course, for the poet can often strain the limits of others' courtesy. But too often, I believe, poets are more concerned with respectability than communication. It's embarrassing to speak from the heart. It's a scandal to try to put truth into words and to constantly fall short, for that is the nature of poetry. Somehow, many poets think, publication will grant them affirmation.

Unfortunately, acceptance and respectability have always been enemies of poetry. Just as secular poets have always been something of a scandal to the world, so most Christian poets, inevitably, scandalize other Christians. St. John of the Cross was criticized for the eroticism of his devotional verse. Donne had to live down his earlier (and sometimes better) love poems. Traherne and Browning were thought too universalistic. Herbert, Southwell, and Vaughan, too mystical. Christopher Smart and William Cowper went mad, and yet they wrote some of the greatest hymns of the church. Blake was one of the most inspired of Christian poets, and yet he was considered insane, or, worse, heretical. But all of them opened people's eyes.

It is too late to make poetry respectable. Respectable poetry ceases to be a revelation; pretty poetry, if it is nothing else, is nothing. Even Christian readers, who have discovered the Good News, can never claim to have discovered all of it; they can never close their minds and spirits to the incredible richness, beauty, and constant newness of God's creation. They need good poets — especially unrespectable ones.

In a time of televangelism, global outreach, Christian celebrities, and high-tech religious marketing, the poet's voice may be the only human one left. Poetry is scary because it doesn't bow to the machine, the sales pitch, or the spotlight. It is seldom impressed with numbers, high attendance, or effectiveness surveys, though many Christians are impressed with such things.

Though generally ignored, poetry is one of the few written forms that can still startle, that can get people out of themselves, that can metaphorically juice those who need a little juicing. The field is ripe for harvest. Like Chanticleer, the local poet must lift up his or her voice — persistently and clearly — to wake the late sleepers and announce the new day.

NOTES

1. Cincinnati: Writer's Digest Books, annually updated.
2. Berkeley, Calif.: Wingbow, 1972.
3. Orinda, Calif.: Scarab, 1980.

SUGGESTED READING

Alexander, Pat, ed. *Eerdmans Book of Christian Poetry*. Grand Rapids: Eerdmans, 1981.

A beautifully illustrated anthology of Christian poetry from the early church fathers to the present. Printed in four colors on slick paper, a classy introduction to the rich heritage of Christian poetry.

Brande, Dorothea. *Becoming a Writer*. Los Angeles: J. P. Tarcher, 1981.

Though written with the prose writer in mind, contains extremely helpful information on inspiration, the creative process, and overcoming writer's block. Full of wise psychological advice and practical help.

Davie, Donald. *The New Oxford Book of Christian Verse*. New York: Oxford University Press, 1982.

A scholarly compilation of the finest Christian poems ever written in English. An especially helpful introduction with guidelines for defining what makes some poetry "Christian." From middle English mystical verse to T. S. Eliot, the best collection of its kind in print.

Hugo, Richard. *The Triggering Town: Lectures and Essays on Poetry and Writing.* New York: W. W. Norton, 1979.

Essays from a late poet who was one of the country's most effective teachers of poetry writing. Practical, personal, and profound — especially helpful in urging poets to discover the untapped and unconscious wellsprings of poetry within themselves. Recommended.

Leax, John. *Country Labors.* Grand Rapids: Zondervan, 1991.

One of the finest Christian poets writing today, with his perennial themes of nature, identity, eternity, relationships, and authenticity in the Christian life. Powerful and startling.

L'Engle, Madeleine. *Walking on Water: Reflections on Faith and Art.* Wheaton, Ill.: Shaw, 1980.

An extended journal-like meditation on the relationship of art and faith; one of the best books available for enhancing creativity. With its companion volume, *And It Was Good*, offers true encouragement to the Christian writer who has doubts about the value of the artist's craft in God's larger scheme. Deeply insightful.

Shaw, Luci. *Polishing the Petosky Stone.* Wheaton, Ill.: Shaw, 1990.

Deeply moving poems with a knack for pinpointing the beautiful and holy in everyday life. A compilation of the best work of one whose name has become synonymous with the best in Christian poetry. Recommended.

Ueland, Brenda. *If You Want to Write.* Saint Paul: Graywolf Press, 1987.

Forthright talk on inspiration instead of discussion of technique. A good cheerleader and encourager for anyone who becomes discouraged, blocked, or otherwise lacking in motivation. In practical ways, able to prod you into discovering the personal and unique things you have to say.

Wangerin, Walter, Jr. *A Miniature Cathedral and Other Poems.* San Francisco: Harper & Row, 1987.

The best poems of one of the best and most passionate writers and storytellers of our time. Intense, thoughtful, elegant, mystical, and always highly enjoyable.

Chapter 28

Denominational Publishing

Kristy Arnesen Pullen

Working in denominational publishing can feel like walking a tightrope. You've always known a net is below you. When you think you might be starting to fall, you just lean to the side where the net is. The only problem is that you notice the hard ground has gotten much closer to the bottom of the net than ever before.

When a religious publisher operates under the auspices of a denomination, there is both the monetary and organizational support that comes from being a part of a larger organization[1] and the responsibility to return income to the "parent" operation. Sounds like a fair arrangement, doesn't it? It may have been fair in earlier days. Now, however, the climate in religious publishing, as well as the state of denominational religious life, makes the old rules no longer realistic. The "hard ground" of balancing the budget is calling denominations to scrutinize all of their operations. The days of relying on the "net" of a large endowment to finance worthy but economically unprofitable activities are all but over.

Kristy Arnesen Pullen is director of Judson Press, the denominational publisher for the American Baptist Churches in the U.S.A. She was previously senior editor for Judson Press and editor of evangelism materials for the denomination and also held management and pastoral positions. She holds a B.A. in journalism from the University of South carolina and an M.A. in religion from Eastern Baptist Theological Seminary.

As the costs of doing business rise, even a large endowment may not generate enough interest income to support the entire ministry.

To understand denominational publishing, it's important to look at not only the day-to-day issues and specific aspects of the work but also the factors that have led to the current state of the enterprise. Economic conditions in the field of publishing have changed. Whereas once religious publishing was a key way for denominations to finance other parts of their mission, now its very existence has come into question. Now the question is less "How much money can we count on from the publishing operation?"and more "Should this denomination still publish books?"

This chapter will examine some of the reasons denominations have been forced to ask the latter question, explain some of the peculiarities inherent in religious publishing within a denominational context, and discuss some of the specific responsibilities a publishing organization must be sensitive to when it is accountable to a denominational constituency. Publishing books can be a tremendously effective way of reaching people with God's message, but the enterprise is laden with risks. Matching the appropriate form of the message with the right person at the right time can be a tricky task. My discussion will focus on both the complexities of denominational publishing and the broader questions of its very survival.

At stake in the analysis of these issues is a denomination's ability to sustain its access to its own members and a much larger group of sisters and brothers of faith through a medium as old as the Bible itself. For those who believe that religious book publishing is itself a ministry and not simply a way for denominations to make money, their very call from God in many cases is being questioned. A person may feel called by God to work in publishing for a particular denomination. If his or her job is eliminated by a lack of funds, what does that say about that person's understanding of his or her call?

Defining the Terms

Although *denomination* is a term familiar to many people, references to the so-called "mainline" denominations may not be as easily under-stood. In this context the mainline churches are those long-established organizations whose members in many cases cover a wide distance on the theological spectrum. Many of these groups have a historic tradition of publishing both scholarly theological works and general readings for the religious community. Their publishing organizations generally have operated in a "trade" environment, meaning they sell their wares to nondenominational bookstores in addition to the members of their churches.

Denominational publishing in most cases includes books, curriculum, and merchandise developed and produced with local churches and their members in mind. Curriculum is unquestioned as an integral part of the educational mission of the church. Merchandise is seen as a financially profitable opportunity to provide needed resources to churches. Since the status of book publishing as a ministry versus profit-making enterprise tends to be more open to debate, this chapter will deal primarily with book publishing.

"Subsidized" publishing refers to publishing activities that are not expected to generate a profit. Financial resources from the denomination are allocated to the publishing operation with little or no expectation of return on the investment. Sometimes individual products may be subsidized, even if the publishing house as a whole is expected to be financially independent.

Background

The strictly defined programmatic functions of a denomination have never been expected to pull their weight financially. Generally the nature of those activities does not lend itself to generating income or in many cases breaking even. For example, if part of a denomination's mission is to provide consultation or training for its members, charging a hefty fee for its services might discourage people from taking advantage of the opportunity. Trying to recover the cost of staff salary, travel expenses, etc., could be counterproductive if the goal is to provide a service for as many people as possible.

At one time subsidizing a publishing operation was not even an issue since religious books sold to broad audiences and generated significant income. Along with mission giving from churches, the publishing operation provided the subsidy for the denomination's "ministry" activities. Today's economic conditions have changed the dynamics. Production costs have risen, magnifying the normal risks of publishing. It has always been difficult to predict what will appeal to book buyers at any given time and how much they will pay for a particular book. In order to make a profit, publishers must print large numbers of copies of each title and sell each copy at the highest possible price that the market will bear. Since choosing manuscripts is an art, not a science, a percentage of the titles chosen are destined to remain unsold. Sometimes that percentage can be quite high, causing the publisher to take a significant loss. The more times this happens, the more dismal the publisher's financial bottom line. This reality can be deadly for small publishers, since they simply do not have the resources to risk printing large number of books that might not sell.

This change in the dynamics has set up a tension. Many denominational workers involved in what are commonly called "program" areas tend to see publishing as a way to fund the ministry and not as a ministry in itself. A program activity (e.g., evangelism) is one that carries out the purposes of the organization rather than one that simply supports the organization itself (e.g., payroll). If the publishing operation has always been expected to bring in dollars and that expectation has never been questioned, workers involved in subsidized activities will feel let down if those dollars don't come in. At the same time, if those working in publishing are producing books to try to meet the needs of the denomination, they will likely feel they are fulfilling a programmatic function rather than simply supporting the work of others. With that understanding it's easy to see where tension might arise.

Evaluating the Current Situation

So what happens when an arm of the denomination that used to generate income no longer does? If it's an operation that has no other purpose than to make money, it's not fulfilling its purpose and should be prevented from draining the organization's resources. If it exists to carry out a purpose of the organization, the traditional approach is to subsidize it. In these lean economic times, mainline denominations hardly have enough money to subsidize what they used to, much less fund projects they had expected to bring in income. Formerly when an activity was deemed worthy but economically unprofitable, the response was "We'll have to subsidize it!" Now that response brings the question "With what?" Given these new dynamics, denominations are forced to evaluate their publishing operations to determine if they indeed can be considered a foundational part of their mission.

It would be difficult to determine the ministry quotient of religious book publishing, but one could get an idea simply by calculating the number of potential readers for a single title. That, of course, can only be estimated, since a book is often read by many more people than the buyer alone. And how often have we heard it said that a life has been touched and changed by the reading of a book? If books as a medium have such an enormous potential for profoundly reaching individuals, the question becomes "How best can such a valuable communication channel be utilized?"

The Dangers of a Shortsighted Solution

Getting out of the business of publishing books may be one way to balance the corporate budget — in the short term. But if religious book publishing becomes solely the domain of publishers that have no denominational affiliation, won't churches risk distancing their members from the specific interpretation of God's message they feel called to proclaim? Mainline denominations in essence would be inviting others to interpret God's mission to their members in their place. What would serve a denomination most effectively would be to have its members reading materials that specifically interpret its mission. Many believe that the decline in mainline denominational membership and involvement evidenced over the years stems from a lack of denominational identity (What sets us apart?) and hence loyalty (If we're really not that different from all the others, why should I limit myself?).

With declining membership comes declining mission giving. In the midst of this downward spiral, the denomination may be asking itself, "Should we still publish religious books?" Those who see the publishing enterprise simply as an operation that should be generating income and isn't doing so would say "Can we afford to?" Perhaps the better question, for two reasons, is "Can we afford not to?"

First, books are an ideal medium in which a denomination can explain its history, its beliefs, its distinctives, and its mission. If religious publishing can provide that kind of direct vehicle for promoting denominational identity and thus hopefully loyalty, can we afford to ignore this channel for enhancing the overall health of the denomination? Through the vehicle that books provide for educating members and potential members, a denomination can develop a strong sense of relationship with people who might not be reached through its other efforts. As those individuals begin to recognize the unique value of membership in that denomination, they become more loyal to its causes and mission emphases. With that loyalty comes a willingness to give of their time and their financial resources. Book publishing at that point has become a vital tool for improving and maintaining the health of the denomination, both financially and, most importantly, in its ability to do God's work.

Second, given the large percentage of a denomination's budget that goes toward activities that return no income, what sources of income does it have? For most denominations one of the significant sources of revenue is the publishers' "backlist" (those books published previously that continue to sell). Often a publisher may continue to sell a book decades after its original printing. The more additional printings a book warrants (provided it does not require costly revision), the greater will be the margin of profit and thus income. The publisher's inventory of already-produced books can be a ready source of income for the organization if the books are effectively promoted. After all, if the money has already been spent to produce them, why not follow through until the proceeds come back in?

Someone might suggest, then, that the denomination sell only the books already produced and get out of the business for the future. That is an option that works for the short term. A few years down the line, however, after the publisher has presented no new titles for a length of time, bookstore owners become reluctant to buy even older titles from the publisher. One reason for this is that bookstores are entitled to return to the publisher, within a designated time period, books they have purchased but have been unable to sell. If the publisher hasn't come out with any new titles recently, most people assume it is in the process of going out of business. Bookstore owners begin to wonder if they will be able to return their unsold stock to a publisher that is on its way out of existence. Before that point the publisher had better choose whether to stay in the business and publish some new titles or be prepared to take a loss on the books it paid to produce but can no longer sell.

In order to survive in the field of denominational publishing today, it is essential to understand the previous discussion. Once those issues have been dealt with, what are some of the specifics an individual faces on a day-to-day basis?

So What Is It Really Like?

What is it like to work in the field of denominational publishing? The clearest picture is again the tightrope image. On one side of the tightrope is the denominational constituency, and on the other is the religious bookselling industry or the "trade." What one "customer" wants and needs frequently is not the same as what the other wants and needs. Can a publisher meet the requirements of both? Sometimes — sometimes not.

The ideal situation for a denominational publisher is to publish books that meet the needs of its own members but that also appeal to a wider market. Unfortunately, the books that sell to a wide audience often are not the same ones that are chosen to meet an identified denominational concern. A book with specific denominational references may be called for but may have very little chance of selling to the trade. Depending on the denomination, the constituency may not be large enough to insure successful sales. In that case a solution is to choose other titles for the broader market that will bring in enough income to balance the shortfall of the denominational project.

Sometimes difficult choices have to be made. The number of requests for publication of projects with limited market appeal is staggering. Some of the requests come from "official" denominational channels, others from individuals. In either case, it is tough to say, "We're sorry, but your book won't sell enough copies for us to be able to make that kind of financial investment." The toughest part is that invariably the requester is convinced that it will.

Sometimes it seems as if every child of a minister or missionary has written a book about his or her parent's life. No doubt the lives of these individuals have been rich and full, but that does not necessarily mean that a book should be written about them. How do you explain that to the author who fancies himself or herself to be the next James Michener and his or her father to have been a person whose contributions to the Christian church are comparable to those of Martin Luther or John Wesley? And what about that denominational saint who has written his (so far it's mostly been men) autobiography, which will surely be lifechanging for millions of readers? These well-meaning writers should not be faulted for their desire to leave a record of such noble lives, only for their lack of objectivity. Their naïvité leads them to false hopes and inevitable disappointment, not to mention heartbreaking conversations for editors who would like nothing better than to make the potential author's dream come true.

The situation is not as delicate when the request comes from someone in an official denominational capacity, mostly because they usually understand the economic realities a bit better. They also have access to funds that can be used to offset the large financial investment of publishing a book. Although they may still disagree with the publisher's estimate of sales potential, they may be willing to underwrite at least part of the production costs in order to see the project marketed and distributed appropriately.

Responding to a denominational constituency raises questions about what it means to be an "official denominational publisher." Are denominational authors given preference over other authors? Are "official" denominational positions supported even when that means part of the constituency may be disgruntled? For instance, a denomination may discourage the use of masculine language when referring to God. An author, who may represent a significant number of churches in the denomination who refer to God only as male, insists on using the language he or she finds most comfortable. Whose position carries the most weight? It's a matter of editorial and political instinct, not an exact science. The deciding factor may be the nature of the book. If the particular project carries some kind of endorsement that would reflect on the denominational leadership, the masculine language may be eliminated. If the book reflects on the author alone, the author's position may be upheld.

As with any enterprise containing political elements, tact and diplomacy are crucial for those working in denominational publishing. They must be willing to listen to different points of view and respond in constructive ways. That's not easy when they are faced with unrealistic expectations. Denominational publishing is a business as well as a ministry. When someone submits an unacceptable manuscript and wants a detailed critique complete with advice to improve his or her writing, is the response based on ministry or business motivation? If motivated by ministry, an editor may take the time to provide the assistance the writer is asking for, even if it means putting other work aside. If that same overworked editor responds from a business mindset, he or she may point the writer in the direction of professional writing help, which is not the free solution the writer was anticipating. A business mindset opens the door to public relations problems while a ministry approach can lead to missed deadlines, burned-out staff, and other business problems. As with other areas of life, balance and judgment are vital.

Is It Worth It?

Despite the balancing act and diplomacy required, denominational publishing can be extremely rewarding work. God has gifted us in a variety of ways. If an individual's vocational gifts happen to lie in the field of publishing, that does not mean he or she must separate ministry activities from his or her livelihood. What better way to answer God's call than by using one's gifts holistically?

Balance and judgment are required not only in the day-to-day decisions that individuals working in religious publishing make but also in the overall assessment of the future of denominational publishing. Denominational publishing was originally begun to meet needs of individuals and structures. It has been and continues to be an important part of God's work. That does not mean, however, that the way it has been done in the past is still the best way to meet those needs. Redefining priorities is a healthy exercise that can keep a ministry healthy. The tightrope of denominational publishing may be the divine way of "keeping us on our toes" to make sure we don't become convinced that we're in charge of God's work. And perhaps that hard ground that we see looming so closely below the net is just God's solid foundation calling us to make sure we stay in close enough touch with God's mission today.

NOTES

1. Sometimes the publishing operation is housed within a particular mission agency of the denomination, an agency that may function as a separate corporation.

SUGGESTED READING

Boston, Bruce O., ed. *STET! Tricks of the Trade for Writers and Editors.* Alexandria, Va.: Editorial Experts, 1986. Pp. 59–64.

Practical tips on working diplomatically with authors, an essential skill for editors in denominational publishing.

McKinney, William. "Revisioning the Future of Oldline Protestantism." *The Christian Century* (November 8, 1989): 1014–16.

An analysis of the funding crisis confronting "oldline Protestantism" that affects so many denominational publishers, with some suggestions for the future.

Noyce, Gaylord. "Mandate for the Mainline." *The Christian Century* (November 8, 1989): 1017–19.

An explanation of the author's "convictions about the continuing importance and vitality of the mainline churches," presenting a challenge for a more clearly articulated witness.

Roof, Wade Clark. "The Church in the Centrifuge." *The Christian Century* (November 8, 1989): 1012–14.

A perspective on the challenges facing mainline Protestant churches, now and in the years ahead.

Wheeler, Barbara G. "Theological Publishing: In Need of a Mandate." *The Christian Century* (November 23, 1988): 1066–70.

An excellent overview of the history of and prescriptions for "serious" theological publishing, focused on denominational publishers.

Chapter 29

Newsletters
A Late Twentieth-Century Phenomenon

William H. Gentz

In the course of a week's mail most households receive several publications that qualify as "newsletters" — the modern age's most prolific kind of publishing. These informal periodicals are used by every kind of group and organization in the country. Many are also published by individuals, including your congressman. Newsletters are also the most prevalent kind of publication in the religious field, far outnumbering books, magazines, newspapers, and other journals. In fact, it would be hard to imagine the religious communities of our modern world functioning without newsletters.

These publications come in all sizes and shapes and look quite different from each other. They vary from the small two-to-four-page sheet sent by the local church to its membership to the large, professionally produced newsletters of large organizations with national and international circulations. Yet there are certain characteristics that all newsletters have in common and that set them apart from other

William H. Gentz has held book editorial positions for five publishers. He is the author or editor of six books, including three editions of *Religious Writer's Marketplace* and two editions of *Writing to Inspire*. He founded and published the *Christian Writers Newsletter* for eight years and for ten years was editor of *Church & Synagogue Libraries*, an interfaith publication for congregational librarians.

publications. They are a very specialized kind of publishing that has burgeoned in the late twentieth century, especially in the religious field.

A Little History

Howard Penn Hudson, one of America's foremost authorities on newsletters, traces their beginnings back to the sixteenth century.[1] The first known newsletter was issued by Count Philip Fugger of Augsburg, Germany. The publication was made up of loose, handwritten sheets reporting business news gathered by agents in the trade centers of Europe. The publication became known as *Fugger Zeitung.* (*Zeitung,* meaning "tidings," later became the German word for "newspaper.") These news reports were sold to paying subscribers. Here, then, are two characteristics of newsletters — specialized information prepared for a subscription audience.

The first newspaper in the United States, founded in 1704, was called the *Boston News Letter.* The colonies were growing fast, and commercial news, such as information on ship arrivals, could no longer travel efficiently by word of mouth. As Mark Beach, a modern authority on newsletters, points out,[2] editor John Campbell of Boston had to be as versatile as his twentieth-century counterparts: he gathered the information, wrote articles, fit copy, supervised printing, and maintained the address lists. Editor Campbell was also aware — nearly three centuries ago — how much readers liked his very personal approach. This is another characteristic of newsletters that is still true today.

However, it is in the late twentieth century that newsletters have come into their own in the United States and around the world. The first modern newsletter of consequence, still being published, was the *Kiplinger Washington Letter* founded in 1923 by Willard M. Kiplinger. Other newsletters followed, and the explosion of this phenomenon came in the 1960s and 70s. As a result of this explosion, there are more than one hundred thousand newsletters of major circulation in the United States today. Some authorities estimate a total of half a million if one includes the thousands of smaller circulation newsletters in all fields.

To coordinate the industry, the *Newsletter on Newsletters* was founded in 1964 and the Newsletter Association of America began in 1977. There are today many publications in the field. The most important of these are listed at the end of this chapter.

The rise in popularity of newsletters is due to many factors. Newsletters provide information that people need and want on particular subjects or areas of specialized interest. They are comparatively simple to produce. And the invention of new forms of duplication and printing as well as computerized publication have made the newsletter the ideal publication for many fields, including religion, in the late twentieth century.

What Is a Newsletter?

Newsletters are published in many varieties, but all of them have at least three common characteristics.

1. *Newsletters contain specialized information for a designated audience.* They contain specific information on one subject or on related subjects not readily available in other forms. To understand this, take a look at the newsletters to which you subscribe or that come to your home. For example, the newsletters I receive are related to the subjects that interest me or in which I am involved. Each month I receive a newsletter from my church and from other institutions that interest me or that I support: a hospital, several organizations that give help to victims of specific diseases (in my case, Alzheimers and cancer), New York's Central Park, the Philharmonic Orchestra, the Metropolitan Opera, the American Scandinavian Foundation, and two museums. I receive newsletters from those branches of stamp collecting in which I am involved: Collectors of Religion on Stamps, the American Topical Association and its American Bicentennial division, and from an unusual philatelic society related to my profession: Collectors of Journalists, Authors, and Poets on Stamps. I receive a monthly newsletter that summarizes and digests information from all religious and church-related magazines and newspapers. There are more — e.g., a dozen charities, but this is enough to demonstrate the very specific readerships that most newsletters seek to reach.

Because they contain specialized news, newsletters are apt to be kept by readers longer than other publications and passed on to friends with like interests. Thus the readership is often much greater than the number of subscribers on the mailing list.

2. *A newsletter contains news.* It differs from a newspaper since it contains news related to one specific area of interest and is published for a specialized audience, but nevertheless, true to the first part of its name, the information in a newsletter must be news. The information is timely and also qualifies on the "man bites dog" principle — it is something new, different, unusual — in other words, "newsworthy."

For example, the *Christian Writers Newsletter*, which I founded and published for eight years, always contained items that were news — new publishers to whom writers could submit manuscripts, changes in editorial staffs, trends in religious publishing that were significant or timely, and new and unusual ways to conduct the business of writing and make it work for the writer. On the other hand, some of the articles in each issue were not news but of an inspirational nature related to the field of writing. Some of these articles were taken from the backlog of material that had been purchased earlier, but the majority of the newsletter was "news."

In the most successful newsletters, the news is usually information that is not obtainable elsewhere — at least in that condensed and specific form. Because of this characteristic of the material in a newsletter, perhaps "informative" is the best word to characterize the specialized news contained in such a publication. The potential subscriber of any newsletter is a person who wants to "keep up with the latest information" on the specific subject of the publication.

A newsletter to be true to its purpose must contain news.

3. *A newsletter is written like a letter* (the second half of its name). Unlike a newspaper or magazine (except for specialized departments such as the editorial page), a newsletter is a personal, informal, direct letter from the editor or other staff member to the reader. Newsletters are usually quite informal publications, written like a letter between friends (with some obviously more formal characteristics). Unlike magazines, newsletters do not have covers. They rarely have more than twelve to sixteen pages.

Most newsletters are even shorter. The subscriber thinks of the publication as a letter. The day it arrives in the mail he or she may sit down and read the whole thing through, then later go back to study certain portions more carefully, clip some article or information for further use, photocopy a specific item to be passed on to friends with like interests, and perhaps put the newsletter into a file or notebook for further reference. Most newsletters are 8½ x 11 inches in page size — another characteristic that makes them seem like letters — and because they are often kept and reread, many of them come with three holes punched to make this easier.

Whatever the format, the most successful of these publications are designed as letters written by the editor to the subscriber. When I sold the *Christian Writers Newsletter* to another publisher a few years ago, I heard from many subscribers whom I had known previously only as names, saying that they were going to miss this regular personal contact with a "writing friend." Newsletters are letters.

The Purpose of a Newsletter

The editor and publisher need a clear idea of the purpose of the newsletter being published under their supervision. What is a newsletter designed to do? The purpose of a specific newsletter can usually be described in a word or two. I am indebted to Mark Beach, author of *Editing Your Newsletter* for the following list of verbs that describe what a newsletter does.[3] No doubt every publisher or editor of a newsletter could add more.

teach	report	impress
inform	analyze	illustrate
announce	clarify	interpret
motivate	advertise	inspire
entertain	solicit	define
explain	praise	justify
recruit	persuade	

Every successful newsletter will have a carefully planned purpose, stated in writing (if not in the publication, at least on the editor's desk). For the *Christian Writers Newsletter*, for example, we had three specific purposes: "to inspire, inform and motivate Christian writers." Everything we published had to fit under one of these three verbs stating our purpose.

The goals of any newsletter are related directly to the subject or field around which the publication is planned and the kinds of subscribers or readers it intends to reach. Many newsletters have as their very specific goal persuading readers to contribute funds to their organization or projects. Such newsletters are filled with information about what the organization is doing, the kind of people it is reaching or helping, and the goals it is accomplishing. All of the material in such a newsletter is written in a style that is highly motivational, convincing the reader that here is a cause to which he or she wants to contribute. Other newsletters not concerned with finances may concentrate completely on the informational aspect of the subject they are dealing with, or the reporting and illustrating of techniques that may help the readers improve their work.

For ten years, I edited *Church and Synagogue Libraries*, a publication designed to help congregational librarians in their task of running a local religious library. About half of every publication was made up of reviews of new books on the market — a major interest of readers. Some of the columns were filled with information about the parent organization, sponsor of the newsletter. But the other major feature was a sharing of ideas about what works and what doesn't work in a local library seeking to reach potential readers of books and publications in their own local faith community. The purpose of any newsletter will determine largely what the content of the publication will be. And the more clearly this is defined in the minds of the editor and publisher, the more successful the newsletter will be.

Types of Newsletters

The content and purpose of a newsletter is determined not only by the audience it aims to reach and the subject around which it is published, but also by the type of newsletter it intends to be. There are basically three types, and all newsletters can be classified under one of the following.

1. *Subscription Newsletters.* A large number of the major newsletters published in the United States fall into this category. These are publications issued on a regular basis and sent to subscribers who pay an annual fee to receive the needed information. Many of these letters are related to *business and investment*. Some of them, having special and restrictive information, charge large fees for subscriptions. Another classification of subscription newsletters is that of *consumer* publications aimed at a general audience and with a broad appeal but offering specialized information to consumers of certain kinds of products — such as newsletters for parents of small children, or those about travel, health, cooking, restaurants, etc. Many religious newsletters fall into this category.

A variation of the consumer newsletter are *affinity* publications that link together groups that share a common passion or interest in a subject such as hobbies, sports, or leisure activities. Some of these letters could also be classified as *instructional*, offering help for either part-time or full-time activities. My *Christian Writers Newsletter* might fall into either of these last two categories of subscription newsletters.

2. *Organizational Newsletters.* These are publications of churches, civic groups, service clubs, etc. These are usually sent free to the members and are often also sent to prospective members. Other such newsletters are sent only to members who have paid their dues for the current period. Such a newsletter is *Church and Synagogue Libraries*, already mentioned. Many religious newsletters are in this category.

3. *Public Relations Newsletters.* These "uninvited letters" may be sent by a company or an association to prospective customers to tell them about an organization or a product. These letters, intended to "sell" the product written about, are often sent to mailing lists targeted at certain age groups or those with special interests but also to general mailing lists to develop new markets. Many religious newsletters fall into this category, especially those of large organizations that depend on contributions for their major income.

The Structure of Newsletters

Guidelines for successful newsletters have developed over the years. The following are the important elements in the structure of these publications.

1. *The Name.* Like the lead in a news story, the name of a newsletter is a very important key to reaching the audience at which it is aimed.

In choosing a name, the newsletter publisher needs to keep the market in mind. Who is the newsletter for? How will the name chosen strike the potential subscriber or reader? Because a newsletter is an informal and personal publication, some very clever names have been devised. There are a few principles that need to be kept in mind. The name should

— identify the newsletter's subject or sponsor,
— describe the contents,
— have impact on the reader,
— be pitched to the needs of the potential reader.

Keeping these principles in mind, the publisher should select a name that is straightforward and simple, something that can be easily remembered. One should not get too clever and disguise the contents and purpose of the newsletter. The *Christian Writers Newsletter,* which I founded and published, had a very straightforward name. It has now been combined with another publication with a clever name that states its purpose symbolically: *Cross and Quill.* Sometimes if a name is somewhat obscure, a subtitle can be used to help establish its purpose in the mind of the reader. *Cross and Quill* uses such a subtitle, stating that it is the official publication of the *Christian Writers Fellowship.*

Because newsletters are often printed on separate unbound sheets, which may become separated, the name of the newsletter needs to be repeated: a banner head on the first page and a masthead usually on page two, with the name appearing again along with page numbers and date of publication at the top or bottom of at least every other page.

2. *Frequency and Schedule.* Because a newsletter is news, it is published regularly so that the information is fresh when it reaches the reader. The frequency of publication reflects the needs of the sponsor as well as that of the reader. Weekly, monthly, and bi-monthly are the most common frequencies — quarterly is too infrequent in most cases. The personal, regular contact between editor and reader is essential to a successful newsletter.

3. *Style.* One of the joys of newsletter publishing is that the style can be quite free-ranging. It is up to the editor and publisher to establish the style that fits the contents and purpose of the newsletter. The only

requirement is that the style be consistent with the material being presented. It can be strictly factual if that is what the material and audience calls for, or it can be as opinionated and controversial as is desired.

But style is important. It will determine the character of the newsletter and the effectiveness of the writing. Howard Penn Hudson quotes James M. Jenks of the Alexander Hamilton Institute on good newsletter style thus:

> Plunge right into your subject.
> Use short sentences.
> Use strong verbs and nouns.
> Use the active voice.
> Use yourself. Remember that you are writing a letter to your
>
> readers. It must be personal. Two words to remember about style are especially important: *Brevity* and *Variety!*[4]

4. *Design.* There is a lot of help available to publishers of newsletters when it comes to design. Some of the sources are listed at the end of this chapter. In 1986 the Newsletter Clearing House, the producer of many of these helps, began a newsletter called *Newsletter Design.* This publication is subtitled, "News and Reviews for the Desktop Generation." Since the advent of the computer and its available software the design of newsletters has taken on new dimensions, and desktop publishing has come into its own.

Just a few of the hints about design of newsletters are given here. The following are principles that operate no matter what mechanical production process is involved:

a. Vary column widths. Paper that is 8½ inches wide can have one, two, or three columns, and there can even be variations within that format. Whether or not to justify lines or keep ragged right-hand edges is a matter of style preference.

b. Use plenty of white space throughout for readability. Don't crowd the type. The larger the type face, the longer the line possible. Avoid dot matrix print at all costs. Remember that italics are less readable than roman — especially in a long paragraph. Using all capitals also makes a sentence less readable. Be sure your type is readable and pleasant to the eyes.

c. The name plate and logo should be attractive and large enough to be read from a distance. It must also be appropriate to the subject of the newsletter.

d. Graphics (illustrations) are important. There is much clip art available to the amateur. With computers the possibilities are almost unlimited. Graphics are attractive and attention getting, and they add variety. *But they are not the most important aspect of a newsletter*. The content is primary.

e. Color can be added in paper or in ink. But be sure that readability is not lost in the process.

f. Headlines should stand out. Type faces can vary here, too, but roman is more readable than italics.

g. Strive for readability above all other aspects of design.

h. Proofreading by more than one set of eyes is an absolute necessity.

5. *Standing Elements*. Like newspapers and other periodical publications, newsletters have several such items that appear in every issue:

a. The name and address in more than one place.

b. Copyright notice and ISSN number if one has been applied for.

c. Page numbers on every page, with date and name of the newsletter on at least alternating pages.

d. Date, volume, and issue number on the front page and in the masthead. The masthead also includes other essential information such as the name and address of the editor and the cost of subscriptions and individual issues.

Subscriptions, Renewals, Mailing Lists

Since newsletters do not usually contain advertising and since they contain specialized information for a designated and often limited audience, the maintaining of accurate subscription and/or mailing lists is a necessity. There are companies set up to provide such service, often for several newsletters.

Most newsletters examine carefully the potential of subscribers before beginning a new publication. The publisher also needs to study the subscription price carefully in order to be sure that a reasonable profit or return for promotion can be realized for the sponsoring organization. Pricing is part of the total budget planning necessary.

The sources of subscribers are many and as varied as the subjects on which newsletters are published. Several types of solicitations are possible to gain subscribers: space advertising in magazines and newspapers, telephone solicitation, and fliers sent to mailing lists purchased or exchanged with other publications. In the case of nonprofit newsletters, there are many avenues open for promotion, such as radio and TV public-service announcements. Mailing lists of all types can be purchased for one-time use from brokers. In most cases special effort is made to reach first-time subscribers. For example, the best source of subscribers for our

Christian Writers Newsletter was the many writer's conferences held throughout the country each year. After obtaining the list of these conferences and their directors, we sent fliers for distribution on the "freebee" table at the conferences. In exchange we offered to run the information about the conference in our newsletter. First-time subscribers were offered a special price if they told us the name of the conference at which they received the subscription blank. We often also extended their subscription one issue if they gave us this information.

Many newsletters, religious and otherwise, offer special discounts to senior citizens if they are subscribers. Some newsletters give discounts to students. Because there is a high attrition rate for most newsletters, the gaining of new subscribers is an important and constant task.

Renewals are also a most important consideration. In fact, someone has said that "the newsletter business is not a subscription business but a renewal business." Renewals after the first subscription period has run out are the most important. Once a subscriber has renewed, the process becomes more automatic. Present subscribers and past subscribers are the best potential for the future success of any newsletter.

For nonsubscription newsletters that are primarily promotional or organizational in nature, all of the above suggestions for obtaining and keeping subscribers apply except the collection of money.

Mailing and Distribution

The final stage in the production of a newsletter is making the proper mailing arrangements to get it into the hands of the subscribers promptly and efficiently. There are many different methods used. Each has some advantages and should be considered.

Because time is important in the production of a newsletter while the information is still "news," many publications are sent by first-class mail. Also because the "letter" feeling is one that should be maintained, many newsletters are stuffed into envelopes as well. First-class mailing with envelopes is more costly, but in many cases the extra effort at the producer's end is worth the cost involved.

For a much cheaper type of mailing, a postal permit may be obtained. A good share of the nation's newsletters are sent by this method. Third-class permits, of course, mean that there are often delays at both ends of the mailing process, and if time is important, this may be a drawback. If the sponsor of a newsletter is a nonprofit organization, the rate for mailing is even less. For any third-class mail there are other complications: a deposit must be made at the post office, the permit number must be placed on all mail, mailings must be at least two-hundred pieces each time and all pieces must be exactly the same; extra material (such as renewal notices) must not be inserted in some of the envelopes. Also mailings must be sorted by zip code by the sender.

Many newsletters are mailed without an envelope. This method affords considerable savings, but the newsletter may not be as attractive in this form and is more liable to be damaged in the mail. Such newsletters can still be sent first class with proper postage affixed.

All of these variations in mailing and distribution need to be weighed by the publisher to make sure that the proper form is used for the kind of newsletter and information being sent.

The Future of Newsletters

Newsletters are facing a technological revolution with electronic transmission of news now possible. The electronic age is in full swing. But, in spite of this, newsletters on paper are not obsolete by any means. One way or another, in the final analysis, most of the electronic procedures are steps toward the printed page.

There is an important future for newsletters. The entire newsletter field in the United States began with one man, Willard M. Kiplinger. His son, Austin Kiplinger, made several observations at the 1980 international newsletter conference in Washington, D.C. He stressed that newsletters are utilitarian, reader-oriented, forward looking, and based on the real needs of the reader. Newsletters are in business to help people adjust to the realities of life. That is the key to all newsletter success and survival.[5]

Getting Help: Resources

The publication of a newsletter seems like a simple procedure. It is true, of course, that many aspects of this type of publishing are easier than those of newspapers, magazines, or books, but many aspects of newsletter publishing are also quite complicated and costly. Therefore, careful planning needs to be done before publication and careful accounting and accurate records need to be kept continually. Anyone planning to publish a newsletter would do well to consult some of the resources in "Suggested Reading" and get all the help possible to be assured of a successful publishing venture in this field.

NOTES

1. Howard Penn Hudson, *Publishing Newsletters*, rev. ed. (New York: Macmillan, 1988), 1.

2. Mark Beach, *Editing Your Newsletter*, 3d ed. (Portland, Ore.: Coast to Coast Books, 1987), 2.

3. Ibid., 2d ed. (1982), 2.

4. Hudson, *Publishing Newsletters*, 41.

5. Ibid., 191.

RESOURCES AND SUGGESTED READING

Books

Beach, Mark. *Editing Your Newsletter: A Guide to Writing, Design, and Production.* 3d ed. Portland, Ore.: Coast to Coast Books, 1988.

Large-size pages, well illustrated with samples, a practical guide. Available from Coast to Coast Books, 1115 SE Stephen St., Portland, OR 97214.

Gregory, Helen. *How to Make Newsletters, Brochures and Other Good Stuff, Without a Computer System.* Sedro Woolley, Wash.: Pinstripe Publishing, 1988.

A breezy guide to the field.

Hudson, Howard Penn. *Publishing Newsletters.* Rev. ed. New York: Macmillan, 1988.

The most complete guide and bibliography available to the whole field of newsletter publishing, from the publisher of *The Newsletter on Newsletters* and other helps from the Newsletter Clearing House.

Nagan, Peter S. *How to Put Out a Newsletter.* Washington, D.C.: Newsletter Services, 1987.

Free sixteen-page booklet prepared by a publisher of a number of Washington newsletters; available from Newsletter Services, 1545 New York Ave. SE, Washington, DC, 20002.

Organizations and Services

The Newsletter Association, 14-1 Wilson Blvd., Arlington, VA 22209.

A nonprofit association of professional newsletter publishers founded in 1977. Conducts annual conferences and numerous seminars on publishing, editorial, promotion, and management topics.

The Newsletter Clearinghouse, 44 W. Market St., P.O. Box 311, Rhinebeck, NY 12572.

Private service organization for the industry, publishing several items, including the *Newsletter on Newsletters* (semimonthly) and *Newsletter Design* (monthly), listed below, and the *Newsletter Directory* and other books. Conducts an annual award competition for newsletters.

Newsletters and Other Periodicals
Desktop. In-House Graphics, Inc., 342 E. Third St., Loveland, CO 80537.
Desktop Graphics. Dynamic Graphics, 6000 N. Forest Park Dr., Peoria, IL 61614.
The Editorial Eye. Editorial Experts, Inc., 85 S. Bragg St. Alexandria, VA 22312.

Also publishes books and guides and conducts seminars.

The Newsletter on Newsletters. Newsletter Clearinghouse, 44 West Market St., P.O. Box 311, Rhinebeck, NY 12572.

Reporting on the newsletter world: editing, graphics, management, promotion, etc., twenty-four issues annually.

Newsletter Design. Newsletter Clearinghouse, 44 West Market St., P.O. Box 311, Rhinebeck, NY 12572.

News and Reviews for the Desktop Generation. Each issue critiques fourteen newsletters. Monthly.

Publish! 501 Second St., #600, San Francisco, CA 94107.

The how-to magazine of desktop publishing.

Chapter 30

You Can Write and Publish Curriculum Materials

Ruth Rorem Schenk

About ten years ago I submitted a short story to a curriculum publisher. Nothing to it. My idea came late one Saturday night as I studied a Sunday school lesson. The Scripture verses in the teacher's guide reminded me of an experience that related to several Bible verses. After all, I'd read take-home papers during church services most of my life. Though more entertaining than most sermons, they didn't seem particularly elaborate or complex. Surely I could write one an editor would welcome.

The project took about an hour: thirty minutes to write, and another thirty to type. I sent the manila envelope off the next day with overwhelming confidence. I thought it was the beginning of a new hobby, possibly even a new career. With an average of one hour per article, fifteen articles per week, sixty per month, and over seven hundred per year, I could earn some extra cash — even at the current rate of only three

Ruth Rorem Schenk works on a variety of curriculum materials for several publishers. Her new book, *Booker T. Washington Goes to School*, will be published by Bob Jones University Press in 1992. She is currently working on a series of Christian biographies for children eight-to-ten years old and a series about black evangelicals for adults. She lives in Louisville.

cents per word. I could visualize some new furniture and Christian school for my children; I even planned to donate some of the money to our church.

The rejection notice came two weeks later. It was a faded mimeographed postcard that explained in twenty-five words that my story did not fit their publishing needs, and no, they could not comment on the merit of the story. Not ever thinking it would be rejected, I hadn't sent a SASE. The story was never returned. I filed the rejection card in a folder in the back of my desk. I hate rejection and it still hurts to open that drawer. So much for my new hobby; so much for a new career; so much for editors with open arms; so much for seven hundred stories per year.

Working with curriculum could have ended with the rejection of that first story. But it didn't, and I have learned that my article invited rejection for many reasons. I have discovered that success in this field is possible, even probable when specific guidelines are followed. However, this very specialized area of Christian publishing receives little publicity, so usually the guides aren't obvious.

In spite of this, such writing is an area of great opportunity. New writers are welcomed. Consideration does not require a recognizable name or an advanced degree. Curriculum writing caters to a wide variety of manageable assignments perfectly designed for the new writer, but still challenging for those more experienced. Since that first failure, curriculum has become my niche in the publishing world. I hope that with the guidelines, suggestions, and plan of action in this chapter, it may become yours also.

What on Earth Is Curriculum?

Curricula are planned courses of study. Any material studied or taught is curriculum. Curriculum is systematic instruction in the things that really count in life; it's where new things are discovered, questions are answered, the issues of life are put in order, and mysteries are solved. We have all studied many different curricula in the course of our education: science, social studies, mathematics, and so on.

Religious curricula involve courses of instruction in the Christian life. Its main goal is to tell the truth about God and how that truth affects lives. It is a vital part of every church program and is designed to influence individual lives from the cradle to the retirement home.

Religious curricula should teach, inform, and inspire. Every day of the week thousands of diverse people of all ages and denominations study curricula. They read and teach Sunday school lessons. They get take-home papers or magazines. Some study Christian textbooks at home or in school. Many attend Bible clubs, youth groups, and Bible studies. Children enjoy puzzle books, coloring books, craft books to use with lessons, and learning aids like flannel-graph and object lessons. The sum total of all these materials is religious curriculum. Although some of these products are written by in-house writers or on assignment, many are not, and there is a niche for every interest. Consider your skills and talents as you read the next section.

Writing Opportunities in Curriculum

1. *Curriculum involves many courses of study and many kinds of material.* These materials must be produced in volume for every age level. Most are designed to fit the calendar or school year. Take-home papers, Sunday school lessons, Bible study programs, and learning aids are produced for all ages for every Sunday of the year. One curriculum publisher has over a thousand items in its 1991 catalog.

With the exception of some teacher's guides and textbooks, these products cannot be written by in-house writers exclusively. To keep publishing costs down, much of the work is done by free-lancers, those writers who can produce the stories, studies, features, or activities needed by editors of the publication. The need for volumes of material for many age levels equals big opportunity.

2. *Most curriculum editors welcome new writers.* In our challenging but needy world, religious materials must be innovative and captivating. They must fill needs. They must be so arresting that they will make a difference in individual lives, not end up as expensive trash outside the church door or convenient paper for notes passed during the sermon. This constant need for new ideas, experiences, features, and stories creates plenty of room for new writers.

3. *Everyone is qualified to write curriculum on some level.* Ever since childhood you have been building up an inexhaustible store of personal experiences, adventures, and interests — the stuff of which writing is made. You are qualified to share those things you have learned.

Within the scope of your personal experience are hundreds of memorable moments. Who can forget how it felt to be the last one chosen for a team in gym class? Remember when you were hurt by a trusted friend? How about the day you became a Christian? Have you ever forgotten the consequences of a wrong decision or choice?

The best material for curriculum comes from ordinary life — ordinary people with ordinary lives. Curriculum publishers are not looking for the flamboyant, the ostentatious, the sensational. They want realistic, well-written episodes of daily life that have meaning for their readers. They want people to nod knowingly or smile as they read. It has happened to them. They want readers to embrace their material, save it in their Bibles, or share it with a friend.

4. *Assignments are defined, restricted, and manageable.* With few exceptions, editors assign the general topic, length, and vocabulary of materials. These mandates cannot be altered because curriculum is a systematic study with specific themes for certain age levels. Layout specifications determine word length. These restrictions give the new writer a great advantage. They narrow an overwhelming field. They give a secure boundary to the challenge to write. They allow time to learn the fundamentals in an orderly fashion, then expand on that work. They keep the writer from wandering and teach discipline. A typical assignment is a character-building story of nine hundred words with a fifth-grade vocabulary. Themes and outcomes must conform to the guidelines of the assignment. The ability to write quality material to specific needs in the market prepares the writer for success in any other field.

5. *Story needs are diverse.* There is room for every interest and skill. Do you enjoy interviews, missionary stories, investigative pieces, true-life dramas, fiction, or biography? Perhaps you enjoy creating puzzles and craft materials to supplement curriculum. In addition to these, there is the opportunity to write self-help articles, how-to pieces, and biographies about sports stars and celebrities.

New writers are often advised to write about things they know best. While that is sound advice, curriculum allows the writer to explore new areas of interest. You may want to research the life of Mary Slessor, a courageous missionary who changed Africa in the 1800s; or you may wish to write about time management at home and in the workplace, qualities of leadership, or prominent Christians who are making a difference. All are possible. Writing curriculum is an adventure.

6. *Curriculum materials reach a large audience.* Even the smaller curriculum publishers reach thrity to forty thousand persons with each issue. That means your message will be heard. It is an exciting adventure with awesome responsibility.

Now you understand the nature of curriculum. You know what it is and why it generates opportunity. You've thought about your own skills and interests. Perhaps you've even read a variety of materials and thought to yourself, *I could do better than that.* While that may be true, it is a grave error to assume that writing curriculum is easy. It was my first mistake on the path to rejection.

While writing curriculum is an open field of opportunity, it does have some requirements. First of all, writers must have a deep conviction about the truth and relevance of the Bible. They must have intense discipline and skill in the English language. Above all, they must have an intimate understanding of people and their needs. To prevent any misunderstandings, writing curriculum is *not*

— tacking a Bible verse onto a story
— overly sentimental, dogmatic, or theological in nature
— simply retelling a Bible story
— the same as writing a tract
— a venture independent of the goals and theme of the publication

Every editor has a box or shelf full of rejected manuscripts. Often they were rejected for simple faults or deficiencies that could be remedied. But few editors have the time to work with authors on an individual basis. The following guidelines will help you write the kind of material that editors will welcome.

Guidelines for Writing Curriculum

You have a 9 x 11 legal-pad list of ideas. You have your favorite pen, a Bible, and a dictionary. Maybe you even have a style manual on hand. You've thought a lot about various topics, types of articles, age level, and your own skills and interests.

The phone is off the hook; the doorbell is disconnected; there's a huge placard on the front lawn that says DO NOT DISTURB. You're ready to write. Sounds like a great beginning, but not necessarily a successful one. The following five guidelines will help ensure success.

1. *Always write to the specifications of the guidelines*. Don't write until you have requested, received, and memorized the guidelines. Study the goals, readership, and interests of the publication. Marketing your idea with a curriculum publisher is a waste of time if you do not understand their educational program and needs. Never leave too much to chance. Even work of high quality will be rejected if submitted to the wrong place at the wrong time in the wrong format.

Note the types of articles currently needed: fiction, interview, humor, anecdotes, or puzzles. Notice those not included. Avoid writing articles not listed with current market needs. There's a logical reason they are not listed: they may not fit in with the educational overview of the program or may have recently been addressed. Sensationalism in the form of unrelieved suspense or gratuitous violence should be avoided as well as profanity or blasphemy. Themes advocating secular attitudes of cynicism, rebellion, or materialism will be rejected. They do not belong in this market.

Pay close attention to detail. Notice word length and vocabulary. Make a mental note of inside tips. Check the practical details regarding submissions. Are computer printouts acceptable? Which editor handles specific age levels? How much do they pay? Do they buy reprint rights?

Failure to follow the guidelines is like telling a child not to worry about specific homework assignments, to just answer any question from any page of any book. It doesn't work in any field of education, and it won't work in curriculum development.

Keep these guidelines in a special file safe from small hands, the family dog, the wastebasket. Update them occasionally. Writing according to the guidelines will save time and energy. It will keep your rejection file (nearly) empty.

2. *Know your readers*. While the rule is usually to write about what you know best, in curriculum the rule is to write for those you know best. One of the primary reasons submissions are rejected in curriculum publishing is that they are not appropriate for the target age group. Write for the age group you know intimately — your own children, kids in your Sunday school class, your friends, your neighbors, your own peers.

Visualize your readers. Do they ride "big wheels"? Do they still cry through Sunday school? Are they plugged into earphones? Were they bodily dragged to church? Are they trying to find their place in the world? Looking for a mate? Are they struggling to keep a family together? Plagued by poor health and loneliness?

If you choose to write for an age group you don't know intimately, volunteer to work with them. Observe. Eavesdrop. Nurture friendships. Take sufficient time before writing to discover what things fascinate and what things bother them. What do they talk about in a group together? What things happening in the world interest them? What do they fear most? Read their magazines and watch their programs on TV. Visit the library. Look at the books they are reading. Listen to their speech patterns. Let them become part of your experience and then write.

Whatever their age and whatever their circumstances, people want to be entertained as well as instructed. It takes courage to write. It takes a special kind of courage to write curriculum. In the educational process you must instruct and motivate and inspire. Added to that, you must somehow make it all interesting and entertaining. Above all, the message must be clear. Although generalities are difficult to apply, suggestions about writing for different age groups may be helpful.

Children from birth to age three enjoy stories with rhythmic sound patterns. Mother Goose rhymes are a good example. Who has forgotten "Not by the hair of my chinny-chin-chin" or "Run, run as fast as you can. You can't catch me, I'm the gingerbread man."

For children at this young age, curriculum generally works to build positive attitudes about God, the Bible, church, their famlies, and themselves. Stories should be simple. Sentences should be short, following the speech patterns of the children — mostly nouns and verbs.

Children from three to five respond well to rhythm and repetition. Story plots should be simple and direct. Action should build quickly. Any dialogue should be short. This is the time to explore basic Bible stories. It is a time to build character and faith.

Six-to-eight-year-olds are just coming to terms with the real world. It's a time when their broadening world brings both disappointment and surprise. It is also the beginning of realism — Mom can't fix everything anymore. There are teachers to obey, friends to get along with, new pressures to deal with, and new skills to learn and achieve. At the same time that they're losing their baby teeth, they're losing their naïveté about the world. Children in this age group love humor and stories about real life. They crave adventure and surprise. In curriculum it's time for them to learn more about God's relationship with mankind. They get to know Bible characters with both their strengths and weaknesses. They learn about God's plan for their lives.

Nine-to-eleven-year-olds are sophisticated. They look for the dramatic, the witty, the adventurous. These kids like stories where weak prevails over strong, where the underdog wins, where the unexpected happens. They also like exaggerated humor and hero tales. Many children over nine look for something that appeals to their developing sense of reason and judgment.

From this point on, curriculum materials are often theme-oriented. What does the Bible say about friends? About money? About sex? About success and materialism? Stories, features articles, and lesson ideas are limitless and as diverse as the people who read them.

Perhaps you have chosen several publications, an age level, and a topic. Now it's time for the real work of writing. General rules of good writing certainly apply to writing curriculum materials.

3. *Wisely use the tools of the trade: words, grammar, and syntax.* Good writing is not casually done. It rarely takes just thirty minutes like my first submission. Curriculum must be communicated effectively within limits of time and space. Most stories, features and lessons are short. Although time and space are limited, the quality of the writing must be maintained. The skill of the writer must make an eight-hundred-word story unforgettable or a five-minute play for six-year-olds meaningful. The following suggestions are from a variety of curriculum editors. These are the hints they would share with authors if individual conferences were possible. Often submissions have promise and generate interest, yet need

refinement. These suggestions are about refining, improving, and perfecting submissions.

a. Always work from an outline. Good material is organized, has purpose, and moves toward a goal. It has a beginning, a middle, and an end, and the three parts are well-balanced.

b. Choose words carefully. Time and space limitations force curriculum to deal with essentials only. Each word must be weighed and counted with the intensity of poetry. Choose strong verbs that will work hard in your sentences. Pack your work with energy and excitement. Make each word precise. Does look really mean stare, gaze, or gawk? Does throw mean hurl or toss? Does your character eat fast or wolf his food down? Use words to paint vivid pictures. Avoid archaic language and obscure words or phrases.

Vocabulary should be simple and direct, yet colorful and entertaining. Put words together with a careful ear. Give the language rhythm, harmony, and color.

c. Carefully plan sentences and paragraphs. Be simple and direct. Take your readers on an adventure they will be eager to follow. Limited space makes it essential that characters and situations be introduced quickly and clearly. The right balance of action and characterization is essential or the story will be too sketchy — a skeleton that says nothing.

Use simple sentences in the active voice. Complex sentences are hard to follow. Curriculum materials must meet needs within a wide range of language skills. This does not mean that theme or plot should be too simplistic or insultingly shallow, but simpler is usually better. Avoid long descriptive passages and dialogues. Although these can be effective in longer works, most curriculum materials don't cater to this type of writing.

d. Create believable characters from a mixture of race, class, and ethnic backgrounds. Your work will stand out if it's about a black hero, an American Indian, or someone from another culture. Above all, avoid sexism and racism.

Make characters seem as alive as your friends and neighbors. Sketch personality traits and habits before writing. Does your character have a loose tooth? Is there always a basketball in hand? Does he or she have bitten nails? A best friend? Laugh a lot? What is your character's voice like? Make characters real enough to be cared about. Don't say, "Tim was a nice boy with a happy smile." It tells us nothing about Tim. Use action instead of adjectives to describe characters. If you want us to know about

Tim, show us how he acts. Does he befriend stray animals? Does he have a favorite snack?

Limit the number of characters to those you can handle in the time allotted. If you have a thousand words, you cannot create ten believable characters. Let dialogue be natural. Avoid stilted conversation.

e. Be professional. Include fully documented footnotes and bibliography when appropriate. Get written permission to use quoted materials.

4. *Rewrite, edit, throw away, expand, and write again until your submission is your best writing.* Read it at least three different times for style, punctuation, and vocabulary. Read it out loud. Cut out unnecessary words. Think about what you've written. Ask yourself these questions:

Is it accurate? All Bible verses and story references must be accurate. Include the translation used. Your editor will thank you.

Have you snagged the reader? Can your story be put down to clean the house, cut the lawn, feed the cat?

Is your theme clear? Is there a good reason to read this article?

Is your work balanced? Is it too emotional? Too academic?

Is it worth remembering? Is this the kind of story someone will repeat? Clip and save? Pass on to a friend?

Submitting Your Work

1. Send perfect, error-free copy.

2. Include your name, address, phone number, and social security number in the upper left-hand corner of the first page.

3. Indicate the number of words in the upper right-hand corner of the first page.

4. Enclose an SASE for each item submitted.

5. Always keep a copy of your manuscript.

6. Enclose an intriguing cover letter stating why you wish to write for that publication. State why your submission will help someone else.

7. Allow four to six weeks for consideration.

Now you understand religious curriculum. You know how to write a memorable story or article. Editors welcome thorough, accurate, interesting work in proper format.

Go ahead. Send for the guidelines. Study them. Choose several markets and write. Enjoy the process. Share what you have learned and observed. Investigate new topics. Create something special that may affect many lives. You have the opportunity, the skills, and the motivation to succeed.

A Word About Textbooks

So far we've considered mostly Sunday school materials, though general rules still apply to Christian school curriculum. As the number of home and Christian schools increase across the country, so also does the need for quality textbooks. Many of these are produced in-house or on assignment. This does not mean, however, that the field is closed to new writers. Query editors to see if your idea has a market and needs to be addressed. Include writing samples and reasons you are qualified to write the book.

Curriculum Publishers Who Welcome New Writers

Christian Education Publishers
9230 Trade Place
San Diego, CA 92126

David C. Cook Publishing Co.
850 North Grove Avenue
Elgin, Illinois 60120-2892

Gospel Publishing House
616 Walnut
Scottsdale, PA 15683

Standard Publishing
8121 Hamilton Avenue
Cincinnati, OH 45231

Newsletter with curriculum updates included:

Cross and Quill
Christian Writers Int'l.
590 West Mercers Fernery Road
DeLand, FL 32720

Christian Textbook Publishers

A Beka Book Publications
P.O. Box 18000
Pensacola, FL 32523

Bob Jones University Press
Greenville, SC 29614

Alpha Omega Publishers
P.O. Box 3153
Tempe, AZ 85281

Rod and Staff
Crockett, KY 41413

SUGGESTED READING

Cheney, Theodore A. *Getting the Words Right: How to Revise, Edit and Rewrite*. Cincinnati: Writer's Digest Books, 1983.

An excellent how-to book for polishing and perfecting work.

Famous Writer's Course by Famous Writer's School, 1960.

A four-volume set with readable chapters from great writers; practical and helpful assignments.

Karl, Jean. *Childhood to Childhood*. New York: John Day, 1963.

Designed for those who wish to write for children, explains the qualities of memorable works and gives helpful suggestions for various age levels.

Provost, Gary. *100 Ways to Improve Your Writing*. New York: Mentor Books, 1985.

A humorous and helpful guide to good writing.

Chapter 31

Writing the Audio-Visual Script

Ken Anderson

The audio-visual producer's primary and most necessary tool is not a camera, not sound recording facilities or an abundance of high-intensity lighting. Nor is this tool to be found on the shelves of a studio supply room, however laden those shelves may be with what is commonly known as professional equipment.

The basic, most valuable aid to the producer of audio-visual materials is a ball-point pen and a supply of blank sheets of paper!

The best of photography and the ultimate in visualizing and recording skills too often fall short for want of good writing in the very initial stages of production. Conversely, many motion-picture and television productions, even with less than award-winning technical embellishments, have succeeded because of good scripts.

Let us briefly examine the elements and procedures necessary to prepare an audio-visual script.

But first, and because of its vital importance, we will look at the foundational element of a good script. To include this element among the

Ken Anderson is the owner and operator of Ken Anderson Films and a director of InterCom, specialists in worldwide audio-video evangelism. He is the author of more than forty books, most recently *Bold as a Lamb*. He has encouraged and taught script-writing for more than fifty years.

395

points that we will subsequently consider might tend to lessen, in the student's mind, that which is so truly foundational.

The foundational element is this: Even though it must, of necessity, involve printed words on a page, the audio-visual script — in every facet of its development — must ever serve as a visual instrument. It is not a work of literature, although it may be eloquent. It does not relate to any of the other arts or divisions of education and experience except in the information and guidance it gives to those artists who will transfer its contents to the motion picture or television screen.

Seek to prepare your script with impact and conviction, to be sure, but always think of your script — first and foremost — as an audio-visual tool!

A Predetermined Audience

Before writing one line of script copy, you must know your target audience. In fact, the more competent you become as a writer of audio-visual materials, the more sensitive you will be to your audience. The more you know about your audience — how they react, what appeals to them and what does not — the more effective will be your writing.

What Is Your Message?

No field of writing is more specialized than that facing the Christian who has a message to proclaim. More than a quarter-century ago, in our own organization, Ken Anderson Films, we coined the slogan "The Message Is Always First." Some have derided us for this, accusing us of producing and distributing little more than sermons.

One of the most scathing reviews I ever received for my work came from a youth leader who, after seeing one of our films, said, "Why didn't you just produce an audio cassette?"

He laid bare a weakness I had struggled with for many years. I often became so taken with the message I wanted to present that I wrote a script of little more than "talking heads."

I had neglected that foundational element — the visual!

But you can make your message very visual. Just know, in the depth of your heart, what the message is you wish to present. Not messages, but message — the single, even simple truth you wish to convey to viewers in your audience.

Once you have determined this message, then you concern yourself with how best to convey this truth to your target audience. You will likely need dialogue or narration in your production, but strong visuals will be your most effective element of communication.

I once struck up a conversation with a United Airlines flight attendant. As we talked, she learned I had written and directed the motion picture *Pilgrim's Progress*.

"I saw that film in my church!" she exclaimed. "When the burden rolled off Pilgrim's back and down Calvary's hillside, I wept, because it reminded me of how the Lord Jesus took away my burden of sin!"

We had simply interpreted author John Bunyan's excellent verbal visualization and transferred it onto the screen in her church!

Germinal Idea

Integral to your script, whether drama or documentary, will always be the germinal idea. Too often the beginner in any aspect of writing settles for little more than a chain of events, usually known as stream-of-consciousness writing. Instead, your presentation must literally hatch from the egg of a decisive, convincing primary idea.

For example, being quite shy by nature, I have long been concerned about effectively sharing my faith with others. I had developed several scripts, and even directed some of them as motion-picture productions, before I learned the simple truth that when a Christian witnesses, the Holy Spirit is the one who motivates and implements. We, as individual Christians, serve only as obedient tools of the Holy Spirit.

This basic truth has, on several occasions, become the germinal "idea" around which we have formed scripts and subsequent audio-visual productions to convey our message.

Content Research

Unless your script develops from your own personal experience, you will need to devote considerable time to research.

In writing scripts with life-drama content, my preference lies strongly with fact rather than fiction. Some of my scripts — such as for our films *Hudson Taylor* and *Fanny Crosby* — involved months of initial research, much the same as a writer of biography would do prior to beginning a book.

In developing contemporary stories, I have learned to steer away from presentations centered on the life of only one person. There have been pleasant exceptions, such as individuals like Stanley Tam, the amazing and effective Ohio industrialist. But on two specific occasions, individuals whose lives were depicted in motion pictures later proved to be less than exemplary Christians. Therefore I have usually found that my research has involved the gathering of many incidents from the lives of numerous individuals. This has allowed me to produce a composite story.

Here especially, the writer keeps in mind the target audience. My research, for example, has involved gathering material from young people — Christians and non-Christians. On one occasion, I received strategic help from members of youth gangs — ranging from drug peddlers to prostitutes — finding them keenly anxious to guide me to material that would help relate Christian truth to their friends.

Organizing Your Material

The best of research, quite obviously, avails little unless that material is organized into the preliminary content of a script. To do otherwise would be like purchasing all the materials required for building a home and then storing them permanently in a warehouse.

In my own writing, I rely on file cards — sketching the proposed scenes and sequences on cards that can be rearranged as needed or abandoned.

Here, most emphatically, you must think visually!

When giving lectures on this subject, I often tell students I have beaded glass — such as used for projection screens — covering the inside of my eyelids so that, as I write, I can project the visualized script content for immediate viewing.

Unless you can "see" what you have organized for your script, your efforts will surely fail. In fact, many audio-visual producers develop what has become known as a story board, sketched drawings of actual scenes taken from the script.

Please note that, even in the possible development of a story board, all production to this point involves only pen and paper. Costly equipment remains on the shelves!

Writing Your Script

Actual writing of your script need not seem so forbidding an effort as might first be anticipated. True, many of the elements of a good script result from long experience — aspects such as visual continuity, pacing, transitions, dialogue, characterization, to name only an illustrative few.

I had been a free-lance author for many years when a motion-picture producer asked me to prepare a script. Although I had written and sold many short stories, I did not have a clue as to the aesthetics and mechanics of a script.

"We'll send you one of our previous scripts," the producer suggested. And he did.

It was a simple script, yet I read it over and over. Then, as I began development of my own material, I placed the example script beside my typewriter and followed its technique. In my naïveté, I think I actually included the same number of scenes in my own effort!

Unless you are familiar with the technique of script writing, be sure to give careful study to professional examples. Some audio-visual producers will provide you with a previous script if you request it. But you can also go to the library. In most large libraries, you will find copies of actual motion picture scripts.

The Ultimate Resource

I cannot overemphasize one final resource at your disposal. Prayer!

Rarely, perhaps never, do I become involved in the preparation of an audio-visual script without coming to points in the work where my only resource is to claim the promise of James 1:5: "If any of you lacks wisdom, he should ask God, who gives generously to all without finding fault, and it will be given to him." In the research and development of our *Pilgrim's Progress* script, I realized that keeping the cost of production reasonable and facilitating the message simply could not be accomplished by scripting the famous book as the author had written it.

But then, after a time of prayer in which I specifically claimed the promise of James 1:5, the idea came to me to let one character — namely, Apollyon — portray all of the evil roles in the motion picture and another character — Evangelist — represent all of the good people Pilgrim encountered on his trek to the Celestial City.

It worked.

I would not dare to claim the success as any accomplishment of my own!

The audio-visual is the church's communication tool of the future. We dare not use it as a means of displaying mere ego and talent. Like all those who serve the Lord, we must see ourselves as *laborers together with God*.

SUGGESTED READING

Books on screen writing are so rare that professionals in this field are sometimes accused of possessively hiding their "trade secrets." It is more likely that the paucity of publications stems from a limited market. Script writers comprise a small segment of the media world. Here, however, are some volumes aspirants will find helpful.

Beranger, Clara. *Writing for the Screen*. Dubuque, Iowa: Wm. C. Brown, n.d.

A text for beginners in college-level cinema classes, written by Cecil B. DeMille's sister. Elementary in its description of studio people and functions, and helpful for beginners.

Brady, John. *The Craft of the Screenwriter*. New York: Touchstone / Simon & Schuster, 1982.

A resource but only in the sense of providing atmosphere; little evidence of technique, but much regarding the plastic world in which secular writers perform. Neil Simon a rare exception of a writer good enough to stand his own ground and bypass lethal "studio committees."

Bronfeld, Stewart. *Writing for Film and Television*. Englewood Cliffs, N.J.: Prentice Hall, 1980.

Brief, to-the-point guidance in the development of scripts for media. Help for beginners to bridge the gap from obvious amateurism to professional know-how.

Field, Syd. *Screenplay: The Foundations of Screenwriting*. Expanded ed. New York: Dell, 1984.

Easily understood guidelines to make film writing accessible to novices and help experienced writers improve their scripts. A step-by-step, comprehensive technique for writing with material in script layout, markets, and production details.

Mankiewicz, Herman, and Orson Welles. *The Citizen Kane Book*. Boston: Little, Brown, n.d.

A treasury of information and guidance for writers, involving the actual script of the motion picture supplemented with detailed background on how the screen story came to be written. Many photographs.

Mascelli, Joseph V. *The Five C's of Cinematography*. Hollywood: Cine/Grafic Publications, 1965.

Probably the best resource available on basic techniques for developing professional audio-visuals. Gives writers a vital frame of reference for script development.

Moore, Sonia. *The Stanislavski System: The Professional Training of an Actor.* 2d ed. New York: Penguin, 1984.

> Although written primarily for actors, clarifies the "method" approach so revolutionary in its time and still in use somewhat today: actors training themselves to "think" like the characters they portray. Familiarity with this system a necessary component for good writers.

Chapter 32

Using Electronic Technology to Write

Michael Pearce Pfeifer

Writing has never come more naturally. I sat quietly as the technician gently slipped a bioprobe filament into the transfacer microchip in my cerebral cortex. Three seconds elapsed as the organic and artificial neurons silently sorted, organized, and verbalized all the knowledge and judgments my brain had stored for forty-five years. The filament communicated and entered the information into the computer. In twelve seconds I had electronically "written" a nonfiction book on business ethics and a novel and had scripted the video adaptation. I read *Publisher's Daily* at the café as my HAL2010 computer corrected grammar, spell-checked the material, and typeset the text for transmission to bookstores. After lunch I electronically faxed manuscript copies to my publisher for audio-taping and visual amplification for cassette tape and video.

Writing is not that easy, yet. Writers still labor over each word, sentence, and paragraph. However, researchers into "artificial intelligence" continually reveal new vistas of the way our minds work.[1]

Michael Pearce Pfeifer edits and ghost-writes nonfiction and biographies. His academic credentials include American Schools of Oriental Research, Harvard University, and the Institute for Social Research at the University of Michigan. His most recent writing includes *Finding Missing Children* and legal articles.

Electronic publishing, with its new uses and applications, plays a role that fundamentally differs from all other technologies and their impact and consequences. Transcending rarefied intellectual environments, the functional reach, width, and depth of electronic publishing affects all professions.

Publication opportunities in electronic form have grown rapidly. Intense research, design, and sales of electronic publishing hardware and software indicate that electronic publishing has evolved into a permanent technology. Consequently, the role played by writers, authors, editors, and publishers, has changed dramatically. The application of electronic publishing to the craft of writing has opened new vistas for individuals willing to embrace change. The same technological advances have propelled established book publishers across the frontier of traditional concepts and into the technology breach.

My purpose is not to recommend hardware and software or explain equipment or tell authors how to use computers when they write. Rather, I will orient religious writers to the electronic universe that directly affects their craft. Since the public uses the terms "electronic publishing" and "desktop publishing" interchangeably and synonymously, a descriptive statement will clarify the distinctions. Electronic publishing denotes a broader concept than the functional aspects of desktop publishing. Electronic publishing means the storage and distribution of information, using electronic media (computers, recorders, telecommunications, etc.). These media store information in machine-readable form so an electronic device can make it readable by people. In research and writing, a computer transmits the data or manuscript so it can be read or seen by readers.[2] "Data" refers to facts or ideas that are controlled by a computer for processing and suitable for communication. Thus a database organizes a collection of information on a particular subject or subjects stored in computer files.

How did the apostle Paul or Jonathan Edwards sound as they influenced so many in their audiences? Handwriting and then print technology allowed us to capture their written words, but not the quality of their voice or the structure of their spoken language. The spoken word is an event. The written word exists — it is a thing. Electronically reproduced, a spoken word also exists. A spoken or visual moment in time can be captured electronically and played repeatedly as a thing. Without innovation and renewal, any tradition — including the writing profession — becomes moribund and meaningless. Yet, without tradition, writers cannot meaningfully infuse innovation and renewal into their craft. Current uses of electronic publishing and the adaptation of communication technologies to come, must fit into the same pattern of tradition, innovation, and renewal.

Handwriting, and later printing, generated change and influenced the behavior and thought of individual people. Five centuries of technology have moved us from Gutenberg to computers. Electronic publishing has altered our notions of intellectual endeavors and redefined how writers expedite their craft. Personal creativity and electronic capability will increasingly drive and determine professional writing and its future. Consequently, bioengineering of the future also will directly influence most religious writers.

Religious writers must understand that an admonition to "publish the good news" means more than putting ink on paper between two cardboard covers. At the end of the twentieth century, the printed word represents only one medium of publication. Religious writers, by the nature of their genre, assert that they are arbiters of ultimate truth. Therefore, they have a responsibility to anticipate innovations in their craft and understand how those changes affect their ability to communicate. If religious writers expect to fulfill their responsibility as witnesses to a watching and reading world, they must continually incorporate the existing electronic methods into their craft. Failure to do so means that they will increasingly lose their potential audience. Both religious and nonreligious writers who utilize electronic publishing to manage writing will more easily and quickly communicate their ideas to the public than those who do not.

Occupational reality and purposeful stewardship dictate that religious writers redeem the time and show readers the paths to spiritual growth. Ironically, soul-less computers help writers make tremendous strides toward these goals. An electronic servant worthy of its hire behaves as a trustworthy, patient companion, helping its master redeem the time. A writer's art demands a persevering, persistent ministry that inspires fellowship and spiritual growth through prudent research and wise judgments communicated by publicly accessible publications.

Research

Novelists and nonfiction writers should deftly use databases available through public libraries, college and university libraries, and on-line services (The Source, Dialog, CompuServe, etc.). These electronic resources offer access to bibliographies, abstracts, and entire articles. They are time-saving options for gathering, manipulating, and digesting information. Religious writers can read John J. Hughes, *Bits, Bytes and Biblical Studies: A Resource Guide for the Use of Computers in Biblical Studies.*

Religion Database (RELI) provides a computerized database that facilitates researching religious topics and may dramatically benefit the writer who uses electronic publishing. Before RELI's computerization, researching and photocopying a bibliography took four hours. Then the writer took another two days to sort, organize, and write out the topics and authors. Now, the RELI searches for, orders, and prints those same bibliographical citations in seventeen minutes.

Writers benefit from perusing or word-searching titles for various topics available in a particular area of interest. This determines who has written on that subject. A check of RELI revealed no citations for Betty Boop. Therefore, one can assume that publishers are not currently evaluating any competing manuscripts on Betty Boop and religious values in the 1930s.

Fiction writers should occasionally tour electronic libraries to learn what information is electronically available. Nonreligious databases such as LISA, Infotrac, MedLine, LegalTrac, and ERIC substantiate factual information and provide mental stimulation. For a novel, I decided to create a fictional character who influenced social values but had little insight into the moral predicament of modern society. Electronically searching Medline abstracts for a defense-industry client, I inadvertently discovered the phrase "macular degeneration." Reading the abstract, I learned that the opthalmological condition "macular degeneration" leads to loss of vision and that "drusen" is the name given to age spots on the eye. I fictionalized a hard-rock band called macular Degeneration with Drusen as the influential pop star.

For writers using extensive public domain materials, scanning a text may be quicker than typing it into a computer. Scanners capture images on paper and convert those replicas into the digital format of a computer system. The system incorporates these digital images into page layouts. Technicians have designed hand-held scanners to capture input of small images limited to scanning areas from 2½ to 4 inches square. They recreate logos, signatures, and small line-art images. Sheet-fed scanners convert line art, text, and photographs.

Writers should exercise caution when selecting a scanning service or purchasing a scanner. They should test the scanner with the exact text that is to be scanned into "place." Poorly scanned materials create more adjustment problems and time delays than manual entry of information. Remember, whether scanning or photocopying, writers have a legal and moral obligation to respect someone else's copyrighted material.

Preparing to Write

How should writers use electronic publishing? No formula exists, so each writer must choose the methods and equipment suited to his or her habits and needs. Using electronic publishing hardware and software involves a steep learning curve. Yet computerization allows a highly efficient way to master research information, manage text, and bolster style and content.

An electronic servant is a patient co-worker who preserves and communicates text and information, provides clerical assistance, facilitates mastery of the writer's craft, challenges the writer's grammatical judgments, and provides limited proofreading. Once mastered, electronic servants open several paths to communicating with people and save time and expense over traditional research, writing, and production methods.

Computers and tape recorders enhance writing talents and simplify procedures. In mundane life, a writer can redeem the time by efficiently devoting work hours to creative and fulfilling writing. How can hardware and software help us accomplish this goal? Always carry a tape recorder and record your thoughts. Tell your idea to a listener who can respond intelligently, elaborate a storyline, or clarify a thesis. Record the entire conversation and transcribe the audio tapes into your computer. Then rearrange the contents into a logically organized structure. For anyone with a worthwhile story who fears the writing process, this technique starts the procedure, and that person avoids facing a blank page.

Writing and Proofing

Computer-assisted writing procedures enhance a writer's capabilities. Writing has changed from a straightforward pen-to-paper method to an interaction with a variety of computer programs. Networking powerfully reinforces interactive sharing with others and reshapes some fundamental aspects of traditional research, writing, and book publishing.

Writing has become much more formidable because of technologically inspired changes in the way we write. Typically, planning, putting ideas into words, and correcting the text occur simultaneously. Writers effectively using electronic publishing employ a wide range of sources and use them more flexibly than they otherwise could.[3] Idea processing has led to computer programs for writers so they can exploit the computer software's capabilities. In composing a manuscript, the writer can easily move between parts of a complex and lengthy piece of writing. Without the computer's abilities, a writer might suffer cognitive overload.

After organizing the text, a writer should use word-processing software to build and qualify the research and expand the text. Minimally, he or she should own a personal computer with word-processing, grammar-check, spell-checker, and thesaurus software. Both a letter-quality dot matrix printer and a laser printer reproduce drafts and final copy from the computer.

Manuscript Presentation

Writers should judiciously target publishers who are most likely to be receptive to their manuscripts. From the editors who will be evaluating their writing they should obtain a copy of instructions for new authors regarding manuscript submission, style, and format. If an editor asks to see the entire manuscript, the author should always send a paper copy of it. However, the editor may indicate that the publisher will accept or prefers to receive manuscripts also in electronic form. If so, the author should determine which operating system the publisher requires. Most publishers prefer ASCII (American Standard Code for Information Interchange), which provides a character set that includes the alphabet in uppercase and lowercase, punctuation marks, and assorted characters. The system assigns a specific code, which, theoretically, remains the same for every computer and software package.

Presenting the finished manuscript in a visually appealing form enhances the potential for a favorable reception by the publisher. Also, should the manuscript be accepted, the writer gains a significant reduction in the time it takes a publisher to edit and print a well-presented electronic manuscript. It also gives the author a better opportunity to participate in determining the appearance of the final product.

Developing and printing a paper manuscript or duplicating an electronic product for resale already lies within one person's capabilities, assuming of course that writer either has the financial resources to hire professional assistance or has mastered the ability to achieve each task well. However, the publishing profession involves far more than attractively placing ink on paper. Copyright protection, marketing, sales, distribution, and administrative requirements are far more complicated.

A myth exists that publishing has become a one-person venture because of the availability of desktop publishing systems, outside electronic services, and free-lancers who create books, audio tapes, and other electronic products. Writers who gather and organize information, compose text, edit, illustrate, design format, and produce camera-ready or copier-ready material reproduce products for distribution and perform functions similar to those of commercial publishers.

With a little imagination, a writer who uses desktop publishing can turn out a well-designed manuscript. Type size, fonts, and general layout visually communicate a manuscript's organizational style, hierarchy, relationships, and identity. Efficient use of visual characteristics not only assists in processing the manuscript but also helps readers find and use the information they seek.[4]

Desktop publishing brings writing, designing, editing, typesetting, and printing into the hands of a single person. Desktop publishing combines a personal computer, page-composition software, and a laser printer to produce printed material ready for reproduction by a printer or photocopier. Its primary value is its enhancement of the ability to control presentation, the speed with which results can be seen, and the versatility and control over typography and graphic design. A writer designs text and graphics on the computer screen for a complete page layout and displays on the screen exactly what will appear on paper.

Using a computer to create publisher-ready documents requires a proper match of software and hardware. A writer who wants to use desktop publishing should own a computer with one megabyte (1MB) of random access memory (RAM), a 40-megabyte hard disk, and a laser printer.

After completing the manuscript, the writer should convert the file to desktop-publishing software; design the page, chapter, and publication layout; and run the file through a high-quality laser printer. Writers who take their manuscript through the entire technical process assume more responsibilities in production by taking on editorial, graphic-design, and print decisions.

Working with Editors

Electronic publishing has caused a reexamination of the relationships between authors, editors, and production personnel. Computerization and coordinated cooperation between writer and editor means that prepress activity becomes more of a smooth, continuous process. For best results, the publisher and the author should use the same hardware and software system. With the author's and publisher's computers linked via a modem over telephone lines, a single electronic manuscript could be sent back and forth until they complete a version that satisfies everyone.

Usually an editor has the author's electronic manuscript, makes editing changes on paper, and returns a corrected copy to the author for approval and further changes. Then the revisions and typesetting codes are entered on the publisher's in-house computer. This gives a publisher control over the editorial and production process.

If an editor prefers correcting a paper copy, then editorial changes can be made in that form and returned to the author to make corrections on the writer's computer. As an author enters the corrections, additional modifications can be incorporated. Many publishers prefer this method because it avoids computer compatibility and software conversion problems. As an added incentive, a publisher saves paying for editorial time for the electronic work because the author assumes that expense. Established authors, however, usually refuse to expedite work traditionally relegated to copy editors. By contrast, some writers may prefer negotiating for a percentage, above other royalty and remuneration considerations, of the publisher's savings.

Product Options

The writer's freedom of mind that generated the writing must take that same creative, imaginative talent and conceptually decide how his or her publication should be communicated to consumers. Electronic publications communicate powerful messages and images. Also, their capacity, portability, and durability benefit writers, publishers, and consumers.

Publishers should provide as many product options for readers as possible. Recent developments in telepublishing and optical publishing indicate that new delivery systems can provide viable alternatives to print publishing. Alternative publishing includes CD-ROM (Compact Disk — Read Only Memory), telecommunications, computer diskettes, laser disks, audio disks and tapes, and other new electronic publishing products. Accessibility to the public, capabilities for capturing and assembling information, cost, marketing, and ease of distribution determine the feasibility of using the electronic media selected.

Electronic media are not appropriate for every author or publication. Scrolling through a computer screen to read a novel or narrative nonfiction, unless it is interactive fiction in which the reader participates in the narrative direction, will not divert readers from preferring paper books. However, reference works are a viable option for electronic publication because users can search and sort the information to locate a specific topic, word, or concept. CD-ROM converges computer, video, and audio technologies. CD-ROM provides the personal computer with the capacity to store an immense quantity of data and permits rapid and convenient access to information. A CD-ROM laser disk can contain five sets of encyclopedias and costs less, financially and environmentally, than the printed books whose contents it stores.

Selecting Electronic Equipment

Efficient, methodical use of computer software can move a writer more efficiently and competently toward successfully securing a publisher and an audience. A writer should have access to the following hardware and software: tape recorder, personal computer, printer, scanner, modem, word processor, grammar checker, spellchecker, thesaurus, database, desktop-publishing software, and laser printer.

Initially, the software-selection process helps a writer focus, define, and prioritize the needs dictated by one's own method and habits. Preplanning and research lead to wise purchasing decisions. If it is financially feasible, writers should hire a knowledgeable consultant who listens to their computer and software needs, understands how they actually use a computer, and comprehends the types and methods of materials entered into the system.

Every writer should extensively research product options, because a mistake in choosing software or hardware inordinately complicates his or her life. To avoid this pitfall, writers should determine what suits their needs. Many popularized computer hardware and software periodicals seem reluctant to negatively critique the inadequacies of some brand-name products. Many popular magazines usually tell the reader what brands out-sell others but not necessarily what may be most appropriate for one's particular situation. An exception, *Infoworld*, objectively and persuasively reviews and rates hardware and software. Examine the "Product Comparison" section and read the evaluations and descriptions of software, hardware, and peripherals. IBM offers a free, elementary guide on how to select a computer: *The Little Blue Book From IBM*. Call IBM's toll-free number for personal computers to order the booklet.

Before choosing a computer, writers should figure out what software they need and then purchase a computer that runs that software. There are over one hundred word-processing softwares priced from $39 to $700; select a brand that several publishers and respected authors recommend. Writers should start with what they need but make sure the hardware system and software can expand the computer's capabilities as expected changes and new requirements arise.

Know how much hardware and software should cost before being "sold" by a salesclerk. Salespeople have a vested interest in selling their stock and may understand only their line of products. Purchase affordable products and select the best quality for the least expensive price.

Summary

Electronic publishing, the storage and distribution of information using electronic media, has altered the roles played by writers, authors, editors, and publishers. If religious writers expect to fulfill their responsibility as witnesses to a watching and reading world, they must continually incorporate electronic methods into their craft.

As computers continue to increase in complexity and functionality, it will become necessary for them to have command of natural languages. They will need natural language ability if they are to be used to their full capacity by human beings.[5] When computers achieve this, they will have reached the rudimentary stages of human existence, and authors will be able to write the natural way.

NOTES

1. Franco Mastroddi, ed., "Information Technologies," in *Electronic Publishing: The New Way to Communicate* (Luxembourg: Kogan Page, 1987). Proceedings of a symposium of the Commission of European Communities.

2. Oldrich Standera, *The Electronic Era of Publishing: An Overview of Concepts, Technologies, and Methods* (New York: Elsevier, 1982).

3. T. F. Carney, "Print Culture in Transition," in *Publishing by Microcomputer: Its Potential and Problems* (N.p.: Peter Francis Publishers, n.d.).

4. Marilyn Martin, "The Semiology of Documents," in *IEEE Transactions on Professional Communications* 32 (September 1989). See 171–77.

5. Gerald Gazdar and Geoffrey K. Pullum, "Computationally Relevant Properties of Natural Languages and Their Grammars" (Stanford, Calif.: Center for the Study of Language and Information, Stanford University, 1985, Report no. CSLI-85-24). Also see Stuart M. Shieber et al., "A Compilation of Papers on Unification-Based Grammar Formalisms," parts 1 and 2 (Report no. CSLI-86-48).

SUGGESTED READING

Easily accessible publications include *Folio, Publish, Personal Publishing, Writer's Digest, Electronic Publishing and Printing, Personal Computing, Infoworld,* and *Publishers Weekly.* Search "electronic publishing" and "desktop publishing" in the Religion Database (RELI) for a bibliography of materials directly applicable to religious writing.

Brand, Stewart. *The Media Lab: Inventing the Future at M.I.T.* New York: Viking Penguin, 1987.

Essays on emerging ideas and future applications of all electronic media.

Hughes, John J. *Bits, Bytes and Biblical Studies: A Resource Guide for the Use of Computers in Biblical Studies*. Grand Rapids: Zondervan, 1987.

An indispensable, practical, encyclopedic-style reference book for religion writers and researchers.

Standera, Oldrich. *The Electronic Era of Publishing: An Overview of Concepts, Technologies, and Methods*. New York: Elsevier, 1982.

A good introduction to the field as applied to book publishing. Although dated in technological competence, asks the proper conceptual questions confronting writers and publishers.

Part 4

Beyond
the Horizon

Chapter 33

The Future
of Religious
Publishing: 1

Eugene H. Wigginton

Religious publishing has an exciting future. The current high level of interest in religion will probably continue and even intensify well into the next century. One journalistic indication of this is in William Moyers's decision to cover "the religion beat" almost exclusively from now on because, he says, that is "where the action is."

This increasing interest is not just for the United States — the spiritual quest is part of the human experience, and people in both traditionally Christianized and traditionally non-Christianized nations will want to know more, read more, and have more resources and information available to them.

However, the focus in religious publishing will not remain constant. As in the past, we can expect trends and emphases to continue to change frequently. In the last thirty years we have seen a shift from "the death of God" to books that tried to make God seem more alive in a radically changing culture to the recent trend that emphasizes experience over

Eugene H. Wigginton is the publisher of Standard Publishing Company, a major nondenominational publisher of Sunday school curriculum, Vacation Bible School curriculum, and religious books. He was executive vice-president of Milligan College and was also a senior pastor for churches in Louisville and Atlanta. He is a trustee of Milligan College and the Cincinnati Christian College and Seminary and a board member of several Christian mission-ministry organizations.

doctrine. Some observers anticipate an imminent shift to a more rational, objective mode.

But, of course, these emphases are not mutually exclusive; they are often reactions to a previous trend. Addressing one recent emphasis may be in reaction to — or even in unknowing anticipation of — another trend or emphasis. Twenty years ago evangelicals had the corner on the market of evangelism, while mainline Christians majored in social action. Now all kinds of mainline literature is dealing with evangelism while evangelicals are looking hard at social issues, from abortion to environmentalism to world peace.

Whenever the focus shifts, the religious publisher must realize that such shifts all reflect the human spiritual quest. Even when men and women appear to be moving away from God, they may be simply going through a momentary knee-jerk reaction of frustration in their search for God. Overreaction to radical theology gives it undeserved credibility. The religious publisher's challenge is to faithfully communicate biblical immutables.

Anyone trying to anticipate the future and position himself accordingly is involved in risk. That holds doubly true for the religious publisher. The leap of entrepreneurial faith will be well rewarded if it is in the right direction. The publishers who make the most significant contributions — and will reap the most benefit — will be those who define their mission and discipline themselves in faithful adherence to that mission.

Exploiting fads will bring only short-lived benefits. Religious publishing companies can learn from Wall Street. The corporations that invested in or took over other companies that were complementary to their own purposes have thrived. With few exceptions, however, those corporations that seemed to sell their souls and their credit ratings for a quick profit were soon in trouble, in terms of both unmanageable debt and disgruntled personnel.

Thus the religious publishing company's constant point of reference is its prayerfully considered and carefully stated mission: "The reason we exist is. . . ." This mission is the guide in selecting personnel, the determining factor in deciding what products to produce, and the basis for choosing which segment of the market to serve. The religious field is vast, and no one publishing company can excel in every segment of the industry. And while expansion is not always undesirable, many publishing houses that have been successful in one specialty found themselves in serious trouble when they expanded into other publishing ventures. If a publishing company is considering expansion or diversification, it must first count the cost, research the field, and honestly evaluate its own strengths and weaknesses.

In the immediate future, the religious publisher can help accelerate the changes that are about to occur as well as provide a solid foundation on which to help build them. The church-growth movement, for instance, will be less concerned with numerical growth and more concerned with the growth of individual disciples. (Paradoxically, significant numerical increases will result from this more substantive approach to building churches.) This emphasis on personal growth will bring with it the desire to have growth emanate from in-depth study of the Scripture with a corresponding application to life. The current emphasis on studying the Bible only to "see what it means to me" will give way to a study that asks, "What is the original intent of the passage and how should that affect contemporary life in the late twentieth century — specifically mine?" Thus professional Christian educators and serious students of the Scripture are looking to religious publishers to suggest creative ways of applying biblical teaching to life. Some leading educators indicate that at least half of religious instruction should focus on application, with a big part of that application being in the form of a stimulus that requires "discovery learning" from the student.

A popular maxim states that "change is growth." But change can also be painful. Religious publishers today face a unique set of challenges that seem to be converging on this decade. The needs of the churched are changing in several ways. For instance, Christians of different traditions are generally more aware and tolerant of others and therefore more open to using materials that come from other sources than their own denominations. Denominational publishers may not have guaranteed customers anymore. And all publishers will be affected by illiteracy problems. One Christian educator predicts that churches will soon need to spend significant amounts of time teaching their members how to read. The demographics of the unchurched are changing: By the year 2000, for the first time in history more people will be living in urban areas than in rural areas. The fastest-growing churches in the world are found in Africa and east Asia, not Europe or America. Will this latter fact, along with increased immigration to the United States, mean that religious publishers need to produce more foreign-language editions? The economy has changed: we are now in a truly worldwide, interlocked market in which one nation's economic health depends on another's. Publishers are discovering that it may be more economical to have a manuscript edited in the United States, typeset in Hong Kong, and printed in Italy. And communications technology is changing almost every day. Few religious publishers can afford the latest equipment; yet in the long term, who can afford not to invest in it? Any one of these challenges demands serious study and strategizing, but with all coming at once it is clear that the publishers oriented to the future will make the most meaningful contributions in the coming decades.

As we consider the future, we can begin by concentrating on three crucial aspects of religious publishing that are distinct but interrelated: the publisher, the product, and the process. More than ever, the publisher can have an impact on what is produced — on the content, on the intended audience, etc. But the quality and distribution of the product will depend on what technology is available, both in terms of capability and feasibility. As conventional methods of production become obsolete, publishers will have to decide between what is theoretically possible and what is economically practical for themselves. And, as it always has done, a publisher's title list will reflect an accommodation between the house's goals (its mission) and its capabilities (its current technology and its budget).

The Publisher

The future of religious publishing will to a large extent be determined by the publisher, the person at the top of the publishing house's organizational chart. This is the key individual for setting policy and is the driving force behind the scenes. As is often the case in other fields, the person who provides the driving force is not highly visible or widely known. (An NFL quarterback is usually better known than his coach.)

In the not-so-distant past, a few exceptional religious publishers have been renowned figures in their field, such as Christian education. Several of these are still quoted as authorities even if they retired or died many years ago. We might conclude — with some justification — that they were leaders who were far ahead of their time, and thus their influence lingers. But upon closer analysis we see some interesting dynamics at work (which, incidentally, are to be found not only in religious publishing).

First we can note that once a person has established his or her credibility as a leader and as an authority figure, his or her devotees develop an unshakable sense of loyalty first to the person of the leader and then to the leader's philosophy. The philosophy becomes a basis on which adherents build assumptions, techniques, and even entire careers. Consequently any real or perceived change is an invasion into a professional and philosophical comfort zone.

Any undue lingering influence of past leaders in religious publishing also indicates that a void in leadership exists. We rely on the philosophies of the former leadership — as dated as they may be — because no one has broken any truly fresh ground and no apparent new leaders are on the horizon. It is as though the industry is collectively holding its breath, waiting to see what bold new leader will emerge to courageously take us into the promised land of the next century.

It is too much to ask for only one or two publishers to take the entire burden of leadership in an increasingly complex business. But what sort of person should we look to for leadership in our particular arenas? What is the profile we should use in our search for those individuals who will chart the course for the years to come?

The religious publisher must be a church person. Theorists and ivory-tower isolationists need not apply for the position. Success depends on consumers having a confidence in the publisher that is born from relationships. Consumers want a peer who has served in the trenches. They want to know that the person providing direction has been a practitioner and has a working knowledge of the professional vernacular. They also need assurance that in his experience the publisher has had more successes than failures.

Part of establishing credibility will involve participation in professional meetings, seminars, local workshops, and national conventions. This may first appear to be crass self-promotion or even political maneuvering. It is actually paying a price of using one's giftedness and discovering the potential contributors to a publishing company's mission. The person who seeks to exalt himself or herself will quickly be exposed and discredited. But the one who humbly seeks to be used of God as a servant leader will be honored as God's person.

The publisher must be a futurist. One strength of book publishing is its potential for timelessness: a well-written, well-edited, well-produced book can — and should — affect the lives of readers and whole societies for decades, even centuries. One strength of periodical publishing is its timeliness: the editor and contributors should have the ability to recognize, report, and analyze important events and trends almost while they are happening. More and more these strengths are being blended. Publishers in recent years have anticipated well enough to produce a substantive book on a subject or a person even as that subject or person was making newspaper headlines. Current technology has enabled mass-market publishers to meet the demand for instant information and produce books about a news event within days after it happened. And mass-circulation magazines seem to be publishing more special "collector issues" that are designed to be reliable references and keepsakes for years to come.

But timeliness is a two-edged sword for a publisher. No matter how fast the technology becomes, publishing will always be plagued by lag time: It is still possible for a concept to be outdated by the time it gets into print as a book or as curriculum.

Religion is no exception, even though it deals in a general way with the most timeless of subjects, eternity itself. Issues arise and become a matter of intense interest only to fade into the background. The death-of-God theology of the 1960s and the debate about inerrancy in the 1970s were "hot topics" that have since cooled. Even now the furor over "secular humanism" seems to be giving way to concern about the New Age movement.

To take another example, the Sunday school movement came on the scene early in this century and grew phenomenally. It began to lose momentum in the 1960s, and home Bible study groups have had an impact on the Sunday school over the last ten to fifteen years. The jury is still out as to what will be the new direction of Christian education in the local church.

To know what issues to address and whom to draw on for material, the publisher must continually ask and answer such questions as: How much creativity do the current popular authors have left? What will be the theological hot topics in the next five, ten, fifteen years? What will be the shape of the church — in North America and worldwide — at the turn of the century? Who is in the next generation of provocative thinkers and writers? What can our company do to discover, encourage, and develop new talent? How can we best utilize the technology available to us?

The religious publisher will be called upon to be a little like a prophet in both biblical senses of the word: he or she must be faithful to the mission of publishing the truth of God, and he or she must have a certain gift of predicting future concerns, needs, and trends in order to prepare to address them. Quite simply, the publisher *in* the future must be a publisher *of* the future. And that future includes a revolution in communications technology that will necessitate a new publishing process.

The Process

When we discuss the future of religious publishing, we must take into account the process. Technology — the *how* — will become a bigger factor than ever in the publisher's decisions of *what* to produce.

Electronic publishing (EP) is now a fact of life. The question about its implementation is not if but when and how, and like other revolutions this one requires major adjustments in thinking and execution. At our company we have switched to a high-end, integrated system that has an electronic trail virtually through all the editing and production processes: manuscripts (hard copy, copy on diskettes, and copy that has come via modem) and art are scanned in and edited or corrected, pages are made up on-screen, and film is output, ready for stripping. Within a matter of months we moved from conventional methods to state-of-the-art processes. The editor of one of our magazines summed up the change succinctly: "We have had to change the way we think about and do almost everything from the point we start working on a manuscript to the time it hits the press."

But this is only the leading edge of greater possibilities. There is a growing consensus that as fax machines with higher resolution are developed, they will play a starring role in publishing. Satellite transmission is already being used by major publishers to print specialized editions of magazines, to send photos across international phone connections, or to simply have their books and periodicals printed more cheaply elsewhere, whether it is on the other side of the continent or the other side of the globe.

While "desktop publishing" has been around for almost a decade, its color capabilities have been very limited until recently. That is starting to change — industry analysts correctly predicted that affordable good color would be one of the big stories of EP by the early 1990s. And what seemed literally unthinkable only a few years ago is now getting off the drawing boards: electronic stripping, for example, and automatic presses that essentially form their own plates on the press.

These developments have several benefits. One major selling point is the increased control publishers of any scale will have. EP will usually reduce production costs in the long run, and that will become increasingly true as prices drop on the more accessible hardware and software. Communication technology will allow publishers to make many imprints or editions of one product quite easily. Licensing and consortium agreements will allow two or more publishing companies to customize a basic text for their own audiences. Publishers may find diversifying easier: the same technology that can be used to print materials can be used to produce visual resources — an important consideration in a video age.

But there will no doubt be several drawbacks. As always happens in a technical revolution, a few valuable skills will be lost. And the growing availability of EP hardware and software will almost certainly have a negative impact on the quality of printed materials. Print technology will still be a slave to the user, and, as one EP seminar leader said, "This can put out garbage like any system — it just puts it out faster." And even the content may suffer in religious publications as the filter of professional publishers, editors, and proofreaders can be easily bypassed. (The concept of a one-person operation has some attractions, but it has some dangers, too.)

In our fascination (or fear) of the technology, we could easily forget the importance of the people involved in the process. But, as always, how well the new machinery works — or, for that matter, how well religious publishing succeeds as a whole — will depend on the personnel involved. What kinds of people will be needed in religious publishing in the coming years?

Religious publishing houses typically have been staffed by loyal generalists, those who work with a sense of ministry and have a hand in many of the operations that take a publication from concept to print. In general, we can see that pattern changing. The technology will require fewer people on a day-by-day basis. This has several implications. First, and more obvious, editors and designers will be competing for fewer positions. That in turn should translate into a work force that is more specialized and better trained. But it could also create a demand for more free-lance editors, proofreaders, designers, etc., since publishers would save labor costs if their work could be done at home and then transmitted to the publishing house.

At this point, publishers will be faced with the fundamental task of organizing the people and procedures involved in production. In the early days of desktop publishing, most observers predicted (and even welcomed) the return of the one-person shop: the desktop publisher as writer, editor, proofreader, designer, typesetter, and printer.

Now, however, it's clear that the EP system works best when it is used as a tool to help specialists do their jobs as they consult with other members of a team. But a warning is needed here: an EP system can either help solve communication problems between, say, editors and production managers, or it can aggravate them. The difference lies in such basics as setting ground rules for how the EP system can be used (and by whom) and clearly establishing lines of communication in the stages of production. (To avoid confusion — or perhaps conflict — a few publishing companies have virtually isolated different phases of production: after the editors have finished processing a manuscript, it is electronically mailed — sometimes across the country — to a designer. In some cases the software program is structured so that the editors cannot retrieve the copy after it has been transmitted to the designers. From the designer, the publication is sent again, sometimes electronically — to prepress facilities and then to the printer.)

While we must consider the impact of technology on our methods of producing materials, we must not forget that the process is the servant of the publishing company and its sense of mission. And ultimately, the publisher's mission is expressed in its products.

The Product

Religious publishing has never had more potential for success — or failure — than it has today. With increasing interest and a growing audience, the influence of and rewards to publishers could be great. But these broader horizons also bring higher expectations. A generation or two ago, many readers would remain loyal to their denominational publisher or another trusted house, especially among evangelicals and fundamentalists. Now the lines between believers have somewhat blurred and readers feel more free to choose from a myriad of options. So customers will buy books, curriculum, and magazines that they perceive to be more valuable, either because of the name on the cover or because it seems to best fit their particular needs. Therefore, while publishers can take heart because of a potentially wider audience, they must also pay closer attention to the quality of their publications. The big fish in small ponds will find themselves thrown into the oceans.

Using Christian education material (one of our company's specialties) as an example, we can describe some of the emerging needs and concerns of religious publishing.

I mentioned before that many researchers expect a renewed focus on objective Bible study. But that is not to say the emphasis on felt needs will diminish, much less disappear. The shift could be described as just changing the starting place. Instead of first asking, "What's my need?" followed by "What does the Bible say?" students will ask, "What does the Bible say?" and then ask, "What does this say about my life, my situation, my needs? How does this apply to our society today?"

With that in mind, publishers will need to offer products that address a wider variety of topics, all with very practical applications. This type of product will require at least three essentials: (1) sound methodology, both biblical and educational; (2) thorough research to determine both the perceived needs of the intended audience and how best to promote the materials as able to meet those needs; and (3) professional presentation.

The product should have a solid biblical basis, but too often it does not. As more churches and Christian leaders emphasize the need to teach the biblical message above all, publishers will be challenged to produce materials that are less denomination-oriented and more Bible-centered.

In terms of educational philosophy, publishers will need to create a balance between presenting only ideals (which alone would discourage people who live in less-than-perfect realities) and advocating only outmoded or popularly accepted methods of dubious value.

Publishers must find out what the consumers think they need before any definite product decisions are made. One of the unresolved tensions in publishing — all publishing — lies in the difference between what the reader wants and what the publisher thinks the reader needs. While a publishing house must remain true to its sense of mission, it must also remain true to its customers by fulfilling the unspoken pledge to provide what they need. A publisher should not make product decisions solely on the basis of a market study, but he or she should take such a study into serious consideration. And if religious publishing continues to follow mass-market trends, then the value of publications will be judged on the basis of how well they address particular needs for specific segments of society. One needs only to compare the fortunes of most general-interest periodicals with those of "niche magazines" to realize how focused readers are becoming.

Fortunately, the technology of national (and even international) communications will make possible the kind of tailored publications that were virtually impossible only a few years ago. The more focused, of course, the more these publications can meet at least perceived needs. The mass-market magazine industry has been one of the first segments of publishing to take advantage of satellite communications. Several national magazines have overseas editions that are produced simultaneously with their American editions, but feature stories can be substituted, expanded, or shortened to fit the particular audience. In the United States, magazine advertisers regularly target geographic regions, demographic groups, and other segments of the reading public.

Religious publishers should not be slow in exploiting this ability. Similar products can now be easily produced in any number of parallel forms without adding excessive production costs. A given study series, for instance, may be published inexpensively for churches, groups, or individuals with tight budgets, using one or two colors and low quality paper. But electronic page make-up and film output devices make publishing the same content in another, perhaps more upscale, version feasible. So while a church with limited resources may opt to buy inexpensive, almost throwaway versions, those that may want to "invest" in printed materials can count on having it in a more endurable form. I will discuss more about the ramifications of technological advances in a moment.

The ability to diversify has more profound implications for the publishing house if it sees its work as a ministry, a service, to the church.

Communication shows us not only how much alike we are; it also reveals how different we are. We may be more aware than ever how every person and every nation needs the gospel — but we will also realize how many different situations that gospel must address. The religious publisher has the ability to continue forming a common ground among consumers with what comes off the press. But he or she also has the ability to target needs and concerns more specifically and more powerfully than ever.

This thinking doesn't imply a helter-skelter rush into every corner of every possible market. It does imply a shift in strategy, to one that will offer a wide variety of formats — traditional Sunday school lessons, home study-group materials, individual study guides, etc. — but only a limited choice of topics within each format. The diversity will come in the presentation or application of a message or lesson, not in the message or lesson itself.

Once the publisher has developed a philosophy and a methodology and has determined what is needed in the marketplace, he or she must ensure that the product reaches the audience in such a way that the audience will notice it and respect it. Although we may hate to admit it, we do judge books by their covers (and other parts): how they look, how they feel, how they read. Good, clear writing, sound editing, and user-friendly (and imaginative) design are almost as essential to getting the message through as is the message itself. Again, as the consumer becomes more familiar with high-quality publishing, he or she will have greater expectations and will be less tolerant of amateurish publications. Some of the most creative editorial and graphic design work is in the religious realm, but much of that effort has been fueled by the need to compete with secular publishers for the attention of readers.

Although it appears here almost as an afterthought, we must realize that video, audio, and eventually computer resources will take up more space in publishers' catalogs. Few experts now predict the demise of paper, but it may not be the dominant medium very much longer. One of the significant felt needs of the late twentieth century is the need for active stimulation. So publishers will be challenged to find innovative ways to integrate printed and electronic communications. Will publishers join with television producers to create cable or video-taped teaching sessions (complete with biblical reenactments) that are correlated to printed resources? What potential benefits are there in establishing modem or fax links between a student, a Christian college, and a religious publisher?

The religious publishing industry is at a crossroads in its history. We live in a time when whole societies are undergoing fundamental changes, when there exists a growing hunger for information, when new communication technologies are emerging every day, and when spiritual hunger is increasing. This combination of circumstances points to the kind of opportunity that may come only once in a millennium, one in which publishing in general — and religious publishing in particular — could have as much impact on our world as any profession, and more than most.

How effectively and significantly religious publishers respond to this opportunity depends on three factors: (1) how committed they are to their sense of mission and sense of service to the church; (2) how much they are willing to experiment, risk, and innovate to provide the Bible-based materials that are needed and wanted by consumers; and (3) how much they are willing to sacrifice and change in their methods in order to provide attractive and affordable materials where they are needed.

A generation ago, Pope John XXIII said, "If Saint Paul were alive today, he would have certainly become a journalist in order to spread Christianity." This statement will have even greater validity in the years to come.

SUGGESTED READING

Anderson, Leith. *Dying for a Change*. Minneapolis: Bethany House, 1990.

Barna, George. *The Frog in the Kettle: What Christians Need to Know About Life in the Year 2000*. Venture, Calif.: Regal, 1990.

Bellah, Mike. *Baby Boomers*. Wheaton, Ill.: Tyndale House, 1988.

Dychtwald, Ken, and Joe Flower. *Age Wave: The Challenges and Opportunities of an Aging America*. Los Angeles: J. P. Tarcher, 1989.

Gallup, George. "What Are the New Cultural Trends and Values?" and "Who Is the Audience and Who Will It Be?" Insights on Videotape. Tyler, Tex.: Leadership Network, n.d.

Miller, Herb. Editorial. *Net Results* (Feburary 1991).

Naisbitt, John. *Megatrends 2000*. New York: Warner Books, 1990.

Towns, Elmer L. "Reaching the Baby Boomer." *Church Growth Today* 5, no. 5 (1990).

Chapter 34

The Future
of Religious
Publishing: 2

C. E. (Ted) Andrew

According to a 1988 Gallup survey, 44 percent of the adult American population has no tie to any church or synagogue, and evidence indicates that this "unchurched" group is increasing each year. (Gallup says the unaffiliated population has grown from 41 percent to the present 44 percent in just ten years.)

To publishers of religious literature, these statistics are bad news. The good news, however, is that Gallup's studies indicate that approximately 90 percent of the United States population say they believe in God and 70 percent believe in the divinity of Christ.

Surveys of the publishing industry reveal that more religious books are published each year and the annual growth rate has averaged about 8 percent over the past decade. Estimates for 1989 show an increase of about 8.6 percent. This growth is in dollars; unit sales are static.

Where does the industry go from here? What are the future prospects for publishers of religious literature? What should they be

C. E. (Ted) Andrew has been involved in the religious book industry since 1940, first in retailing and subsequently in publishing. He has been a field representative, sales manager, and vice-president and president of a publishing house; from 1980 to 1987 he served as executive director of the Evangelical Christian Publishers Association. Currently he is a publishing consultant.

doing to enlarge the market in the 1990s and into the twenty-first century?

Recognizing that no one person has all the answers, I turned to a number of key professionals in the publishing community and this chapter is the result of their combined wisdom and understanding of the challenges and opportunities facing publishers.

We recognize that although there are some factors over which publishers have no control (e.g., inflation, interest rates), there are many things that the industry can do to assure future growth. Good planning for the long term is the most important.

Although the number of people patronizing Christian book stores is increasing, studies indicate that only a relatively small percentage of the potential buyers of religious literature frequent them. How to reach the unchurched 44 percent of the population poses a challenge to publishers and booksellers alike.

1. A number of publishers have addressed the need to expand the audience and tap new markets. Here are some of their comments:

"Yes, the market continues to be strong, but we are reaching basically a Christian market. In the early to mid 70s the industry did a superb job moving Christian books to the secular market. We got incredible secular media attention. This all resulted in many being exposed to the Good News for the first time, and many of these became believers.

"Christian publishers must somehow regain the ability to tap the secular media and market. Only then will there be meaningful growth."

— Hugh R. Barbour, President
Barbour and Company

"I believe that the key issue facing religious publishing in the coming decade is the need for increased sophistication in the ability of the religious publishing houses to reach those people in the general population who are searching for spiritual insight through the general bookstore's distribution channel. There is increasing evidence that millions of Americans are open to genuine spiritual insight. And unless religious publishing units can make their books visible in the mainstream of the culture, the thirst for insight will be met only by those volumes that are sensational in tone and exploitive in content.

"The growing market is among the restless, spiritual searchers — not among those who sit comfortably in the pews. And it is the common task of the publishers of substantive religious books to meet those readers where they are — in the midst of the mainstream of the general culture."

— Clayton E. Carlson, Vice President and Publisher
HarperCollins San Francisco

This unchurched segment of the population is recognized by one publisher who writes:

"As we move into the 90s, the economy is good and fewer people are attending church because there is more money for 'toys' to be enjoyed on weekends. Also, more mothers are working and they need the weekends to 'escape.'

"Many companies are doing well and will continue to do so as long as they publish books that meet the needs of people."

— Robert H. Hawkins, Chairman
Harvest House Publishers

A successful writer, and one-time publisher says:

"In my opinion, the future of Christian publishing rests equally in the hands of authors, publishers, and book dealers.

"Publishers [should] continue to carve out alternative markets and distribution channels, working with rather than against progressive dealers, who will see the value of using those channels themselves."

— Jerry B. Jenkins, Writer in Residence
Moody Bible Institute

Other publishers wrote:

"With church affiliation declining, where does a publisher find the market for the nineties?

"Publishers need to break down the 'us/them' barriers and start to listen to the unchurched; hear their spiritual cries. . . . Feeding their hunger is a challenge that religious publishers must face. Fantasy fiction may be the most ground-breaking and effective publishing direction in that area."

— Marilyn Moore, Vice-President and Publisher
The C. R. Gibson Company

"I believe that the key issues for Christian publishers to address in the years ahead boil down to focus, penetration, and reach. These issues, interestingly enough, are also high on the list of secular publishers if I read PW correctly. . . .

"Our studies show that 80 percent of the people who do shop in U.S. Christian bookstores live less than 11 miles away. These shoppers would buy greater amounts of our product if it were available in closer places where they normally shop (department stores, grocery stores, catalogs, etc.). Obviously, the same is true for the countless Christian shoppers who live more than 15 miles from a Christian store. How much product would they buy if it were available somewhere close?"

— David L. Orris, Director of Book Division
David C. Cook Publishing Co.

2. Some in the industry see a need for quality writing that will compare favorably with general books — both fiction and nonfiction. They comment as follows:

"If publishers continue to publish quality books on relevant subjects, with aggressive marketing, we see no reason why this upward trend should not continue well into the 90s."

— Richard L. Baker, President
Baker Book House

"I would emphasize the need to publish only books of real quality. We should ask ourselves continually, 'Does this book have something significant, new, and important to communicate, or is it just a rehash of material that is already available?' The publishers that strive to publish only those books with fresh new content that will make significant new contribution are the ones that will do well in the 90s and into the coming century.

"I think there is also a growing potential for 'crossover' books. We are seeing some remarkable inroads with our fiction, which is now being carried extensively in leading (secular) chains. Again the key here is the quality of books being published. If they are really outstanding they will go in the general marketplace as well as the CBA market."

— Lane T. Dennis, President
Crossway Books

"In the 1990s it will be necessary to create a greater desire within the hearts of individuals to read, study, and know more about the Word of God. Self-help books will continue to sell, and certain novels. . . . The aggressive Christian publishers who meet the needs of the people will be the ones who survive."

— Robert H. Hawkins

"Fewer and better books with wider and deeper sales will spell success for the survivors and health for the industry as whole."

— Jerry B. Jenkins

"I believe booksellers are finally beginning to realize that the public is satiated with the contribution of a limited number of national personalities. As a result the message will eventually get back to the publishers that what a person has to say is more important than who he or she is in the eyes of a hero-worshiping public. Couple that with the higher educational level of the baby boomers in the church, and the stage is set for books richer in content and more demanding for the reader. This baby-boomer generation will also continue to be heavy consumers of family-oriented books.

"Finally I believe we are seeing the beginning of a dramatic resurgence of quality fiction (also tied to the higher educational level of baby boomers). Such fiction will be more realistic despite being more creative in plot development and presentation of the theme."

— Leslie H. Stobbe, President
Here's Life Publishers

3. And what is the outlook for products other than the traditional "book"? Educational materials, including Sunday school and vacation Bible school curriculum materials, are important. Also audio tapes and videos are factors in this market. Some publishers see a growing opportunity in the marketplace for educational materials:

"Ours is a wonderful ministry. As those involved — whether bookstores, dealers, or publishers — are driven by the desire to provide product that will reach the unsaved for Christ, Christian publishing will make a tremendous impact on the world.

"Curriculum has played, and will continue to play, a major role in the Christian publishing ministry."

— James R. Grogg, formerly Vice-President, Marketing
Standard Publishing

4. American publishers, as part of the world community, have new opportunities, in the international arena. The new political climate in Eastern Europe bodes well for the Christian church, in my opinion. And changes elsewhere must be considered. A number of publishers see a new challenge, as the following comments indicate.

"European Common Market policies scheduled to go into effect in 1992 will affect a publisher's global policies."

— Richard L. Baker

"And what are U.S. publishers going to do during the next decade to develop effective Christian publishing in less privileged countries?"

— Hugh R. Barbour

"Eventually this nation and the world will see that there is a need for Jesus Christ. There are some exciting things happening in the Third World and in several countries in Asia. We must and we will find a way to service these millions of new converts and prospective converts. For that reason I am optimistic about the growth in the long term."

— James R. Grogg

5. Publishers see new opportunities in a changing United States. Here is food for thought from one:

"Historically, in the United States, the church has been the single greatest protector and preserver of 'decent people' values — a partner for parents who have struggled to hold families together in the face of the Great Depression, wars, and other adversities. . . . The children and grandchildren of these white Christian families now direct much of the religious publishing industry's operations. We are testimony to the American Dream.

"But there is a new and different generation of American famlies that need the bulwark of Christian values for survival. . . . Families in the barrio, middle- and low-income-class blacks in our cities and suburbs, new refugees from Asia — these comprise some of the most active, vibrant, and loyal church communities in the United States today. If our industry would break the invisible racial barriers, . . . a real boom in religious publishing could occur."

— Marilyn Moore

6. A healthy industry must be a profitable one, and in the eyes of a number of publishers, Christian books are often underpriced. There must be an adequate profit for publishers if they are to survive. There is a familiar cliché that says, "A product is not necessarily *overpriced*, it may be *underdesired*." It may be that publishers of Christian books do not have a sufficient gross-profit margin to support the advertising and promotional programs of which they are worthy. Are Christian books "underdesired" because of this?

I quote one publisher:

"Pricing is going to continue to be a major problem in Christian publishing. For example, our house had a book simultaneously on the New York Times list and the Christian Bestseller list. The book was the least expensive book on the secular list and the most expensive on the Christian list. Unfortunately, there are no book manufacturers that offer special discounted prices to "Christians" nor do we get special rates from the trucking companies that transport our books. And the paper manufacturers continue to move up their prices regardless of our mission statement."

— Robert D. Wolgemuth, Chairman
Wolgemuth & Hyatt Publishers

I am confident that, having read the comments of people "on the firing line," you will agree that the opportunities for publishers of religious literature are tremendous.

To summarize: the future of religious publishing can be bright indeed if publishers of Christian literature make it so. The publishers' emphasis must be on editorial excellence, deeper penetration of the existing market, and a concerted effort to broaden the market through the other channels open to them. To reach those who have no religious background, we must produce books in their idiom, and we must formulate and implement plans to reach the unchurched 44 percent. We must look at the changing world both here at home and around the globe and be prepared to meet the needs of people where they are. I, for one, am confident that the leaders of this industry will make the intelligent decisions that will assure future growth. That is our mission!

SUGGESTED READING

Christian Book Publishing and Distribution in the United States and Canada. Scranton, Pa.: Center for Book Research, University of Scranton, 1987.

ECPA survey: A Study of the Market for Christian Books. Tempe, Ariz.: Evangelical Christian Publishers Association, 1984.

Religion in America. Princeton, N.J.: Princeton Religion Research Center, 1991.

Index of Persons

Subject Index